J. D. At...
School of ...
The Institute For Advanced Study
Princeton, New Jersey 08540
U.S.A.

S0-CAR-512

J. D. Atlas
School of Historical Studies
The Institute For Advanced Study
Princeton, New Jersey 08540
U. S. A.

ACT
&
QUALITY

A Theory of Literary

Meaning and Humanistic Understanding

Charles Altieri

The University of Massachusetts Press   Amherst

Copyright © 1981 by
The University of Massachusetts Press
All rights reserved
Printed in the United States of America

Library of Congress Cataloging in Publication Data
Altieri, Charles, 1942–
Act and quality.
Bibliography: p.
1. Hermeneutics. 2. Semantics. 3. Literature—
Philosophy. I. Title.
PN81.A453   808′.00141   81–2147
ISBN 0–87023–327–0   AACR2

Contents

Acknowledgments

I first began planning this book during moments of despair, rage, and intense pleasure at Literature and Philosophy Colloquia sponsored by The State University of New York at Buffalo. I hope the finished work reflects and celebrates the spirit of inquiry fostered during those years. Still present in their absence are Eugenio Donato, Lionel Abel, Joe Riddel, Norman Holland, Irving Massey, Ed Dryden, Homer Brown, Murray Schwartz, Neil Schmitz, Art Effron, Al Baum, Jim Bunn, and Ken Dauber. Absent in their presence, on the other hand, are the extremely capable and devoted editorial staff at the University of Massachusetts Press and the following editors who worked with earlier versions of some of these materials—Richard Macksey (*MLN*), Michael Hancher (*Centrum*), Ralph Cohen (*New Literary History*), Tom Mitchell (*Critical Inquiry*), and Paul Hernadi, who edited *What is Literature* (Bloomington: University of Indiana Press, 1978).

The work necessary to organize and develop this project was sponsored by a summer grant from The New York State Research Foundation and a Younger Humanist Fellowship from the National Endowment for the Humanities. (I want also to mention the productive anger created by several organizations who rejected my applications for support.) The many revisions were facilitated (and guilt reduced) by the unfailing kindness of the secretarial staffs of SUNY Buffalo and the University of Washington. Their work and mine was made more difficult by the sharp criticisms of those who read parts or all of the manuscript at various stages—a task only partially imaginable by those who complete this version. For this I express special thanks to Carl Dennis, David Tarbet, Eric La Guardia, John Webster, Renato Rosaldo and, above all, to Leroy Searle who read it all twice and offered penetrating remarks (as did one especially kind and thorough, but nameless, reader for an academic press). Finally I want to thank my wife Joanne who read most of the book despite her wishes and best judgment, and who put up with the anxieties and angers created by my private reactions to the criticisms I acknowledge above.

I would like to dedicate this book to the spirit of the Buffalo English department. It exemplified for me, and still exemplifies, the ideal of affection and respect for others based on the intensity and clarity of their expressions. In the spirit of conflict we learned self-delight, and in working to maintain that self-delight through conflict we all learned to appreciate complexity almost as much as I did the dream of "truth."

Some certified nut
Will try to tell you it's poetry,
(It's extraordinary, it makes a great deal of sense)
But watch out or he'll start with some
New notion or other and switch to both
Leaving you wiser and not emptier though
Standing on the edge of a hill.
We have to worry
About systems and devices there is no
Energy here no spleen either
We have to take over the sewer plane—
Otherwise the coursing clear water, planes
Upon planes of it, will have its day
And disappear. . . .
                              You
Really have to sequester yourself to see
How far you have come but I'm
Not going to talk about that.

JOHN ASHBERY, *"As We Know"*

Introduction

1. *The purpose of this study*

This book offers a theoretical examination of literary meaning. It is devoted to three basic questions—how one can define the constituent units and principles of organization that make literary texts coherent semantic and aesthetic experiences; how the elements of meaning make it possible to derive criteria for distinguishing the roles that various interpretive acts play and for judging the validity of those acts; and how one can use an account of meaning and interpretation in order to understand and defend the values traditionally attributed to literary experience.

The last of these questions is the one most responsible for both the shape of my argument and the contribution I would claim for it. I see this book as developing semantic principles capacious enough to lead coherently into models of consciousness which make obvious the cognitive roles literature might play and the satisfaction involved in such cognitive activity. We are not without contemporary theories which pursue the same goal, but most of them, I shall argue, neither provide accounts of meaning that will stand up to philosophical analysis nor correlate meanings with the values I consider most important for literary studies. Unless we can recover the *force* that writers intend by their efforts as artists and interpreters of action, I do not think we can justify appeals we make to their authority and wisdom. And without such appeals, I doubt that humanistic education or its objects have much claim upon the attention of society.

In working on semantic and hermeneutic questions I hope to show how literary meanings can be seen as actions that we assess in terms of qualities projected in representative situations. The correlation of meanings, acts, and qualities, in turn, serves as a foundation for describing what it means to treat literature as a humanistic discipline. It establishes a clear definition of how human attributes reside within textual structures, and it enables me to show how one's understanding of a range of human attitudes is enhanced by attending to these structures. In order to make these transitions I must reconcile two conflicting traditions in literary theory and philosophy. My analyses of the nature of meanings derive, with some modifications, from the Anglo-American tradition fostered by Wittgenstein's later thought, but I am constantly aware that such methods are valuable for literary theory only to the extent that they focus and preserve the speculative energies and thematic concerns that continental philosophy shares with the literary imagination. Indeed, I consider one basic measure of the value of using *action* as a central theme to be the capacity of the concept to integrate the concerns of both traditions, without falling back on a purely relativistic pluralism.

One could say, in fact, that only by such syntheses can one hope to speak adequately about the humanities or even to define one's particular version of what it means to be a humanist. On the one hand, no currently acceptable, technical philosophical language will allow one to describe properties of depth, complex values, and circularity, which we will see are necessary features of humanistic views of literary experience. On the other hand, the descriptions we have of such properties tend to be vague and pious, precisely because humanists reject the philosophical languages which seem to dispel everything that they think matters. Moreover, the humanities are by nature forms of thinking which in articulating values also invite narcissistic fixations on the terms used in one's self-representations. To speak of humanities is to put a stake on one's discourse that makes one strongly resist fundamental criticisms, especially when it is so easy to yield to the temptation of taking oneself as seriously as one takes the works of genius one loves and identifies with. As Derrida might put it, the language employed for the humanities is used and usurious coin: the more we rely upon it, the cheaper and more inflated both it and we seem to become. Yet to do without such terms for self-representation is to succumb to what Stevens called the pressure of reality. We leave ourselves a very limited set of predicates for describing actions; we lose any way to recognize the dignity and complexity of

certain acts or roles; and we leave ourselves with only myths of demystification as attitudes we can identify with. Yet even on this last point we
cannot really explain our urgency to have a myth of ourselves, or to
claim authenticity for a given position.

Because I want to continue to use such coin, I need to describe here
what I shall mean by *humanism* and how I hope to recover the force of
humanist values. Humanists since the Renaissance have shared an ambivalent relationship to philosophy, desiring its authority and speculative reach but suspecting its analytic energies as substitutes for commitment and action. As a result, there is no single humanist position.
Among self-styled humanists one can find virtually contradictory positions on everything from the nature of consciousness to the harmony—
or lack of it—between the moral and the aesthetic. Nonetheless, I think
it is possible to identify some ideals shared by most humanist positions,
so that we can imagine it very difficult to accept as a traditional humanism a position that does not hold some of the following values—which
are, of course, the ones I make basic in my identification with this tradition. The humanist is devoted to ideas of education because she be-
lieves that (1) certain forms of knowledge transform one's powers to
act and to understand others through their actions; (2) education plays
the role of creating "noble" models and leading someone to want to be
able to represent his value as a person in terms of those models; (3)
both the models and the terms for discovering actions are richest when
one can recover, from pieties and historical positivities, the energy that
works of genius can give to the present; and (4) one can recover and
use these works of genius because they do not simply make statements
or reflect historical conditions—being neither philosophy nor history,
they present concrete, nondiscursive qualities of actions in representative situations, so that the human images they embody remain significant as images for those in other cultures.

The difficulties inherent in maintaining these positions produce two
positions that are perennially antagonistic to humanist stances—first, a
sceptical anti-idealism which sees all discourse about values as only a
series of masks for the play of unrationalizable desires, and, second, a
somewhat desperate rationalism (or now-scientism) which is willing to
settle for almost any ground it can defend, however sterile, so long as it
can maintain some secure terms for describing and judging human behavior. In order to avoid this Scylla and Charybdis of my quest, I need
first a philosophical model for showing how acts and qualities can be

seen as properties of meanings. This, I shall soon argue, one can find in Wittgenstein, a philosopher obsessed with adapting and resisting analytic traditions. For now, though, the pressing need is to explain the general strategy I use to reverse roles with the demystifying critic, and to indicate the blindness to which this form of demonic piety is prone. Again, Wittgenstein will serve as a model. He imagines the errors of traditional analytic philosophy as lights illuminating the shadowy areas where reside the familiar processes within which philosophical problems can be dissolved. I do not aim at dissolving problems. But I think one can turn the tables on scientism and scepticism by continually exposing their inadequacies with respect to literary meanings and then using those inadequacies as what I call a *contrastive frame* setting off the properties and forces gestured at by humanistic pieties. Since Derrida is the contrastive figure I find most useful, I shall return to his metaphors: one can hope to restore the luster and exchange value of humanistic critical ideas by insisting on the inflationary features of newly minted currencies, which do not allow it to serve the same critical functions as the apparently outmoded assumptions. If this contrastive method works, it will also resolve a feature of my humanistic commitment that I find troubling. This book is motivated by a sense of urgency that looks somewhat ridiculous in retrospect, and that always appears to me difficult to reconcile with the philosopher's ideal of disclosing timeless truths. Yet by insisting on contrast as the vehicle for such urgency, I can at least hope that the resulting disputes will clarify perennial issues and test fundamental strategies for resolving them.

2. My general criticism of contemporary theories and an outline of my argument

A brief indulgence in this contrastive method should prove helpful now for two basic tasks. It can quickly clarify the major theses I shall work into my account of meaning and should make evident the stakes I see involved in the arguments. As a first example of how views of meaning affect one's sense of the values served by literary texts, I quote from the previous editor of PMLA explaining how a specific issue is a "mirror" of how literary critics now understand their profession: The articles " 'discuss' Milton and Keats, Dryden and Blake, Dickens and Lampedusa, but the issue is really about Freud, Heidegger, Greimas, Todorov, Derrida, Frye, de Man, Hartmann, Holland, Fish, Bloom and the many other scholars and critics who helped inspire its contents." [1] The motives here are laudable: the editor celebrates the rejection of narrow academic and formalist concerns in favor of critical discourse which promises to give our literary heritage a substantial role in discussions of pressing intellectual concerns. But the result is an odd canon and a strange set of priorities. Texts become relevant by virtue of the conceptual contexts one adapts them to rather than because of the distinctive versions of experience they present. Instead of a professional commitment to describing the depth and variety of literary renderings of experience in perennially useful ways, enriched by theory but not displaced into theoretical questions, we have only a pluralism of critical methods, each of which reduces texts to its own concerns. How damning this mirror is becomes apparent if one tries to imagine Milton or Keats or Dryden or Blake reacting to the cultural roles the editor sees them as playing. I suspect that Yeats might serve as a spokesman for them all:

> All think what other people think.
> All know the man their neighbour knows.
> Lord, what would they say
> Did their Catullus walk that way?

Such statements in PMLA do not self-consciously derive from a single coherent theoretical position. That, indeed, is one reason why I find this one so disturbing. It depends on a set of contemporary assumptions about the meaning and value of texts which in fact make it very difficult to defend the values I think the editor actually subscribes to. The nature and scope of these assumptions will become clear if we examine three problematic statements by influential literary theorists who hold quite divergent positions:

> Meaning—whether we are talking simply of putting black marks together to form words or the much more complex process of putting words together to form themes—does not inhere in the words on the page but, like beauty, in the eye of the beholder.

> The net result is to understand language as an intentional structure signifying a series of displacements. Words are the beginning sign of a method that displaces another method.... The text is trans-

---

1. William Schaefer, "Editor's Column," *PMLA* 93 (1978):355. I should add that Schaefer's recent talks indicate that this remark was probably more editorial politeness than conviction. Yet this vacillating may be even more indicative of the price we pay when we lack a comprehensive theory of literary studies.

formed from an original object into a produced and producing structure whose laws are dynamic not static, whose materiality is textual
not genetic, and whose effect is to multiply meaning not to fix it.
... Writing is the production of meaning, never its achievement.

The distinction stated between the confession stated in the mode of
revealed truth and the confession stated in the mode of excuse is
that the evidence for the former is referential (the ribbon), whereas
the evidence for the latter can only be verbal. Rousseau can convey
his "inner feeling" to us only if we take, as we say, his *word* for it,
whereas the evidence for his theft is ... literally available.... The
distinction is that the latter process necessarily includes a moment
of understanding that cannot be equated with a perception, and
that the logic that governs this moment is not the same as that
which governs a referential verification.[2]

In some respects these statements are fairly innocuous: there is a
tautological sense in which meaning requires an interpreter, or writers
only produce meaning a reader completes, and there is obvious truth in
distinguishing between referential and performative discourse. But these
authors, Norman Holland, Edward Said, and Paul de Man, intend a
good deal more. For Holland the beholder's character constitutes essential aspects of the meaning; for Said the production of meaning never
reaches resolution; and for de Man introducing performative considerations into semantics creates the continual possibility of an ironic level
which becomes "the systematic undoing of understanding." All three
critics, then, share, with significant variations, two basic premises which
I consider the source of many contemporary problems.

The first is fundamentally a relativist assumption about how we determine the intelligibility of a literary utterance. At its simplest, this is
a strange version of historicism, with all the burden of relativity or difference put on the interpreter rather than on the changing cultures in
which texts are written. Thus, we find each critic asserting a radical dis-
continuity between some putative objectivity in a publicly assessable
structure of signs and the constitutive acts which give meaning to those
signs. It seems that only interpreters act, not authors, at least not in intelligible ways, so that attributing meanings involves a continual process

2. Norman Holland, *Poems in Persons* (New York: Norton, 1973), p. 98; Edward Said, *Beginnings* (New York: Basic Books, 1975), pp. 66–67, 261; and Paul
de Man, "The Purloined Ribbon," *Glyph* 1 (1977):30. The quotation below from
de Man's essay is on p. 46.

of displacement—into the eye of the beholder, into an endless chain of methods created by both authorial and interpretive desires, or into the endless duplicities of words defining the status of other words. Reading is less interpreting meanings than creating various substitution sets for the multiple possibilities signs produce.

The most sophisticated forms of this way of thinking involve returning to problematic features of a view of meaning Foucault shows is shared by Marx, Nietzsche, and Freud, but often suppressed by their disciples.[3] What we now take as a vulgar view of these thinkers insists that contemporary languages have superior explanatory power to the languages authors actually employed. We can, therefore, distinguish superstructure from base or manifest from latent content and read the former categories as a symptomatic expression of forces we can explain. Now, however, the flaw in that picture is all too obvious. We cannot allow the critic to escape the models of symptomatic displacement once attributed only to the text. The observer and the explanatory framework the observer uses must be subject to the latent forces they purport to describe. In analytic terms, general accounts of meaning in terms of manifest and latent content cannot both be true and explain their truth on the manifest level of discursive argument. One obvious conclusion is to reject such theories as contradictory. But they do locate obvious phenomena, so an alternative interpretation arises. One takes these explanatory systems as metaphors or examples which indicate the presence of forces in discourse which discourse itself cannot explain or even adequately describe. Then, instead of a limited, explainable model of displacement, one is constrained to posit endless substitutions and masks: language becomes a multilevelled dance among forces one can participate in but never completely control or fix. There is only the production of meaning or the impossibility of equating understanding with perception. Consequently, not only is discourse indeterminate, but also it is impossible to state clearly the appropriate constituents of a discourse, especially the balance between signs of intention or act and textual properties on which coherent semantic analysis might be grounded.

This insistence on instability and displacement gains a good deal of its force and plausibility because it participates in a second assumption deeply rooted in modernist thought. I refer to the dichotomy between referential and expressive or emotive discourse. This dichotomy is a

3. Michel Foucault, "Nietzsche, Freud, Marx," in *Nietzsche* (Paris: Editions de Minuit, 1967), pp. 183–92.

commonplace in the empirical tradition: only what can be verified as a true description of a state of affairs can have determinate meaning while discourse expressing emotions or beliefs depends on unstable associations or analogical leaps by which we try to infer the processes of other minds. The exemplary version of this dichotomy is Russell's theory of types, where determinate meaning and clear reference depend upon unravelling all self-referring aspects of an utterance. Most contemporary thinkers recognize that however powerful Russell's principles are for specifying descriptive functions, the dichotomy cannot be extended to all forms of discourse. Yet literary theory finds it very hard to escape such a model, in large part because the model once allowed reversals through which one could attribute special properties to literary discourse. Thus, both Richards and the New Critics accepted positivist dichotomies, in order to show how important it was to have a "poetic logic" capable of combining description with emotion. The Romantic dream of unifying subject and object became, through metaphor, the role literature could play in saving us from the abstractions of scientific description and the empty associations cultivated by public and private rhetorical effulgence. Literature's truth was its "miraculous" capacity to supplement the truth of science. But now this dream of a special union of the emotive and descriptive comes back to haunt us. The dream had little philosophical substance and thus is easily demystified (and this helps give authority to the idea of criticism as demystification). We find the expressive and extra-logical properties of metaphor now used to insist on inescapable oscillations between reference and the force of desire, at once expressed in and concealed by metaphoric utterances.[4] This is why each of the theorists quoted can base his generalization on some force which displaces any objective properties in a discourse: for Holland the force is that of a constitutive subject expressing an identity theme; for Said it is the productive aspects of signification which overdetermine meanings; and for de Man the displacing expressive force is the performative function, where the desire to appropriate merges with the desire to describe and "truth" can be verified only through another's word. So as other disciplines work their way out of positivist dichotomies, our demystifying irony ironically leads us to extremely sophisticated denials that any cognitive power resides in a discourse condemned to producing an endless regress of symptomatic displacements

4. The best version of this reversal I know is Paul de Man, "Form and Intent in American New Criticism," in his *Blindness and Insight* (New York: Oxford University Press, 1971), pp 20–35.

and substitutions. Interpretation only invites reinterpretation. This leads to a final irony. When metaphoric or dense forms of discourse, like literature, become the primary instances of unstable meanings, anyone seeking knowledge from literature must reverse the New Critical dream of finding it in the most complex forms of language. If there is to be knowledge it must reside in analytic discourses with at least the possibility of controlling or perhaps of deliberately using the forces of desire released by metaphoric acts. We run the risk of finding as the only possible alternatives to demystifying ironies a sentimental escapism that rejects all theory, a structuralist scientism, or a variety of critical stances that insist on the authority of a sociological or political perspective to treat texts as primarily symptoms of the network of social practices and interests which they reflect and reinforce.[5] Without a common sense of what texts offer as objects of knowledge, we cannot appeal to the authority of literary traditions, we have no shared idea of the ends of criticism, and we have no principles for showing how the different kinds of interpretation critics produce illuminate the riches of a work.

Generating an alternative framework for viewing meaning will take most of this book. My basic strategy is to adapt for my purposes Wittgenstein's treatment of meaning as use, and then to connect use with recent thought on the nature and interpretation of actions.[6] In doing this, I must ignore some of Wittgenstein's subtlety and must turn into arguments what are for him indices of ways of viewing and dissolving philosophical problems. Given the confusion and sloppiness in literary theory, our need for discursive clarity justifies abstracting Wittgenstein from his own intricate self-consciousness. (I will, nonetheless, also try to explain why Wittgenstein's method demonstrates principles that can make sense of the circularity inherent in discourse within and about the humanities.)

Wittgenstein provides, first of all, a way of viewing meanings that avoids the referential/emotive dichotomy, and, thus, enables one to at-

5. For versions of social criticism based on this line of thinking, see Edward Said, "Reflections on Recent Left American Criticism," *Boundary* 2 8 (1979):11–30; and Frederic Jameson, "Marxism and Literary History," *New Literary History* 11 (1979):41–74.

6. The two best works of literary theory directly relying on Wittgenstein are John Casey, *The Language of Criticism* (London: Methuen, 1966), and John Ellis, *Theory of Literary Criticism* (Berkeley: University of California Press, 1974). The former is especially useful in opposing the referential/emotive dichotomy and other positivist progeny, while the latter makes a good case for a procedural definition of literature and a Wittgensteinian view of culture. However, I shall disagree strongly with Ellis' version of pluralism.

tempt grounding meaning in terms not dependent on the endless displacement of interpretive schema. In his later work the objective meaning for an utterance does not depend primarily on picturing states of affairs or locating the proper, fixed sense of terms. Rather, the crucial category is one of appropriate sense that depends on what I call a procedural approach to meaning. This approach emphasizes methods of projection rather than pictorial lines of projection, as the mediation between words and world. This means that referential criteria apply in some procedures, but in many contexts other methods of projection can establish secure senses for emotive or expressive terms. We learn how to distinguish appropriate senses because our education in a native language is also an education into a culture. We develop "grammatical" powers to understand how terms are characteristically used in contexts and how we can test among possible uses by projecting ways of going on within the culture.

The concept of grammar, in turn, allows me to develop a dramatic or dramatistic sense of meanings, because it explains how we can recognize and respond to the actions speakers perform in a discourse. Technically this will cast speech act theory as less an analysis of rules than a pragmatics, although in order to make pragmatics applicable to literary meanings I need the further step of extending Grice by showing how expressive features of a discourse can be interpreted. Then I can make my transition from semantics to literary theory by suggesting that literary texts are best viewed as actions performed on a variety of levels for our contemplation. With such a model we need not treat texts as primarily thematic constructs which encourage ideas of substitution and of conflict between action and description. Capturing a sense of the production of meaning is part of the way meaning is achieved in a performance, and, because we have a grammar for understanding acts, there is a good deal more than words which serves as evidence for assessing these actions. A dramatistic approach to meanings reorients critical attention from ideas to the qualities manifested by acts in situations.[7] Even when a

---

7. I cannot be as clear on the concept of *quality* as I would like, but I think I employ it in accordance with ordinary usage. *Quality* has two overlapping general meanings—one descriptive and one normative—which it is hard not to exploit. Descriptively, *quality* is the opposite of *quantity*: it refers to an act or object considered not as merely a member of an abstract class, but as a particular, with its distinctive *qualis* or whatness. Quality is whatness *quo modo*, whatness as characterizing individuality (perhaps Heidegger's *being* emerging through particulars), and not as reducible to general categories of the understanding. Normatively, I understand *quality* as an attribute of an action or a phenomenon that seems worthy of

writer seeks to convince us of ideas, we fully understand her performance as a literary one when we reflect on how the writer uses her medium, how judgments are made and qualified, and above all how the interpretive act presented affords an adequate intellectual and emotional response to the levels of the dramatic situation the text invites us to construct. Critical interpretations do not appeal simply to ideas, but to the complex and flexible assumptions about actions developed in our grammatical understanding.

This correlation of performances and grammatical frameworks for understanding has important consequences in two different areas. First, it helps establish principles which clarify criteria we can use for judging interpretations. If we have a grammar for understanding actions, we can describe how it is possible to make plausible hypotheses about authorial intentions in a text. This allows us to decide what patterns of coherence are probably internal to a text, and which derive from concerns brought primarily by the interpreter. We can put distinctions between meaning and significance on a secure foundation, yet we can show how we need a wide variety of critical positions to deepen our grasp of the qualities projected or required in imagined and historical situations. Second, because we are speaking about acts when we make these judgments, we can avoid the tendency to turn texts into thematic constructs, which then invite the claims about indeterminacy and substitutions which we have observed. By concentrating on actions I can recover traditional ideas of the nondiscursive properties of literary meaning without problematic appeals to a poetic logic or the incarnational power of metaphor. Literary texts are not reducible to abstract themes simply because we are invited to read them by concentrating on the complex features of what

---

special attention because the particulars descriptively established stand out from other instances in some way considered significant for the interpretive procedures being employed. Both descriptive and normative uses blend when we apply the term *quality* to human actions. These various meanings of *quality* have in common, I think, the fact that predicates asserting them are not easily stated in discursive or propositional language. This is why British philosophers from Locke to Ayer have suspected that no objectivity is possible about them, and why early Wittgenstein insisted that everything important existed outside philosophy, as conditions of the world rather than as facts within it. If qualities do not admit propositions, but depend upon careful attention to particulars, internal relations, and (normatively) comparisons, it does not follow that we have no public ways of identifying them or discussing their value. Making this clear will be the burden of my second chapter on Wittgenstein's concept of grammar. The best philosophical descriptions of quality I know are Aristotle's essay on "Categories" and a section of the "Preface to Hegel's *Phenomenology*," trans. A. V. Miller (Oxford: Clarendon Press, 1977), pp. 23–39.

they display in their performance of a range of actions. And it is as actions that texts can preserve an identity across cultures. For the action lives in its specificity: even if we bring different ideas to it, we do so largely in order to recover the qualities of feeling and judgment the text creates within the worlds it asks us to imagine. Conversely, the need to recover this specificity makes us disposed to explore through the text possible ways of viewing experience which are not available in our contemporary thinkers or identity themes.

We now approach what I take to be the fundamental value of my work—both in itself and as a measure of the way a dramatistic approach makes available a coherent progression from semantic to hermeneutic to teleological themes. My view of meanings provides or integrates terms which allow us to describe the cognitive functions which literary texts serve, and, thus, it leads to at least one powerful social goal for literary criticism. I shall show how the performances in literary texts may exemplify attitudes which represent possible ways of acting or making judgments in ordinary experience. Texts afford knowledge not because they describe particulars but because they embody ways of experiencing facts. Their truth is one of possible labels, not of accurate propositions. So instead of grasping texts as ideas, we come to possess them as features of a complex cultural grammar, which extends the power to make discriminations that we learn when we learn a language. Moreover we can treat as cognitively significant both the holistic and non-discursive attributes of texts normally emphasized only in formalist approaches. Yet we can also propose a basic social role for criticism to deepen our sense of what is involved in literary performances so that readers develop complex terms they can project as means of understanding their own actions, those of others, and the ways culture makes possible this range of discriminations. By beginning with Wittgenstein as the grounds for a dramatism, we end with a secularized version of Hegel's description of the ends of reflective consciousness. The identity we can claim depends on our capacity to identify with and reflect upon the performances of the finest and most capacious minds.

3. Provisos, qualifications, and apologies

If I am to avoid piety while making claims like these, I will obviously need a good deal of careful philosophical analysis. Yet it is unfortunately just as obvious that I am not a trained philosopher and cannot hope to present a logically rigorous case based on necessary and sufficient conditions. It helps build my confidence, if not my arguments, that what philosophy I have imbibed is sufficiently laced with Wittgenstein and Husserl to make me suspicious of such methods. But suspicion is only self-defense unless I can make clear the ways I intend to use philosophy and the criteria I think are appropriate to my enterprise.

I shall explain later how I take from the differing perspectives of Wittgenstein, Austin, and Nelson Goodman a view of philosophy which is concerned more with the conditions of rightness or fit than with traditional criteria of truth. As Goodman puts it, "For a categorial system, what needs to be shown is not that it is true but what it can do." [8] I see my own work here as adapting Goodman's statement in two basic ways. First, my goal in making specific claims is only to offer phenomenological descriptions, which can be tested in terms of their plausible and representative fit with the experience of persons we can take as competent in the relevant practice. Then I hope by arguments to show how it is philosophically consistent to hold and to build upon the relationships I establish between semantic, literary, and axiological issues. In both spheres of discussion, I try to employ philosophy only as a tool which breaks down issues into the relevant constituents and tests whether or not one can consistently relate concepts to one another that are derived from descriptions. I cannot avoid using the authority of philosophy with respect to matters of consistency because if one tries to relate concepts to one another only philosophy serves as a norm for judging whether one can do what one attempts. However, when I offer descriptions, I make no pretense to ground my claims in some more systematic context—whether it be a formal logic or explanatory hypotheses borrowed from some scientific discipline. [9] Like Husserl I be-

---

8. Nelson Goodman, *Ways of Worldmaking* (Indianapolis: Hockett Publishing Company, 1978), p. 129. An excellent model for the form of discourse I think I am practicing, and an excellent account of the need for this discourse, may be found in Richard Rorty, *Philosophy and the Mirror of Nature* (Princeton: Princeton University Press, 1979). I am on balance glad that this book appeared after I had finished this work.

9. One might argue that Chomsky invites the recent critiques of his emphasis on syntax, because his fidelity to a rationalist explanatory model severely limits the descriptive facts he can thoroughly consider. Examples like this, and the strong sense I give to *explanation*, account in large part for my ignoring the hermeneutic claims of Marx and Freud. Their forms of descriptions depend on large explanatory claims which I distrust, because I see no way of testing them as systematic arguments. One can, of course, use their work as guides to problems one must consider, but this is true of any good imaginative work and does not constitute grounds for hermeneutic theory. In this respect, these thinkers have simply become part of our grammar for locating relevant features of actions.

lieve that we cannot even dream of explanations until we are reasonably sure that we agree in describing the phenomena to be explained. Moreover, I rarely venture into arguments on the subtle and thorny issues which fascinate philosophers. For the most part, I remain on a level where there is a good deal of agreement among Anglo-American philosophers. They are interested in how one characterizes the elements allowing this agreement, while my concern is primarily with showing literary critics that such agreement exists and can have significant consequences for our understanding the nature and value of what we do. The task I propose still involves a good deal of hubris, but, if the statements on literary meaning I have quoted above are at all indicative of the state of literary theory, there is considerable room for, and need for, theoretical discussions from a dramatistic point of view, even though they are not defended with trained philosophical precision. I harbor the hope, in fact, that humanists can rely on philosophy in the way I do in order to develop the conditions and implications of their work without feeling the discomfort that permeates these remarks.

Given my discomfort, however, I need to elaborate some of the concepts I employed in the preceding paragraph—in particular the idea of competent observers making commonsense judgments in terms of criteria of plausibility and representativeness. Appeal to ordinary or commonsense judgments is an ancient strategy for supporting fairly nonsensical claims. Yet we cannot do without the idea. For while there is no way to "prove" the claims of common sense, there is also no way to escape endless regress—of justifying theories by other theories—unless one can specify some appeal to prereflexive or pretheoretical experience shared by those in a community with the relevant power to perform certain actions. Wittgenstein provides a useful example of how common sense determines descriptive criteria because it involves standards different from those employed in judging systematic explanations. He asks his audience to imagine the consequences of denying what we take as fundamental truths in areas of experience not laden with ideology (as, say, religious beliefs are). There is no way to prove that one knows he has two hands, or that time is a fundamental condition of experience, or that some discourse must have clear, public meanings. One cannot stand outside these conditions to posit the independent facts by which a proof might be supported. Yet if one contradicts these fundamental assumptions, he condemns himself to proceeding purely by abstract connections which will probably not be able to describe or to explain any matters in experience which depend on the denied assumptions. And with assumptions so fundamental, the price is very high. Suppose that a scientist tells us that the floor we stand upon is not solid, but made up of atomic particles and empty spaces. In one—scientific—sense, he is correct. Nonetheless, Wittgenstein argues, he wrongly applies his picture if he uses it to deny our experience of solidity because, from the point of view of ordinary practices, it is precisely this sense of solidity which his scientific model must explain. The scientist can show the inadequacy of commonsense explanations, but he cannot easily contradict the basic terms in which the phenomenon itself is commonly understood.[10]

Hempel

My task is compounded by the fact that I must appeal to two different kinds of practices and grounds for judgments—one a large community, which can reflect upon its capacity to communicate in language, and the other a more specialized group, which one can claim is competent to judge interpretations of literary texts. The first case holds no difficulties in terms of criteria. The ultimate test of claims about meaning is whether they are consistent with ordinary speech practices. Communication through language is not a natural fact: we cannot tell from observation whether communication takes place, at least in many cases, unless we take into account what people say or how they interpret their experience. Thus, no purely abstract argument on the nature of meanings can compel, as it might with natural laws, unless it makes sense to those whose behavior it describes. Suppose, for example, that one of the theorists I cited should come along to assert that my last few sentences produced meaning without achieving it. However strong his logical case, the claim would obviously have to be qualified in order to account for what a given group of competent readers might agree that they understood—of performative as well as strictly lexical features in the discourse. There are obviously dimensions of my discourse which are not clear and not overt, but the test of that is a community's practice, not

---

10. In my first chapter, I will give bibliographical information for the works of Wittgenstein I use. Here, though, I must point out that the solidity example derives from *The Blue and Brown Books*, p. 45. And I must note an essay of mine completed after this book which greatly expands on the following discussion here and distinguishes my idea of consensus and practice from that argued by Stanley Fish in *Is There A Text in This Class* (Cambridge: Harvard University Press, 1980). My thesis, in "Going On and Going Nowhere: Some Uses of Wittgenstein for Literary Theory," forthcoming in a collection edited by William Cain, is that we must distinguish several levels of community which do not all change consistently or coherently. Fish would have trouble, I think, attributing expectations like those I describe here to specific ideologies.

a theory's prescriptions. At the same time, these descriptions have no scientific weight except as challenges to the adequacy of explanatory accounts. Descriptive semantics can provide facts and tests for psychology, but it cannot presume to offer its own claim to explain the mental operations that make us capable of determining meaning.

With literature, however, the issue of an audience competent to judge gets more complex because we have no clear test of literary competence. Very few theorists ask themselves the apparently simple, but actually appallingly difficult, question of what exactly theory can hope to describe. One answer is "properties of texts," but that seems to depend on what readers expect to find in texts, at least if the theory is to have much depth. I find it hard to imagine claiming that cultural entities like texts are governed by natural laws, which can be stated in universal terms without concern for changing forms of understanding their contents, so I must turn to the alternative pole: theory describes the experience of readers, or changes in the history of reading. But how do we know which readers are worth describing? Obviously many readers simply ignore what seem to others the richest features of texts. So an empirical or historical study of reading, however useful in its own terms, will not be much of a literary theory. The fact is that we have no simple test of *whose* common sense a theory is to be measured by, as we do with general models of behavior. The basic reason for this, I think, is that literature has an inescapably ideal aspect. Writers address imagined, eternal audiences as well as real, historical ones, and readers tend to become more dissatisfied with their reading skills the better they learn to glimpse what great texts elicit. Similarly, theorists are usually concerned with focussing on educating as well as describing. The best analogy I know is moral philosophy, where pure empirical description of what people in fact do, without attention to how they might idealize or orient behavior, seems to miss the point of the discipline. This leaves me with only an imaginary object at the center of my analysis. I want to construct an idea of competence which captures powers my audience can accept as necessary to make sense of fundamental properties in texts. Properties have a claim to be fundamental when we see writers rely on them in making evaluations or functional claims about their work. My object, then, is a ratio between reading and textual properties, based on the norm of what a history of literature has idealized as its own potential significance. Such a goal should at least keep my analysis focussed on central, if not essential, problems.

While my object is imaginary and idealized, it is not without plausible and testable connections to the common understanding of a group of competent readers. I propose two measures for locating these readers, whose experience and judgment must be the arbiter of my claims. The first measure allows considerable empirical analysis. As I shall explain later when I discuss Chomsky, one can propose a literary analogy to semantic competence if one grants the power of society to authorize judges. Since we have institutions for studying literature, it seems plausible to imagine as competent readers those most honored by the institution and those whose readings of texts they might take seriously, even if they disagree with the specific claims. Those whose differences in judgment matter to us are those whose competence we clearly respect. This imaginative licensing act is clearly not definitive, but it helps focus issues and it at least describes some concrete judges for theoretical claims. We can supplement this with a second imaginative test for competence which puts more emphasis on judging textual features. Every theory proposes, at least implicitly, a canon by which it is to be judged, and such a canon contains an image of the theory's ideal reader. But not every canon is equal, at least if one wants the theory to have general application. The theory I propose purports to describe the expectations about literature we can attribute to readers concerned with preserving a range of values they locate in a standard version of western literary history. The paradigmatic core of such readings can be imagined as the activity by which someone fairly widely honored as a major writer goes about constructing terms for attributing the same status to several other writers. We might differ on some candidates for this canon, but it is hard to imagine a literary theory in our culture which would be representative while not taking responsibility for Dante and Shakespeare. The canon, in turn, establishes criteria to the extent that it gives us a range of understandings and valuations to account for.

My concern here may seem too obvious to bother with. What else could theorists describe? Yet I often think that the deconstructionist canon begins with Lautréamont, at least to the extent that these theorists specify writers who share the sense of language and purposes of literary activity they affirm. And Harold Bloom's work clearly cannot pretend to be literary theory in my sense, although it is often very suggestive criticism, because it explicitly banishes on its own authority a wide variety of texts most readers value as instrumental to their sense of the shape of literary history and their ways of valuing literary experiences. Moreover, by raising these issues I can make clear the boundaries of my own ambition. I make no claims to describe general principles beyond those one can locate in the canon I mention. And I think this discussion shows what I mean by criteria of plausibility and representativeness, while allowing me to introduce a third criterion of consistency. Each criterion involves imaginative tests, and each suggests that theories are not only true or false but also possess degrees of rightness for different communities with different ambitions. *Plausibility* I take as a measure of phenomenological descriptions: a description is plausible when it connects relevant features of a subject so that a competent audience agrees it is an adequate account of their practical understanding of a procedure or, on another level, of a set of relations among procedures. Plausible descriptions account for the elements and terms of judgments that often are not explicitly conscious but can be brought to self-conscious reflection. *Representativeness*, then, is a measure of the relationship between plausible claims and the actual problems which elicit theoretical inquiry in the first place. Descriptions can be plausible but not representative if they reduce complex issues to trivial ones or pertain only to isolated cases. In my view, a representativeness criterion for literary theory requires that descriptions be adequate to a variety of basic operations trained readers perform when engaged with a large class of the texts which constitute a rough canon of masterpieces preserved as such by our culture. Representativeness also has the important property of requiring judgment, and, thus, of not depending on arguments for necessary and sufficient conditions. Isolated counterexamples will not refute the usefulness of a theory that represents a significant body of cases. The counterexamples might indicate the limits of the theory, but often the ingenuity that goes into the example serves as an ironic measure of how deeply entrenched and typical is the case it takes such efforts to deny. Finally, I mean by *consistency* as a criterion of theory both internal coherence (relative to the nature of one's critical language) and the power of one's language to connect with other languages. A literary theory is not necessarily falsified if its account of literary meaning is incompatible with standard accounts of ordinary semantic practices. But such a condition leaves the theory incapable of making any claims for how the texts plausibly connect with such forms of linguistic action in the world. Similarly, psychologies like Bloom's or even Frye's are difficult to connect to the discourse carried on by the discipline of psychology. This may be because of the narrowness of that discipline, but such a claim could be supported only by a language richer than Bloom's or Frye's. It goes without saying that other theorists need not accept either my specific criteria or my general sense of the importance of philosophy to theory. But I think it fair to ask that they try to state what criteria they do accept, what they are trying to account for, and what plausible consequences would follow if their claims held up. If a critic rejects traditional ideas of theory, the burden is on him to show how another set of grounds is more powerful or more accurate.

My concern for criteria of representativeness and consistency leads to one feature of this book (or, at least, one I am aware of) which many readers will find disturbing. I rarely discuss literary texts and I offer only one extended literary discussion. My aim is not to provide new ways of reading, to display my own sensibility, or even to celebrate literary texts. All are valid enterprises, but all distract from what I consider the goals of theory. I want to explain what is essential to the reading suggested by the canon I propose as common, so I shall simply assume that the few examples I give indicate how I read and suffice as a test of concrete agreements. Were I to spend more time on texts, I would face three uncomfortable options—boring readers with obvious comments, trying to impress them with original readings, or trying to show how theoretical questions can lead to new thematic or methodological perspectives. None of these, however, would help meet the tests of representativeness and consistency I have been discussing. In literary theory, as in ordinary experience, too much emphasis on originality makes us lose sight of the values we share and of the grounds by which we might judge the adequacy and scope of significant original hypotheses. The stress on originality overemphasizes either a scientific or a fashion-conscious model for literary discourses, while destroying our sense of shared problems and criteria. Moreover, such emphases lead us to base our thinking on the work of professional critics. These critics are important to me as competent readers, but their competence as general readers is least evident when they are most professionally ambitious and working at the limits of what can be added to readers' views of texts. So, while I will make suggestions about the ends and logic of practical criticism, my main purpose is not to produce a new methodology, but to bring conceptual order and significance to the variety of critical perspectives we adapt in our ordinary reading.

This is not a humble project. The kind of work I propose is instrumental in establishing the terms by which we rationalize the critical and educational practices of literary studies and explain the values it fosters. There need not be a single literary theory, just as there need not be only one set of values by which people represent themselves as moral beings. But the depth and power of our representations depend in large part on the philosophical pressure we put on our theoretical langauge. There is a sense, then, in which I can be content if this work simply provokes by its errors sharper and more responsible arguments than now occupy literary theorists. I hope, of course, for more. My self-justification, which I almost believe, is that if my theoretical model holds up we will have a philosophically defensible perspective which frees us from narrow theories and returns us to the varied and dense concrete life of literary texts. Then, while the necessary means remains tedious abstraction, I can hold out for my reader the same promise of an end which got me through this book.

ONE

It is so difficult to find the beginning.
Or better: it is difficult to begin at the beginning,
and not try to go further back.
(WITTGENSTEIN, *On Certainty* 471)

1

Wittgenstein and the Nature
of Linguistic Signs

1. *Wittgenstein on methods of projection, and the importance of Derrida as a contrastive figure* Self-reflexiveness about beginnings is virtually unavoidable in the current literary climate. That one faces a blank page, and yet one writes among all too many full books, is problem enough. Even more oppressive is the problem of authorizing a point of departure. If literary theory is to be anything more than a farrago of observations and practical monitums, it clearly must establish itself by a coherent philosophical account of its grounding terms. Yet, as the statements on meaning I cited in my introduction indicate, an aporia of groundlessness easily gives way to a more serious and blind aporia caused by relying on problematic and inadequate philosophical grounds.

Wittgenstein's later work is the fullest treatment I know of the problem of grounds and beginnings. Wittgenstein makes it clear why the statements we have been considering founder by seeking too abstract, absolute, and inflexible a principle grounding the intelligibility of meanings. And, more important, he constructs a framework within which we can recognize the ways signs in ordinary and literary utterances come to convey sharable and coherent meanings. Wittgenstein bases meanings not on reference or picturing, but on our capacity to register the roles signs play in contexts within forms of life or conditions for acting. Thus, his semantic analyses sustain the dramatistic perspective on meanings which I shall show allows us to describe in philosophical terms both the role of qualities in literary discourse and the cognitive functions one can attribute to works foregrounding such qualities.

The best way to begin discussing Wittgenstein on grounds and beginnings is to concentrate on his criticism of his own earlier logical atomism. Whether one takes his *Tractactus* as essentially empirical (as Russell did) or essentially a formalist treatment of logic, it expresses a conceptual framework imposing the sharp dichotomy between referential and emotive meaning which is fundamental to modern literary theory—from I. A. Richards' affective theory and its heirs, to unstable New Critical attempts to show how emotive meanings could actually constitute or refer to nondiscursive features of experience, to the sceptical ironies of Derrida and his allies. The later Wittgenstein, on the other hand, formulates what will become a pragmatic approach to meanings: shared meanings (or what I shall call "secure" meanings) are possible to the extent that we can agree on the place of the utterance in a general practice and then establish its intention in relation to the specific context. The key to this transformation, and one of the basic themes of this study, is Wittgenstein's claim that approaches to questions of meaning depend not on *lines of projection*, but rather on *methods of projection*. Where the former privileges a referential correspondence model for assessing meanings, the latter allows us to speak of assessment as dependent on procedures appropriate to the specific activity performed in the discourse. Then, in order to be able to speak coherently about procedure as ground of meanings, Wittgenstein elaborates concepts of *forms of life, meaning as use*, and *philosophical grammar*. These concepts link questions of meaning to concerns for the nature of actions and help explain how actions can be publicly intelligible and assessable. Thus, by appropriating Wittgenstein's basic concepts, I hope here to establish a foundation for the next two chapters. *Philosophical grammar* and *meaning as use* should enable us to develop a model of speech acts sufficiently complex to handle questions of literary meaning while avoiding arguments dependent on sharp oppositions between referential and emotive uses of language. And the grammatical foundation of speech acts should help ground recent discussions of action in order to show how actions are intelligible and, more important, how viewing literary texts as the presentation of actions for qualitative reflection enables us to elaborate a notion of literary knowledge free of the problems that arise when we must posit some special nondiscursive realm of truths.

It is possible and tempting to abstract from Wittgenstein's torturous dialogues with his sceptical demon a fairly straightforward account of how the various concepts I have just mentioned connect with one another and provide a defensible perspective on questions of meaning and the intelligibility of human actions. But I think doing so immediately would be both a philosophical and a rhetorical mistake. Philosophically, we need a sense of the complexity of the issues before we can fully appreciate the need for a modified, essentially procedural, approach to beginnings. Rhetorically, it seems to me necessary to convince literary theorists and critics of the contemporary relevance of pursuing the narrow and technical matters which must be comprehended if we are to secure a Wittgensteinian perspective and to earn the right to go beyond or modify it.

Both purposes can be served, I think, if I defer my own conceptual beginning to make a detour around and through the influential presence of Jacques Derrida. Where most philosophies have to invent sceptical demons in order to test their claims, those interested in recent Continental thought and literary theory find perhaps a richer demon ready-to-hand. Moreover, Derrida's work is not simply an abstract philosophical scepticism; it is the most thorough and subtle contemporary attack I know on the basic elements of the traditional Western humanism, the broad outlines of which I hope to restate and to defend.[1] Indeed, Derrida's attack often is based on attention to those dimensions of speech acts which will play a central place in my defense. I hope, in fact, not so much to dismiss Derrida as to attempt the bolder strategy of showing how we can employ his work within a perspective on speech acts that evades his metalinguistic scepticism. Finally, my elaborate detour is justified because Derrida and Wittgenstein have a good deal in common, deriving primarily from shared suspicions about traditional Western philosophy's concern for logically established beginnings. I hope that what they share will focus their differences clearly, will make compelling the significance of Wittgenstein's basic moves for avoiding scepticism, will warrant necessary changes I shall propose for speech act theory, and, finally, because of Derrida's current popularity among literary critics, may define a place within literary thought for the more speculative dimensions of Wittgenstein's work. If the reader feels already aware of

---

1. For an explicit claim to represent an *other* to Western traditions of thought, with an immediate qualification of the idea of a "claim," see Jacques Derrida, "Limited Inc," trans. Sam Weber, *Glyph* 2 (1977); 162–254, p. 211 in particular. I shall refer to this text below as LI. I shall also use in my discussion of Derrida the following abbreviations: "Differance," in *Speech and Phenomena: Introduction to the Problem of Signs in Husserl's Phenomenology*, trans. David B. Allison (Evanston: Northwestern University Press, 1973), pp. 129–60, Diff.; and "White Mythology: Metaphor in the Text of Philosophy," *New Literary History* (1974), 5–74, WM.

such issues, he will lose nothing but some possible entertainment by skipping to my discussion of Wittgenstein.

2. *The relation between performance and argument in Derrida*

I shall confine myself now to clarifying Derrida's thinking on the topics of the meaning and assessment of utterances. Later, there shall be plenty of criticism both of Derrida and of what I shall call, following Lionel Abel, the textualist theories his work has fostered. Just restating Derrida is chore enough, since one of his main purposes is to call into question all descriptive uses of language. Perhaps the only way out of the traps he lays is to distinguish strata within his work and to inquire into their possible uses. At its most complex Derrida's writing is pure text, a circulation and recirculation of language which multiplies possibilities of meaning while refusing any single form of projection onto the empirical world. On this level Derrida's texts exemplify a form of pure constitution, of writing on other writing aimed to manifest the way we can make the seams in one discourse the creative ground of another. Such writing also calls attention to the radical difference between the thinking in imaginative acts and that devoted to reality testing or aimed at practical action. Derrida demonstrates beautifully the danger of holding any position since having an *interest* in systematic truth pulls against any traditional ideal of "truth" as impersonal. At his cleverest Derrida makes his reader, and by implication the dream of seeking philosophical "truth" seem a version of the spectator who leaps on the stage in order to save Desdemona. Such a quest for "truth" might be called a category mistake, but this would blind us to the power his writing has to make us suspect the possibility of having clear categories in the first place. Perhaps the most we can say of this level of his texts is that Derrida makes such rich, self-aware and playful internal twists on the sceptical tradition that scepticism itself seems no longer merely a parasitical negation of philosophical assertions. As one of his disciples (or petits supplements) put it "Aux thèses, Derrida substitute l'inscription qui déjoue toute position." [2] Yet the undermining also opens a space of complex intercourse, or other means of exploring *jouissance* among positions.

2. Sarah Koffman in Lucette Finas, Koffman, Roger Laporte, and Jean-Michel Ray, *Écarts: Quatre Essais a propos de Jacques Derrida* (Paris: Fayard, 1973), p. 130. I am indebted to Frederick Bogel for the reference quoted here. I am also indebted to Henry Slatin for pointing out that my work on Derrida had ignored his pure textualism.

It remains possible, however, to desire a discursive understanding of the nature of Derrida's writing and of its possible uses in relation to other texts and practices. Here we must, I think, perform the same operation I suggested for Wittgenstein. We must see how the arguments which seem abstractable from the rich play of consciousness might hold up as possible descriptions of experience implicated in but not totally congruent with the bracketed realm of free play. Thus if one wants either to explain how it is possible to discuss a description of Derrida like the one I just gave or to show why Derrida matters in relation to realms of experience not so confined to textual conditions and aesthetic attitudes, it is probable that one must find ways of employing Derrida within the very practices whose authority he challenges. Such a move is not without problems, but the alternative seems sustainable only by madmen and creative geniuses. If we reject that, or seek to supplement it, we need to specify concrete grounds of inquiry where there can be pragmatic tests of the appropriateness of one's claims. In order to do this with Derrida, I must assume some familiarity with his work. Derrida's text is so closely interwoven that quotations often seem absurd when taken out of context. So while I will try to clarify what I take to be possible arguments derivable from his work, my discussion will depend on some willingness on the reader's part to see the terms in Derrida's contexts. This task will be made more difficult because of another operation I need to perform. I want to acknowledge Derrida's significance within the speculative tradition in which he situates himself—the questioning of metaphysics and transparent self-reflection in Nietzsche, Freud, and Heidegger.[3] But I do so largely to justify the further step of placing his themes within the formulation of issues related to questions of meaning and intention as they have been developed in recent Anglo-American philosophy. In this context and on this level I feel justified in treating Derridian arguments as a sophisticated form of scepticism.

No treatment of Derrida can get very far, however, without first acknowledging the importance of his strategies as a textual performer and reflecting on their possible significance. These are interesting in their own right, and they provide a powerful test case for speech act theory.

3. The best commentaries I know in this vein are Gayatri Spivak, "Preface" to her translation of *Of Grammatology* (Baltimore: Johns Hopkins University Press, 1976), and Joseph Riddel, "From Heidegger to Derrida to Chance; Doubling and Poetic Language," *Boundary* 2 4 (1976):571–92. For a sharp commentary on some of the oversights that arise from remaining within this tradition, see Newton Garver, "Derrida on Rousseau on Writing," *The Journal of Philosophy*, 74 (1977):663–74.

One of Derrida's basic aims in his calling attention to performance is an insistence on what Sartre saw as the irreducibly situated and positional features of an act of consciousness. In Derrida it is discourse, not consciousness, that is positional, because insofar as discourse involves an act, it embodies desires which disrupt or manipulate repeatable truth conditions. Thus, the challenge for me is to grant these performative disruptions of a referential order and still to explain how they remain intelligible as productions of meaning open to public assessment.

Sartrean versions of the performative dimensions of speech acts become the focus of attention in Derrida's admirably baroque reply to John Searle's critique of his attempt to appropriate speech act theory. This essay clearly exemplifies how Derrida the performer goes about undermining specific positions, and through them the idea of philosophy as a coherent discipline. The debate format is a perfect vehicle for this enterprise. It enables Derrida to point out and to play upon the multiple codes, structures of desires, and repetitions and variations of previous thinkers that complicate any simple presence of clear philosophical argument. Derrida creates an almost inescapable scenario, in which philosophical procedures either blindly ignore the actual egoistic and social forces at play or are ultimately subordinate to the will to power. Philosophy becomes a mask which one wears out of self-deceit or the desire to deceive. The status of the argument becomes enormously complex because one can never fix precisely which of the levels of the discourse is motivating segments of the exchange. Consider the following passage from Derrida's conclusion:

> I have promised (very) sincerely to be serious. Have I kept my promise? Have I taken Sarl seriously? I do not know if I was supposed to. Should I have? Were they themselves serious in their speech acts? Shall I say that I am afraid they were? Would that mean that I do not take their seriousness very seriously?
>
> What am I saying? What am I doing when I say that? (LI, 251)

This passage will not sit still for analysis. Where do the claims reside—in the assertions, in the allusions, in the tone? Yet all are relevant, for the issue is whether or not speech acts admit clear interpretation, especially because it is always possible in them to confute normal and parasitical, serious and nonserious, uses, and because context is always possibly problematic. Moreover, even when one thinks he has caught Derrida in a contradiction, the complex tonal play has so undermined the ground that it is plausible for Derrida to claim that he has planted the contradiction. After all, contradictions serve to illustrate the inherent duplicity in lines of argument or the desire to preserve the sexual pleasure of philosophical debate, that encourages philosophers to resist any cure for their blindness (LI, 169 ff.). Yet we have so far only considered self-conscious tonal play and contradiction; once we admit in the loosest terms some kind of unconscious forces, we multiply the codes operating in the text severalfold, and in several folds (an expression that reintroduces the code of sexual pleasure).

This half-serious dispersal of the argument has strange effects on the unsympathetic reader of Derrida's text, effects which reinforce Derrida's undermining of philosophical positions. As the passage quoted above indicates, Derrida lets no term, however innocuous, go unexamined. In addition, he does not respect the economy of someone's argument. If the discourse involves multiple codes, it may be one's subordinate claims that most reward careful scrutiny. The effect is to make one despair of ever providing a philosophical analysis sufficiently self-protective to justify its claims against scepticism, and it calls into question the possibility of communicating at all—for how can one start to communicate if he neither knows what terms need clarifying nor can predict which of his arguments will be taken as crucial? Thus, Derrida comes close to winning even if we do not believe his arguments. With so many confusions possible, it hardly seems worth the trouble to do "serious" philosophy. Seriousness may be so narrow a reduction of discourse that its conclusions are purchased only at the price of blindness to human activity. Whichever way we turn, questions of philosophy entail rhetorical decisions. We come to see how rhetoric entails the will to power, because its main task is precisely to wield power, to limit the endless questioning which is "serious" philosophy, and to provide, by ideology, social authority, metaphor, and charm, a termination to a discourse which reality testing cannot produce. One is tempted to say that in Derrida the open society encounters at once its greatest representative and its greatest contradiction: the endless openness of argument is a continual invitation to assertions of power, whether they be blind propaganda or the sly wisdom of Nietzschean free play.

One cannot, however, reduce Derrida to his performative functions. His originality in the sceptical tradition resides in his development of two principles by which the sceptic can actually state, if not argue, the grounds of, and possible values in, a sceptical perspective. The first is the concept of *sous rature,* or erasure, basic to Gayatri Spivak's account of Derrida. This concept enables Derrida to make assertions while bracketing or crossing out the implicit claim that they are adequate to any task except revealing their own inadequacy. Philosophical terms are used to invoke all of their associations, but no attempt is made to defend a single meaning or to connect a given meaning to testable hypotheses. The effect of this erasure is to increase what is available for the mind to play with, while allowing the terms to collapse into overdeterminations. Derrida's concept of difference, of a grounding nonconcept determining the endless supplements preventing signifier and signified from coinciding, at once states why erasure is necessary and demonstrates the very process of erasing any single way to test an idea. The idea of crossing out and yet preserving concepts becomes an ironic version of Hegelian negation. The second sceptical strategy is not so carefully hedged and can be evaluated. This strategy is crucial, because it provides a conceptual link between Derrida's performances and his actual arguments. I refer to his stress on the importance of taking the possibilities surrounding a concept as inescapably tied to it and as thus undermining any secure applications of the concept:

> A corruption that is "always possible" cannot be a mere extrinsic accident supervening on a structure that is original and pure, one that can be purged of what thus happens to it. The purportedly "ideal" structure must necessarily be such that this corruption will be "always possible." This possibility constitutes part of the *necessary* traits of the purportedly ideal structure. The ("ideal") description of this structure should thus include, and not exclude, this possibility. (LI, 218)

Conceptually, this stress on possibility is intended to combat what Derrida sees as the central deception necessary for traditional Western philosophy—the assumption that one can pose, without sustained argument, ideal cases which represent the "normal" referent of an abstract concept, like *truth* or *speech act* or *context.* Such normalizing, Derrida argues, not only evades the complexities of experience, but also covertly establishes hierarchies of relevance in oppositions like "normal-eccentric," "serious-nonserious." Thus, traditional philosophy ignores the complex issue of what forms of power authorize these oppositions in the first place, and constrains itself to repeating as discoveries the very hierarchies of oppositions assumed as grounds of the analytic discourse (LI, 234–

36). Searle, for example, wants to account for speech acts, but then assumes a normal case, which in turn justifies his arguments for the clarity of intentions and contexts. Yet it is these concepts which actually establish his criteria for normality and justify his banishing other "possible" speech acts as abnormal or parasitic.

The point of Derrida's performances is to enact within philosophical discourse the range of possibilities which that discourse tries to exclude. Whatever he can express, like the complexity of forces in a speech act, becomes then a necessary field for testing and revealing the limits in the grounding assumptions that allow philosophers to make "secure" oppositions and thus to "prove" their case. We see why Derrida is sincere in expressing his admiration for Austin's problematic, because of its challenge to simple oppositions like true/false as adequate dimensions for assessing what Austin tried to convince himself were a specifiable range of convention-bound speech acts. For Derrida, as we have seen in a different context, once you multiply possibilities as conditions of a subject matter and terms for assessment, you make philosophizing such a complex, interminable discourse that you reveal its dependence on an interminable dream of cure. In the process you dramatize the dependence of philosophy on powers to limit a discourse, which themselves cannot be philosophically grounded (without stopping possibilities), but must depend on the power of will, ideology, or social structure.

3. Derrida's "position" on meaning

One cannot avoid metaphilosophical issues in discussing Derrida, but it is important to see also how his metaconcepts, like *possibility*, are derived from close philosophical analysis of standard questions. Two of his basic doctrines are especially significant for specific problems of meaning—his attack on *origin* and *presence*, and his metaphoric use of the notion of writing. These "doctrines" (again, erase if you will) in turn deepen the performative qualities and the bite of his claims about possibility, because each seems intended once again to reveal the overdetermined and yet fundamentally ungrounded nature of traditional philosophical arguments.

It is obvious, for example, that unless philosophy can explain how its propositions can assert clear, testable ideas, the discourse is condemned to endless vacillation between masked versions of a will or wills to power, working in and on the rhetorician's art rather than with the analytic scientist's rigorous heuristic methods. Thus, in attacking the notion of presence, Derrida feels he is taking on the basic possibility that meanings can be securely grounded and assessed independently of the discourse situation in which they are created. The attack has two objects —analytic versions of a correspondence model of assessing and determining meaning by reference, and psychologistic phenomenological accounts of meaning as anchored in the power of language to embody and to express an agent's intentions:

> The possibility of a certain non-presence or of a certain non-actuality pertains to the structure of the functioning under consideration [proper names], and pertains to it necessarily. . . .
>   What is valid for intention, always differing and deferring, and without plenitude, is also valid, correlatively, for the object (qua signified or referent) thus aimed at. However, this limit, I repeat ("without" plenitude) is also the ("positive") condition of possibility of what is thus limited. (LI, 195)

Against correspondence theories of truth, Derrida argues that we can never posit—without the continual possibility of error—either an adequate correlation of a philosophical signifier to the signified or of the signified meaning to clear, repeatable factual situations. Thus, we cannot establish secure meanings, at least for abstract terms, which would enable us to treat them as pictures of facts, nor can we verify the pictures by repeating as present the state of affairs referred to. Referring depends on naming, and, for Derrida, proper names are the test case for the possibility of true descriptions: "A name is a proper name when it has only one sense. Or rather it is only in this case that it is properly a name" (WM, 48). But, following Saussure, he proceeds to argue that to have one name we must have a system of names which *qua* system displaces any single pictorial line between name and object into the differential operation of systematic oppositions, which are always possibly multiple: "The signified concept is never present in itself, in an adequate presence that would refer only to itself. Every concept is necessarily and eventually described in a chain or a system, within which it refers to another and to other concepts, by the systematic play of differences. Such a play, then—differance—is no longer simply a concept, but the possibility of conceptuality" (Diff., 140). A similar case can be made, as we shall see below, by deconstructing the opposition between proper name and metaphor, so that traces of metaphor can always possibly displace reference into the overdetermined structures of metaphoric chains.[4]

The attack on intention as a form of presence will likewise become more clear as the problem is repeated in other contexts. For now, the outline of the case can be made by simply considering the ironic pun inherent in the French expression for meaning—*vouloir dire*. Here we see in another form the problem of clearly treating claims for existential properties within a structure of intelligibility for signs that has its own order. If meaning is *wanting to say*, what guarantees that the wanting and the saying will be congruent with one another? (cf. Diff., 147). The speaking and the desire differ from one another not only in the expression *vouloir dire*, but in any attempt to find in words—which are infinitely repeatable as the conditions for speech—the presence of intentions, which one assumes must be specific psychological forces in distinct situations. One cannot deny the presence of intentions, but neither can one see them as fully present. Speech depends on a desire, from which it must differ if it is to be intelligible beyond the private desire. Yet, as intention becomes at once present and absent, the discourse, too, is divided—both under and overdetermined by a necessary, yet indefinable, genesis it cannot fully re-present. Thus Derrida casts Searle in the complementary roles of inadequate philosopher, unable to say what he intends, and self-deceived protagonist in a power struggle which ironically reveals itself in the intentions unconsciously expressed in his discourse. What should be present is absent; what one desires to absent from himself becomes disturbingly present.

Derrida uses the notion of writing as a basis for his most general attempt to pose the conditions which render *presence* so problematic an ideal. In conventional terms, we might describe these general claims as substituting a coherence for a correspondence model of truth. Then Derrida sceptically inverts any possible arbiter of coherence and denies clear links between the system and some independent realm of facts. (Coherence theory is the Hegelian dynamic Derrida continually uses and subverts.) Writing is the condition in which one recognizes that signs are

---

4. The general outline of Derrida's attack on reference repeats a constant theme in arguments for correspondence models of truth. Compare, for example, Nicholas Rescher's account of the quarrel between Stoics and Pyrrhonian sceptics in his *The Coherence Theory of Truth* (Oxford: Clarendon Press, 1973), pp. 12–16. I should add that I consider Rescher's version of a coherence theory of truth a formally defensible and sophisticated version of what I stumble toward in my attempts at a Kantian reading of Wittgenstein's procedural model.

deprived of presence (in contrast to phenomenological idealizations of speech) and thus require one another in systematic relations in order to preserve intelligibility. Yet, the mutual dependence of signs is also a mutual displacement that, in the absence of correspondence, overdetermines the signs and prevents any coherent single chain of meanings from developing.

I stress the analogue between Derrida and coherence theories because I think that the theme of writing and the correlative themes it generates are most clear and resonant when placed in the light of Kant's basic effect on subsequent philosophy. It is through Kant that we can at once see Derrida's work in the context of traditional philosophy and recognize the general structure of inquiry giving him affinities with Nietzsche, Freud, Marx, and, indirectly, the later Wittgenstein. The relevant aspect of Kant's thought is his powerful and inescapable articulation of the difficulties in linking structures of representation to some *other* of representation, some *"ding an sich,"* which simultaneously activates or motivates the representational structure and escapes its terms.[5] In other words, closer to Kant's language, Kant saw clearly how difficult it would be to show how the a priori could also be synthetic; once one posits a realm of phenomena dependent on a priori constitutive powers of mind, he creates a nearly unbridgeable gulf between these and some noumenal reality external to these images. The direct heritage of Kant is German Idealism, on the one hand, with its denial of any external reality not ultimately identical with mind, and, on the other hand, Schlegel's Romantic irony, insisting on the inevitable gulf between representations and actual empirical references. Similar oppositions, then, emerge in the many ways subsequent thinkers distinguish between manifest and latent content—not only Freud and Marx, but Nietzsche on metaphor and morality, Bergson on abstraction and *élan vital*, and even Heidegger on beings and the presence of Being. And it is by stressing this problematic that contemporary thinkers articulate the difficulty of Freud and Marx

5. I apply to Kant this dilemma taken from Michel Foucault's account of problems facing contemporary human sciences in the last chapter of his *The Order of Things* (New York: Random House, 1970). For a reading of German Idealism as emerging out of Kant's attempt to resolve a priori and synthetic, see Josiah Royce, *Lectures on Modern Idealism* (New Haven: Yale University Press, 1919). For clear examples of how Derrida's thought depends on and leads to problematics involving the notions of representation and what I call its other, see *Of Grammatology*, on supplement, pp. 141–64, and Eugenio Donato, "The Idioms of the *Text*: Notes on the Language of Philosophy and the Fictions of Literature," *Glyph* 2 (1977):1–13.

actually naming, within the manifest structures of analytic discourse, the specific nature of the displacing and motivating forces revealed in latent content and economic infrastructure.

Derrida's concept of writing, with its associated metaphors of trace, hymen, supplement, restance, parergon, and dissemination, can be seen as a precise rendering of this problematic relation between representation and its other. Derrida alters his heritage by shifting the basis of representational structures from properties of mind to properties of language, as defined through Saussure's differential method. Thus, because language re-presents and does not picture what it purports to refer to, meanings depend on structures of signs or other meanings, none of which is securely anchored in a reality outside language. And this general picture of writing as representation enables Derrida to achieve a kind of freedom within the Kantian tradition. Derrida does not "naively" try either to reconcile a priori and synthetic, or to argue, as Bergson and Heidegger do, for the priority of one pole of the opposition over another. Instead, he makes the necessary constitutive power of that opposition the fundamental condition of all thinking, and hence ground for a sceptical treatment of meanings as always partial and always producing further possibilities of discourse. Thinking is the production of an interminable discourse desiring to bridge the gap between the structures of a written textuality and the realm of experience it continually displaces as it *names*. The clearest evidence for this approach to Derrida's thought is his description of *differance*, the nonconcept which is necessary ground of the play of presence and absence in all concepts:

> Differance is what makes the movement of signification possible only if each element that is said to be "present," appearing on the stage of presence, is related to something other than itself but retains the mark of a past element and already lets itself be hollowed out by the mark of its relation to a future element. This trace relates no less to what is called the future than to what is called the past, and it constitutes what is called the present by this very relation to what it is not, to what it absolutely is not; that is not even to a past or future considered as a modified present. . . . And it is this constitution of the present as a "primordial" and irreducibly nonsimple, and therefore in the strict sense nonprimordial, synthesis of traces, retentions and protentions . . . that I propose to call protowriting, prototrace or differance. The later (is) (both) spacing (and) temporalizing. (Diff., 143)

4. *Deconstructive hermeneutics*

If *differance* is the ground of meanings, it demands a form of hermeneutic activity not bound by delusions of presence in either referential or intentional terms. This is Derridean deconstruction. But in order to see what deconstruction can do, we must first be more clear on the nature of signs as constituents of a primordially written textual foundation for acts in language. Here the crucial concepts are *iterability* and *dissemination*. Iterability is a rich notion for exhibiting the problem of any discourse claiming presence. On the one hand, pure iterability seems a necessary condition for any scientific account of truth. In Husserl, for example, the test of the truth of a statement is its being permanently repeatable and verifiable in other languages and situations. But for Derrida, pure repetition is not defensible, because linguistic codes and contexts always raise the possibility of alteration (cf. *Speech and Phenomena,* and LI, 190 *ff.*). Yet, some form of iterability is inescapable, because of the need for language to remain intelligible, independent from the private experiences of individual speakers. This principle becomes the wedge for splitting Searle's claims about intention and determinate contexts:

> Iterability makes possible idealization—and thus a certain identity in repetition that is independent of the multiplicity of factual events —while at the same time limiting the idealization it makes possible: broaching and breeching it at once.... The very factor that will permit the mark ... to function beyond this moment—namely the possibility of its being repeated another time—breeches, divides, expropriates the "ideal" plenitude or self presence of intention, of meaning (to say) and, *a fortiori* of all adequation between meaning and saying. Iterability alters, contaminating parasitically what it identifies and enables to repeat "itself"; it leaves us no choice but to mean (to say) something that is (already, always, also) other than what we mean (to say), to say something other than what we say and would have wanted to say, to understand something other than ... etc. The *mis* of misunderstandings ... must have its essential condition of possibility in the structure of ... oral and written utterances. (LI, 200)

In order to say what I mean (*vouloir dire*), I must use terms that can mean without my presence (thus the analogue of writing). But then the direct experience of the I is contaminated by the need to express that experience in terms repeated from other contexts not proper to the exact occasion or capable of strictly constraining how an auditor attributes presence to the terms (LI, 194–95). Neither experience nor intending self can remain undivided. This condition is exemplified for Derrida in the plight of Austin's discourse on speech acts: because Austin could not separate his vision from the borrowed terms needed to express it, his discourse is simultaneously under- and overdetermined. It says less than he meant and offers more possibilities than he could control, creating a field of meanings to be appropriated differently by Searle and by Derrida. Because the possibility of corruption is a necessary condition of intelligibility, iterability explains why discourse can be seen as dissemination. If discourse were the communication of a presence, and hence real conversation rather than interminable dialogue, it might warrant the metaphor of insemination. But, in its divisions within itself, discourse continually produces meanings which never fertilize reproduction but invite further dispersal in ultimately narcissistic acts.

Deconstruction, then, is a (non) method for interpreting the interplay of iterability and dissemination in a piece of discourse or, because of the absence of an identifiable intending agent, of a text. If we must say something other than what we mean to say, the role of interpretation is to trace the mechanisms by which the displacements occur and to give examples of the possibilities they disseminate. Texts exist in complex fields of iteration and variation, inviting further versions of those properties. Thus, deconstruction rests on three preconditions: the transformation of intentional act into textuality; an emphasis on the necessarily intertextual field of dependencies that a text enters when identity proves a divided interplay of repetition and difference; and the recognition that the interpreter himself is similarly divided and cannot claim the authority to correct another's illusions. (At best, he can reweave the object text so that its inadequacies stand clear, but not as dialectical negations allowing a "better" solution to the problem.) The object of interpretation, then, is not acts, or even single texts, but textual fields and folds. Deconstruction aims (ideally?) at revealing the structural seams of a system, so that one can see how contradictions are not simply negations of an argument's validity but inescapable duplicities that ground and disseminate the specific enterprise of trying to make a coherent argument:

> The task is, not to consolidate the position . . . by setting up a symmetrical position at the other, systematic pole, but rather to dis-

mantle the metaphysical and rhetorical structures which are at work in this position, not in order to reject or discard them, but to reconstitute them in another way, and above all in order to begin to identify the historical terrain—the problematic—in which it has been possible to inquire systematically of all philosophy the metaphorical credentials of its concepts. (WM, 13)

One of Derrida's best deconstructions should serve both to exemplify these strategies and to summarize his case on the inadequacy of models that base secure meanings on correspondence or phenomenological versions of presence. "White Mythology" takes as its subject the possibility of making sharp philosophical distinctions between names, which denote single referents, and metaphors, which duplicate and contaminate any single direction for empirical inquiry. Unless names can be secured, basic distinctions between normal and abnormal, direct and parasitical, even referential and emotive (*emotive* at least in the sense of having ineradicable traces of desire), all become problematic. Derrida's strategy is to show that the field of oppositions can never be resolved or reduced to a single hierarchy, because the concepts of name and of metaphor depend on one another. Neither can claim priority (logically or temporally), without basing its claim on its opposite: "Philosophy as a theory of metaphor will first have been a metaphor of theory" (WM, 56). Aristotle, for example, uses the concept of proper name as emblem of secure meaning or *propre sens*, in order to distinguish name from metaphor, yet the concept itself relies on a metaphor which disperses the name into several subversive codes. Let us ignore the duplicity of *sens*, although its foldings from French to English are fascinating, and concentrate simply on *propre*. The sign invokes at least two linguistic codes or sets of oppositions—one implying economic possession and the other social authority. *Propre*, then, introduces as aspects of its meaning precisely those properties of external determination and wills to power which idealizing philosophy seeks to exclude from the realm of testable truths. The attempt to purge from philosophy the contamination of sophistic rhetoric and to distinguish philosophical inquiry from desires for power requires implicating traces of threats to clarity which should be excluded. This does not mean that all uses of proper names are suspect, but it does insist that the concept of proper name gains authority only at the cost of what is, for philosophy, a most egregious impropriety. Moreover, once we recognize the necessity of this opposition, and perhaps the message it proclaims, we find it somewhat silly (and an exercise in claiming truth as one's property) to attempt to spin out one more attempt to resolve the problem in terms of one of the two opposites. We will choose neither Aristotle nor Gorgias, but will content ourselves with the somewhat perverse *hope* (Diff., 158) that gay wisdom resides in accepting, as the only satisfying form of philosophy, the disseminating process to which we are condemned.

Whatever the specific problems in his arguments, Derrida is an inescapable thinker because he so thoroughly and complexly sounds the implications of our growing awareness that a kind of death bell has been tolling for traditional philosophical argument in our culture. Bacon's complaint, that philosophy in effect disseminates a plethora of words without ever producing fruit, may not be wholly true, but our culture more and more recognizes the limits of a discourse doomed to be interminably about and round about itself. Derrida's ultimate irony is his repetition of the dream that philosophy is the ideal example of human discourse, but as an image of its inevitable disease rather than of enlightenment. There remain, of course, several forms of analytic philosophy which state their claims carefully enough to avoid Derrida's charges. But it seems to me probable that any renewal of a speculative philosophy capable of fully treating literary values must face Derrida's challenge and must give a coherent picture of the grounds and implications of the multiplicity and duplicity that characterize human language.

5. The idea of meaning in *Wittgenstein's* Investigations

Wittgenstein's later work provides a framework for meeting Derrida's challenges. No philosopher is more aware of the complexities of language, but for Wittgenstein complexity itself becomes a stage on which to recover new, more pragmatic, ways of understanding how we do in fact make sense of the duplicities and folds of discourse. These complexities sustain Derrida's scepticism only if it is possible to support Derrida's two basic philosophical claims—that philosophy requires a notion of *propre sens* and cannot secure the concept, and that discourse is always plagued by overdetermined possibilities which cannot be adequately constrained. I want to argue, instead, that Wittgenstein can handle these claims—indeed, it is precisely Derrida's pressure which reveals the significance of the model of philosophical thinking projected by Wittgenstein's later writings. Wittgenstein shares with Derrida a profound hostility to traditional philosophical and psychologistic versions of referential presence as the criteria for defining the sense and use value of utterances. For both philosophers, these suspicions even lead to similar explorations of therapeutic metaphors for philosophy—with Wittgenstein, however, holding open hope for a possible cure.[6] The terms for such a cure derive primarily from replacing the dream of *propre sens* with a framework capable of specifying appropriate senses and uses for linguistic acts. In rejecting his earlier logical atomism, Wittgenstein turns from a pictorial model and referential criteria to a reliance on the concept of methods of projection grounded in the ways people come to share a culture. And it is the grammatical competence which education in a culture produces that enables us to establish criteria for appropriateness and then to rely on practical considerations for defining degrees of probable relevance in hypotheses about meanings. Grammar, then, establishes expectations where probability is not a matter of statistical regularity but of specific contextual judgments about plausibility and adequacy.

Within these procedural frameworks, Derrida's ontological scepticism is not so much refuted as revealed to be irrelevant for the rough grounds that sustain human communication. It may well be the case that we have no absolutely secure grounds for *truth*, but the more important question is whether we need these grounds for coherent discourse, even on the self-reflective levels within which philosophical analysis takes place. Without such forms of truth, we may not be able to produce single, systematic accounts of human behavior capable of resisting sceptical attacks. But on procedural grounds, and within a model of appropriate senses, it is the sceptic who must face up to the burden of showing his relevance. It will not do to undermine abstract philosophical positions, because that process only brings us back to the need for explaining the forms of intelligibility and coherence we do in fact rely upon in a nonphilosophical, practical world. Derridean scepticism may undermine the unity of philosophical systems, but it leaves us with multiple forms of coherence and probabilities which still demand explana-

6. For good discussions comparing Derrida and Wittgenstein, see Marjorie Greene, "Life, Death, and Language: Some Thoughts on Wittgenstein and Derrida," *Partisan Review* 43 (1976):265–79, and Newton Garver, "Preface" to *Speech and Phenomena*, pp. xix–xxix. Garver elegantly demonstrates how both thinkers base their attacks against traditional Western philosophy on a denial that logic is prior to rhetoric.

tion, and, more important, which provide limited criteria for these explanations. Most important for my purposes, by showing the necessity for strategies like Wittgenstein's that can account for probabilistic criteria (and through these for basic certainties, where no alternative model of behavior is conceivable), Derridean scepticism ironically brings out the significance and the power of interpretive strategies and methods of projection based on old-fashioned humanistic virtues, like sensitivity to context and the capacity to make perspicuous practical judgments. Simply stating the need for such virtues will not suffice as explanation or defense. But Wittgenstein is no pious humanist. What pieties I can derive from his work will depend on exploring his ways of establishing how we learn to recognize and to employ methods of projection. Through Wittgenstein, we shall begin to develop terms for establishing a fully dramatistic account of meanings and qualities, within which these humanistic virtues are at once necessary and defensible.

6. *Forms of life and grammar as the grounds for philosophical descriptions*

Wittgenstein's later work can be defined largely in terms of a simple conceptual consideration: if there are to be determinate and assessable meanings and uses of language, the terms for understanding meanings must derive from some kind of common world. Either this common world is based on an image of an essence outside of language—whether it be Platonic ideas, or the protocol facts and direct observations of the empiricist and positivist traditions—or it develops in some form from the ways people learn to use language through the activities and procedures they have in common. Thus, in denying the former alternative, he is not left with Derridean oppositions between natural origins and free play, or between names and metaphors. But he takes on the difficult burden of explaining these forms of agreement without relying on some Kantian model of a priori mental structures.

Wittgenstein is so powerful a figure on the nature of meanings because he won his later position only by conquering both the positivist in himself and the latent scepticism that follows upon a distrust of positivist ontology. Thus, the clearest context for approaching his later work is its relationship to the *Tractatus*. There, it is crucial to note, Wittgenstein accepted the traditional oppositions Derrida feeds upon as the only alternatives: either words could be shown to refer to substances that existed independently of language, or truth and falsity were mere constructions of an endlessly regressive process of signification:

2.02   Objects are simple.
2.201   Every statement about complexes can be resolved into a statement about their constituents and into the propositions that describe the complexes completely.
2.021   Objects make up the substance of the world. That is why they cannot be composite.
2.0211 If the world had no substance, then whether a proposition had sense would depend on whether another proposition was true.
2.0212 In that case we could not "sketch" out any picture of the world (true or false).[7]

Wittgenstein's later withdrawal from this position can be described simply, in terms of four basic claims warranting a procedural approach to meaning: (1) that logical simples, or basic facts, cannot be discovered independently of *methods of projection* which guarantee their status as facts; (2) that one can develop what I shall call an ontology based on *forms of life* which explains why analytic and empirical methods are not sufficiently subtle or complex interpretive tools; (3) that one can describe the ways these procedures operate in terms of a *linguistic phenomenology* which Wittgenstein termed *philosophical grammar*; and (4) that these moves avoid any grounding opposition between the Kantian dichotomy of representation and its other, which, by negating correspondence, leaves only ironic tensions between an impossible dream of presence and an "arbitrary" structure of signs displacing one another.

---

7. I shall use the following abbreviations for Wittgenstein's work in my text: Wittgenstein, *Philosophical Investigations*, trans. G. E. M. Anscombe (New York: Macmillan, 1958)—PI; *Notebooks, 1914–1916*, trans. G. E. M. Anscombe (New York: Harper Torchbooks, 1969)—NB; *Tractatus Logico-Philosophicus*, trans. D. F. Pears and B. F. McGuiness (London: Routledge and Kegan Paul, 1961)—TLP; *The Blue and the Brown Books* (New York: Harper Torchbooks, 1965)—BB; "Lecture on Ethics," *The Philosophical Review* 74 (January 1965):3–12—LE; *On Certainty*, ed. G. E. M. Anscombe and G. H. Von Wright (New York: Harper Torchbooks, 1972)—OC; *Lectures and Conversations on Aesthetics, Psychology, and Religious Belief*, ed. Cyril Barrett (Berkeley: University of California Press, 1972)—LA; *Zettel*, ed. G. E. M. Anscombe and G. H. Von Wright (Berkeley: University of California, 1970)—Z; and G. E. Moore, "Wittgenstein's Lectures in 1930–33," in his *Philosophical Papers* (New York: Collier, 1962), pp. 247–318—PP.

Wittgenstein's denial of the empirical dream of simple objects to which names must correspond gives his *Philosophical Investigations* a starting point very similar to that of Derrida, whose philosophy begins with an attack on Husserl's quest for apodictic essences.[8] But Wittgenstein had seen enough of Derrida's polarities in the *Tractatus* to develop strategies for replacing secure simple objects with something more stable and communal and less demonically theological than the concept of free play. He recognized that the concept of simples has a linguistic and an ontological aspect. Linguistically, a desire for simples leads to what might be called a *label* view of language, such as the Augustinian view Wittgenstein criticizes in the opening of the *Investigations*. This view assumes that the basic function of language is to name objects and actions on the model of ostensive definition. This clearly won't do for expressive and connotative dimensions of language (and hence helps explain why labelling or correspondence theories tend to banish these dimensions from the realm of objective meanings), but there is also a deeper problem that leads to ontological considerations. For, as Hegel showed in a different way, the possibility of making ostensive definitions is not a pure, unmediated relationship between mind and nature. It presupposes the existence of categories and procedures that enable the hearer to know precisely what is being pointed to in a given situation. If I say, "That is called a cow," how does my auditor know I am speaking about the whole object, and not its shape or color, or way of standing (PI, 33–36)? Philosophy that assumes the proper way to ground the meanings of words is by showing they can be analyzed into logical simples essentially reverses the way ostensive meanings actually function— "Only someone who already knows how to do something with it can significantly ask a name" (PI, 31)—so one source of determinate meanings must be in the forms of speaking rather than in the objects pointed to.

The same argument against the possibility of reducing composites to logical simples independent of human actions can be put in more formal epistemological terms:

8. I find Anthony Kenny, *Wittgenstein* (Cambridge: Harvard University Press, 1973), the best supplementary text for understanding the basic themes of the *Tractatus* and for appreciating the considerations leading to the changes from his earlier position. Kenny's specific discussion of pictorial form in the TLP makes clear the possible parallels to a mimetic aesthetics. For a brief general description of positivism and the reasons British philosophers came to reject it, see G. J. Warnock, *English Philosophy Since 1900*, 2d edition (New York: Oxford University Press, 1969).

But isn't a chessboard, for instance, obviously, and absolutely, composite? You are probably thinking of the composition out of thirty-two white and thirty-two black squares. But could we not also say, for instance, that it was composed of the colors black and white and the schema of squares? And if there are quite different ways of looking at it, do you still want to say that the chessboard is absolutely 'composite'? Asking "Is this object composite?" outside a particular language game is like what a boy once did, who had to say whether the verbs in certain sentences were in the active or passive voice, and who racked his brains over the question whether the verb "to sleep" meant something active or passive.

We use the word "composite" (and therefore the word "simple") in an enormous number of different and differently related ways. Is the colour of a square on a chessboard simple, or does it consist of pure white and pure yellow? And is white simple or does it consist of the colours of the rainbow? . . . (PI, 47)

How then can words have determinate meanings, or propositions any verifiable truths, if their contents are always open to reinterpretation from other perspectives? (In other terms, how do we escape the central feature of modernist consciousness?) Wittgenstein's answer—through the concept of language games—is well known. I find the best way of formulating the change from an ontology of logical simples to one based on language games contained in Wittgenstein's remark that in the *Tractatus* "he had confused the method of projection with the lines of projection." [9] He had argued that truth functions depended on demonstrating a logical form, which could operate pictorially by arranging aspects of a statement in a mirror relation to states of affairs. Logical form, then, captures lines of projection between propositions and the world they purport to represent. But Wittgenstein came to see that this logical form was not the only, or even the most characteristic, way language projects a relationship to the world. Thus, the lines of projection he had so carefully traced to logical atoms and their internal potential for interrelationships were not the only conditions for valid speaking,

9. Peter Winch makes very nice use of the distinction between lines and methods of projection in "Introduction: The Unity of Wittgenstein's Philosophy," in Winch, ed., *Studies in the Philosophy of Wittgenstein* (New York: Humanities Press, 1969), pp. 1–19. As one example of the difference between the two forms of projection, compare the *Tractatus* metaphor of logic as a ruler held up to the world (2.1512) with PI, 430, where the ruler is "in itself . . . dead, and achieves nothing of what thought achieves."

but simply one valid method of projection. What should most concern the philosopher is not the state of objects, but the many established ways there are of dealing with them. The philosopher's role is not to analyze propositions into a truth-functional logic in order to test whether they picture and mirror the world. Rather, he must examine the way utterances and descriptions fit in specific contexts or operations, and *fit*, in turn, is not a mirroring relationship but a matter of appropriateness to specific forms of acting on objects. The central ontological concern of the philosopher is no longer with objects but with ways of acting, and the language game is the means for explaining how actions are essentially public and grounded on agreements that must be prior to any process of checking statements about objects. Language games tell us what aspects of objects might constitute relevant proof for a given proposition: "I shall call the whole, consisting of language and the actions into which it is woven, the 'language game'" (PI, 7), and "To imagine a language means to imagine a form of life" (PI, 19), not to imagine a set of grounding objects and logical relations.

The shift from lines of projection to methods of projection involves a different vision of the form of knowledge most fundamental to philosophy. The *Tractatus*, like most empiricist treatments of knowledge, concentrates on how we know *that* something is the case. The *Investigations* tries instead to understand our knowing *how* to do a variety of things with language.[10] Knowing how is logically prior to any specific claim that something is the case, for we must have mastered techniques before we can meaningfully point to objects and understand utterances. The consequence for philosophy is substantial. Analytic logic can not be treated, even implicitly, as a means for specifying ultimate terms or determining the authority of philosophical arguments. Such logic is a tool, a line of projection that cannot interpret its own relevance as a method. Analytic logic assumes an ideal relationship between mind and world not influenced by methods of projection, and thus posits ideals which ultimately oversimplify the complexity of experience: "We have got on to slippery ice where there is no friction and so in a certain sense the conditions are ideal, but also just because of that, we are unable to walk. We want to walk so we need *friction*. Back to the rough ground" (PI, 107; cf. 89–133).

What would an ontology adequate to this rough ground look like? There are at least two basic features—a concern for actions rather than

10. The best discussion of *knowing how* and *knowing that* is Gilbert Ryle's in *The Concept of Mind* (New York: Barnes and Noble, 1949).

propositions as primary objects of attention, and a model of certainty which relies on human procedures and conventions rather than correspondence to facts, but with no possibility of standing outside these conventions to call them "arbitrary" and to posit a deeper reality beyond them, of which they are interpretations.

Consider Wittgenstein's most abstract and general statement of the ontology required by his vision of methods of projection: "If we construe the grammar of the expression of sensation on the model of 'object' and 'designation' the object drops out of consideration as irrelevant" (PI, 293).[11] The point here is not to propose a new idealism, but to allow philosophy to account for the multiple modes of projection that constitute the rough ground of experience. There are language games we play which depend on correlating names and objects, but it is the *form* of sentences and contexts which tells us that, and not the specific elements referred to. We name things or describe sensations because we know how they can be used in language games: "Children do not learn that books exist, that armchairs exist, etc., etc.,—they learn to fetch books, sit in armchairs, etc., etc...." (OC, 476), and: "So one must know that the objects whose names one teaches a child by an ostensive definition exist! Why must one know they do? Isn't it enough that experience doesn't later show the opposite?" (OC, 477; cf. OC, 144, 410). The point is not that objects do not exist, but that there are two reasons why it is useless for the philosopher to bother himself with them and with methods of checking for ways language corresponds to them. First, what we mean by *objects* and *exist* is not fixed and simple but de-

11. Although I resist the temptation to develop analogies from Husserl on bracketing objects, I do assume here that Wittgenstein's statements like this one can be made the foundation of abstract claims (I do not know how else to take them), even though he clearly does not argue them as such. I think it is this uncertainty how to take Wittgenstein that is a major factor in the current disfavor with which analytic philosophers regard him. They do not refute his work, but find it insufficiently rigorous and verifiable, and they may be right from their perspective: Wittgenstein may not have propounded views that can be tested or followed up by analytic philosophy. He would say, of course, that this is because their questions cannot be answered within the only grounds there are for certainty about human experiences, the rough grounds of procedure. It should suffice here to say that I do not claim that Wittgenstein's ontology is in any sense ultimate; we might discover empirical laws for procedures and for the constitution of objects. But I do claim that if we are interested in the concepts of experience, his ontology makes a coherent and defensible foundation, one not yet seriously threatened by the forms we have for proving empirical object statements and general laws. For a fuller treatment of Wittgenstein's relationship to science and many of the topics in this discussion of ontology, see my "Wittgenstein on Consciousness and Language: A Challenge to Derridean Literary Theory," *MLN* 91 (1976): 1397–423.

pendent on the methods of projection used. Is the color white on the chessboard an object? And, second, there is something absurd in checking statements that people agree are meaningful, and in terms of which they can act against some abstract notion of objectivity: our experience of what we trust as objects and relationships is more immediate and secure than might be a philosophical analysis of abstract and rarely used terms (outside of philosophy) like *object* and *exist*.[12] This is not to say that specific methods of projection, like those used in scientific inquiry or logic, might not clarify or change the meanings of such terms within the relevant disciplines, but scientific discoveries about the constitution of matter are not likely to change our ways of dealing with tables and chairs as objects to be manipulated in conventional ways for our ordinary experiences (cf. BB, 45).

It is crucial, then, to recognize that when we consider objects as irrelevant we do not do away with forms of secure knowledge, but simply alter the grounds for determining what we know and can trust as secure and meaningful. Instead of rooting essences in nature, Wittgenstein insists that "Essence is expressed by grammar" (PI, 371). "Grammar tells us what kind of an object anything is" (PI, 373), and the philosopher's task becomes what he calls explicating the philosophical grammar informing human ways of using language. Philosophical grammar is the process of analyzing the ways in which we make sense of our experiences by relating them to established language games or by modifying language games in accordance with specifiable contexts. Philosophical grammar is the means for analyzing methods of projection—rather than lines of projection—and thus for exploring the activities which constitute a human world (cf. PI, 29).

Philosophical grammar is a concept that can best be clarified in my forthcoming discussion of speech acts, because this concept provides procedures for understanding the link between methods of projection and Wittgenstein's statements on meaning as use. For now, though, we can see the basic ontological status of the concept by contrasting the criteria it provides with concepts of representational thinking that lead to Derrida. For Wittgenstein's approach also raises questions of linking an a priori grammar to synthetic features of actual experience. How can he then avoid the charge that in renouncing presence and correspondence he finds himself relying on forms that are essentially "arbitrary"

---

12. For a good statement of the priority of experiential over analytic grounds for certainty with respect to fundamental concepts, see Stuart Hampshire, *Thought and Action* (London: Chatto and Windus, 1959), pp. 48–49.

or mere interpretations that easily slip into the displacing free play of signifiers? Paul Ricoeur makes essentially this claim in an interesting comparison of Husserl and Wittgenstein. He argues that Wittgenstein's stress on analyzing signs according to the ways they are used ignores the more fundamental issue of the ontological status of the sign. Once we raise this issue, Ricoeur continues, we cannot ignore the arbitrary systematic qualities of language pointed out by Saussure, and we must recognize that the very fact we recognize a sign as only an arbitrary element indicates the unbridgeable and problematic "distance between thought and life." This distance, for Ricoeur, at once requires language —a system trying to bridge thought and life—and renders language continually problematic.[13]

Wittgenstein's response, I think, would be to turn the tables on Ricoeur by inviting him to recognize that his own philosophical language is more problematic than the language of ordinary experience on which philosophical grammar operates. Making abstract pronouncements about a gap between *thought* and *life* leaves us unclear about both the terms of the problem and ways to adjudicate among competing analyses, while philosophical grammar has at least a set of operations by which to explain difficulties that arise in existential contexts. Ricoeur abstracts language into a reified, monolithic formal system, and leaves himself with no way of examining the variety of uses to which language is put in *life*. The basic terms of his argument, like *life* and *arbitrary*, make sense within philosophical traditions, but Ricoeur can give us no way of adapting them to account for actual behavior. It is precisely to blunt the force of Ricoeur's kind of language, and to demand that it be tested in existential contexts, that Wittgenstein developed the strategy of posing *intermediate cases*. Thus, in the following sequence we find

13. Ricoeur, "Husserl and Wittgenstein," in A. Lee and M. Mandelbaum, eds., *Phenomenology and Existentialism* (Baltimore: Johns Hopkins University Press, 1968), pp. 216–17. For another argument about the arbitrariness of signs, surprising from such a fine critic, see Jonathan Culler, "Literary History, Allegory and Semiology," *New Literary History* 7 (1976). He follows Paul de Man in seeing symbolism as "the desire that poetic meanings be true, inherent, and natural rather than artificial and arbitrary" (p. 265), and sees allegory as a recognition of the gap between the world and arbitrary signs (p. 268). F. E. Sparshott's refutation is precise: *arbitrary* makes sense when applied to language only if it means that no present user of a language knows an ontological reason for using a specific linguistic form, but it makes no sense to treat arbitrariness as a practical problem. All speakers inherit that condition and the ways we have learned to make distinctions within it. See his *The Structure of Aesthetics* (Toronto: University of Toronto Press, 1963), p. 367.

Wittgenstein anticipating Ricoeur's claim. The meditation begins with a remark that echoes the abstract pronouncements of Ricoeur and Derrida: "But if you say: 'How am I to know what he means, when I see nothing but the signs he gives?' then I say: 'How is he to know what he means, when he has nothing but the signs either?'" (PI, 504). But Wittgenstein then examines what possible opposite there could be to the practice of dealing in what might be arbitrary signs:

> I say the sentence: "The weather is fine"; but the words are after all arbitrary signs—so let's put "abcd" in their place. But now when I read this, I can't connect it straightaway with the above sense. I am not used, I might say, to saying "a" instead of "the," "b" instead of "weather," etc. But I don't mean by that I am not used to making an intermediate association between the word "the" and "a," but that I am not used to using "a" in the place of "the" and therefore in the sense of "the". (I have not mastered this language).
> (PI, 508)

How easy it is to lose our place when we think from the outside. If the object can drop out as irrelevant, then the whole problematic of arbitrariness cannot be resolved by abstract analysis. If the signs have a characteristic use, they have the only kind of existence they need.

The possibility of defining language as arbitrary really requires the corollary possibility of standing outside language and judging it by reference to some more inclusive and more established form of certainty. In other words, we must be able to say "arbitrary in relation to something." The deeper issue here is the kinds of doubt that can possibly make sense in human experience. Descartes provides a prototype for a typical form of philosophy in his careful doubting of all the certitudes of ordinary experience, in order to reach a deeper reflective ground for certainty. But this form of absolute doubt logically entails scepticism, since it begins by denying the only possible grounds for resolving doubt. If I want to suspect that everything may be arbitrary, how can I ever find a ground on which to stop doubting, without some recourse to faith? For a doubt to really make sense, it must itself accept its second-order status as a move within an established system for testing and confirming. Doubt only makes sense where certitude is possible; doubting the possibility of certitude is a doubt with no possible resolution, and hence not a doubt but an ungrounded metaphysical statement. The following quotation exemplifies Wittgenstein's many remarks on this subject in *On Certainty*: "What would it be like to doubt now whether I have two hands?

Why can't I imagine it at all? What would I believe if I didn't believe that? So far I have no system at all within which this doubt may exist" (oc, 247; cf. oc, 115, 117). The doubt in such a case, we might say, has no meaning because it has no use or produces no way of going on.

Wittgenstein's argument here—that radical doubt logically entails scepticism or God—applies equally well to Derrida on possibility. Once we see that doubt itself requires a language game, we should recognize that the only workable ground for a general philosophical analysis of human experience is what we can describe as the regular, shared forms of behavior that constitute these experiences. This is why, as we shall see, the notion of human actions is of crucial importance. For now, though, we only need the observation that general claims about total arbitrariness or total possibility cannot be checked and are very difficult to use. Given this alternative, both practical and theoretical discourse are condemned to seeking probabilistic agreement, often by indirect methods, even when we would like to exhibit the necessity of certain assumptions, like those involving properties of our bodies. If we are to locate such agreements, we must accept distinctions between the normal or probable and the unlikely. This runs the danger of reducing philosophy to an examination of social proprieties, but it also provides the only tests I can imagine, in a world without metaphysically established essences, for positing determinate public experiences by which to judge general philosophical descriptions and claims. It is precisely because absolute doubt itself proposes an impossible standard for judgment that we must learn to accept more limited, probabilistic criteria dependent upon shared experience:

> You must bear in mind that the language game is so to say something unpredictable. I mean: it is not based on grounds. It is not reasonable (or unreasonable). It is there—like our life. (oc, 559)

> If the true is what is grounded, then the ground is not true, nor yet false. (oc, 205)

> ... As if giving grounds did not come to an end sometime. But the end is not an ungrounded presupposition: it is an ungrounded way of acting. (oc, 110)

Such statements echo Kant's a prioris, but what if these are not forms of representation, but a variety of established ways of acting which can be described and recognized without metaphysical or epistemological hypotheses? Here we reach the center of Wittgenstein's implicit ontology. The essence of this center—with its claim that the irreducible bases for human certainty are a variety of ways of acting (PI, 224)—is the vision that there is no center and need not be one. We arrive, then, at a perspective on origins which avoids the whole problem. Wittgenstein simply accepts the fact, so much lamented in Continental thought, that we are twice removed from the Christian doctrine of an original Logos. There is no divine word grounding the free play of human words, and there is no way to discover any luminously present object anchoring words to the world. But the remaining alternatives are not just nostalgia and free play, because these themes depend on the absence of what we never had. Instead, we can recognize the error so deeply embedded in traditional philosophy and try to restructure philosophy so that it need no longer attempt to ground itself by posing abstract principles. The hardest task in philosophy, then—one never achieved by French critics of the doctrine of essence, from Bergson to Sartre to Derrida—is to cease asking the old questions. If we are to speak of origins at all, we must learn to stop at what can be recognized as a valid beginning for philosophical reflection, and that beginning lies not beneath the signs but in the relationships and contexts of action which they carry with them:

> It is so difficult to find the *beginning*. Or better: it is difficult to begin at the beginning. And not try to go further back. (OC, 471)
> ... The real discovery is the one that makes me capable of stopping doing philosophy when I want to. The one that gives philosophy peace, so that it is no longer tormented by questions which bring *itself* in question. —Instead, we now demonstrate a method, by examples, and the series of examples can be broken off. Problems are solved (difficulties eliminated), not a *single* problem. (PI, 133)

It is important to add that beginning at an accessible starting point with the ways men construct their world does not entail pure conventionalism. Conventions are no more a necessary alternative to origins than is free play. The crucial point is that there are problems in philosophy, not a single problem, so even the arguments for an ontology based on actions and procedures must be considered less a *statement* of the fundamental structure of being, than a *program* for locating ways to handle specific problems. Grammar, for example, can be more or less a matter of strict conventions, depending on how closely tied a problem is to established social institutions. It is easier to do a philosophical analysis of law than of the kinds of behavior law courts must consider. Thus,

Wittgenstein, unlike the Oxford philosophers, did not trust in language itself or in established conventions as the primary object of grammatical analysis. He was careful to link the metaphor of language games with the looser one of *forms of life,* because he saw that philosophy's ultimate subject was not language but the ways men used language. Grammar is ultimately the analysis of how we can reach public agreement about the placing of modes of behavior "among the concepts of experience" (PI, 193). Wittgenstein defined his own philosophy as an investigation of the foundations of psychology (PI, 232). And his true heir, albeit with substantial methodological differences and a more explicit reliance on Kant, is the Strawson who defined the ideal of descriptive metaphysics:

> There is a massive central core of human thinking which has no history . . . ; there are categories and concepts which, in their most fundamental character change not at all. Obviously these are not the specialities of the most refined thinking. They are the commonplaces of the least refined thinking; and are yet the indispensable core of the conceptual equipment of the most sophisticated human beings. It is with these, their interconnexions, and the structure that they form, that a descriptive metaphysics will be primarily concerned.[14]

14. P. F. Strawson, *Individuals* (Garden City: Doubleday/Anchor, 1963), p. xiv.

2

Grammar, Speech Act Theory, and Gricean Pragmatics: The Foundations of a Dramatistic View of Language

1. *The program for this chapter: from use meaning to the concept of action*

We now have a stance toward philosophical problems that can avoid both the radical empiricism that fosters the referential/emotive dichotomy and the scepticism that insists upon unbridgeable gaps between the free play of signifiers and determinate practical uses for linguistic acts. But we have yet to make the ideas of grammar, methods of projection, and appropriate senses do very much actual work. In this chapter I want to test the value of this Wittgensteinian framework by using it for a general account of the different aspects of meaning necessary for literary theory. I shall begin by staying fairly close to Wittgenstein.

The first step for a theory of meaning is to get clear on how we learn the meanings of words. On this matter I think we can rely upon a statement in which Wittgenstein nearly offers a straightforward definition: "For a large class of cases—though not for all—in which we employ the word 'meaning' it can be defined thus: the meaning of a word is its use in the language" (PI, 43). This use criterion replaces denotational and pictorial models of a term's *sense*, and in employing it we shall begin to analyze features of philosophical grammar which explain how qualitative features of discourse can be publicly determined. But the ascriptive nature of meanings only takes us a short distance toward a theoretical account of meaning that might be adequate for literary discourse. We clearly need to go beyond Wittgenstein's explicit concerns in order to consider a sense of use meaning appropriate for analyzing the ways in which speakers adapt meanings for specific utterances in concrete contexts. Thus, I shall move from Wittgenstein to the theories of speech acts proffered by Austin and by Paul Grice. My ultimate concern is to show how we can use Wittgenstein's ideas of grammar and fit in order to extend Grice and to postulate what I call a dramatistic approach to speech acts. This approach consists of treating certain kinds of speech acts, which I shall call expressive implicatures, as the purposive use of semantic and illocutionary conventions so that the qualities of the agent's act in a specific situation are offered for the assessment of an auditor. Elaborating this approach will eventually take us beyond speech act theory to the following chapter on the philosophy of action, because we need a fairly complex conceptual framework for talking about purposes, contexts, and judgments about qualities. But before we can appreciate the ways Grice leads us to the philosophy of action, we must work through Austin's groundbreaking analyses. Austin will be extremely useful for providing basic definitions and for establishing conventional, institutional aspects of speech acts, which I shall rely upon later when I attempt to define the methods of projection elicited by works we take to be literary. My primary concern here, however, will be to discuss unresolved tensions and problems in Austin's work. These will establish a context in which we can understand the pressures Grice is responding to and will allow us to weigh his proposed resolutions. But I am equally interested in simply delineating the nature of the difficulties raised by speech act theory. Some of the difficulties are probably insuperable; others, I think, derive from the fact that often neither the proponents nor the opponents of the theory take sufficient care in describing the kinds of criteria relevant for testing descriptions of the behavior which speech act theory analyzes. These problems in establishing relevant criteria will continually affect the shape of my arguments in subsequent chapters, and they will require that I repeatedly invoke Wittgenstein in contexts which illustrate his significance for humanistic inquiry.

This may seem an inordinately indirect and abstract way of entering into literary theory. I would reply, however, that we have seen where more direct speculative forays into literary issues leave us. There is good cause to think that an adequate literary theory depends in large part on getting straight about the semantics of ordinary language before engaging more complex issues. This path promises to call attention to specific difficulties where various formulations can be evaluated, and, positively, it should make clear basic similarities between literature and the ordinary experiences it proposes to elaborate, dramatize, and interpret.

Two basic issues in particular seem to me to require patient general analysis. We need a sense of what constitutes the coherence of any unit of discourse before we can begin to speak about the unity and functions of literary discourse, and we need a general picture of interpretive competence before we specify distinct features of literary methods of projection. The first of these issues, for example, establishes a perspective from which we can describe how literary texts project qualities, and can adjudicate between intentionalist and formalist strategies for specifying the hierarchy of semantic elements in a text. Yet it makes little sense to speak about qualities, purposes, and forms of coherence until we have a reasonably well-developed grasp of what constitutes a community's competence for interpreting discourses in publicly testable terms. Dramatistic semantics depends on showing how a version of Wittgenstein's philosophical grammar establishes our ability to go beyond formal rules and to produce dense synthetic accounts of what occurs in a speech act. But there is no easy or direct way to analyze this competence. Rather, we must proceed in an essentially circular fashion, by drawing out of examples and analogies the ways in which we learn to recognize the properties of speech acts when we learn how to use a language in a culture. One powerful element in Wittgenstein's work is his capacity for revealing shared powers and realms of agreement which cannot be directly argued for. Consequently, I must work through each of the three areas of semantics I mentioned in order to draw a thorough picture of the forms of competence we can rely upon in formulating reasonable and perspicuous criteria for literary interpretation. Once we have a decent sense of what our grammatical competence consists of, we shall have a context for specifying and analyzing claims about literary texts which are often posited in a conceptual vacuum or naively tied to general abstractions which have not been sufficiently tested.

The specific thesis I shall maintain through the various analyses of this chapter is that when we learn a language in a culture we develop powers to understand semantic properties in relation to several kinds of dramatistic contexts. A lexical sense of use meanings involves recognizing general scenarios in which the terms characteristically have force, and the pragmatics of speech acts gives us a framework for describing how actors in specific contexts can use the lexical potential of the language in order to project or perform particular qualities for an audience.

Then, in determining the relationship between purposes, situations, and typical expectations, we have a coherent stage on which we can recognize and assess the qualities displayed in the act.

If my thesis proves defensible, it has at least two important consequences. It will make clear the limits of formalism—both aesthetic and textualist—because a dramatistic perspective makes coherent sense of a broader range of examples and of a deeper range of qualities in those examples than do alternative theories. And by drawing out similarities between literary texts and typical speech acts in ordinary existential contexts, a dramatistic semantics makes it possible to argue for distinctive ways in which a literary education fosters and extends our capacity to describe, appreciate, and assess the complex properties of human actions.

2. Forms of lexical meaning: descriptions, institutional rules, and dimension terms

Speaking about meanings requires, first, that we clarify what the object is that we propose to analyze. It is crucial, then, to recognize that there are at least three levels of possible meaning required for an adequate description of most utterances.[1] Take the utterance, "This is my red pen." On one level the statement is intelligible as it stands: we know how a speaker might use it, even if we do not know what "this," or "my," or even "pen" specifically refers to. The second level includes these specifics—let us say I hear the words uttered in a concrete situation, so I know the speaker and see the pen. And the third adds to specifications of reference those of performative force: suppose different stress patterns or punctuation (e.g., "!" or "?") which indicate the relationship the speaker takes toward his materials and his audience. Or imagine that one makes the statement to warn his auditor not to take this pen because it is not the auditor's. As we move from use as an impersonal semantic measure to use as a category for specifying referential and performative dimensions of a specific speaker's meaning in a situation, we obviously come closer to the kinds of conditions that make for a fully dramatistic sense of language. In so doing, we avoid the tendency

1. I take these levels from P. F. Strawson, "Austin and Locutionary Meaning," in Isaiah Berlin, ed., *Essays on J. L. Austin* (Oxford: Clarendon, 1973), pp. 46–48. Derrida makes ironic use of similar distinctions in his initial essay on Austin, "Signature, Event, Context," *Glyph* 1 (1977):183–85, hereafter abbreviated, SEC.

in literary theories to emphasize only one of these levels of meaning. For example, both Jacobson's structuralism and versions of Derridean textualism tend to rely entirely on a diacritical method which Saussure invented only as an account of ascriptive meaning. The result is that they are logically constrained either to ignore the actual speech act (Jacobson on "Les Chats") or to find it indeterminate. A method devoted to possibilities for meaning will produce only possibilities and will see no way of moving from text to acts, which give purpose and function to what otherwise must remain ambiguous.[2] Other theorists, like Norman Holland and the Stanley Fish of "Affective Stylistics," tend, on the other hand, to see only the pragmatics of creating and construing meanings, so they ignore constraints on interpretation imposed by public ascriptive dimensions of a discourse.

A theory of lexical meaning is, first of all, an account of the ways names are intelligible. For a use theory, this entails spelling out the different ways in which we can characterize a grammatical competence for recognizing meaning in terms of "the overall use of the word in language" (PI, 70). Take the simplest kind of name, like *apricot*. If I wanted to show someone what the term meant, I would first have to make sure that he had mastered general procedures for understanding the place of ostensive definition and of categories like *fruit* in our normal behavior. Then the definition would be largely a matter of describing the physical properties of the fruit and perhaps of having him taste it. But suppose I want to teach him what a pawn is in chess. Here pointing to physical criteria would not be very helpful. One who understands what fruits are would easily grasp what an apricot is and can be used for, but one who understands that carved objects can be given various representational uses cannot first see a *pawn* as a particular type within the larger category. He cannot really learn what a pawn is without learning the specific set of conventional rules and goals that characterize playing chess.

The distinction between the procedures invoked by these different types of name has generated what I take to be one of the most important and productive distinctions in modern philosophy—that between brute and institutional facts. The distinction not only clarifies grounds for meaning, but has produced significant work overturning classical dichotomies between *value* and *fact*, at least in areas where it is appro-

2. For a critique of structuralist views of meaning along lines similar to mine, see Peter Caws, "Critique of Structuralist Semantics," *Diacritics* 1 (1973):15–21. For discussions of Holland and Fish, see my chapter below on indeterminacy theories.

priate to speak of institutional facts. *Brute facts*, as John Searle states the case,[3] are those which we take as features of the physical world (including immediate sensations) and can be described by the physical sciences. The good Wittgensteinian would add that recognizing these depends on established procedures, but the procedures only regulate our ways of describing—they do not constitute aspects of the facts which could only be known from cultural analysis. *Institutional facts*, on the other hand, depend on what Searle calls *constitutive rules*, which "do not merely regulate, they create or define new forms of behavior" (SA, 33). The rules for games do not simply describe brute facts, but create the conditions determining what will count as relevant facts and are not subject to empirical contradiction, as are laws proposed by science. They do not say this is what a pawn does, but what it can do, and pawns have no significance outside the possibilities the rules create for them. Apricots, on the other hand, exist and can be described in terms of other facts. We may have rules regulating how to talk about them, or how and when to eat them, but these rules do not constitute special kinds of facts about apricots (though they may about apricot users—e.g., they may constitute class differences). Searle defines the formal procedure characterizing institutional facts as that which makes us aware "x counts as y in context c" (SA, 52).

An example should make this clear. Imagine a scientist from an alien culture describing chess (the example in SA, 52 is football). He could record all the natural facts and regularities, the dimensions of the board and the pieces, the average time of the moves, the gradual reduction of pieces on the board. But, without understanding the constitutive rules of chess, without sharing this aspect of chess-playing culture, he could not comprehend all that gives chess its point. He would not understand, except perhaps statistically, what moves are possible, or the point behind them, or the meaning of terms like *pawn, castle,* and *check*. He would not understand, ultimately, what makes this game *chess*, and not some curious diversion being invented extemporaneously by two bored hominoids.

The concept of constitutive rules affords a very useful way of charac-

---

3. John Searle, *Speech Acts* (Cambridge: Cambridge University Press, 1969), pp. 31–42, 50–53, and, on facts and values, pp. 175–98. For Wittgenstein's rough formulation of the same principle, see BB, pp. 102–04. Searle, I should add, sees the slogan "meaning as use" as responsible for a good deal of confusion in modern philosophy (pp. 146–49), but, as we shall see, his alternative, reliance on rules, fares even worse. I shall hereafter abbreviate this book as SA.

terizing aspects of meaning which are publicly determinate and yet not based simply on impersonal observations of empirically testable properties of phenomena. Objects known in relation to constitutive rules are distinctly cultural entities, dependent on people learning an established set of practices. From this foundation, then, I think we can make a transition to a third kind of name, which depends on shared cultural understandings but is not reducible to rules for its definition and cannot be fully understood simply by observation. Rather, such names, which I call *dimension terms*,[4] are objects which depend on interpretations of behavior and are therefore determinable on several different levels of complexity, which derive from degrees of depth available to an observer and attributable to a human agent. As paradigm cases of such terms we might consider words like *jealousy* or *love* or *knowledge*. These terms may be distinguished from my other two categories by two features. First, they involve minimum conditions of intelligibility, but in many cases they are not reducible to these conditions or to a sharp distinction between minimal observational conditions and specialized knowledge. Thus, while a scientist clearly knows more about an apricot than an ordinary person does, we can define the special conditions of the scientist's knowledge while separating the clear public object of attention. Similarly, one could insist that terms like *jealousy*, *love*, and even *knowledge*, can only be applied when clear behavioral criteria are satisfied. But if we assume a complex agent who is jealous, etc., we are not likely to insist that his or her manifestations of these traits reveal the same kind of behavior as would the actions of a different kind of person. Similarly, we do not assume there is a common object for interpreters of the experience who have different capacities to understand the relevant emotion. The public object referred to implicates aspects of actions which change in degree and quality, depending on what we attribute to the agent and on the interpretive competence of the observer.

These differences are also manifest when we examine how we learn to understand dimension terms in relation to the ways they are used in a

---

4. I do not think that we yet have an adequate descriptive term for the phenomena I classify as dimension terms. Other alternatives are *funded wisdom* or Polanyi's *tacit knowledge*, but, while both seek to explain the same data as I do, the former is too pompous and the latter too tied to Gestalt psychology and Merleau-Ponty on what it means to have a body to be of much use to me. I think we need cultural terms, like *grammar*, rather than natural ones, like those of Gestalt theory, to ground the intelligibility of these depth dimensions. I shall feel more comfortable later when I discuss a grammar for intensional language, because that is the general class of phenomena to which dimension terms belong.

culture. *Apricots* and *pawns* depend on fairly specific use criteria, in which qualitative considerations are essentially irrelevant for applying the terms. But while dimension terms depend on observable phenomena, they are not reducible to them. We learn to combine the various phenomena in different ways, often with qualitative considerations a central concern. Our understanding of the specific application of the term will take into account our sense of the agent and our possible experience of dense or complex models of the phenomenon in question. We do not stop with behavioral signs or overt properties; we synthesize them in a variety of interpretations. Being *in love*, for example, applies to a wide variety of cases only loosely connected with one another. The more one knows about a cultural grammar for speaking about matters like love, the more fully he can recognize qualitative features which actually constitute the phenomenon. Constitutive factors here are features of the object, as with elements like pawns, but they derive from one's awareness of cultural models and his capacity to synthesize them. These factors are not clearly specifiable in relation to rules, but require narratives or scenarios in which the individual phenomenon is compared to a wide variety of types (PI, 75).

Dimension terms, in short, are functions which vary in relation to how actions are understood. Thus, they depend ultimately on features I shall discuss later as elements of action descriptions. For now, the crucial point is that action descriptions involve a distinct form of grammatical understanding, in which terms vary in depth and quality in proportion to a competence that contains more than powers of classification or the capacity to apply rules. The term *knowledge* is the best example here, because it contains in a reciprocal way the various aspects of dimension terms. Recent philosophy has delineated fairly clear behavioral criteria for using the term. For example, we accept claims to knowledge only if someone can give adequate reasons for a claim or can make predictions that follow from it. But these behavioral criteria leave undefined the ways in which we make qualitative considerations about the nature or complexity of knowledge in given areas. In many cases, we attribute qualities to knowledge and apply it as a dimension term precisely because the knower herself displays a capacity to appreciate the complexity of other dimension terms. And our own powers to attribute dimensions to knowledge depend on our grammatical competence to appreciate distinctions in a given area, even when the distinctions cannot clearly be attributed to features of natural objects or to formal procedural rules.

3. A contrast between use and label theories of meaning and the burden on the concept of competence

This first theoretical gambit has significant consequences for indicating the different kinds of operations that comprise adequate understanding of the sense of a word and of possible sentences using the word. It clearly reveals the inadequacy of label theories of meaning, makes us reconsider versions of psychology and learning based on them, and prepares the way for elaborating a model of semantic competence that at once grounds the basic properties of literary meanings and indicates one crucial role they play in our culture.

A label theory of ascriptive meaning, like St. Augustine's, assumes that we understand all ascriptive meanings as we do that of *apricot*. Wittgenstein's counterexamples of numbers and commands refute the semantic argument, but it is equally important to point out how this mistaken semantic view affects general claims about the nature of mental activity. As we have seen with Derrida, once one assumes that *propre sens* depends on ostensively fixed names, he finds it easy to become sceptical about secure grounds of meaning for terms which do not fit this model. And, as Augustine himself shows, it is hard not to extend the label model so that one posits some realm of essences or metaphysical entities to explain how we understand the meaning of abstract and dimension terms. Moreover, a similar logic leads empiricist psychology to treat expressive and emotive terms either as publicly determinate, because they label sensations and stimuli, or as indeterminate, because they are subjective interpretations of these fundamental sensations.

Notice how different the implications are when we take as a basic criterion for ascriptive meaning a Wittgensteinian formula like William Alston's:

> A meaning statement of the form "x" means "y" is to be tested by determining whether "x" and "y" can be substituted for each other in a wide variety of sentences without, in each case, changing the job(s) which the sentence is used to do, or, more precisely, without changing the suitability or potentiality of the sentence for performing whatever job(s) it was used to perform before the alteration.[5]

5. William Alston, "Meaning and Use," reprinted in Jay Rosenberg and Charles Travis, eds., *Readings in the Philosophy of Language* (Englewood Cliffs, N.J.: Prentice-Hall, 1971), p. 408.

Here words are neither labels nor simple functions of diacritical oppositions to other words. Rather, words relate to other words as they become established in task-related contexts. This means that criteria depend on loose webs of coherence rather than on isolated name-object relations. A psychology attentive to this perspective would then have to grant the mind synthetic powers that begin to account for the complex foundations of meaning which enable us to understand constitutive rules and dimension terms. And there remains no rationale for ascriptive versions of the referential/emotive dichotomy. Our many different ways of understanding names are measured not in terms of the presence or absence of pictorial elements, but by the degrees of possibility by which one makes them cohere with other sample sentences and images of behavior. We understand what it means to say that someone is in love, for example, not by trying to recall a specific sensation or picture, but by considering possible scenarios and behavioral patterns which we then try to adjust to the situation in question. Consider the difference between establishing a representative example of an apricot, a pawn, and being in love. For the last we would need several cases and, even then, one can easily imagine continual dispute about which features of the cases make them representative or about what degrees or qualities a representation must include. In the case of knowledge, for example, we have certain behavioral expectations which distinguish between, say, acquaintance, general knowledge, and a high degree of mastery. This last condition entails not simply knowing what someone has said, but being able to explain the coherence of what was said and perhaps to use it in other contexts.

The crucial point here for both semantics and literary theory is that we need not sacrifice complexity for determinacy or public assessability of meanings. We can show that complex expressive utterances are publicly determinate simply by showing that those educated in a culture and its language develop in common a reasonably high degree of semantic competence. Semantic competence is precisely the ability to understand grammatical relations among terms functioning within an elaborate system of projections which make labelling as well as other kinds of activity intelligible. Labels, emotive expressions, and other kinds of dimension terms, then, all have determinate ascriptive meaning to the extent that a community can be expected to know how to use and respond to a specific term in particular situations. Hannah Pitkin offers a concise summary of this semantic level of Wittgenstein's thought: "Grammar . . . establishes the place of a concept in our system of concepts, and thereby in our world. It controls what other concepts, what questions and observations, are relevant to a particular concept." [6]

We have, then, an initial formulation of semantic competence. When one learns a language, one learns to make discriminations about relevance along the lines Pitkin indicates. While the term *competence* has its contemporary significance primarily because of Chomsky, it has broader applications than are contained in his treatment of syntax. I think that any coherence theory must rely on hypotheses about competence, precisely because it cannot ground meanings on any purely pictorial or behaviorist model of ultimate simples. However, if one refuses to base competence on Chomsky's a priori structures, one must face difficult problems of circularity. One must identify forms of shared understanding and then claim that the understanding requires the hypothesis of a shared grammar. Our norm for the shared understanding must presuppose the very competence it must explain, since only those who share the understanding can be its judge. This circularity often tempts philosophers to independent referential tests for semantics, but, as Wittgenstein shows, if logical simples are impossible, the positing of referential tests will only presuppose a shared competence on a different level (for example, shared ideas of ostensive definition), often a level that tends to be reductive. Therefore, I see little choice but to grant that a circularity which is inescapable is not necessarily vicious, especially if within the general hypothesis about competence one can distinguish levels and make clear explanations of why certain forms of transcultural communication require learning the procedures of a distinct culture. If the powers to make determinate semantic judgments cannot meaningfully be doubted in certain kinds of cases, we have a clear warrant for hypothesizing forms of shared competence. We can roughly define competence, then, as a capacity that is attributed to someone who shows the ability to master tasks and carry on operations within methods of projection for which a community has fairly clear standards for proper and for unsuccessful activities. Competence need not be opposed to performance; rather, it is a hypothesis on another conceptual level for explaining how agents within practices can assume a wide range of shared assumptions and make efficient predictions about subsequent behavior. And in many cases there are two clear checks against vicious circularity: there is the fact that tasks are performed or continued to

6. Hannah Pitkin, *Wittgenstein and Justice* (Berkeley: University of California Press, 1972), p. 119. This book is the best application of Wittgenstein I know to practical aspects of understanding behavior.

everyone's satisfaction, and there is the fact that judges of competence are often institutionally certified. Institutional certification is not an absolute standard, but we are describing how people make sense of their world, not how some ideal, secure, metaphysical picture of the world might dictate our behavioral norms.

The most obvious general class of procedures in which competence must be attributed includes those dependent on constitutive rules. For here specific boundaries can be drawn between those who have and have not mastered relevant semantic operations and the connection of these operations to possible forms of behavior and to institutionally established values and ends. But we must be careful not to attribute competence only to those who have self-consciously mastered specific rules. Many forms of competence, like riding a bicycle, are achieved in largely intuitive ways through practice. It may be, in fact, as J. M. Moravcsik asserts, that we usually invoke the notion of competence only in procedures where the skills are not simply automatic but involve intuitions and judgments,[7] which, I add, derive in turn from something like a grammatical sense of possible relationships among the elements within

---

7. J. M. Moravcsik, "Appreciation, Care, and Understanding,": 14–15. I cite a typescript of material that will appear in two essays in *Dialectica*, 1980 and 1981. For further descriptions of institutional practices from an anthropological point of view that makes similar hypotheses about competence, see Clifford Geertz, *The Interpretation of Cultures* (New York: Basic Books, 1973), and the debate between Peter Winch and Alasdair MacIntyre, in Bryan Wilson, ed. *Rationality* (Oxford: Basil Blackwell, 1970), pp. 3–17, 65–77. Dell Hymes, "Modes of the Interaction of Language and Social Life," in John Gumperz and Hymes eds. *Directions in Sociolinguistics* (N.Y.: Holt, Rhinehart and Winston, 1972, pp. 53–65, develops an explicit idea of "communicative competence" that I think supports my way of using the term. In my treatment of competence I have no need to rely on Chomsky's abstracting competence from performance so that he can propose an object of analysis that can be treated in formal, rule-governed terms which are more comprehensive than any analysis of performances within a given culture. Because a competence derived from learning institutional practices obviously cannot be used to make authoritative statements about regularities that cross cultures, one can be content with aspects of competence simply embedded in whatever makes performances intelligible. Even on this level, however, we must not take competence as a single abstract term. We must speak about forms of competence—some of which turn out to transcend many cultural boundaries (for example, the capacity to read gestures or to translate), while others are culture-specific. Some competences may be part of our genetic makeup, others purely culturally learned, and so forth. Moreover, there are levels of competence. As I shall develop more fully in chapter five, there is a good case for arguing that some very general literary procedures make it possible to use conventions which involve highly specific competences. In all these matters, the crucial points are to know why we need the hypothesis, to make explicit how it can roughly be tested, and to avoid making generalizations from only certain forms of competence.

a procedure. And where it is appropriate to speak of flexibility as a feature of competence, it is usually also appropriate to distinguish among
degrees of competence. Competence, in short, is not a fixed level of skill,
but a capacity which can develop and grow complex or subtle. Again,
chess is a good analogue for semantic competence: there are basic skills
and capacities for judgment needed to perform at an ordinary level, but
there are also many degrees of skill—each with a smaller class of those
who can adequately judge competence.

The general properties of semantic competence are easy to indicate
by observing the ways in which we learn the meanings of words by
mastering the grammar of their use. If one only learned words by ostensive definition, we would have trouble explaining flexible or original uses
of language. But, as Wittgenstein argues and M. A. K. Halliday has confirmed in a recent empirical study,[8] this flexibility is explainable by the
fact that we learn through a constant process of adjusting meanings,
picked up in connection with various examples of behavior and changing
social contexts. Meanings, again, are learned not by the assignment of
propre sens, but by constant exercise in judging appropriate senses. This
model of learning procedure at once leads to and supports Wittgenstein's concept of family resemblances as a principle of *grammatical*
definition. Features of experience cluster about a term or exemplary
situation in a wide variety of ways not reducible either to necessary and
sufficient conditions or to dependence on an original *idea* with clearly
marked lines of derivation:

> I can think of no better expression to characterize these similarities
> than "family resemblances"; for the various resemblances between
> members of a family: build, features, colour of eyes, gait, tempera-
> ment, etc., etc. overlap and crisscross in the same way. . . .
> And for instance the kinds of number form a family in the same
> way. . . . And we extend our concept of number as in spinning a
> thread we twist fibre on fibre, and the strength of the thread does
> not reside in the fact that some other fibre runs through its whole
> length, but in the overlapping of many fibres. (PI, 66–67)

We come now to the feature of a use model of semantic competence
most significant for dramatistic analysis and for justifying a category of
dimension terms. I refer to Charles Fillmore's treatment of meanings as
relativized to scenes: "We need to know for each word what scene, or

---

8. M. A. K. Halliday, *Learning How to Mean: Explorations in the Development
of Language* (New York: Elsevier, 1977).

cluster of linked scenes, is to be activated by it. A given real-world scene is perceived according to the degree to which it matches some paradigm or prototype outline scene. Prototype scenes can be thought of as scenes from simple worlds, worlds whose properties simply do not take in all the facts of the real world." [9] With this as his theoretical base, Fillmore shows the different strategies for interpretation that arise from degrees of distance between auditor's and speaker's knowledge. He demonstrates how, in any of these cases, inferences drawn from our various sources of knowledge about the topic of a sentence shape the ways we construe and test hypotheses about both text meaning and text coherence or, in more general terms, the relationship between semantic and rhetorical structures.

Fillmore's ultimate concern, of course, is a literal equation between semantic competence and the actual grammatical operations definable by a case grammar. But his work clearly illustrates both how much we share simply by learning a language in common cultural contexts and how a form of dramatistic interpretation is a basic feature of semantic activity. It is, then, not a large jump from Fillmore's illustration of the forms of knowledge needed to understand the semantic import of utterances to the claims I have been making about philosophical grammar.

We can conclude this section with a brief summary of some basic implications of taking a grammatical approach to analyzing the descriptive senses of terms. First, it provides support for what will be a constant theme in my argument—the need to go beyond purely formal, rule-governed analyses of both semantic and pragmatic aspects of language use. As David Antin dramatizes beautifully in a performance piece called "Tuning," our semantic competence comprises so many oppositions and lines of relationship that there are virtually an infinite number of possible binary oppositions for which an adequate system would have to account. Moreover, among the complex interwoven fibers we have no guarantee, or even likelihood, that all codings take the form of binary oppositions. Both Saussure and experimenters in derivational semantics, like Fodor and Katz, must explicitly reject aspects of meaning—like context—not

9. Charles Fillmore, "Topics in Lexical Semantics," in Roger W. Cole, ed., *Current Issues in Linguistic Theory* (Bloomington: Indiana University Press, 1977), pp. 89, 87. For similar analyses based on situation types and a notion of competence connected with the idea of *potential* uses of a language, see M. A. K. Halliday, *Language as Social Semiotic: The Social Interpretation of Language and Meaning* (Baltimore: University Park Press, 1978).

explicitly marked by rules in the linguistic code. Formal semantics cannot explain the grammatical properties that allow us in our culture to distinguish immediately between the kinds of shoes in "our store sells horse shoes" and "our store sells alligator shoes." Other kinds of semantic operations simply elude the logic of derivation rules. These rules can explain why "I am two years older than my father" is anomalous, because *father* is semantically marked as positing precedence in time in relation to son. But the anomaly of "My father is two years older than I" is not so encoded and depends upon a cultural grammar for the uses of *father*. The case becomes more compelling when we consider the complex distinctions philosophers like Austin can find in the ordinary use of terms like *deliberately, intentionally,* and *on purpose.*[10]

Breaking with formalism gives us a perspective from which we can see how it is possible to claim a high degree of determinate public meaning in complex discourses which often depend on implicit dimensions. Examples can carry a good deal of weight in shaping our capacity to set the scenic stage required for these discourses. Hence, there need be no less clarity in emotive expressions or metaphors or connotations than we find in propositional statements. A full exposition of this claim must wait until we consider the theory of speech acts, but connotation provides a fairly clear semantic example. At least a core of connotative associations of a name depend for their intelligibility not on subjective additions to some basic proposition, but on patterns of behavior and social contexts in which the term is often used. Connotations are objective properties of meaning, to the extent that the contexts they invoke connect with both the grammatical ways we learn to use a given term and the grammatical expectation about their relevance in a given context of utterance. The choice of *shovel* or *digging implement* or *filthy spade* can be a deliberate choice of publicly determinate associations. In other contexts, as we shall see, the choice may not be intentional, yet may still publicly affect meaning. Indeed, a good deal of the most penetrating analysis of signification systems along structuralist lines, in the vein of

10. I list together the references in this paragraph. David Antin's "Tuning" has been given in his performances and will be in a forthcoming book from New Directions. For Fodor and Katz, see "The Structure of a Semantic Theory," and for the *father* example, see Charles Fillmore, "Entailment Rules in Semantic Theory." Both essays are in Rosenberg and Travis, eds., pp. 482–83, and p. 536. For Austin's distinctions, see "Three Ways of Spilling Ink" and "A Plea for Excuses," in his *Philosophical Papers* (London: Oxford University Press, 1970), hereafter abbreviated as PPA.

Barthes' *Mythologies*, depends precisely on locating implicit, yet publicly testable, structures of connotations.[11]

Finally, we can make self-reflective use of examples, to represent for ourselves our grammatical capacity and to try out fresh ways of disclosing the implicit understanding we share. This, indeed, is one basic feature of Wittgenstein's description of his stylistic strategies:

> A main source of our failure to understand is that we do not *command a clear view* of the use of our words. Our grammar is lacking in this sort of perspicuity. A perspicuous representation produces just that understanding which consists in "seeing connexions." Hence the importance of finding and inventing *intermediate* cases.
>
> The concept of a perspicuous representation is of fundamental significance for us. It earmarks the form of account we give, the way we look at things. (PI, 122)

Philosophy here plays a role very close to that of literature, and it enables us to postulate an initial claim about the cognitive powers literature can develop. If we learn to make discriminations and reflect upon our grammatical understanding through perspicuous samples, literary scenarios become vehicles for extending our grammatical capacity. *Grammatical competence* itself is ultimately a dimension term, because it changes in quality as it becomes increasingly capable of recognizing the ways multiple interrelationships help situate specific uses of terms in complex clusters of meaning. How these clusters are formed and understood will be a central topic of this study, but the consequences of their capacity to be formed should already be evident. If poets are not legislators of the race, they may still be considered its educators. For, as Hannah Pitkin puts it, "Confronted with words like 'God' and 'love' and 'beauty,' we today are like children, knowing a few uses of the terms and having some notion of their meaning." Our passage into a fully adult understanding depends in large part on our effort to meet the demands on our grammar imposed by the complex perspicuous samples which poets and philosophers create.[12]

---

11. For good accounts one can use to draw links between the binary cultural oppositions studied by structuralism and their foundation in a form of competence based on or compatible with a use theory of meaning, see John Ellis, *Theory of Literary Criticism*, and Jonathan Culler, *Structuralist Poetics* (Ithaca: Cornell University Press, 1975).

12. Pitkin, p. 109.

4. *A second sense of use: transition to speech acts*

Wittgenstein's treatment of meaning clarifies how we understand the possible sense of words and utterances. But in order to account for the actual meanings of specific utterances, we must turn to a second sense of *use* which leads us to speech act theory and to the grammatical grounds on which we interpret speakers' meanings in concrete situations. This field is now in turmoil. There are specific arguments about the nature and classification of speech acts, and, behind these, a general debate about the place of speakers' meanings in semantics and about the kinds of criteria—formal or pragmatic—which one should accept as conditions for adequate theoretical explanations.[13] I cannot treat these in the depth required of philosophical argument, but I think I can present a defensible case for a coherent view of speech acts we can adapt for literary issues. Thus, my goal in this chapter is to make as much sense as I can of Austin's most ambitious statement of his project: "The total speech act in the total speech situation is the *only* actual phenomenon which, in the last resort, we are engaged in elucidating."[14] This ideal, however, is as difficult to achieve as it is initially tempting for literary theorists. Austin's own analyses will provide some necessary insights and terms, but his work will be most useful here for indicating problems that arise when one tries to speak about acts and forces in terms of conventions and rules. If we are to discuss speech acts, phenomenological and pragmatic procedures prove more rewarding than formal and institutional ones. Instead of rules, we need a critical norm for what Austin calls *uptake* that takes as its descriptive stance a perspective like Wittgenstein's: "Ask yourself, in what sort of cases, in what kind

13. See, for example, John Searle, "Indirect Speech Acts," in Peter Cole and Jerry Morgan, eds., *Syntax and Semantics: Speech Acts* (New York: Academic Press, 1975), p. 82: "neither the philosopher's paradigm of logically necessary and sufficient conditions nor the linguistic paradigm of generative structural rules seems adequate to the various phenomena raised by discussion of speech acts." See also the introduction to Peter Cole, ed., *Syntax and Semantics: Pragmatics* (New York: Academic Press, 1978), p. xii: ours is "a new era in the study of meaning and grammar, one in which the issues are more complex and the problems more trying than had been imagined previously."

14. Austin, *How to Do Things With Words* (New York: Oxford, 1962), p. 147; hereafter abbreviated HTD. See also "Performative Utterances," in PPA, pp. 233–52. For recent, Gricean accounts of the pragmatics of reference, see Peter Cole, "On the Origins of Referential Opacity"; Keith Donellan, "Speaker Reference, Descriptions, and Anaphora"; and especially David Kaplan, "Dthat*," all in Cole, ed., *Syntax and Semantics: Pragmatics*.

of circumstances, do we say, 'Now I know how to go on' " (PI, 154; cf. PI, 141). Thus, I shall use Austin primarily to set a stage for developing and modifying Grice's pragmatic approach to speech acts. Grice is by no means a follower of Wittgenstein, but his basic insights seem to me to depend on a framework very much like Wittgensteinian grammar. By making this explicit, I think I can show how we can use Grice to elaborate a dramatistic theory of speakers' meanings that satisfies most of the spirit, if not the letter, of Austin's ideal.

5. Austin's speech act theory and its problems

The philosophical climate that eventually leads to speech act theory begins with reactions to the logical atomism of Russell and early Wittgenstein. For here we recognize some of the philosophical pressures that require a reassertion of the importance of speakers' meanings and of the contexts of utterances. P. F. Strawson, for example, takes on Russell's denotative criteria for establishing the meaning of particular descriptions by insisting that Russell ignores categorical differences between meaning and referring. For Strawson it is reference, not meaning, which is context dependent. *Meanings* are values of expressions and sentences; thus, they depend on the conventions we learn as we learn a language. *Reference*, on the other hand, is a property of statements and depends on how we use sentences in particular situations. To give the meaning of an expression or a sentence, Strawson says, "is to give general direction for its use" in mentioning particulars or making assertions that can be true or false:

> The meaning of a sentence cannot be identified with the assertion it is used, on a particular occasion, to make. For to talk about the meaning of an expression [or a sentence] is not to talk about its use on a particular occasion, but about the rules, habits, conventions governing its correct use, on all occasions, to refer or to assert. So the question of whether a sentence or expression is *significant or not* has nothing to do with the question of whether the sentence, *uttered on a particular occasion*, is on that occasion, being used to make a true or false assertion or not.[15]

Thus, taking the handkerchief out of my pocket is not showing you the

---

15. Strawson, "On Referring," reprinted in Rosenberg and Travis, eds. I quote from p. 181.

meaning of *my handkerchief,* for without knowing the meaning of the expression, you would not know what I was waving or why. Similarly, to take Russell's classic example, there are enormous differences between the meaning of "The King of France is wise," which remains constant, and the truth values of the utterance in different historical periods.

Austin's work, then, adapts Strawson's strategies to questions of the meaning of specific utterances. For matters of context can also play a role in deciding what conventions allow utterances to have determinate meaning, even when they do not lead to propositional claims and truth/ falsity assessments. There are, Austin saw, two different methods of projection that control how we interpret meaningful utterances—performative and constative acts. Each involves a different way of using language and invokes different kinds of assessment and *uptake: performatives* are ways of doing something in the act of saying under appropriate conditions, while *constatives* are statements or reports or descriptions (PP, 246), which by saying something propose a possible correlation between the statement and states of affairs. Because performatives accomplish something in the act of speaking, they do not depend on adequacy to external states of affairs, but rather on adequacy to conditions that affect the felicity of the statement, conditions that point to conventions that characterize and qualify the stating, not to independent facts. Later, Austin would see that these two acts are not mutually exclusive. He reinterprets performatives as constituents of any utterance which, in saying something, establish the nature of an illocutionary act (HTD, 91–99). This *illocutionary force* functions as an index of the way a speaker is using his referential claims. Then, if one's illocutionary act poses the reference in a way that (purposefully) produces "consequential effects upon the feelings, thoughts or actions of the audience . . ." (HTD, 101), one also performs a perlocutionary act.

At first glance Austin's distinctions seem enormously promising to literary critics. The distinction between what is done in saying and a concentration on perlocutionary effects seems to establish an ordinary language parallel to endless attempts to distinguish special foregrounding effects of literary language. And even in Austin's weaker, later formulations of a performative force within utterances that is determinate and yet points back to contexts and actions rather than depending on reference there seems to be a powerful instrument for denying Said's claim that the production of meaning is incompatible with the achievement of meaning. Language use has its own areas of intelligibility, its own functions, and its own possible criteria of assessment. But Austin takes pains not to allow these easy equations. His task is to convince philosophers, not to encourage literary critics, and thus he must use a good deal of caution. I think this caution leads Austin into trouble, but before I can demonstrate this I must make clear the obstacles Austin puts in the path of literary critics.

Austin's first need for caution involves methodological issues. He must provide conditions that allow determinate means for identifying illocutionary forces and for describing how they can be assessed. He must do so in a way that preserves clear connections between the illocutionary and constative features of an utterance. Austin proposes two basic tests for the presence of illocutionary force. True illocutions can be rewritten in either of two forms. The sentence should be able to be stated in the form, "in saying x, I hereby x," and a performative verb should fit the schema, "In saying x, I was x'ing." [16] Thus typical performative utterances, like "I promise to come," "I find him guilty," "I apologize," and so forth, all admit a *hereby*, and all allow perfect correlation between the saying and the doing. But other predicates, like "I jump," "I want to jump," or, more important, "I am sad," fail these conditions. I call attention to the last example because it shows why expressions of feeling do not necessarily involve illocutionary forces, although they seem to fit Austin's initial claims about performatives and do not sit well as constatives.

Austin now also needs a set of conditions that will explain how the illocutions we identify can invoke determinate criteria for assessment within behavioral frameworks and so need not depend only on abstract truth function analyses. This need produces what Austin calls six *felicity conditions*: (1) "There must exist an accepted conventional procedure having a certain conventional effect" achievable in an utterance; (2) "the particular persons and circumstances ... must be appropriate for the invocation of the particular procedure"; (3) all participants must execute the procedure correctly and (4) completely; (5) when the procedure suggests appropriate thoughts and feelings, the participants must have these thoughts and feelings, along with the proper intentions; and (6) the participants must conduct themselves in accord with (5). The first four conditions determine whether the act comes off at all; the last two determine whether the procedure is abused or not, even if it stands as accomplished (HTD, 14–16).

16. For a good discussion of these conditions and some problems they encounter, see Steven Davis, *Philosophy and Language* (Indianapolis: Bobbs-Merrill, 1976), pp. 21–27.

Beneath Austin's methodological prescriptions lies a deeper caution occasionally revealed in his complex ambivalence about doing philosophy. Having formulated an idea of performative force, he had two choices: he could turn to grammatical competence and probabilistic criteria on the model of practical judgments as a means for talking about total speech situations, or he could reduce the variety of ways one does something in saying something to explicit, rule-governed, illocutionary procedures. Austin clearly chose the second in HTD. Thus, he denied the relevance of expressions or fictional utterances (which include irony) and eliminated from consideration "primitive" performatives, in favor of those that can be made explicit (HTD, 32, 69). I assume that he did so because he had to confront the Nietzsche in his own thought. If performatives are not confined to purely conventional contexts, they open the door to a variety of rhetorical considerations and to the possibly endless regress in matters of competence and the interpretation of intentions behind a performative. Conventions and rules shape discourse and provide a clear nonreferential ground for determinate meanings, without requiring that one specify intentions beyond the conventions or that the interpreter make probabilistic assessments of the speech act. Conventions to some degree entail intentions, while confining them to social practices, and, thus, establishing pure interpretive rules analogous to those in Searle's formal institutional practices.[17] Why risk all the problems of hermeneutics, Austin probably thought, when even his limited account of illocutions would be sufficient to challenge the primacy of Russellian analysis? Moreover, Austin had other stakes in mind. He wanted the notion of performatives to reinforce Ryle's claims against empiricist versions of the ghost in the machine. In their reliance on referential models of meaning, empiricists must posit discrete mental events as the objects of psychological verbs like *promise, apologize, believe,* and, most important, *know*. Austin, on the contrary, envisions such verbs as simply enacting mental states or bringing them into being by expression: "The one thing we must not suppose is that what is needed in addition to the saying of the words in such cases is the performance of some internal spiritual act, of which the words then are to

---

17. Michael Hancher, in a review of Mary Louise Pratt, "Beyond a Speech Act Theory of Discourse," *MLN* 92 (1977): 1081–98, makes an interesting case for the difference between Austin's constitutive sense of illocutionary force and Grice's "regulative" use of pragmatic implicatures. It may be, then, that one source of Austin's caution was a desire to preserve conditions for genuinely constitutive features of performative force.

be the report" (PPA, 236). Such claims are radical enough, especially in their affinity to idealist views of expression like Croce's, without inviting the further burden of explaining nonconventional intentions.

Austin's, nonetheless, seems to me a misplaced caution. Instead of securing his claims, it only renders them more problematic by incurring obligations to explain rules and to make distinctions among types of conventions which Austin could not meet. In limiting his ontology to satisfy conditions on methodology, Austin, in effect, disclosed features of linguistic behavior which simply will not admit an analysis based entirely on conventions. This can be shown in two ways—by arguing that Austin's account of conventions is not clear or complex enough to explain the institutional features of illocutions, and by arguing that no analysis based on purely conventional grounds can do justice to some of Austin's legitimate insights.

The first of these charges is the easiest to explain, and perhaps to correct, because the difficulties of using Austin's sense of rules are close to the surface. Austin apparently did not see that his illocutionary acts depended on two different kinds of conventions, both of which satisfied the identification conditions discussed above.[18] Those illocutions, like "I bid four no trump," or "I find him guilty," which most clearly rely on the first four felicity conditions, depend for their uptake on conventions not inherent in the semantic code. In order to understand them, one must know both the use meaning of the words and the specific, nonsemantic conventions which they use. Other illocutionary acts, like "I promise," or "I apologize," which can be made explicit performatives, rely only on semantic conventions and may require no special analytic apparatus. This oversight leads to criticisms like L. Jonathan Cohen's: insofar as performatives can be made semantically explicit, they require no special speech act theory, and, insofar as speech acts do not reduce to semantic rules, the conventions and practices they rely upon become too

---

18. Austin is not very clear on what he means by convention. He seems (HTD, 118–21) to equate *convention* with the conditions that allow us to determine what was said if we know only the words and the context, only the features of an utterance available to any observer without any special knowledge of the speaker of his private intentions. For a sharp sense of convention, to which I shall try to be faithful (and which will force me to stress looser terms like *procedures*), see Max Black's analysis of the four properties contained by pure conventions in "Austin on Performatives" in Fann, ed., p. 407. Conventions are rule-governed, self-validating (i.e., to follow them is to achieve something) determiners of significance, within their parameters independent of empirical facts, and (loosely) claim-generating (i.e., to do x is to assume one has whatever privileges and responsibilities the rules give to x).

vague and diffuse for clear analysis.[19] But this criticism is based on too narrow a view of analysis, so that ironically it does not go far enough in criticizing what is loose about Austin. I do not see how one can dismiss aspects of meaning that rely on institutional practices—and this is precisely the cutting edge of Austin's attack on traditional theories of meaning and his defense of felicity conditions. Some consideration of institutional methods of projection is clearly necessary for large classes of speech acts. The question is whether an account of institutional practices in terms of rules will suffice to explain the various forms of cultural understanding that create felicity conditions. Moreover, even purely semantic treatments of explicit performatives encounter some serious problems in specifying the appropriate rules. J. R. Ross, for example, tries to accommodate illocutions by arguing that all declarative sentences have an underlying structure in which the highest verb is a general verb of stating, that controls the semantic relations possible among subordinate terms. Ross can explain many of the selection constraints in sentence types controlled by verbs like *warn,* but the general value of his position is seriously undermined by its failure in some cases to produce identity of meaning between the embedded sentence and the actual utterance. According to Ross, *prices slumped* presupposes a deep structure "I state that prices slumped." But the deep structure sentence logically entails only that an assertion is made, not that the assertion is a proposition about actual prices.[20]

19. Cohen, "Do Illocutionary Forces Exist," reprinted in Rosenberg and Travis, eds. The following quotation states his fundamental position: "What Austin calls the illocutionary force of an utterance is that aspect of its meaning which is either conveyed by its explicitly performative prefix, if it has one, or might have been so conveyed by the use of such expression. Any attempt to piece off this aspect of meaning, and regard it not as meaning but as something else, leads to paradox and confusion." In essence *it* ignores the way language comes "to express more and more subtly diverse shades of meaning" (p. 587). It also avoids all problems of intention. The best responses to Cohen I know are Strawson, "Intention and Convention in Speech Acts," reprinted in Rosenberg and Travis, eds., and Mats Furberg, "Meaning and Illocutionary Force," in T. K. Fann, ed., *Symposium on J. L. Austin* (London: Routledge and Kegan Paul, 1969). For a more elaborate attack on Austin and Searle as failing to provide an adequate account of rules, see Joseph Margolis, "Literature and Speech Acts," *Philosophy and Literature* 3 (1979):39–52. Below I shall quote from p. 41. I heard Margolis give a version of this essay in 1977; the published version is much closer than was the original to the general claims I make in this chapter. I regret that I saw this version too late to include it in my arguments.

20. I take this analysis of Ross from Steven Davis, pp. 122–30. For Austin's awareness of this problem with *I state,* see PPA, 245.

These problems are primarily technical matters. But when we turn to some of Austin's most suggestive ideas, we find them not easily reducible to analysis in terms of rule-governed conventions. Austin's forays into the theory of truth are a clear, if somewhat complicated, instance of this tendency. For here Austin's resistance to Russellian standards leads to an essentially pragmatist notion of truth, in which illocutionary force establishes contextual criteria for testing the propositional features of an utterance. This move, in turn, provides a focus for several themes in my study. Austin argues that there is a necessary interdependence between illocutionary force and the kinds of tests applicable to its propositional component. In my view, this is the key to a dramatistic treatment of utterance, but the manner in which Austin proposes this interrelationship is indefensible. For he is probably wrong in asserting his proposals as a theory of truth, and, because of this error, speech act theory has branched in two general directions. On the one hand, we find Searle's attempts to draw sharp distinctions between illocutionary force and propositional content. And, on the other, the consequent narrowing of illocutionary force leads to speculations, like Grice's, on a thoroughly pragmatic sense of how the stance of the speaker can in many cases dictate conditions of uptake which cannot be confined either to matters of convention or truth-functional analysis. These issues are crucial to my case, because they make it clear that if one is to accept Austin's contextualism, one must not so much propose alternative theories of truth as insist that philosophical truth criteria have limited uses. Austin leads, in short, to proposing for many utterances a thoroughly dramatistic sense of appropriate criteria for assessment.

The range of possible consequences makes it worth our time to consider Austin's argument at some length. Austin's contextual theory of truth derives from his attempt to treat *I know* as performative, or as a way of relating to a discourse, rather than as a term referring to psychological states, as he proposes that an empiricist must take it. First-person claims to knowledge, in short, are not simply states of awareness but enactments in a social context. Because *state* is an illocutionary verb, it invites assessments according to felicity conditions as well as truth conditions. Thus, by contextualizing truth claims (in a formulation where arguments about conventions will clearly be inadequate) Austin hopes to ground in a model of mind and linguistic action the pragmatic, contextualist perspective he used so effectively against Ayer in *Sense and Sensibilia*. The conditions of an observer, here in relation to an audience, in large part determine how descriptive claims are to be judged.

Austin's strongest claims on this matter occur in "Performative Utterances" (but see also HTD, 146–48): "True and false are just general labels for a whole dimension of different appraisals which have something or other to do with the relation between what we say and the facts. If, then, we loosen up our ideas of truth and falsity we shall see that statements, when assessed in relation to the facts, are not so very different after all from pieces of advice, warnings, verdicts and so on" (PPA, 250). Austin here comes very close to Wittgenstein's concern for methods of projection as a basic condition on the adequacy of descriptions: "There are various degrees and dimensions of success in making statements: the statements fit the facts always more or less loosely, in different ways on different occasions for different intents and purposes" (PPA, 130). We need, in short, both truth conditions and appropriateness conditions—the latter described by Austin as a happiness/unhappiness dimension of assessment. Thus, to repeat Austin's example, a surveyor's map is generally a far more accurate picture of a landscape than a road map, but there are situations when the surveyor's map would be inappropriate and perhaps misleading—as when a stranger wants to traverse an area as quickly as possible.

Pragmatic themes, however, are not adequate to handle the topic of truth conditions. Lawrence Davis gives a brief and perspicuous explanation of Austin's failure: it is not acts of stating but signs which are judged as true or false. Propositions or statements, not utterances, bear truth values. We can, for example, imagine different statements or utterances of a descriptive statement, like "water boils at 212° F." But the proposition itself does not admit of different tokens; the speakers all utter the same statement, because the order of propositions is abstracted from behavior. And we can use qualifiers on the act of stating, like *hurried* or *careless*, which cannot formally apply to the actual statement. Therefore, Austin is simply wrong in assuming that felicity conditions appropriate to the act of stating pertain to actual propositions.[21] Yet we cannot easily dismiss his illustration of the force of these conditions in affecting uptake.

We find ourselves now faced with the two alternatives I mentioned above. Aware of the problems Davis points out, John Searle tries to save some of Austin's case by making sharp distinctions between the propositional or locutionary aspect of an utterance and the illocutionary frame, which he treats as the expression of propositional attitudes. Thus,

21. I rely on Steven Davis, pp. 46–53, for the criticism of Austin.

one can clarify what elements of an utterance bear truth values, and one can separate them from the elements which entail other dimensions of assessment. Moreover, once one can separate the illocutionary features, one can make a strong case for viewing them as subject to purely semantic conventions which should be explicable in terms of generative rules. But this alternative pays a considerable price for its clarity and its preservation of analytic criteria for assessing truth values. Searle to a large extent emaciates illocutionary force. He ignores the aspects of Austin's work on illocutions that produce uptake not by virtue of reference but as expressions within social practices (where the empiricist epistemology supporting truth-conditional analysis seems inappropriate, and where we begin to see some of the more radical aspects of Wittgenstein's ideas about how expressions differ from descriptions). And, more important for our purposes, Searle preserves the most cautious features of Austin's work, thus reducing what one does *in saying something* to merely functional, typical attitude types. There is no room for viewing what one does in the utterance as having significance because it might comprise a particular expressive act or qualify the propositional content in possibly nonconventional ways. Searle preserves a philosopher's world by insisting on an abstract model of the components of speech acts, which one can argue has very little to do with actual conversations.[22]

The second alternative involves a dramatistic and Wittgensteinian recasting of Austin's arguments about truth. Clearly philosophers like Davis are correct in attacking Austin's confusion of truth conditions as a property of signs and use conditions as a property of utterances. But it seems just as clear that Austin's concern for appropriateness dimensions of propositions calls our attention to a significant pragmatic aspect of how some propositions are uttered and assessed. I want to suggest that while matters of relevance do not affect the truth value of signs, they do often affect our judgment of the speaker and at times our understanding of how literally to take a proposition that may be true, but is situationally irrelevant or inappropriate. Moreover, if Stephen Toulmin's use of Wittgenstein is correct, it may well be that an analysis, like Davis', of truth conditions ignores a wide variety of cases in which we coherently make truth judgments, even though there is not a clear relation between sign and appropriate referent independent of a given procedure. Toulmin argues that the ways in which grounds "are capable of supporting

22. The best critique I know of Searle's various essays on speech acts is Dennis Stampe, "Meaning and Truth in the Theory of Speech Acts," in Cole and Morgan, eds., *Syntax and Semantics: Speech Acts*, pp. 1–39.

conclusions" may vary between fields.[23] Each field (which I take to be something like a method of projection) has its own standards for making transitions between aspects of data, grounds, or "warrants" invoked, and the kind and quality of conclusions it can make (UA, 234). One might decide that *truth* applies technically only to some pure criterion of demonstrability, but, even with such a criterion, one must still grant some term for confirming certain propositions by practical judgments. Toulmin puts the case succinctly: "Every logical word has, on the one hand, its extra-philosophical use, in which it is applied with an eye to field-dependent criteria; and, on the other hand, its inter-philosophical use, in which the criteria for its application refer solely to entailments, contradictions, and consistency" (UA, 233). For Toulmin, there must be a field of comparative logic analogous to comparative anatomy: a monkey's hand would be misformed on a man in much the same way that rigorous Cartesian standards misform the discussion of practical epistemological issues (UA, 255).

Austin's theory of happiness dimensions for propositions serves, then, to indicate the importance of recognizing the place in discourse of ways for assessing descriptions which do not allow purely truth-functional criteria. One basic area of these assessments is pragmatics, and pragmatics involves both matters of indirect or implied reference and matters of dramatistic analysis, in which an agent is judged by his awareness of conditions of relevance. In both cases, what an agent intends or what a situation requires will not determine the independent truth value of a statement, if it can be established, but they will effect *uptake* of both the statement and the status of the agent. We are all familiar with cases where too literal an insistence on narrow truths distorts one's grasp of the whole, or where true statements can nonetheless be used ironically. Imagine a scenario in which it is true to say "prices slumped," but the other economic factors have changed so that in effect prices really increased relative to costs. Or even imagine a situation where prices have in fact slumped, but not so much as expected, so that an ephebe planner who blithely announced the slump would be judged inexperienced or worse, unless he saw how to place his observation in context. Finally, imagine in the same situation an utterance "prices slumped" as true and yet used ironically to indicate the gap between the small slump and

23. Stephen Toulmin, *The Uses of Argument* (Cambridge: Cambridge University Press, 1964), p. 42. Toulmin defines his position as a form of pragmatism that simply ignores the kinds of concerns about truth that can foster scepticism; cf. p. 232. Hereafter, I shall refer to this work as UA.

the expectations of disaster. In all these cases, the statement may be distinct from the utterance, but its use—and appropriateness as a use— remains contextually dependent, and thus the statement must be assessed in both of Austin's dimensions.

This is where literary theory can use Austin. A typical claim about literary contexts is that two kinds of contextual pressures—from the dramatic situation and from authorial patterns eliciting qualitative inferences about characters and acts—affect the uptake of statements uttered within literary texts. Because of this contextual pressure, the adequacy of statements to situations becomes a crucial second-order index of the qualities of the agents making the utterance and of the possible ways the literary text itself may be related to experience. Consider the brutal lucidity of Anna Karenina's last visions in the railroad station. These are no doubt accurate assessments of the objects of her attention, but their truth and their power are dependent on Anna's context and on the contrasts between her and Levin. Anna's vision, then, is significant primarily as a vehicle for assessing perceptions under dramatistic conditions. While such visions are not typical of ordinary speech situations, their power in large part depends on their evoking and filling out a potential attitude toward utterances that is basic to our standard procedures for correlating propositions and contexts. It is always possible to prise statements off the act of utterance, but this is probably the extraordinary rather than the ordinary procedure.

I am tempted here to propose a new felicity condition for the analysis of ordinary utterances: do not treat the proposition as an independent philosophical statement if you have any desire to describe how communication takes place, or even how practical truth judgments are usually made. Russell somewhat ironically understood this when he insisted that an adequate truth-functional analysis of statements required recasting ordinary sentences to capture their possible independent validity as propositions. Russell saved philosophy from speakers of the language; Austin, in reaction, tried to save speakers of the language from Russellian criteria for philosophy, but in the process he became so ambivalent about philosophy that his particular formulations stand largely as indices of work still to be done. Yet focussing the direction for this work and indicating general lines for recognizing how the production of meaning can be its achievement is itself no small achievement. Austin leaves us with formulations that can easily be modified to fit a Wittgensteinian sense of grammar (which, in fact, his formulations actually help us to flesh out). In general, we need to replace Austin's reliance on conventions with more flexible forms of determinacy derived from grammatical competence. This entails, first, making clear that illocutions relying on social conventions can either directly employ formal rules (as in bridge, or judicial verdicts) or depend on a general sense of a practice. Thus, as Toulmin indicates, it is plausible to view our ways of deciding on what is significant in a discourse and how it should be assessed, both as partially determined by the practices the discourse is engaged in. More important, we must show how our grammatical competence enables us to understand and to assess the full performance of a speech act. What one does in saying something must be viewed as an act in context which can be dramatistically understood and which can dictate a wide variety of assessment dimensions.

6. Grice's pragmatic analysis of speech acts

In this last respect, Paul Grice is the heir of Austin most relevant for literary theory. He insists that a speaker's meaning must ultimately be seen in terms of actions. Because talking is "a special case or variety of purposive behavior," [24] a full semantics of the ways speakers use a language requires concepts and criteria taken from the philosophy of action. Grice views meaning as dependent on the communication of an agent's purposes, and his specific work on speech acts tries to establish the ways we interpret these purposes. Thus, he prepares the way for a fully dramatistic account of linguistic behavior which can be adapted to expressive performances.

Grice distinguishes himself from Austin in two basic, interrelated ways. Because he insists on utterances as acts, Grice locates his version

---

24. My treatment of Grice is based on his "Logic and Conversation," in Cole and Morgan, eds., *Syntax and Semantics: Speech Acts*, pp. 41–58; hereafter abbreviated LC. I quote from p. 47. Grice's other relevant essays include "Further Notes on Conversation and Logic," in Cole, ed., *Syntax and Semantics: Pragmatics*, and, on his theory of meaning, "Meaning," *Philosophical Review* 86 (1977):377–88, and "Utterers Meaning and Intentions," *Philosophical Review* 78 (1969):147–77. It is striking that Grice, despite his distrust of formal rules, seems to be bearing fruit for linguistics in a way Austin did not. This may derive in part from the fact that Grice functions on a more abstract and encompassing level of generalization than did Austin. For a very useful, but somewhat narrowly focused application of Grice to matters of literary theory and literary interpretation, see Mary Louise Pratt, *Toward a Speech Act Theory of Literary Discourse* (Bloomington: Indiana University Press, 1976). For shrewd comments on this book, see the essays by Hancher and by Margolis cited above.

of performative force in maxims rather than rules, so he concentrates on nonconventional rather than conventional models of implicature. The concept of nonconventional implicature, in turn, has as its context Grice's insistence on human meanings as nonnatural, and hence as based on intentional properties that entail hermeneutic analysis. Where Austin vacillates, Grice is firm: speakers' meanings are not decoded but interpreted, and interpretation requires correlating in probabilistic terms a particular synthesis of agents' purposes with features of a situation or context.

The basis for Grice's correlation of semantics and pragmatics depends on replacing Austin's rules with a single general principle, which Grice projects as governing standard interpretations of conversational behavior. This principle is called *the cooperative principle:* "Make your conversational contribution such as is required at the stage at which it occurs, by the accepted purpose or direction of the talk exchange in which you are engaged" (LC, 45). This principle serves as a guide for communication, because a speaker can assume his auditor will apply it, and, thus, he can exploit it in various ways. Grice then proposes four general maxims which clarify how speakers and auditors might employ the cooperative principle in different contexts in order to clarify the pragmatic dimensions of a discourse. The categories for the maxims are borrowed from Kant—*quantity, quality, relation,* and *manner.*[25] Each maxim's function is to clarify meanings in situations where the explicit semantic information is not sufficient and yet where no clear conventional context dictates the appropriate force and felicity conditions. Felicity now depends on accurate strategic use of the cooperative principle. The category of *quantity* applies to uses of the cooperative principle that affect judgments pertaining to the economy of information. Auditors assume that a speaker will make his contribution as informative as is required and will not add unneeded information. (Conversely, the auditor will have to test hypotheses about the speaker's intention which will enable

25. Kant's categories, in turn, derive from an analysis of the properties of judgment. But, in the light of recent work on practical judgments, it is important not to stress the exclusive nature of categorical distinctions. As I specify below, I take Grice's maxims as exemplary forms of practical interpretations, not as an exhaustive and precise definition of the only maxims employed in conversation. For a suggestive reformulation of Grice that treats the maxims as only instances derivable from a single principle—*be relevant*—and varying contextual criteria of relevance, see Diedre Wilson and Dan Sperber, "On Grice's Theory of Conversation," pp.11–13, 18–22. I cite a typescript of a yet unpublished essay that will be part of a forthcoming book by the two authors.

him to interpret what information is given as relevant.) The category of *quality* produces the supermaxim, *be true,* and two specific maxims— one expects a speaker not to speak falsely and not to say what he lacks evidence for. The category of *relation* involves the maxim, *be relevant,* so we assume that semantic units are coherent contributions to an on- going process. And, finally, speech is governed by a maxim deriving from the category of *manner* that entails conditions of perspicuousness like the assumed imperatives, *avoid ambiguity, be brief,* and *avoid obscur- ity of expression.* (Grice proposes his maxims as exhaustive and as im- peratives for the speaker. In my summary, I have emphasized their fea- tures as shared understandings between speaker and auditor, and I have tried to express them in a way that treats them only as examples of gen- eral strategies deriving from the cooperative principle.)

Grice's basic example should enable us to get clear on three central issues—what the maxims explain, how they are used in such explana- tions, and their status in contrast to Austin's and Searle's rules. Because he stresses pragmatics, Grice's example is not a type sentence (which invites formal analysis) but a snatch of conversation: "Suppose that A and B are talking about a mutual friend, C, who is now working in a bank. A asks B how C is getting on with his job and B replies, 'Oh quite well, I think; he likes his colleagues, and he hasn't been to prison yet' " (LC, 43). What needs explanation here is the final clause, for in it B has "implied, suggested, meant" something distinct from what his ut- terance overtly says and states (LC, 43). Taken as a direct utterance without implicature, B's proposition would be true and irrelevant. There is, however, an implied proposition that is the intended, but not the stated, assertion, namely that "C is potentially dishonest" (LC, 50). B's meaning is obvious, but it is not straightforward; it is intelligible as an act, but not as a conventional semantic unit. The statement has a prag- matic force that is neither an explicit nor a conventional performative. We interpret this force by taking the utterance as a particular act and by asking what the speaker can expect us to know about speech be- havior which would allow us to see what he intends. What we know is that he knows we can interpret him by assuming that he is indirectly exploiting maxims common to conversational behavior. Maxims of man- ner and of relation provide a path to interpretive coherence here, because they make it clear that the final clause can be relevant and not am- biguous only if we take it as a purposefully indirect or ironic comment on C's character. Moreover, the maxim of relation suggests that B has rea- sons for calling attention to C's possible dishonesty instead of other traits, and the maxim of quality leads one to expect that B has some evidence for his implied doubts. All these maxims, however, will be applied differently if we know more or different aspects of A's relation to B. For example, if A knows that B actually admires c's honesty (or perhaps if A knows that B thinks A admires c's honesty), conversational implicature requires that we take the remark about prisons as a joke. Here we begin to enter more complex dramatistic frameworks, sanctioned by Grice's model but not fully enough considered in his work.

Now why do these Gricean moves matter? First, this is a simple example standing for (or opening up into) more complex cases in which the speaker's purposes in context are crucial determinants of what is in fact said and stated. A dramatistic account of speech is incipient here, because *motive* is a central factor in interpreting the utterance. Neither formal analysis nor attention to constitutive rules and conventions will be adequate to such cases. Instead the speech act is a purposive *exploitation* of assumed interpretive strategies, and its uptake depends on granting the auditor a reasonably complex grammatical competence to use maxims and to relate them to behavioral expectations about purposive acts in this kind of context. While the example is simple, it exemplifies a perspective on language that can give a central role to figurative expressions. Figures are neither mere deviants from ordinary usage nor radically privileged moments of *original perception*. Rather, figures are simply basic possibilities of exploiting standard maxims in order to describe or express perceptions or states of mind in a distinctive, yet clear, way.

Second, the relation between maxims and speakers' purposes should make clear the central differences between Grice and Austin. While Grice often speaks as if his maxims were exhaustive and represented formal rules for pragmatics, it seems to me likely that maxims are neither rules nor conventions.[26] Rather, Grice's maxims represent what Wittgenstein might call features of the grammar of linguistic activity: when we learn how to use language to communicate, we learn not only semantic rules, but general practices and expectations relating to how we construe relevant contexts and implications of speech acts. When we learn to use

26. For critical arguments that link Grice with Austin and attack their inability to specify rules and maxims, see Margolis and Jerrold M. Sadock, "On Testing for Conversational Implicature," in Cole, ed., pp. 280–96. For Margolis, the maxims reduce to "attenuated versions of moral maxims," and for Sadock, the cooperative principle and the maxims do not adequately constrain possible relevant contexts or establish calculations distinctive to conversation.

a language, we learn how these expectations might be relied upon or exploited because we know how we would react to similar utterances. Grice neatly captures these grammatical implications in his use of the term *maxims*. *Maxim* is a term from moral practices, where we do not expect to be presented with the formal descriptive statements that typically characterize rules, for example, in games, legal settings, or formal languages. Rather, maxims are guides for practical reasoning: they do not by themselves account for phenomena, but instead a speaker relies on them because he knows that his hearer can use them as principles or strategies for making a probabilistic judgment. In Austin, implicature is conventional, because if one knows the relevant semantic rules and (in some cases) the social conventions felicitously invoked, he knows what the speech act means. One does not need interpretive hypotheses or a process of tentatively trying out general expectations in order to locate the best fit. Indeed, one might say that Austin confined himself to conventions in order to stay within what Michael Hancher calls a *constitutive* rather than a *regulative* framework, where problems of interpretation and intention might arise. Maxims, on the other hand—in moral reasoning and in the pragmatics of nonconventional implicature—are used to project hypotheses which must be adjudicated so as to fit the vagaries of specific sentences and contexts. Maxims do not project type sentences or generative semantic patterns, tokens of which are uttered in particular cases. Because of their abstract, pragmatic status, it is unlikely that one could produce an exhaustive list of maxims or specific rules for applying them in all cases. Grice's maxims, then, are perspicuous examples of how the cooperative principle works. (We can easily imagine a case for maxims in literary language which would not usually apply in ordinary conversations.) The maxims are specifications of some pragmatic principles which a speaker understands as conditions of communication and which thus establish the probable hermeneutic strategies he assumes his audience will apply. The maxims do not have the same kind of objectivity as semantic or social conventions. They are embedded in social practices, as expectations deeply interconnected with our concepts of person and communication. These concepts clearly resist any overt sense of rules. Thus, it is simply a category mistake to hold Grice accountable to the charges of vagueness levelled against Austinian claims about rules. Austin's claims founder, in fact, partially because he tries to correlate formal semantic principles with tentative assays into pragmatics, while not recognizing fully the different criteria involved. In fact, charges against Grice, like Joseph Margolis' claim that his maxims are only principles of common sense, may indicate his strength rather than his weakness. A *sensus communis* is not a bad ground on which to base our capacity for understanding the pragmatics of speakers' meanings. There remain empirical problems in establishing what in fact is common among speakers and their audience, but Grice indicates the field of assumptions and practical consequences where the possibility of shared grounds can be tested.

7. *Expressive implicature and the need to modify Grice*

We still have to ask what Grice has not done in his analysis of his basic example. There are crucial ways in which he does not exhaust his model of nonconventional implicature and the implicit grammatical frameworks that allow for full uptake in practical judgments about the utterance. In analyzing what B implicates by stating that C has not been to prison yet, Grice ignores an entire realm of possible aspects of meaning, connected with the fact that B has chosen to speak indirectly and to exploit conversational maxims. In fact, what B says is fairly clear; why he puts his statement this way and what the choice itself may *mean* is tantalizing. Is B calling attention to his own perspicuity, making a joke, or trying to convince A that he can maintain a balanced judgment in which suspicion is tempered by ironic self-awareness? These practical questions involve further theoretical issues: must such questions be determined if we are to understand the speaker's meaning, and does the relevance of these matters depend upon whether B wants A to recognize them as his intention? Once we begin to take seriously the pragmatic aspects of an utterance as features of meaning or *total signification,* how do we formulate the relation between the act and the explicit statement, and how do we know when to stop? Questions like these explain Austin's conservatism, but they cannot be ignored. So here I want to develop a conceptual model for these dramatistic forms of nonconventional implicature. I am not sure about the limits of this model, but at the least I will have identified an issue and shown why it matters for literary theory.

Grice's work on pragmatics concentrates on interpreting the ways in which context helps determine the actual content of the speaker's message. So he analyzes those features of an utterance which are independent of any specific concern for what is implied about the speaker in his manipulation of the cooperative principle. Like Austin, Grice confines his analysis of what one does *in* saying *x* to what affects the semantic content. He ignores what is actually done in the specific way *x* is said. Grice's emphasis is clearly adequate to many uses of language, but not to the most interesting cases of implicature. These are the cases where literary texts most fully connect to the potentials of ordinary language and where the complexity of our pragmatic grammar is most in evidence. For such cases involve *uptake,* in which one recognizes how what Valery calls *the voice in action* projects its qualities in its manipulation of language. In order to establish a model for such cases, I propose here to supplement Grice by sketching a concept of expressive implicature appropriate to speech situations where the qualities of an agent become part of the meaning of the utterance, because they are implicated in the contextual exploitation of the cooperative principle. When we ask why a maxim is flouted, we often discover that the reasons are not simply to say something indirectly but to employ the specific indirectness as an index of the speaker's intention to project his identity in a distinctive way. When maxims are flouted, we can ask not only what someone means but also why he has spoken indirectly. Because speakers can use this possibility to project intentions, there are many cases where semantic theory has no alternative but to enter the muddy waters of dramatistic analysis.

For an initial example of some aspects of implicature comprised by my stress on expressive features, I shall turn briefly to the work of M. A. K. Halliday. Halliday does not use Grice—indeed, Halliday lacks a fully philosophical account of meaning—but he does define areas of discourse in which different forms of nonconventional implicature can be located. These three areas are *field, tenor,* and *mode.*[27] *Field* comprises shared expectations inherent in a pragmatic or institutional context, that dictate what an auditor should bring to the literal statements. When linguists talk, for example, many things are clear, yet implicit, which would require painful elaboration for the uninitiated. *Tenor* consists of role relations in a situation: situations allow a variety of implicit features depending on how "interpersonal options" are selected "in the systems of mood, modality, person, key, intensity, evaluation, and comment and the like." Finally, *mode* involves implications that derive from a variety of second-order categories, by which the metafunction of a discourse can be described. Each discourse can be seen as an internal organization of linguistic elements, in which choices can be characterized

27. For a full account of these, see Halliday, *Language as Social Semiotic: The Social Interpretation of Language and Meaning.* Here I rely on Halliday's summary, pp. 143–45.

with respect to other structures sharing the same principles of organization. For example, we can view a specific speech act as a particular strategy for achieving a standard rhetorical purpose or for realizing a genre in a distinctive way. Each of Halliday's categories, in turn, requires an appropriate set of what I shall later describe as grammatical types of predicates, which enables us to place the particular dramatistic instance within a general set of expectations. And when we begin to consider the possible interplay among these functions and their enabling types, we recognize just how far nonconventional implicature takes us from rule-governed contexts into general questions about interpreting human actions.

Expressive implicature applies clearly in utterances where aspects of tenor or mode are foregrounded. I take paradigm cases of expressive implicature to be those in which one is invited to see a speaker as intentionally focussing pragmatic, nonconventional implicatures of an utterance in order to call attention to qualities of the agent-speaker revealed *in* the act of saying something in a particular way. Expressive implicature, then, is a way of developing Austin's initial account of performatives in a fashion that may ultimately show the utility of Grice for questions of style in literature and in ordinary experience. On Gricean foundations we can speak of linguistic choices as ways of exploiting deviations from norms which entail behavioral as well as semantic and syntactic frameworks of expectations.

The best way for me to illustrate the parameters and significance of this definition is to elaborate a single example through a few increasingly complicated scenarios. Let us take the utterance, "I warn you that I shall come." As a standard type for an illocutionary act, this is an explicit performative, readily assessable by Austin's model, by Searle's codification of it, and by generative semantics. Because there is no nonconventional implicature at this level, Grice is irrelevant. Now, let us take the same utterance intended as a somewhat ironic, self-deprecating promise. The speaker, A, knows that his auditor, B, knows that A made a drunken fool of himself at the last party, so A can exploit the irrelevance of warning here in order to commit himself to coming to another party B is throwing. I suspect that Austin would have to write this example off as an ironic one, parasitical on ordinary illocutionary acts. Warnings are *exercitives*, while promises are *commissives*, so no clear illocution is made and no coherent conventions are invoked. Searle might be able to handle this example as an indirect speech act, like "Can you pass the salt?," but the explicit performative is not clearly conventional and the utterance seems to vacillate between what it says and what it conventionally accomplishes. In any case, the dramatic import of the saying is beyond the ken of Searle's analysis, as Derrida somewhat over-exuberantly makes clear. Finally, generative semantics might be ingenious enough to locate a relevant deep structure that synthesizes *warn* and *promise,* but the necessary ingenuity would belie the simplicity of our actual understanding and probably still not account for what the speaker projects about himself in the saying.[28]

My example offers no apparent difficulties for Grice, since his model can explain from context and the cooperative principle the relevant sense of *I warn you.* Indeed, from Grice it is possible to shift to Sperber and Wilson's elegant argument that implicature here makes us see *I warn you* as not a *use* of ordinary semantic conventions but a *mention* of those conventions in order to integrate them within a second-order ironic use. Sperber and Wilson, in short, show how Halliday's tenor and mode can be interpreted as controlling mentioning aspects of a discourse. But Sperber and Wilson's model also makes it possible to clarify the limits of Grice's typical analysis. Grice's nonconventional implicatures will explain how we see the need to shift from a use to a mention of *I warn you,* but it will not explain many of the features of the utterance that follow from the shift. Grice can show how a warning implies a promise, but he does not pay much attention to how the tone in which the mention is used becomes a qualifying feature of the promise that allows A to project a representation of his self-knowledge and his apology to B. In addition to the nonconventionally implied message, A projects aspects of tenor and of self-conscious modal control over the typical forms of accepting an invitation, in order to invite B to recognize and to assess his dramatic stance, as both a form of self-knowledge and as an

---

28. There are some features of my example that invite a formal semantic analysis because *warn* and *promise* share a future-committing dimension. But, as Austin's placing the terms in different categories suggests, these apparent similarities allow a good deal of play between the terms and require that one be able to specify the act before he can fully determine the relevant weight and stress given to the similarities and differences among the terms. The aspect of threat in *warn* can be modified or suspended by the pressure of *promise,* or *promise* can take on overtones of threat not a typical feature of its semantic force. Moreover, as I shall argue, these mutual modifications require that the two terms be correlated as a single complex act. The complexity of that act may be described semantically as suspending *warn* between use and mention, between a literal and a second-order interpretation of its typical semantic roles. My own use of *use* and *mention* derives from Dan Sperber and Diedre Wilson, "Les ironies comme mentions," *Poetique* no. 36 (1978), 399–412.

expression of deference to his auditor. I see no way of not taking these matters of expressive implicature as aspects of speakers' meanings and as indices of where literary and existential understandings interact.

In order to bring out this last point and to further complicate questions of implicature, I shall risk an inappropriate sexual pun and wring one further twist on my example. Now A and B are rivals for a woman who will be at B's party. A's "I warn you that I shall come" in this context can be a complex dramatic utterance. The performative here can contain three distinct acts—a promise, a warning, and an attempt to imply that although they are rivals A wants to acknowledge the rivalry and keep it within civilized terms of a mutual understanding that will not destroy their friendship. Yet to speak of three acts is to miss two important aspects of tone as a feature of dramatic contexts. The speaker does not perform three acts, but one complex one in which the three dimensions of performative force modify or qualify one another. No formal analysis can capture this integration. Moreover, when we consider the kind of dense synthesis such tonal complexities entail, we begin to understand the grammatical context necessary if such utterance is to have *uptake*. B cannot comprehend A's utterance without projecting and testing hypotheses about A's intention. And, most important, B will not get the intention right unless he has a fairly complex behavioral grammar—unless he is a good reader. B must understand the nature of complex intentions, must know how civility and threat are compatible (thus specifying the appropriate lexical sense of *warn*), must grant A the capacity to make complex utterances, and must be able to recognize that terms like *warn* can simultaneously be used in this direct sense and mentioned in a second-order, somewhat self-ironic context. The fuller B's sense of this grammatical complexity, the more the message recedes in importance, to be supplanted by a grasp of the qualities of understanding and concern A has projected. Because A can combine use and mention, he can integrate into his utterance both first-order practical communications and second-order projections of his qualities as a human agent. Because B has developed a complex grammar, he has the ability to compare A's way of handling the situation with other possible ways, and thus he can recognize and appreciate the distinctive qualities of A's act.

By elaborating expressive implicature in this way, we establish three crucial aspects of human understanding in speech situations not emphasized in Grice's groundbreaking work. We understand how speech is a mode of human presence, in which messages are not merely functional exchanges of practical information, but, rather, serve to allow the projection of qualities that cover the full range of human agency. We begin, in short, to make clear the kind of potentials in ordinary discourse fully exploited by literary texts and, conversely, we begin to put basic areas of literary experience on firmer semantic grounds. If we can correlate literary and semantic theory, we also prepare a hermeneutic model of communication that acknowledges dramatic differences between *use* and *mention*. Pure *use* of semantic codes suggests the agent's subordination of qualities of self-consciousness to literal features of the utterance. *Mention*, on the other hand, stages a complex, second-order relation to the semantic code, by which the agent calls attention to his way of staging himself as possessing and manipulating communicative potentials, in order to show something about his qualities as an agent. *Mention* requires for its uptake complex models of self-conscious actions. It leads to two matters I shall elaborate in subsequent chapters—how an authorial act can control mimetic features of a literary text, and how agents become seen as fully purposive, self-defining characters. As we shall see, it is possible to move from expressive implicature to Charles Taylor's powerful distinction between first- and second-order desires with respect to agents' self-presentations.[29] First-order desires are largely empirical judgments about immediate goods, while second-order evaluations are judgments about the value of particular desires: by reflecting on his choices with respect to *uses*, an agent can place his actions within coherent, self-consciously contrastive accounts of values that project him as a certain kind of person. In literary texts, these strong evaluations are usually suggested by complex patterns of implicature rather than stated in overt (and often casuistic) pronouncements.

Finally, a model of expressive implicature begins to reveal the complex forms of coherence necessary for making sense of acts people perform in speech. This I consider a crucial point, because it indicates what are probably inescapable limits in formal semantic analyses and in more general analytic models of thought. As implicature becomes dense and self-referential, part/whole relations become extremely complex. Therefore, analysis into parts and rule-governed relations is not sufficient to account for the kinds of syntheses produced. As my examples became more fully dramatic, the model of coherence they entailed was neither

29. Charles Taylor, "Responsibility For Self," in Amélie Rorty, ed., *The Identities of Persons* (Berkeley: University of California Press, 1976), pp. 281–300. For another useful treatment of persons in relation to second-order operations, see, in the same collection, Daniel Dennett, "Conditions of Personhood," pp. 175–96.

semantic nor, strictly speaking, conceptual, but instead required a scenic or imagistic sense of how actors might behave. We rely on a sense of action types, that lead back to dimension terms and require as their ground of intelligibility a grammar developed precisely by meditation on the nature of actions and of possible choices in contexts.[30]

8. Expression and intention: the problem of interpreting the act in its contexts

We have surveyed a variety of performative forces, ranging from the invocation of social conventions, to explicit performatives governed by semantic conventions, to two models of nonconventional implicature. The further we go from conventions whose determining force can specify uptake and establish intention, the more we enter the correlative spheres of hermeneutic interpretations and the philosophy of action.[31] And the more we have approached a correlation between traditional (and intuitive) senses of how people behave, the messier, more

30. This point brings me into conflict with Grice's desire to preserve a form of argument by necessary and sufficient conditions. If forms of coherence derive from situation and agent types and paradigm scenes, the lines of interpretation often will not fulfill Grice's condition: "The presence of a conversational implicature must be capable of being worked out; for even if it can in fact be intuitively grasped, unless the intuition is replaceable by an argument, the implicature (if present at all) will not count as a conversational implicature; it will be a conventional implicature" (LC, 50). This statement contains what appear to me to be odd notions both of conventions and of agency. It assumes that the only nonconventional model of implicature, and of interpretations of actions, depends on arguments, that all nondiscursive forms of coherence are conventional, and that an agent's nonconventional acts derive from intentions that can be recovered as rational chains of argumentative inferences. The intending agent simply does not always work this way, but instead often leaps among images of types of actions as narrative or dramatic models of what he might achieve in his self-presentation.

31. For various ways of distinguishing among performatives, almost all of which argue for some purely conventional model and some kind of explicit illocution but rarely consider expressive forces, see the essays by Black and by Furberg in Fann, ed., by Strawson and by Warnock in Berlin, ed., *Essays on J. L. Austin*, (Oxford: Clarendon Press, 1973), and Stephen Schiffer, *Meaning* (Oxford: Clarendon Press, 1972), pp. 94–101. Warnock's essay is very good on the different kinds of information needed to understand conventional performatives and explicit illocutions. The only philosophers I know who approach the idea of implicit performatives, neither of whom develop it, are L. W. Ferguson, "Austin's Philosophy of Action," in Fann, ed., p. 165; Warnock in Berlin, ed., p. 77, and Strawson, "Intention and Convention," pp. 602–03. I have also found Strawson's essay very useful for its attempts to mediate between Grice and Austin and for its discussion of intention and non-avowable features of a discourse.

complicated, and more uncertain have been the models proposed for analyzing general phenomena and for making specific judgments. I take all this as an existential parable revealing, and I hope supporting, my commitments. I also take this as a necessary prolegomena to one last muddying of the waters. If we are to speak about *expressive implicature,* we must at least recognize the possibility that equating meaning with intention will not always be sufficient—at least if one takes intention as some version of *rational plan.* Because I shall not discuss *intention* fully until I take up the philosophy of action, I want to indicate only here the problems raised by my use of *expression.*

Alan Tormey suggests that in practical contexts expression is always the expression *of* some property.[32] But the *of* here admits both subjective and objective genitives: an expression can articulate a self-conscious presentation of a property or quality, or it can reveal some symptomatic aspects of the agent's condition which comes to the surface despite his consciousness. Expressions can be deliberate communications, or symptomatic betrayals of one's intentions, or they may be indeterminate in relation to avowable intentions. It may be the case, for example, that A did not deliberately intend to project certain qualities of concern in his warning. He just said it as a way of responding to B, and his just saying it may have been only a warning or may have been a nonreflexive way of expressing the combined acts discussed above. What B knows about A and the situation may or may not allow a strongly probable reading of what he "really" expressed. (Even if B asked A what he meant to express, A might have to interpret his act on the same inferential grounds as B does.) Or A may have actually made a slip in his statement. He may have desired to say only "I promise to come," but his hostility may have emerged. There would usually be evidence of this slip: A would blurt, or stammer, or try to smooth over the mistake. But still, A would have expressed a warning, I think, whatever his conscious intention.

We find ourselves, then, needing at least two supplementary discussions. We must clarify different aspects of expressive implicature. Where rules or other strict discovery procedures are not available, the best theory can do is make it possible to specify the typical conditions and rough probabilistic criteria relevant for the interpretation of specific cases. Second, because expressions can be meaningful despite intentions, we must turn to considerations for judging inquiries that depend on cri-

32. Alan Tormey, *The Concept of Expression* (Princeton: Princeton University Press, 1970).

teria not definable solely in terms of the agent's purposes. Purposes, as I shall argue later, are central to identifying the act, but a thorough description can show how the apparent intention is thwarted or complicated by other factors. I can be mercifully brief here, in large part because the issues do not allow much accurate generalization.

First, it is necessary to distinguish between deliberate expressive uses of implicature and another class, best defined in general terms as nonavowable expressive features of an utterance. Intentional exploitation of maxims becomes expressive implicature when the speaker calls attention to qualities of the action she is performing in her utterance as a way of responding to a context. Here, the full speaker's meaning of the act is simply not understood until the auditor can grasp the fit between the performed qualities and a probable intention. As is not the case with explicit performatives, this recognition depends on a complex grammar of person predicates not coextensive with a simple semantic competence. When we turn to nonavowable expressive forces, we cannot employ our usual sense of the speaker's meaning, because that depends on intentions. I am not sure what to coin as a name for the kind of comprehension involved, but it has affinities with E. D. Hirsch's notion of *significance*, because it depends largely on an interpreter's needs and desires. Nonetheless, if we are to give any credence to concepts of implicature and total speech acts, we must at least see what is involved. (It may be that once we acknowledge these features we can find a way of denying or limiting their relevance.) Thus, I distinguish four subtypes of nonavowable expressive implicatures—cases of nonintentional features of style, cases of unintentional behavioral indices (like signs of showing off or of contempt for one's audience), cases where there is evidence a speaker is lying and in the process signifying things about his desires and concerns, and cases of symptomatic signs (like Freudian slips or betrayals of class attitudes) which are definable within specific interpretive strategies.

Since these various expressive features have different relations to the speaker's intentions, we must also register the kinds of situations in which these expressions characteristically count as significant. In essentially formal contexts, where Austin's conventional performatives might be expected, neither intentional nor nonavowable expressive implicatures are likely to be acknowledged—at least within the conventional procedures. These procedures are usually impersonal and involve formal or legal consequences, so the typical interpretive strategy is to reduce possible uncertainties and to rely on strong rules of evidence for establishing what meanings count as operant. (Conversely, what does count is extremely difficult to reverse.) The criteria differ in ordinary conversational contexts, where the usual standard is simply the need to recognize those implicatures necessary to keep the conversation going in a cooperative manner. In the examples of conversation I have given, the expressive implicature clearly affects how an auditor should respond. Finally, there are a wide variety of cases where an interpreter wants the greatest possible information about the speaker—at least in one context, for example, his psychology or class situation—and, thus, he will try to understand every relevant expressive feature of the utterance. Literature clearly intersects with ordinary discourse at this level, but with a significant difference that reminds us how art is not life, no matter how we deny essentialist definitions of art. For it is frequently impossible to carry on a cooperative enterprise if we either ignore expressive qualities or concentrate too intently on them, especially on their nonavowable aspects. This stricture holds, however, only for first-order, practical, cooperative enterprise, and it thus makes clear why literary discourse projects a cooperative enterprise only on a second-order, reflexive level, in which qualities are not communicated but performed or displayed and then contemplated.

This second-order level, I shall argue, takes the form it does in literary experience because literary discourse is illocutionarily marked by its typical contexts as requiring fairly loose, but still generally shared, procedures for reading. Here Austin's work has its literary payoff. But what really matters is the way these procedures call attention to the dramatistic quality of the acts they frame. Here Grice provides the stage for elaborating how literature at once reflects typical existential concerns and extends our capacity to identify and reflect upon these concerns. Moreover, because Grice's work enables us to describe what takes place in fully dramatistic contexts for achieving meaning by producing it, he enables us to use the insights of textualist theory without being constrained to its metalinguistic claims. A concept of expressive implicature enables us to examine the multiple codes Barthes discloses as "the stereographic space of writing," [33] while integrating these codes as features of human actions. We need no longer treat nonpropositional elements of a discourse as parasites, either banished from a philosophically secure sense of meaning or cancerously destroying secure meanings. To the extent that one can interpret these multiple significations as coherent

33. Barthes S/Z, trans. Richard Miller (New York: Hill and Wang, 1974), p. 15.

dramatistic features of an act, a critic reveals both the complexity of our dramatistic understanding and the limitations of an essentially formalistic dissemination of differences. Derrida at his best can survive Searle's criticisms of his philosophical position by elaborating Searle's insensitivity to the expressive features of the speech acts he purports to analyze. But now it becomes possible to account for Derrida's success in terms deriving from the philosophical contexts Searle unfortunately emaciates in his pursuit of methodological certainties. Derrida is an accomplished performer whose performance depends on his ability to recognize and enact a wide and complex range of expressive implicatures. As is most evident in "Coming into One's Own," his recent, superb dramatic rendering of Freud's attempt to rationalize his own torments, this master of Nietzschean ironies proves ironically human, all too human. His insight as an observer of human actions becomes a sign of his blindness as a philosopher.

3

The Concept of Action, and the Consequences
for Hermeneutic Theory

1. *Introduction: the argument of this chapter* When questions of meaning begin to involve pragmatics—applying to both how we understand the sense of certain terms and how we assess uses of language—we must engage the larger question of what human actions are and how they are intelligible. This is both a welcome and a difficult chore. It is welcome because it connects discussions of meaning with a fully dramatistic framework, where as we clarify the concept of action we also develop the nature of the grammatical competence required to understand how we interpret and attribute qualities to actions. But because we must rely heavily on grammatical concerns and forms of life, we find ourselves entering an area of discourse much vaguer than that establishing the procedures and problem environment in linguistics. As we shall see, there seem to be only two alternatives for the philosophy of action, both undesirable; one can purchase a clear extensional terminology and analytic model at the cost of cutting away many of the more interesting or problematic aspects of the subject, or one can be faithful to the dense texture of complex dramatic examples only by groping for paradigms among the detritus of an outmoded traditional philosophical vocabulary, consisting of mentalist terms like *will, decision,* and *judgment,* which are imprecise at best. This difficulty, of course, suits my case, because it makes clear the probable need for relying on a Wittgensteinian sense of the power of perspicuous samples and examples if one desires to move from the slippery ice of logic to the rough ground of experience. Nonetheless, the tension between these languages puts a heavy analytic bur-

den on the second and third sections of this chapter, where I shall work through some of the specific conceptual issues in order to justify my reliance on a looser vocabulary and a dramatistic methodology. After these sections, the path will grow easier, as I take up the constituents of an intensional language appropriate for the dramatistic analysis of actions and then show how these constituents help us produce what I hope is a defensible resolution for two of the most fundamental questions in hermeneutic theory—the problem of a concept of intention adequate for establishing the meaning of complex utterances, and the corollary problem of adequately characterizing E. D. Hirsch's distinction between meaning and significance.

Since this will be a long, involved, and dense chapter, I want to begin by explaining what is at stake. First, although literary critics rarely inquire into the philosophical foundations for the concept of action,[1] this sphere of inquiry is extremely useful for clarifying theoretical disputes and for elaborating the cognitive dimensions of literary experience. Of this we shall hear a great deal later. But even more important now is a set of issues that lead far beyond literary theory. How we understand actions will shape our view of what a person is; thus, the question of the nature of actions is a necessary element in any analysis of human behavior or of the kinds of explanations adequate for interpreting this

1. Only two literary critics come to mind—Wayne Booth, *Modern Dogma and the Rhetoric of Assent*, and Teun A. van Dijk, "Action, Action Descriptions and Narrative," *New Literary History* 6 (1975):273–94, hereafter abbreviated AAD. Paul Ricoeur is the best philosopher I know who brings the philosophy of action to bear on hermeneutic questions directly related to literature. See his "The Model of the Text: Meaningful Action Considered as a Text," *New Literary History* 5 (1974):91–117 and the first chapter of his *Conflict of Interpretations*, ed. Don Ihde (Evanston: Northwestern University Press, 1974). We can begin to appreciate the importance of the concept of action by observing the difficulties confronting those who try to analyze literary texts using only a speech act model. As we shall see more fully in the next chapter, Richard Ohmann's definition of *literature* as the imitation of speech acts ignores forms like monologues and meditations which, at least according to Austin, would not be speech acts because they involve no audience. Such works are purposive acts, however. In a similar vein, Ohmann tries to invoke social concerns by stressing them as contexts for speech acts, but this does not distinguish between actual societies and images of society constructed by an author for given purposes. For fuller discussion of both these concepts, see my "The Poem as Act: A Way to Reconcile Mimetic and Presentational Theories," *Iowa Review* 6 (1975):103–24. Barbara Hernstein Smith, "Poetry as Fiction," *New Literary History* 2 (1971):259–82, takes a different tack from Ohmann, but it is equally problematic. She views the text itself as a speech act, which is perfectly coherent, but then it is extremely difficult to explain how a complete imaginary world is constructed—this entails a notion of mimesis of something more than speech acts.

behavior. Because hermeneutic strategies ultimately involve ways of characterizing actions, one's hermeneutic choices also implicate stances toward fundamental questions about values. The nature of some of these values should become obvious after a brief consideration of the two modes of understanding behavior most clearly opposed to my dramatistic perspective. On the one hand, the values inherent in a dramatistic approach are not easily reconciled with any type of structuralist formalism, and, on the other, they challenge the often disputed but by now almost standard tendency in the social sciences to imagine that adequate explanations of human behavior must take the form of causal laws on a scientific model.

The outlines of a dramatistic case against textualism should already be clear. Textualism's insistence on the priority of signifying codes affords no place for describing the nature of human agency or the roles that concept plays in our experience. When textualism discusses agents and actions, in fact, it is confined to ironic treatments: if there are no means for establishing *propre sens*, the ensuing aporia of meanings contaminates the concept of agency. Agency becomes a position within the play of texts, and there is no way to see agency as a factor in the determination of meanings. When we describe an event as an agent's purposive act, we are really only imposing a representation, produced by unnameable desires in an interpreter and posing a misleading unity on the play of desires working upon the actor in ways which cannot in fact be represented or determined. Such analyses eventually lead beyond practical descriptions to a host of joyous effusions on the death of man.[2] However, when we ask what supports claims like these, we find the arguments are not the results of descriptions but are the consequences of an essentially programmatic chain of reasoning. The conclusions derive from decisions to give primacy to textual functions and to view texts as linguistic units separated from pragmatic considerations. If we ask for the rationale behind these decisions, we are given Saussure's

2. The loveliest of these is Michel Foucault's: "Rather than the death of God —or, rather, in the wake of that death and in a profound correlation with it—what Nietzsche's thought heralds is the end of his murderer: it is the explosion of man's face in laughter, and the return of masks. . . . Since man was constituted at a time when language was doomed to dispersion, will he not be dispersed when language regains its unity? . . . Man had been a figure occurring between two modes; or, rather, he was constituted only when language, having been situated within representation and, as it were, dissolved in it, freed itself from that situation at the cost of its own fragmentation: man composed his own figure in the interstices of that fragmented language" (*The Order of Things*, pp. 385–86).

diacritical model, but the model is extended far beyond the methodological limits Saussure imposed on himself. Now we come to the basic
problems. The methodological assumption, itself not tested, dictates
the view of texts as only bundles of possible meanings, and that view
tautologically produces the conclusion that there is no sense in a dynamic view of agency and no means to explain how these possibilities
take on a single coherent communicative or expressive role in specific
situations. One has precluded from the start any possible force or principle for generating or interpreting this coherence. The effect is to
banish any framework for using determinately the predicates we normally use for human desires, purposes, and evaluations. Therefore,
textualists eliminate the possibility of qualitatively assessing the ways
agents exhibit the properties signified by those predicates.[3] Finally, the
worst result of this grounding tautology is that it affords no analysis of
actions within which one can fully appreciate the ironies and complexities about purposes disclosed by the best deconstructive work. In fact,
Derrida's richest essays, like the response to Searle and the analysis of
Freud in "Coming into One's Own," depend precisely on locating the
agent's purposes and revealing the complexities which disseminate them
into the folds and supplements inviting deconstruction.

Ironies compound when we recognize that textualist distrust of concepts like action may itself participate in the very positivist and empiricist climate Derrida scorns. Beneath the textualist position on the
human subject lie decades of insisting that actions be analyzed not in
terms of what a person thinks he is doing, but in terms of the latent
forces underlying epiphenomenal states of consciousness. This insistence takes two forms—a general theoretical requirement for causal explanation or covering laws,[4] and a variety of specific empirical practices

---

3. Fillmore succinctly states what I take to be the theoretical alternative: we
need a concept of speech acts, because we need some way of handling the question
of why in specific circumstances a person says what he does. See "Topics in Lexical
Semantics," p. 78.

4. The basic argument for the necessity of a covering law model is succinctly
stated in Carl Hempel, "Rational Action," in Norman Care and Charles Landesman,
eds., *Readings in the Philosophy of Action* (Bloomington: Indiana University Press,
1968), pp. 281–305. Opposition to this model is standard in what I shall later
describe as a Wittgensteinian analysis of actions. The following representatives
of that view (with abbreviations I shall employ in my text) are those I find most
useful: George Henrik von Wright, *Explanation and Understanding* (London:
Routledge and Kegan Paul, 1971)—EU; Hampshire's *Thought and Action;* Anthony Kenny, *Action Emotion and Will*, (New York: Humanities Press, 1963)
especially chapter eight; John Cook; "Human Beings," in Peter Winch, ed., *Studies
in the Philosophy of Wittgenstein* (New York: Humanities Press, 1969), pp. 117–

that define the causes of behavior in terms of some analogy with the physical sciences. In one sense, at least, these models are not naive: they find a behavioral warrant in the manifest fact that people are rarely, if ever, rational agents, and they have a strong methodological appeal by negative contrast to the sloppiness of approaches to behavior that rely on empathy or proceed in a chain of concepts that never gets tested against empirical evidence. Empiricists, at least, have a paradigm example in the physical sciences of what a defensible explanation looks like, so it seems logical to attempt to concentrate on aspects of human behavior where similar regularities and a rough predictive adequacy seem available. This typically entails making a sharp distinction between manifest or epiphenomenal properties, like self-consciousness, a property extraordinarily difficult to define, and either latent forces or behavioral regularities which justify explanatory abstractions about how actions may be interpreted or controlled. Examples of this attitude can be located in perspectives as divergent as Skinner's behaviorism, vulgar Marxism, and policy-oriented political science. I consider it naive humanist piety to ignore the validity and power of these methods in several areas of experience. But I also think it is too easy to slip into the vulgarity of hard-headed poses which ignore the reductionism inherent in these perspectives when they claim dominance over forms of expressive or reflective actions, where the nature of the individual actor is projected as a significant factor. If we trust too much to explanatory models we tend either to ignore the differences I assert or to banish such cases to the shadowy realm where anomalies and irrelevant particulars wander in search of subjective responses. I want here to concentrate on these "strong" cases of action and to discuss ways of preventing the reductionism inherent in forcing significant particulars into premature generalizations. This entails specifying principles for understanding as publicly determinate the terms in which agents might understand and describe the purposive qualities of their acts. Once we have ways to insist upon

---

51; A. R. Louch, *Explanation and Human Action* (Berkeley: University of California Press, 1969)—EHA; Charles Taylor, *The Explanation of Behavior* (New York: Humanities Press, 1964)—EB; and "Interpretation and the Sciences of Man," *Review of Metaphysics* 25 (1971):3–51—IS. Anthony Melden, "Action," in Care and Landesman, eds., shows how the philosophy of action continues and develops the concepts elaborated in work on constitutive rules as its means for combatting Hempel's empiricism. For a good presentation of the relationship between analytic philosophies of action, which he calls the work of the new teleologists, and earlier reflections on the subject by Hegel, Marx, and Dewey, see Richard Bernstein, *Praxis and Action* (Philadelphia: University of Pennsylvania Press, 1971).

this phenomenological texture of a dramatistic perspective, we can indicate the power of art (and life) to keep complicating the data to which any science of man is ultimately accountable. This has the ironic effect of tempering both the confidence of behavioral science and the scepticism, or at best tolerant pluralism, that follows the failures of purportedly scientific accounts of behavior to make accurate predictions, as we see in the second-generation versions of Freud and Marx I discussed in my introduction.[5] We are reminded, instead, of the rich potential inherent simply in our cultural grammar and the disciplines which foster it. And we recognize the cultural significance of the hermeneutical methods we need as supplements to explanatory models.

2. Three basic problems in defining what an action is and Donald Davidson's way of handling them

It is deceptively easy to establish the general concept of action required to make sense of the pragmatic and performative aspects of discourse we have discussed and to focus the questions about explanation I have touched upon. Almost all philosophers commenting on the subject agree roughly on the basic opposition which gives sense to the term *action*: a distinction between happenings which do not involve person predicates, and the sphere of actions where an event is in some sense qualified by the effects of an agent's wants or beliefs or reasons. The modern foundation for this distinction is Wittgenstein's question: "What is left over if I subtract the fact that my arm goes up from the fact that I raise my arm?" (PI, 621). There are two ways of answering this, which disclose the range of properties that must be covered in discussions of intentions and human agents: raising one's arm can be either a movement motivated by a simple desire or a gesture that depends upon a complex process of deliberation. In either case, the logical difference from happenings is clear. In the case of "my arm went up," or versions of "I raised my arm" where the adverb *unintentionally* is appropriate, an adequate account would consist simply of describing a physical movement in relation to some physical cause or stimulus. In other cases, where *intentionally* is implicitly present, a description of what happened

---

5. The best example of these sceptical inversions of empiricism is the work of Michel Foucault, especially the last chapter of *Words and Things* and his recent analyses of the use of discourses to maintain power, for example, in *Discipline and Punish*, trans. Alan Sheridan (New York: Pantheon, 1977).

involves questions of what the agent contributes to the event.[6] Physiological reasons still explain what allowed the arm to move, but there remains a question *why* the person raised his arm, which will lead to far more complex aspects of causality involving the agent's interpretation of his situation.

The consequences of this simple distinction can be enormous. Consider a case in which the movement from physical explanation expands to a fully dramatistic account. When a hungry person simply sits down and eats, there is little need to go beyond simple causal explanations of the behavior in physiological terms. But suppose he deliberately refuses to eat. Now even characterizing the activity becomes a complex task, inseparable from making hypotheses about his intentions and relating his intentions to long-term plans or projects.[7] Hypotheses about purposes will establish possible reasons for taking the negative act as dieting, as preparing for an athletic event, as religious fasting, or as a political gesture. Moreover, once we put the activity in such categories, further questions arise, which lead to qualitative assessments. In what way is this act consistent with the agent's earlier behavior, how appropriate is it for the situation, how sincere is the gesture, how well does the agent perform it in comparison to similar acts in similar situations by other agents? Such questions often make us decide that our original hypothesis was wrong. We recognized the physical gesture, but we misapprehended the intentions or their relation to the act. Yes, the agent is fasting; but some features of the activity and context reveal it to be showing off, or hypocrisy, or masochism. If one is asked how he knows the reinterpretation is appropriate, he will have considerable difficulty generalizing the grounds for his judgment. It seems reasonably clear that such judgments depend upon a complex grammatical framework of aspects of forms of life relevant to employing predicates about persons in loosely related conjunctions of typical scenarios and expected behavior patterns. I refer to these conjunctions in using the term *dramatism* to mean a perspective on human actions which emphasizes locating an action in terms of specific motives, plans, judgments, etc., and then assessing in qualitative terms what predications about motive en-

6. I take this way of testing for differences between happenings and action from Van Dijk, AAD, 282.

7. It may be because acts of negation most clearly indicate human agency and require the description of intentions that thinkers from Hegel to Sartre and Lacan use the idea of negation as their basic means for characterizing self-consciousness and the nature of human freedom.

able us to say about the agent's way of dealing with a particular situation.

While the grounds for proceeding to a model of dramatistic analysis seem reasonably clear, the way will prove uncomfortably difficult. For, with the stakes I mentioned earlier, no single account of how one might characterize actions has escaped serious challenge. For my purposes, the most important dispute is one between Wittgensteinian views of action as teleological—or depending for their definition on an agent's appraisals and purposes—and logical or extensional views, which insist on formulating action descriptions in terms of a truth-functional analysis compatible with causal models of explanation based on covering laws. My own basic loyalties should be obvious, but Davidson's work has made it impossible simply to rely on the standard post-Wittgensteinian accounts. It seems to me necessary, then, to go through the relevant arguments as carefully as I can, in the hope that I can illustrate the inadequacy of an extensional perspective for our purposes and can make some qualifications now necessary for a defensible use of Wittgenstein. I have no doubt that there are more precise means for this than I shall provide, but by attending primarily to what is necessary for describing moderately complex examples of action, I think I can develop a plausible and defensible view of hermeneutic strategies for presenting an intensional language which can capture the expressive dimensions of speech acts. Examples are crucial in these matters, because many of the terms I shall employ, like *consciousness, choice, motive,* and *grammatical uptake,* do not admit of precise analysis. What these terms implicate cannot be readily established, except by relationships to other terms and activities whose properties are much more easily exemplified in perspicuous cases than rigorously delineated by scientifically adequate definitions.

I shall proceed by outlining what I take to be the three basic conceptual problems involved in discussing human actions, and then I shall work out my own position by contrasting the two general perspectives I have been discussing—the model of logical analysis represented by Donald Davidson and a teleological-appraisal model of action explanation shared by a variety of post-Wittgensteinian philosophers. We can assume the general agreement described above about the distinction between happenings and actions. But the first conceptual problem is immediate and inescapable. If actions are not simply happenings, how do we identify a specific action and the relationships among the constituent elements? What enables us to distinguish relevant parts, explain how they form a whole, and describe that whole as a unified action? Happenings, in principle at least, are simply physical events, and as such should be clearly determinate and identifiable in relation to one another. But if actions involve considerations of wants, attitudes, and possibly an agent's constitutive reasons, how do we decide what makes it possible to identify the act in question as a discrete entity one can make predications about or put modifications on? [8] This problem is further

8. I take this way of putting the question from two essays of Donald Davidson, on which I shall comment later at length: "Actions, Reasons and Causes," in Care and Landesman, eds., pp. 179–98, hereafter abbreviated ARC; and "The Logical Form of Action Sentences," in Nicholas Rescher, ed., *The Logic of Decision and Action* (Pittsburgh: Pittsburgh University Press, 1967), pp. 81–95,—LSA. A brief summary of some different ways of characterizing actions, in addition to Davidson's and the Wittgensteinian position which I shall now elaborate, should help place my claims in context and indicate some of the stakes, and the difficulties, involved in this discussion. Roland Barthes, for example, indicates how views of action change from structuralism to textualism. In his structuralist phase, Barthes equates an action with a nameable sequence which "opens when one of its terms is lacking an antecedent of the same kind, and it closes when another of its terms no longer entails any consequent function." A typical "homogeneous set would be the movement from ordering a drink to consuming it and paying for it." See "An Introduction to the Structural Study of Narrative," *New Literary History* 6 (1975):253. This definition affords both a test of coherence and a way of admitting different sequences depending on the generality of terms one posits as playing the incipient and concluding functions. But Barthes has no model of grammar that can account for the intelligibility of such functions. Thus, he now switches to textualist indeterminacy, in a formulation that again reveals the positivist undercurrent in this mode of thinking. In "Style and its Image," in Seymour Chatman, ed., *Literary Style: A Symposium* (New York: Oxford University Press, 1971), pp. 3–14, and in S/Z, trans. Richard Miller (New York: Hill and Wang, 1974), pp. 10–16, he argues that action cannot be a useful analytic concept, because actions are not observable facts: the fact is that something happened, while the features that might warrant calling it an action are mere interpretive contexts relative to an interpreter's purposes. This position has interesting affinities with Davidson's treatment of an act as an event identical across a variety of descriptions. But at least some analytic philosophers have accepted the challenge Barthes raises, by trying to specify formal models for defining the unity and intelligibility of an act. Alvin Goldman, *A Theory of Human Action* (Princeton: Princeton University Press, 1970), hereafter THA, rejects Davidson in favor of a perspective that breaks actions down into basic act tokens, which exemplify basic act properties. Then he describes more complex acts in terms of level-generating operations, that take the form of a tree diagram illustrating the forms of internal coherence in the description. Acts can be shown to constitute unified sequences in terms of four types of relations— causal generation, conventional generation, simple generation, and augmentation generation. Thus, where Davidson views flipping a switch, turning on a light, and warning a burglar as the same event, differently described, Goldman analyzes the sequence as a basic act of flipping the switch that causally generates turning on the light and augmentally generates warning the burglar (because this was not the agent's intention). Other philosophers, like H. A. Prichard, *Moral Obligation* (Lon-

complicated by a feature not often considered in recent discussions—the adequacy of the empiricist assumption that there are, in principle, logical simples which allow us to speak abstractly about the identity of physical events, without self-consciously recognizing the limited perspective of a given method of projection. A modification of Wittgenstein's example should illustrate some of the conceptual options. Suppose I raise my arm to signal I am making a turn. Is this one act, or is it a series of act tokens combining properties in some fixed relation, or is it only a segment of some larger action context? And what can be the principle of identification—a physical event to which we attribute various descriptions, a set of type properties (tokens of which we find in the act[s] or the agent), or a set of physical signs given meaning and identity only by interpreting the agent's probable purpose from the context, assuming we can tell what a relevant context is? Is it an act of signalling if the agent only puts his arm out the window casually and someone reads the gesture as a signal?

The second problem is already implicit in the first. Whatever account we give for identifying the act, we must also explain how we understand the relation between the agent, his physical act, and the context. Here one's answer will depend partially on what he sees as necessary for simple identification, but three options seem plausible. One can say that the agent causes both the raising of his arm and the signalling. But what do we mean by *cause*—do we mean that the agent caused the movements (and the meaning of the second movement) by willing them or exercising volitional thoughts, or do we take cause as not referring to or implicating mental states, but simply providing an explanatory context in terms of the wants and beliefs of the agent? Finally, if one is uncomfortable with the mentalism of the first sense of *cause* and the opening to behaviorism in the second, one could try to evade the notion of cause entirely by arguing for some kind of analogy to constitutive rules. That

---

don: Oxford University Press, 1945), insist that actions must be identified in relation to a causal event of willing, and Bruce Aune, *Reason and Action* (Boston: David Reidel, 1977), presents a tentative case for dismissing all talk of the identity conditions for events. Instead, he suggests that we can avoid problems of reference by characterizing acts in terms of predicates about agents. None, however, is as consistent and thorough as Davidson. Goldman, for example, provides what I take to be a richer model of action descriptions, but he does not adequately explain criteria for deciding on generations, and the last part of his book seems to me much more reductive than Davidson. These questions are all reviewed in a recent, largely Davidsonian, work, Lawrence Davis, *Theory of Action* (Englewood Cliffs, N.J.: Prentice-Hall, 1979). The book appeared too late for me to use here.

is, just as rules do not cause but regulate behavior and make it intelligible in a game like chess, acts are not so much caused as constituted by the intentions, so that in recognizing constitutive features of the context we can finesse questions of cause and view the act in relation to reasons the agent might provide for it.

Finally, these two questions both shape and are shaped by the more general issue of what kind of explanation one will take as adequate for a human action. Here there are really two issues, or two levels of the same issue. First, what are the phenomena requiring explanation, and what criteria—of evidence and for the correlating of pieces of evidence —will suffice for an explanation? The second level of the issue emerges as soon as we begin to wonder what I have presupposed in using the term *explanation* in the last sentence. What are one's purposes in seeking an account of actions and what model of philosophy justifies those purposes? If one relies on a concept of explanation, she is likely to insist on forms of analysis that produce firm discovery procedures, and this will shape her view of identity conditions and the principles for explaining agency. On the other hand, a version of philosophy that privileges phenomenological exploration is likely to seek concepts that stress the dense description of particulars, and it is likely to emphasize distinctively human forms of action where self-consciousness plays a large role.

Given these differences, the central issue is locating a sphere of common ground where competing accounts are responsible for the same phenomena. If we do this properly, we may avoid some of the oppositions and define a limited area where one can securely rely on a single perspective. Since the most specific differences between Davidson and the teleological view of actions occur with respect to identity conditions, I will concentrate on that question. I want to show that there are kinds of acts, roughly those we take as expressive because they involve self-conscious performances or nonconventional implicatures, for which Davidson cannot fully account. This will justify claiming the need for accepting modifications of the teleological view with respect to at least these actions, and it will help clarify by contrast the nature of the intensional language required in describing the relevant features of these expressive acts.

In order to understand Davidson's position on actions, one must first recognize his methodological commitments. (Indeed, most of my quarrel will be with the limits I think inherent in these commitments.) Davidson wants to explain the logical form of sentences describing ac-

tions in such a way that it is possible to give "a coherent and construc-
tive account of how the meanings (truth conditions) of these sentences
depend upon their structure" (LSA, 92). The spirit, then, and much of
the actual methodology derive from Russell and from Carnap: one can
only meaningfully make predications about phenomena like actions to
the extent that one can show how the operant terms satisfy the criteria
of a logical empiricism. What is not confirmable in a scientific or logical
calculus is only a pseudo-problem about which nothing meaningful
(testable) can be said. Davidson's particular vehicle for his calculus is
an insistence on extensional terms and adaptability to a mechanical
logical notation. What he means by *extensional language* is best clarified by contrast to the concept of an intensional language. As Steven
Davis describes the difference, the former is truth-functional because it
contains only terms from the theory of reference and none from the
theory of meaning, while an intensional language contains only terms
from the theory of meaning. The key analytic concepts in the theory of
reference are *reference, extension, satisfaction, true,* and *true of,* all
roughly adaptable to pictorial tests of adequacy. Terms in the theory of
meaning, on the other hand, are specifiable in conjunction with Carnap's notion of terms relating to the concept of derivation; the central
ones are *meaning, analyticity, synonymy, necessity, entailment,* and
contradictoriness.[9] Intensional sentences are the opposite of pure observation sentences. Their truth values depend on the formal nature of a
language. The appeal of extensional terms, then, is the promise of a
kind of ontological security: we can avoid what the *Tractatus* posed as
the danger of the truth value of one proposition depending on the mean-

9. Davis, *Philosophy and Language,* pp. 180–81. When I shift below from his
logical account to my metaphoric elaboration of intensional statements in terms of
an agent's interpretations, I am making as precise as I can the use of the term
intensional by Wittgensteinian theorists, who to my knowledge never actually
define the concept. Van Dijk (AAD, 281–83) gives a good description of that view
of intensional descriptions. See also Bruce Aune's discussion of extensionality, pp.
33 ff., and his attempt to show how a concept of agency can be treated extensionally, pp. 90 ff. My own concern for an intensional language derives in large part
from the fact that many philosophers who have influenced literary theory use distinctions analogous to that between extension and intension—for example, Gabriel
Marcel on the contrast between a problem and a mystery, Bergson on extensive
and intensive manifolds, and Coleridge on *natura naturata* and *natura naturans.*
But each of these models requires problematic versions of a Romantic metaphysics,
because the models are not content with phenomenological distinctions and want
to attribute features of actions to more general forces. I think that an intensional
model of action descriptions preserves the force of their concerns in a more limited
and specifiable sphere.

ing of another, with an attendant infinite regress unless the system is a closed one.

There is also a fairly clear operational test for the presence of an extensional statement. Extensions are pure denotations, so that reference is *transparent*. Statements with the same truth value can be substituted for one another without changing the truth value of the sentence, and thus any singular term is replaceable by another term with the same referent. For example, the statement "Scott visited Napoleon at time t" is truth-functionally equivalent to, or makes the same descriptive proposition as, "The author of Waverly visited the victor at the battle of Jena at time t." Why this matters for our discussion will immediately become clear if we contrast the example with a sentence like "Scott intended to visit Napoleon." Here intending to visit Napoleon does not entail visiting the victor at Jena, because Scott may not have intended to visit the victor at Jena. Scott may not have known Napoleon won that battle, or may even have thought Napoleon lost the battle. When we introduce verbs that state someone's thoughts or desires, we cannot perform complete truth-functional tests. We can only perform such tests if we rewrite the sentence. Thus, Russell developed his theory of types to avoid problems like the Cretan liar paradox, where the presence of a term in the subject qualifies the descriptive properties of the object. A great deal will depend on whether such rewritings are possible with action sentences which typically contain verbs involving the *opaque* reference of my last examples. In order to capture the differences such opaqueness creates, I shall spend time here trying to work out a specifically hermeneutic version of an intensional language. I say "specifically hermeneutic" as a justification for the fact that I shall offer a largely metaphorical version of the technical term *intension*. I want to be able to move from attitudes, beliefs, and other properties of agency that make reference opaque, to the idea that these form the internal *intensional* coherence of what can be characterized as an expressive act. "Intensional" as a hermeneutic concept, in other words, applies to cases where ideas of meaning and entailment depend on relations established primarily by elements internal to the context of the action. This metaphoric use of *intensional language* affords several advantages: it establishes a clear shorthand opposite to *extensional*; it allows me to defend similar uses of *intensional* by teleological theorists of actions; and, because the strict definition of *intensional* depends on a theory of meaning, it provides a good analogue for discussing both utterances and properties of utterances that depend on intentions. Intension refers metaphorically to the opaqueness created by the need to interpret intentions, and, thus, to rely on internal criteria of fit when we assess action descriptions. Once we have this analogue we can see how a dramatic approach is in many ways a coherence theory applied to hermeneutics and based on the operations of grammatical understanding.

Davidson makes clear his view of the implications of this contrast, between intensional and extensional terms for action descriptions, in an exchange with Roderick Chisholm. Chisholm asks, "How are we to render, 'he made it happen that p' in terms merely of relations among events"? In other words, can an extensional language fully capture the relation between an agent and an act, if its commitment to truth-functional descriptions requires only terms that describe observational phenomena one can clearly denote? Davidson's reply insists that concepts of agency needed to go beyond extension are doubly ambiguous: the concept itself cannot be operationally defined, and one cannot be sure how to decide in particular cases what the agent makes happen. If one were to use *agency* as a term determining truth conditions, he would leave "no way automatically to produce the right description from the original sentence." *Made it happen that* clauses are extremely difficult to describe, because we cannot be clear on what the object is (as in the signalling example), or whether the agency is physical or psychological or some combination of the two (LSA, 85–90). This leads Davidson to propose his own challenge: can Chisholm "produce in a reasonably mechanical way, for every sentence of the form 'He raised his arm,' another sentence of the form 'He made it happen that p' where p does not have the agent as subject"? Only then is a particular truth-functional description possible. For Davidson, the reduction Chisholm resists has at least the advantage of resolving a clear philosophical problem. Davidson can offer a testable model of the logical form of action sentences. However, if one persists in seeking "an analysis of the concept of agency using other concepts, then he may be pursuing a chimerical task we have no reason to assume can be successfully accomplished." This process of definition by concepts, I infer, is doomed to the infinite regress of definitions justifying definitions which plagues inquiries where no extensional tests can be proposed.[10]

---

10. I have based this paragraph in the discussion following Davidson's LSA in Rescher, ed. Chisholm's statement is on p. 114, and the relevant comments in Davidson's reply are from pp. 119–20. This discussion also contains an elegant, concise, logical summary of Davidson's essay, provided by H. N. Castaneda, pp. 104–05.

We can test whether Davidson's analysis suffices for our purposes by summarizing his position on the three issues I described above—identifying an act, relating the act to a concept of agency, and proposing criteria for explaining the action. Each of his answers tries to maintain the principle of treating a sentence describing an action as philosophically defensible only if it is truth-functional by virtue of its logical form. Identifying an action entails binding the event variable by establishing an extensional singular term which can take on quantifiers and modifiers. Action sentences are not strings of predicates, but the application of modifiers to a core event. Thus the sentence "Jones did it slowly, deliberately in the bathroom," where *it* equals "buttering his toast," must admit an extensional equivalent for *it* which serves as common syntactic element for the other modifiers (LSA, 81–85). Now comes Davidson's central move. If one is to speak about the truth value of an action sentence, one can speak only of the event aspect of the sentence. The occurrence which might make the sentence true cannot be called the object, however intensional, of some desire statement or *bring it about that* clause. An event like raising one's arm must occur "at a precise moment in a particular way—every detail is fixed. But it makes no sense to demand that my want be directed at an action performed at any one moment or done in some unique manner" (ARC, 182). Wants can be satisfied by "an indefinitely large number of actions." Therefore, because the event statement and the want statement are *logically independent*, the want statement does not truth-functionally constate the event, but can be used only to give a reason why the event statement is true (ARC, 182). I assume, then, that want statements can be translated by Carnap's principles into testable calculi, along the lines of any causal hypothesis.

The consequences of this separation of want statement and event statement are far-reaching. First, the separation means that any truth assessment of the action sentence requires precisely the move to which Chisholm objects: the action sentence must be rewritten so that it is not dependent on a concept of intentional agency and has only terms that invariably produce descriptions of states of affairs by virtue of their status as singular terms or bound variables. Action sentences must be rewritten in the logical form of propositions about an event. John raised his arm becomes $(\exists x)$ (Raised (John, arm, x). Now we know what event taking place would make the proposition true (assuming a temporal quantifier) and we have a logical form that can take on endless modifiers. Notice that attempting the same strategy with terms involving intentions would produce an unfortunate result. If we want to insist on keeping such terms in the logical notation, then the only referential test would be whether an event took place that was an act of the will (LSA, 87). And how could we know that, or substitute for it extensionally?

Once we know what is necessary for an act to have a truth-functional identity, we can describe the logical relationships between different versions of the act. Suppose we have an act consisting of John wanting to kill Smith and pulling a trigger which fires the gun which shoots a bullet that kills Smith instantly. We do not need to speak about complex acts, or means and ends. Rather, the various clauses in this action sentence are related by logical identity. The same event is true of all of them; the different versions of the event are possible descriptions of it, which do not change its truth value so long as the logical, extensional event statement can be established.[11] Events are treated "as entities about which an indefinite number of things can be said" (LSA, 91). And what we do say about the event may require further evidence, depending on the demands of an explanatory calculus. Thus, "when it is pointed out that striking a match was not sufficient to light it, what is not sufficient is not the event, but the description of it—it was a dry match and so on" (LSA, 93). With these further details, causal explanation becomes possible. It is, then, not a special feature of human actions that they admit a range of descriptions; this condition is true of event descriptions in general. Redescription does not change truth conditions, which remain attributions about extensional event properties. This view of identity conditions, I should add, produces a very neat account of some basic categories for the discussion of actions. Excuses, for example, often take the form of an agent's stating that he was not aware of the identity between two events, like shooting the gun and wounding Jones. Or a typical argument of self-defense would try to expand the identity among events: Brown shot the gun and wounded Jones because Jones was shooting at him (LSA, 84). These redescriptions add modifiers to an event, or correlate different aspects of the identity, but they do not alter the general form of truth-functional analysis: each can be tested, and their conjunction can be related to a possible system of explanatory regularities.

One might still think that Davidson's case for identity conditions leaves him painted into a corner. For, as Chisholm argued, Davidson's

---

11. See Goldman's first chapter for a critique of Davidson's analysis of event identity as an adequate model for action descriptions.

identity thesis seems to deny any logical difference between events and human actions. Davidson, however, is not so easily refuted. He addresses the essence of Chisholm's charge by turning to what I posited above as the last two issues involved in the discussion of actions. After remarking that "it may now appear that . . . the analysis . . . has simply omitted what is peculiar to action sentences," he shows that the concept of agency contains two basic elements which his schema can account for (LSA, 93–94). The activity of the agent can be extensionally captured in the semantic features of certain verbs and in the condition that one "argument place in the verb is filled with a reference to the agent as a person." Then, in order to handle attributions that the agency is intentional, Davidson insists that intentionality is not "an extra doing of the agent," but a hypothesis proposed by further descriptions of the action that place it in a causal relationship to the beliefs and attitudes of the agent. To take any other logical view of intention is to founder on the fact that there is no way short of claiming events of willing in order to mechanically assume that an action like signalling is intentional (ARC, 187).[12] If an arm is raised in the appropriate way, one has signalled a turn whether or not he intends it. But if an observer is not sure what the event is, it may help to offer the further information that the person wanted or intended to signal, or thought he was signalling. This does not change the event, but it may clarify it by introducing a causal hypothesis about the context that leads us to examine testable features of the agent's behavior. In general, wants and beliefs are not features of the event but information that suggests how the event might be explained in terms of dispositions or other events:

> Someone might be tempted into the mistake of thinking that my flipping of the switch caused my turning on of the light (in fact it caused the light to go on). But it does not follow that it is a mistake to take "My reason for flipping the switch was that I wanted to turn on the light" as entailing in part "I flipped the switch and the action is further describable as having been caused by my wanting to turn on the light." To describe an event in terms of its cause is not to identify the event with its cause, nor does explanation by redescription exclude causal explanation. (ARC, 191)

12. Davidson's point here is that expressions like *make it happen that* are ambiguous with respect to intention and do not entail the actual event unless the description is made extremely complicated. See ARC, 87, for another example similar to the case of signalling.

Indeed, quite the contrary. By demystifying intention and showing its relation to an extensional event language, Davidson provides a coherent and conceptually parsimonious model for justifying covering law models as the principle of action explanations. If attributions of intention are features of a causal redescription which imply the relevance of other events, then there is here no substantial difference between scientific and practical or historical explanation. Events are explained causally when a high degree of regularity exists in the conjunction of the relevant details and when other distorting variables are ruled out. Opponents of this position claim it is extremely difficult to produce the relevant causal laws for actions. Davidson replies that we rarely find even descriptions of physical occurrences actually producing causal laws and reliable predictions; rather, such descriptions typically provide only "evidence for the existence of a causal law covering the case at hand" (ARC, 194). Precise predictive laws involve highly technical analysis and mathematical properties, and these require translation out of an ordinary phenomenal language. But, within that language, we function with considerable confidence that the relevant law can be produced: "A generalization like 'Windows are fragile, and fragile things tend to break when struck hard enough, other conditions being right' is not a predictive law in the rough—the predictive law, if we had it, would be quantitative and would use very different concepts" (ARC, 193–94). But we proceed with certainty that the window broke because we saw it struck by a rock. Similarly, we treat events like signalling or like John shooting Smith in self-defense as explainable, because we assume we can produce evidence that they are instances of standard general regularities in the relevant sphere of behavior.

3. The competing teleological account of actions and its power to make difficulties for Davidson

It seems to me very difficult to attack the internal coherence of Davidson's thinking on actions. In fact, as I turn to the Wittgensteinian position I want to defend, we will notice a marked slackening in philosophical rigor. The real question, then, is whether such looser, more metaphoric groping is required by the nature of the subject. After all, if there are versions of actions that require a different, intensional form of analysis, not easily made compatible with scientific criteria of description or causal explanation, then the philosophical framework for such descriptions must be correspondingly more fluid and open-ended. The issue boils down to whether examples can convince us that even if no explanation is possible that meets Davidson's standard, the phenomena are significant enough, and the interpretive language sufficiently clear, to warrant a competing framework. Here, then, are two statements, by Charles Taylor and by A. R. Louch, which describe the general lines of argument I shall defend and which illustrate the problems I mentioned with respect to finding an adequate philosophical language:

> Because explanation by intentions or purposes is like explanation by an "antecedent" which is non-contingently linked with its consequent, i.e. because the fact that behavior follows from the intention is not a contingent fact, we cannot account for this fact by more basic laws. For to explain a fact by more basic laws is to give the regularities in which this fact causally depends. But not being contingent, the dependence of behavior on intention is not contingent on anything, and hence not on any such regularities. (EB, 44)

> Conclusions or actions are rational only if they are right. If they are wrong, it is supposed that the person acting or making a claim is succumbing to desires, interpreted as quasi-physical or Humean internal impressions, as events which could be linked causally to actions or speech. As a result, insufficient attention is paid to the possibility that rational action, and morality itself, might be defined or characterized in terms of procedures. . . . On the procedural view, a man whose actions are guided by his assessments, and his understanding of his own and other actions by the grounds he finds for those actions in the situation of the actor, is looking at behavior morally. . . . He acts or describes action not by seeking temporal antecedents or functional dependencies, but by deciding that the situation *entitles* a man to act in the way he did or is likely to do. (EHA, 51)

These quotations propose a principle for identifying actions in such a way that they are not reducible to events, but reflect some intrinsic relationship between the agent and his deed. Because these proposals clearly rely on a form of Kantian reasoning, they require special justification. What is there lacking in Davidson's account that would warrant this dependence on a more problematic language? I can envision two related ways of elaborating my opening remarks in order to work this out—one methodological, and one concerned with differences among kinds of actions. The methodological point has several aspects. It is clear, first of all, that Davidson's philosophical strategies combine a methodological and an ontological reductionism. But it is difficult to establish exactly the authority he has for these reductions. If one insists upon a truth-functional account of action statements, then Davidson offers a compelling argument. But it may be that his arguments beg a very important question—he may collapse human actions into event descriptions because, in fact, only event descriptions allow a purely extensional truth-functional analysis. Davidson does find a place for agency in his logical notation, but it is not clear that his two ways to describe agency account for all the ways agents enter into action descriptions. In fact, reductions like Davidson's motivate the equally overgeneralized vagueness we see in Taylor, on contingency, and Louch, on right and therefore rational acts. Both schools of thought end up ignoring the possible need for different strategies and generalizations for different kinds of actions. This need to keep one's options open is even clearer when one examines Davidson's ontological claims. Davidson seems to proceed as if we had a clear choice between mysterious mental events and a causal physicalist model. Yet we have little idea of what the real natures of brain structures and events are, so it seems terribly premature to rule out phenomenological accounts on the basis of a version of logical and ontological commitments, which themselves have no clear basis in descriptions. I could sympathize with Davidson if the reductionism were required for countering opponents who used phenomenological complexities in support of outlandish metaphysical claims. But the typical teleological case does not, or need not, try to defend Kantian metaphysics; rather, it can use Kant's model of rational actions as a somewhat metaphoric way of generalizing about properties of actions that do not fit available reductionist or physicalist strategies. It is simply too early to rely on any single ontological picture, before we become clear on what phenomenological properties action sentences exhibit in a variety of modes and circumstances.

So far I have not so much refuted Davidson as tried to clear a space in which we can examine examples with a fairly open mind. I want now to turn to some of these examples where it seems to me Davidson's account of identity in terms of events *cum* descriptions seems implausible. Then it should be possible to speculate about the need for a hermeneutically intensional descriptive language for kinds of actions which seem to require identification in qualitative terms—either because of the nature of the intentions involved, or because the needs of an interpretive method lead us to view what an agent projects of himself in the doing as conceptually inseparable from the event.[13] Davidson's case, after all, has strong resemblances to traditional empiricist needs for logical simples, and any such claim demands to be tested across a variety of methods of projection.

My first example is from Bruce Aune's attempt to show that certain kinds of actions cannot be identified with a physical event. Consider the case of an action "where no physical movement is even intended": "If a man deliberately blocks a door way by not moving away from where he is standing, there need be no movement—not even an unintended one, such as the tensing of certain muscles—with which his action could plausibly be identified. His activity, his doing, *seems* to be purely mental." [14] Here, because there is no clear event, there is probably no mechanical way to produce the appropriate event description. Yet, it is hard to deny that an action has taken place. However, what the action is depends on how one interprets the relationship between the agent, his not moving, and the context. While there is no distinguishable event, we possess here, as was the case with my fasting example, ideas or examples of what Alvin Goldman calls action type properties, which upon a reasonably thorough description would enable us to agree on the nature of the action, even though we could not rely on an extensional analysis.

A second example should further bring out the qualitative considerations probably necessary for a full description of these kinds of actions. Here my example is one Goldman proposes against Davidson's identity thesis. If acts are identical, Goldman argues, they should co-exemplify a given property—in the following case, the property of being supererogatory:

Suppose that I owe Smith two dollars. Seeing him on the street, I reach into my pocket for some cash and discover two single dollar

13. My example of procedures requiring attention to intensional qualities is literary discourse, where the whole point of the enterprise is to take discourse out of an extensional context—indeed, this is why synonymy is much more implausible in literary texts than it is in ordinary discourse contexts. With literature, the interpreter's job is to understand why substitution of co-extensive truth values (within this text's imaginary world) would ignore crucial features of the text. In these cases, one could argue that it is the intention signalled by the use of literary conventions which dictates the appropriate mode of reference, but there are cases I shall cite later where literary procedures apply despite the author's intention. I will elaborate these matters much more fully in chapter five.

14. Aune, *Reason and Action*, p. 19.

bills and one two-dollar bill. I like to collect two-dollar bills myself, but I recall that Smith simply goes wild over them. Bearing this in mind, I pay Smith the money with a two-dollar bill. Now consider my act of giving Smith the two-dollar bill and my act of repaying Smith two dollars. The former is supererogatory, while the latter is not supererogatory in the least. . . . Since one of them has a property which the other lacks, they cannot be one and the same act. (THA, 4)

I must confess that, as stated, this example is not convincing. I do not see why different descriptions must entail the same nonphysical properties, if the identity is asserted only for the physical event as analyzed into extensional terms. But suppose that part of the actor's intention is to have Smith recognize the supererogatory gesture. Then it seems to me that it will not suffice to identify the act in extensional terms: the act is not a physical event with a variety of possible descriptions. But the act here is what it is only under a description that recognizes the intention and clarifies the doing as a deliberate supererogatory gesture. Two tests for identity should confirm this. Very different modifiers and very different relations among the terms would be appropriate to a deliberately supererogatory act and a simple act of repaying a debt. And, if one were to use Wittgensteinian strategies, one could show that each description would demand very different ways of going on or imagining adequate uptake. Moreover, the supererogatory act raises questions the other doesn't, about what an adequate causal explanation might look like. On one level, the relevant causal question might be, "Why are the two dollars given?" But we cannot ask the right causal question until we identify the action properly: the right question here involves a matter of why the giving took place under a certain understanding and not merely in a certain physical way. Specific terms modifying manner may require recognizing the state of the agent as well as aspects of the giving. Here, in other words, the reasons are constitutive of features of the act, and their interconnection with the physical event suggests that only qualitative frames of understanding are appropriate. (There may eventually be a way of describing how the context is perceived in terms of quantitative neurological events that explain these qualities, but we will only know that if we do not prematurely translate them into a pure observational model that precludes hermeneutic issues.)

I have supposed that we know what *cause* means in this case. But, in fact, there are further complexities here that raise doubts whether any single idea of causal explanation is sufficient. There may be causes for the event of giving the money, causes motivating the manner of the giving, and some reason *why* the person chose the supererogatory gesture and chose to want it recognized. The latter questions seem less matters of locating regularities or signs that a law is present than matters of specifying which of the regularities might fit the case and might be intended to be seen as fitting the case. Intentional agents, after all, can manipulate causal expectations as well as physical movements.

4. A modified teleological perspective on expressive actions

It should now be possible to spell out an abstract rationale for a modified version of the teleological position which attempts to account for complex actions, like the ones we have seen will not easily fit Davidson's model. At one pole of a continuum, whose other pole is simply cases like raising one's arm, we might establish a class of what I called expressive acts, which require qualitative analysis because what the agent projects of himself in the doing seems inextricable from or partially constitutive of the physical event in question. At least three types of acts fit this class—speech acts with expressive implicature, performances in which self-conscious control over the end or means of the act is offered for appraisal as a central element of what is in fact achieved,[15] and a type I shall discuss later, which Charles Taylor calls strong evaluations, where the reasons for the act are not first-order empirical desires but second-order exhibitions of an agent's sense of his own fundamental ends. Because in these cases what is enacted in the doing gives the event a qualitative dimension, it seems *prima facie* implausible that these qualities can be rendered as simply descriptive modifications of the physical event. To the extent that qualities are constitutive of the nature of the action, they are not supplementary concerns, but are required of the description of the action. There can, of course, always be supplementary descriptions of any act, but there are some acts where what is supplemental depends conceptually on identifying the act in terms of the agent's intention and interpretations.

We find ourselves needing the basic idea, although not the purely moral context, of statements like the following, from Louch: "If we deprive ourselves of words because of their possible use to form attitudes or incite actions, we deprive ourselves also of what is often the relevant

---

15. Louch's EHA is really devoted to performances, as p. 233 makes clear.

description, the man or situation is not seen and then appraised, or appraised and then seen in distortion: it is seen morally. Value and fact merge" (EHA, 54). I suspect that Davidson would want to dismiss as meaningless the echoes of earlier battles between Wittgensteinians and certain positivists. But, by so generalizing his commitments to truth-functional analysis, Davidson perpetuates, if he does not condone, both the problems Louch describes and the need for an ideological thrust to competing analyses. The facts are clear: a commitment to the exclusive authority of an extensional language, and hence to the substitution of identicals, greatly reduces one's power to describe or to understand the full range of person predicates often needed for our ordinary experiences. Even on the simplest analytic level, a purely extensional approach to actions may banish precisely the terms needed to specify what the action is or, if *is* is too problematic a term, what the event must be taken as in order to produce coherent connections to the other predicates that can modify it or the ways one might go on in response to it.

There remains, however, a significant contrastive function played by Davidson's insistence on extensional analysis. The limits of his position help us understand why philosophers like Taylor and Louch argue that human actions require an intensional language for their analysis. The teleological philosophers keep uneasily gesturing through Kant and Wittgenstein, because the object of analysis is ultimately the nature of our competence at making practical interpretations. We need to rely on this competence, because the crucial feature in establishing the characteristics of an intensional language is the condition of opaque reference. The opacity derives from the fact that what matters in these complex actions is less the physical identity conditions than contextual features, which depend upon the nature and quality of the selections that constitute them. So the grounds for interpretation involve recovering those characteristics of the act which are only suggested in what one can extensionally refer to. I am tempted to adapt here the literary notion of self-reference or contextual interdependence. When reference is opaque —in cases like expressive acts—physical event properties are subordinated to properties of the act that are self-referring, because they are determinate only as parts of a whole; we understand what is physically relevant by how features fit into a hypothesis about the agent's overall beliefs and intentions. *Self-reference* is another, only slightly less problematic, term for teleological properties. Self-reference is the principle by which we come to understand the dimensions of an act which make substitutes impossible, by imposing on the details a distinct form of coherence. The Napoleon whom Scott wants to visit and the two-dollar bill the agent gives Smith are not replaceable by other terms with the same reference, because they take on meanings which are not carried only in the pictorial properties of the utterance. The meanings are caught up in decisions and beliefs which are only intelligible by virtue of what we can infer about the agent's appraisals of his situation, and the terms for these appraisals require trying out different organizations of the available contextual information. Intensional languages, then, can neither be mechanically applied nor assessed only in truth-functional terms. Indeed, they can never be definitive because contexts are never definitive, especially since how one views a given context will depend on how he compares it to other scenarios.

I seem now to be verging on the Continental traditions in hermeneutics that lead to Derrida, because I have posited the identity of some actions as dependent upon interpretations. But rejecting formal logical analysis in favor of a hermeneutic form of intensional language does not entail indeterminacy, as I shall elaborate later. Insofar as we can agree about interpretive purposes and methods of projection, we can also reach probabilistic agreement about relevant contextual details and models of coherence or fit among them. Indeed, it is dissatisfaction with Davidson's methods for establishing truth-functional standards of certainty that returns us to the importance of Wittgensteinian grammar as a ground for reaching agreements in probabilistic terms. Davidson, in fact, provides a concise summary of Wittgenstein on this subject, which can be used both as a description of how intensional coherence is determined and as a transition to my next topic, the question of causal explanations:

> When we ask why someone acted as he did, we want to be provided with an explanation, a new description of what he did which fits into a familiar picture. The picture certainly includes some of the agent's beliefs and attitudes; perhaps also goals, principles, general character traits, virtues or vices. Beyond this, the redescription of an action afforded by a reason may place the action in a wider social, economic, linguistic, or evaluative context. To learn, through learning the reason, that the agent conceived his action as a lie, a repayment of a debt, an insult ... is to grasp the point of the action in its setting of rules, practices, conventions, and expectations. (ARC, 186)

Davidson goes on to warn against drawing "two conclusions that do not follow," namely that Wittgenstein's reasons are not causes and that talk of patterns and relying on contexts can answer the questions of how reasons explain actions. Having a reason may not be the actual cause for and by which someone does something. Yet, even if Davidson is right that the setting of rules, reasons, and so forth, cannot substitute for a causal explanation, such contextualizing may be a necessary feature for describing how a sense of *cause* appropriate for expressive acts requires intensional consideration. Notice that in proposing causal explanations for events, we have a fairly clear sense of what *cause* means. There is no confusion between a cause for doing something and a cause by which something takes place. And if we cannot easily produce causal laws for physical events, we know roughly what is being explained and what general shape that explanation would take for a particular science. Finally, we have no trouble using different levels of causal laws; we know that particular laws about gases changing under pressure are themselves functions of more general laws about molecular changes. But when we turn to actions, talk of cause becomes loose and analogical. In the example of the broken window cited above, Davidson posits a case where, while we do not know the specific law by which the stone has its effect, we do know essentially the kinds of forces and relations that would be quantified, we are interested primarily in a general explanation of why windows break, and we have a history of successful predictive uses of the kinds of laws we assume prevail. But if we shift the question from why the window broke to why the boy broke the window, we enter a realm where scientific notions of cause are only metaphorically appropriate. Even if we treat statements about the latter act as having the logical structure of an event statement, we must deal with several different levels of causes—from the mechanics of breaking the window, to the boy's psychology, to general theories relating to his psychological type, to situational details. As the causal field grows complex, we do not know where to begin dividing the event into quantifiable forces and testable empirical data, nor do we have patterns of lawful explanation that as generalizations have the authority earned by repeated successful prediction.[16]

16. The best conceptual attack on a scientific model of causal explanations by one of the teleological theorists is Von Wright's, EU, chapter two and pp. 131–41. A full causal explanation in the scientific sense (and hence in a behaviorist or determinist view) has two properties which cannot easily be carried over into discussing actions. First, it must correlate facts which are initially independent by proposing necessary and sufficient (or at least probabilistically sufficient) conditions for the result produced when they are combined. And second, the conditions must be expressible as predictive lawful generalizations which can be repeated in subsequent

I have neither the desire nor the ability to argue, as philosophers like Taylor and Melden do, that causal explanations are inappropriate for human actions. So long as we know we are using a metaphor and know what the particular is we are trying to explain, a concept of cause may help us describe what I called intensional fit. We may, though, have to use *cause* in several senses—as a specific motive term, analogous to the metaphor of will Davidson is so bothered by, and as what Burke would call a scenic term, that calls attention to general contextual conditions as giving a specific motive the power to motivate.[17] The important thing here is to avoid the category mistake of assuming that we are speaking of cause in the same sense, and with the same criteria, as scientists use it. On the contrary, when we apply a term like *cause* to complex actions we rely not on the formal procedures of science but precisely on the setting of rules, practices, and the like, which Davidson opposes to causal languages. *Cause* is one of the terms we learn to use in action contexts

---

experiments. Thus, a scientific causal explanation could show that if the separate elements *gasoline* and *a spark* are present, a fire will necessarily result unless some specifiable condition is not also present. But it is difficult, if not impossible, to break down the basic constituents of action into separate elements. What causes what, or even what basic elements are present depend on the very conditions we want to explain, on the purposes of the agent and the means chosen to achieve them. We are not analyzing combinations of natural facts but combinations of ways of organizing natural situations. We might say that actions are not reducible to elements in an experiment, because they are constituted in much the same way as the experimenter's choices when he manipulates his variables to locate regularities. As Von Wright puts it, what makes an action a unity is not a sequence of events but an intentional complex, a coherent set of purposive beliefs which must be determined anew for specific cases (EU, 81).

It is, then, this complex context for an action which also invalidates the second or nomic component of a causal explanation. Empirically, it seems fair to say that we have not yet developed any adequate laws for predicting purposive behavior. We can describe contexts and show, after the fact, how purposes are adapted to them, but we cannot draw necessary and sufficient conditions between the elements of a situation and the human behavior that will result. The causes of actions are not constants, like physical features; rather, general conditions only become causes when motivated by particular desires and purposes that themselves partially define what are the relevant circumstances. Actions are instances of practical reasoning, and, hence, are causally indeterminate before the fact. Goldman's confusions between statistical and specific action descriptions, as he tries to work out a deterministic sense of *cause* (THA, 170–89), might serve as a negative example of what occurs when we ignore Von Wright's arguments, at least in the case of expressive acts.

17. Aune, *Reason and Action*, pp. 51–102, is very good on the complexities involved in describing the actual motive or decision to act, which cannot be only a propensity or even a want, because we must decide to act on a want and often what we do goes against immediate wants.

in order to invoke the framework of expectations associated with expressions that use terms like *he did it because* or *she had that motive because*. The metaphoric sense of *cause* is one of the constituents of grammatical competence which is loosely adapted in making coherent intensional descriptions that fit particular contexts. *Cause* in these contexts actually invokes grammatical regularities, not law-like ones—that is, what we take as regular depends on forms of experience and type images of behavior that may be specific to a culture or community and are often malleable. This is why we can adapt generalizations to particulars and treat individual actions as significant specific ways of organizing details (or even selves), and not as simply instances of general conditions. It is hard to care much why this particular window broke, but, conversely, it is hard to be content with an explanation of the boy's breaking the windows which tells us under conditions *a* and *b* boys will break windows eighty-three percent of the time. We want to know how the particular boy might say he did the deed because he had these particular beliefs, desires, intentions, and goals.

5. Summary of my answers to the three questions given above

Let me summarize this lengthy, abstract discussion by proposing my own answers to the three basic questions about actions with which I began. (1) There are certain types of expressive acts which cannot be sufficiently identified in extensional terms. Rather, descriptions of such events depend on identifying a purposive act (which, as we shall see, may not prove to be the action consciously intended) on the basis of a framework of cultural expectations, which allows us to synthesize information about the agent's intentions, situational details, and general grammatical models for correlating intentions and details. (2) Various notions of cause may be needed to explain different features of the agent's relation to his deed, ranging from the specific motive to the way contexts lead us to posit interpretations of why the motive has the power it does to motivate in such situations. In these explanations, *cause* is not a scientific or quasi-scientific term, but a grammatical one which gains its force from paradigm cases, from one's understanding of dimension terms and the act properties they correlate, and from a variety of schemes for explaining actions that constitute a good deal of the intellectual life of a culture. In the contexts that concern me, *cause* is a term defined by assumptions about motives; motives are not rationalized and judged by an empirical model of causal relations. (3) Because the identity conditions for an action depend on an agent's interpretation and on interpretations of the force and quality of those interpretations, and because *cause* is a grammatical term, the description of expressive actions will include some explanatory elements, but it will be coherent only in terms of an intensional language that focusses on the power of motives to constitute opaque referential conditions. Such descriptions will not provide certainty, but will not therefore be indeterminate or dependent entirely on an interpreter's purposes, because there are probabilistic grammatical grounds for judging interpretations in relation to the patterns of rules, purposes, types, and so forth, established by the hypotheses about the agent's purposes which are necessary to define the act. The initial definition is defeasible—that is, it can be revised or defeated by further information about the agent or by a more coherent fit among details, purposes, and types. But it is some version of an intentional act which must be the focus of further descriptions that try to explore the significance of the act—either in relation to the interpreter's purposes, or in relation to hypotheses about general cultural or historical forces. If these strategies do not get us very far toward general explanations of actions, they do perform the equally important task of saving the features that make the phenomena of special interest in the first place.

6. *The basic constituents of action descriptions: the case for agency*

So far, I have been concerned with justifying the use of concepts whose practical value for criticism remains to be tested. One reason for this is the need, in a time of conceptual confusion, for coherently rationalizing practices so that their grounds and the values deriving from them may be tested. But equally compelling for me is a fear of overrationalizing practice, by turning a way of viewing into a firm discovery procedure, where it is the procedure rather than the wisdom, care, and subtlety of the interpreter that promises significant results. The Wittgensteinian framework I have been using suggests, on the contrary, that grammatical competence is extremely flexible. Discussions of hermeneutics should provide a general set of criteria which explain how someone might formulate and defend a given case, but, ideally, the criteria will be abstract enough to allow a wide variety of ways for correlating purposes, events, and explanations or supplementary descriptions. In other words, I want to suggest that there are implicit in explanations of action that achieve a high degree of agreement some fairly general assumptions, which can be analytically described. I want to suggest norms, without deriving a single set of norms from a problematic hypothesis that poses a single model of motives or of the effects of context. I think this can be done, and my arguments now directed toward more practical concerns, if I specify the kinds of considerations and warrants for using evidence which are implied by the three basic constituents of intensional action descriptions—the intending agent, the range and possible relevance of situational details, and the type predicates or terms for different levels of action properties which serve as hypothetical universals for shaping our ways of organizing hierarchies among details in accord with expectations about *fit* or interpretive adequacy. Then, I can test the value of these considerations by showing how they apply to some basic contemporary disputes about criteria for interpretation.

The concept of intentional agent, as it relates to questions of interpretation, seems the most important of these constituents. For, if my preceding arguments about speech acts and performances are correct, the idea of an agent's purposes is a conceptual requirement for identifying the act as a particular, about which further hypotheses can be made.[18] The identification need not be final, in the sense that the act intended is necessarily the act achieved. Rather, the act intended is the necessary descriptive term for focussing discussion on what is, in fact, achieved in the actual performance. We must know that not eating was conceived as fasting, or that the agent wanted his act to be seen as a political gesture, before we can say whether the act was performed and whether it requires a further description, as hypocritical fasting or as a power ploy. That the event of not eating took place may be a necessary condition, but it is not a sufficient condition for deciding what further description predicates are appropriate to statements about the event as a self-conscious action. There is here a fairly close analogy between the inadequacy of formal semantic rules for characterizing certain speech acts and

18. A good example of the price one pays for not specifying the nature of purposes may be found in Walter Davis' interesting *The Act of Interpretation; A Critique of Literary Reason* (Chicago: University of Chicago Press, 1978). Davis sees clearly the need for a concept of purposes—indeed, my criticisms of textualism echo his case—but he immediately leaps from purpose to an equally problematic notion of form. Then, because form is not an adequate term for avoiding critical circularity, he ends up with a premature case for pluralism, not unlike the pragmatic relativism I discuss below. It may also prove useful to contrast my emphasis on grammatical flexibility with Davis' apparent view that understanding means relying on one of several well-defined interpretive frameworks.

the inadequacy of physical description for specifying the parameters of purposive acts in general.

Being clear about what will not suffice is a good way to begin defining the work a concept of human agency must perform in our ordinary practices. We need hypotheses about a purposive agent in order to use person predicates in making three kinds of discriminations: delineating appropriate descriptive terms in cases where we interpret deeds not as caused by external coercion, but as involving notions of responsibility; establishing a locus for attributing qualitative predicates when the responsibility is not simply legal, but allows other forms of judgment; and developing consistent connections among a person's statement about purposes, a particular deed, and other acts and statements by the person. Each of these three types of case traditionally involves the idea of free will. I want, nonetheless, to bracket such metaphysical concerns in order to avoid the dichotomy of rejecting the forms of behavior because of a metaphysical position or of buying the position to save the assumptions about behavior. I cannot imagine an approach to practical social life which denies such experiences or tries consistently to do without an idea of agency. We must have a conceptual basis for distinguishing degrees of responsibility, adapting ourselves to expressive implicatures, and analyzing incongruities between statements and deeds. Thus, while I am by no means sure what psychological or ontological foundation to give to such attributes, I assume that one can rely on such compelling phenomenological evidence.

Such an assumption still leaves us with the problem of describing criteria for concepts, like intention, which are required to make assertions about agency. Even if we ignore outright denials of the concepts of person and human agency,[19] we have a fairly simple but serious di-

---

19. I refer here, of course, to textualist theory, which insists that agency is a function of discourse produced by an interpreter, not a larger framework for defining the unity or purpose of a speech act or text. I have already given some reasons why this claim won't hold up in Derrida's work. Jacques Lacan is in some ways a more problematic case, because he provides a fairly full psychological picture of the internal divisions which separate the agent of experience from the agent's representation of himself. The structures of signifiers intervene between "the subject of the enunciation and the subject of the utterance": "It happens that 'it' (ça) thinks there where it is impossible for the subject to articulate: therefore I am, because, there, it is structurally out of the question that the subject should accede to consciousness of self (naming oneself as being he who speaks). I think where I cannot say that I am, where I must posit the subject of the enunciation as being separated by a line from the being ... I say that the letter (la lettre) succeeds being (l'être)." Nonetheless, Lacan seems to run into the same problems as Derrida: to know that

lemma: too rational an account of agency and intentions simply ignores the many ways reason serves as pander to will, and it gives us no coherent strategy for describing how we interpret such evasions, while views thoroughly suspicious of human powers to determine actions in relation to reasons cannot make sufficient discriminations among either phenomenological differences in types of actions or the various moral and qualitative judgments we make about both actions and agents. Philosophers like Karl Popper or Martin Hollis can develop a concept of the human agent which justifies a clear notion of responsibility and strict, consistent connections between deeds and statements about purposes, because acts are derived from and explained by a rational series of decisions.[20] But then, all acts not clearly rational are written off as externally caused symptomatic behavior. We have a version of Kant's ethic, and we get the same tendency to produce a radical, ironic, and suspicious alternative one can observe in subsequent German thought. Where rationality seems difficult to locate in an act, thinkers either attribute the difficulty only to their method of analysis or become suspicious of all ideas of agency. This leads to treating all action as symptomatic. But, then, we have no way of distinguishing degrees of self-control or deliberate and responsible activities. The only way out of this dilemma, I suspect, is to give up the idea of rationality for a looser, grammatical sense of reasonableness, which can be located in how an agent correlates means with statements about ends. Instead of a single coherent image of self-determined actions, we must grant the possibility

---

"it is from his partition to his parturition" that the subject proceeds, to understand what the child desires in Freud's description of the Fort-da game, or to develop a subtle model of psychoanalytic practice as resisting the patient's desire to turn the efforts at cure into reinforcements of his imaginary self, all require using a coherent notion of agency, in order to show the duplicities to which it is subject. Derrida, in fact, devotes "The Purveyor of Truth," *Yale French Studies*, no. 52 (1975):31–114, to criticizing Lacan's assumption that the analyst can grasp the truth about his patient's needs and desires. Yet Derrida has no trouble in quite clearly understanding both his own purposes in his critique (at least those giving it an identifiable shape as an act) and Lacan's purposes in his writings. I quote Lacan from Anika Lemaire, *Jacques Lacan*, trans. David Macey (London: Routledge and Kegan Paul, 1977), pp. 76, 51–52, 77.

20. See Karl Popper, *The Open Society and Its Enemies*, 4th ed. (London: Routledge and Kegan Paul, 1962), vol. 2, chapters fourteen and twenty-five, where the concept of situational logic is developed, and Martin Hollis, *Models of Man* (Cambridge: Cambridge University Press, 1977), chapters six through eight. My first quotation from Louch above clearly exemplifies the tendency to draw sharp distinctions between rational and externally motivated acts.

of establishing nonsymptomatic qualities of actions simply by virtue of placing the act a posteriori in a context of examples of plausible and responsible human behavior. The measure of coherence in these contexts is provided not by the existence of deductive, rational plans, but by images of character and situation types (which I shall describe below). With such a measure we need not choose between rational or symptomatic acts, but we can attempt to correlate aspects and degrees of conscious control. We can grant a variety of levels and mixtures of motives, and, thus, we can make obvious the need on some occasions to show an agent that he was mistaken about his motive or about the act he, in fact, performed.

Elizabeth Anscombe helps show the way to such an account, by separating intentions from psychological acts of deciding (where any analysis would find it difficult to evade the infinite regress of intending to intend). She argues that acts are intentional when observers think they can ask for a person's reasons *why* he did something. Intentions are forward-looking motives which can be understood more as the context of an act than as its cause. They depend on how an action can be viewed in retrospect, not on what literally must happen in a decision-making process.[21] Questions about intentions arise when we think we need to understand specific particular reasons for a deed, and they are resolved when further descriptions of the person or situation seem to provide a reason that makes an act's relationship to other acts in a context intelligible. In my terms, the grammar for the act relies on types of behavior where we assume reasonableness, as with self-conscious expressive acts. Wittgenstein, as usual, makes the concept clear and concrete: "Why do I want to tell him about an intention too, as well as telling him what I did?—Not because the intention was also something which was going on at that time. But because I want to tell him something about *myself*, which goes beyond what happened at that time" (PI, 659). Exactly this process occurs in Henry James' description of his characteristic procedure of constructing a novel. He begins with an image of a scene. Then he constructs a complex intentional field for that scene, by giving the agents personal histories and providing the context of other related scenes. Thus, James alters the condition of our interest, from a concern with what happens (the material of chronicle narration) to a concern for the specific motives that might explain why people do what they do

21. Anscombe, *Intention* (Ithaca: Cornell University Press, 1969), especially pp. 17–22, 28–45. See also pp. 8–9 for the public aspects of behavior by which we recognize intentions.

and what the doings reveal about qualitative changes in the agent's characteristic attitudes. He rarely illustrates those decisions through specific dramatic scenes; we usually find ourselves suddenly confronted by a choice, and must go back to work out the appropriate contexts explaining the possible motives.

In this light, I propose as the most general idea of intentional agency a description of an act that interprets its intensional features by attributing the selection and organization of details to some specific predicates typically used to characterize human motives. We require a distinct concept of motive, because intentions are not just propensities to act, but a determination to allow a specific propensity to initiate and govern a series of physical acts. Yet, we cannot simply equate motives with reasons in any technical sense, because behavior can be purposive even when not the result of clear deliberations (cf. ARC, 197). By using the correlative ideas of selection and organization, we leave open the specific rationale for the decision and we allow for the whole range of motives, from symptomatic to purely rational. Yet we preserve a fairly secure basis of evidence for our interpretations. Because we employ types, we have standard images of characteristic ways of making selections from situational details, and we have as the basis for discussion both the situation and the actual selections made. We may have to make hypotheses about mental events, but we know what the behavioral consequences of different putative events may be, and we know what expectations such hypotheses are responsible for. Thus, patterns of selection and organization transcend individual cases. They provide a coherent way of talking about character in relation to a history of actions, and they enable us to make concrete correlations of *fit* between an agent's past acts and the specific deed in question.[22] We have a form of evidence for what the agent means in practice when he gives his reasons, because we can examine the selections they involve. Yet we are not constrained to view the character as repeating the same processes of selection, but here, as with types, we have ways of deciding what the significant variations are that require further interpretation. The agency attributed to acts has significant parallels to the agency we attribute to stylistic choices. In both cases, we have a rough sense of deviances and degrees of coherent

22. For Wittgenstein on *fit* as criterion for descriptions, see PI, 182 and 537. For specific application to a concept of expression, see PI, 527 and Z, 164; and for a general contrast between motives and causes and ways of assessing each, see LA, 13–14.

organization that dictate our purported motives, and we allow for a variety of contexts for these motives, ranging from ad hoc particular decisions to repeated or characteristic ways of viewing the world. And, as the example of Henry James again indicates, we can make qualitative assessments of both the agent and the adequacy of his selections without necessarily attributing the motives to a deliberate chain of practical arguments. It suffices that the pattern of selection follows from attributes of agency, which we take as indications of the person's abilities and commitments.

Finally, equating intentions with a class of motivated selections makes it clear why, in many cases, we must finally deny the adequacy of an agent's stated reasons. They simply do not correlate with his repeating a characteristic pattern of selections he frequently performs under different rationales, or the deeds fit much more clearly into different grammatical expectations the agent's culture shares. Here we need to try out various redescriptions of the actual selections made, in the hope that the agent will provide further reasons for the discrepancies, or will accept as valid the community's understanding of the fit between purported motives and actual selection. The agent may not, in fact, agree, but it is strong support for this criterion that we do not long respect someone's judgment and self-interpretation if the person consistently denies a community's descriptions without giving acceptable reasons for his denial.

My claims here largely repeat the arguments I adduced in discussing nonavowable expressive forces in an utterance. Analogous examples should clarify my claims, although it is obvious that extremely complex cases will often arise. Imagine criteria for deciding whether or not a Freudian slip affects the actual meaning of an utterance in a situation. Or take a more extended case of observing a tight-lipped, red-faced parent seriously beating a child whom we have watched pull apart a potted plant. The parent might state his intention as teaching the child property rights or respect for others, but we could not avoid the suspicion that the parent is largely giving vent to anger or frustration. This bare amount of information and a single case do not warrant a strong conclusion. Yet, repeated beating of the child would lead us to take action against the parent, even though we cannot bring him, in fact, to agree to our description. On the other hand, more information about the value of the plant or the child's behavior could lead us to accept the parent's statement of purpose as adequate.

7. *Situation and type: the other basic constituents of action descriptions*

Because action descriptions involve ratios among elements, I have had to presuppose a clear sense of situation and type when I discussed agency. Now I can be brief in presenting what I take to be the relevant aspects of these practical concepts. *Situation* is, in most respects, an obvious term. Since acts differ from pure unexpressed thoughts by involving a public dimension, in which some change of physical state occurs (or, in some cases, is prevented from occurring), there must be some event properties appropriate for a Davidsonian analysis. However, insofar as the action requires an intensional interpretation, describing the situation can be a complex task involving taste, tact, and a grasp of dimensional features of relevant type terms or images. Expressive gestures are an obvious example, because they range from delicate aspects of intentions to nonavowable features of an act. Describing a situation consists of articulating the nature of the events, contexts, and consequences in relation to which the agent's selections can be shown to have significance. The situation can be a simple one, can involve institutional or conventional contexts, and may depend on bringing to bear other, related contexts from the agent's past or from general cultural frameworks.[23] The properties one locates clarify the act either by simple de-

---

23. The complexity of situations makes me dubious of Burke's tendency to treat scene-act ratio as homologous. This will be the case in systematic thought about the nature of motives, but in practical life I do not see why scenes cannot be seen as contradicting what the actor thinks or desires. In order to avoid confusions between rhetorical analysis of systems and specific situations I collapse Burke's pentad into my three categories of action description. I do not think that his term *act* should be a separate category, since act is the total object of analysis. I also treat purpose and agent as necessarily correlative rather than separate because in constructing these terms we make both depend on a single account of type and intention. I also treat both agency (i.e., means chosen) and scene as details of the situation. Burke remains, nonetheless, the master at illustrating the different levels of generality on which these terms can be construed, and he shows how manipulating these levels is one crucial aspect of rhetoric. On actions as combinations of physical and mental aspects, see Hampshire, pp. 154–55, and EU, 87.

Virginia Woolf, in *A Room of One's Own* (New York: Harcourt Brace, 1929), pp. 96–97, provides an interesting concrete case of how situations are necessary for making qualitative judgments about an author's skills: "All this was to the good. But no abundance of sensation or fineness of perception would avail unless she could build up out of the fleeting and the personal the lasting edifice which remains unthrown. I had said that I would wait until she faced herself with 'a situation.' And I meant by that until she proved by summoning, beckoning, and getting together

scription or by elaborate contrasts that indicate how the particular act varies from typical forms of behavior. On the most general or reflective level, positing a situation involves some of the metaphoric dimensions elicited by Burke's concept of *scene*. Situational features may include conceptual, social, and psychological generalizations about conditions which bring out the full dimensions of the problem an agent is responding to by his action. These factors, in turn, can be crucial in assessing the qualities projected in a performance. An agent may submit to the limits imposed by his culture's standard evaluation of his situation, either by failing to judge the situation correctly or by fully understanding the constraints upon him, or he may construct a strategically effective way of resisting or escaping those pressures. In either case, who he is and what he makes himself in his action depend on our being able to recover what is at stake.

This last consideration leads to a very important point about intensional descriptions of actions. Insofar as one accepts Davidsonian reductionism, *situation* is a passive concept, consisting simply of referring terms. But if one wants to explain how reference becomes opaque and the consequences of that in relation to an agent's selections and ways of projecting himself in his act, positing the situation becomes perhaps the most important aspect of an action description. For it is in relation to the situation that the qualities of the motives and the possible complexities in the act take on meaning and significance. For this reason, I shall later rely on a concept of *power to situate* as one measure of the cognitive values in a humanistic education. Situating is a process of placing acts in context, so that one can measure the range of pressures the agent faces in making and carrying through his choices.[24] It is in this light that I find deconstructionist work often extremely valuable, despite what I have argued is its inadequate general theory of meaning. For it articulates recurrent difficulties and traps facing an agent as he tries to use a given conceptual scheme or to manipulate ideologically or psychologically recalcitrant features of discourse. Deconstruction, for

that she was not a skimmer of surfaces merely, but had looked into the depths. Now is the time, she would say to herself at a certain moment, when without doing anything violent I can show the meaning of all this."

24. For a concrete instance of criticism as situating, which adapts Wallace Stevens' concept of the *pressure of reality*, see the last part of my "Poem as Act," and my "From Experience to Discourse: American Poetry and Poetics in the Seventies," *Contemporary Literature* 21 (1980):191–224. I would cite as an excellent example of this general kind of work Richard Poirier, *Robert Frost: The Work of Knowing* (New York: Oxford University Press, 1977).

me, deepens drama. The more we know, for example, about the problems of signification, the more deeply we can appreciate how writers like Wordsworth (say in book seven of the *Prelude*) come to grips with those features of experience resistant to their desired conclusions. The more we see Freud so easily deconstructed, the more we are forced to take one of two dramatic perspectives on his work. Either we see that Freud's own purported discoveries are stated incoherently, or we can appreciate how Freud's career is a continual attempt to recast the complex situation his insights created into a rational framework accounting for the play of details.[25] However, if one grants that deconstruction's primary role is to deepen situations, one must substantially alter its theoretical foundation. Deconstruction is no longer a specially privileged analytic method deriving from a sceptical theory of meaning. Rather, it is one among a variety of dramatistic strategies, justified only to the extent that it produces a probabilistically defensible reading of a particular act. Similarly, it is tempting to claim that most pluralistic views of meaning are valid less as accounts of meaning *per se* than as reminders that a variety of situational contexts shed fresh light on the complexity and the corresponding qualitative dimensions of actions, once the acts have been roughly identified as particulars.

My final category—that of the types or paradigms for properties in an action that one learns to recognize when he learns a language, especially its dimension terms—is the most difficult of all to explain fully. My goal, however, is simply to point out the general shape of such types. I must rely here on Wittgenstein's model of learning a culture and leave refinements of the issue and empirical accounts of how we learn and function with types to other studies. Goldman is the one philosopher of action I know who recognizes the need for a concept of types. He describes a specific action as an act token, in which an agent exemplifies at a given time an act property. Act properties, in my view, require that we possess a grammar of types that gives shape and coherence to the properties. But Goldman's concern is for fairly simple descriptions, so he concentrates only on defining and using basic act types. A basic act

25. See Derrida's "Freud and the Scene of Writing," *Yale French Studies*, no. 48 (1972):74–115, for a virtually Hegelian description of how Freud comes to reconcile features of his enterprise whose antithetical qualities a deconstructive method makes clear. Similarly, Jeffrey Mehlmann, "How to Read Freud on Jokes: The Critic as Schadchen," *New Literary History* 6 (1975):439–61, shows how, while Freud is not aware of the complex interrelationships between his concepts of jokes, ego, and sexuality, these interrelationships become dimensions of his mode of discourse with which he must continually grapple.

type is a property that can be exemplified at will without level generational knowledge or belief (THA, 10–17, 65–69). In order to describe the levels of competence I have been relying on, we need to consider the opposite end of the spectrum. We must describe a concept of types capable of explaining how we identify complex act tokens where one must relate the event to desires and beliefs, often in a way that forces us to speak of an original act for which no clear type is available. In other words, a notion of types that can explain our obvious ability to characterize actions in intensional terms must be capable of explaining how dimensional features enter into the classification and how, at times, the features become complex enough to combine types, as if types themselves functioned like metaphors to allow us to clarify properties that do not fit any established class. Goldman at one point admits that analyzing a complex act (which to him means using an elaborate act diagram) requires answers to counterfactual questions, so that one can get at relevant contextual details (THA, 33). In my view, an adequate notion of types must explain how we process these counterfactual and contextual details in order to establish in dimensional terms or through Geertz's thick descriptions what relevant synthesis of properties enables us to characterize the act. Therefore, I stress in my account of types those elements of a grammatical capacity to classify and integrate act properties which are established by examples and paradigm cases and employed as provisional universals for organizing and testing probable relations between situational details and evidence about intentions.

The concept of types, as we shall see, allows analyses to be characterized in terms of degrees of generality. There are highly general type constructs or properties, like capitalism or sainthood, and a virtually infinite variety of subclasses. In order to capture some of this range with respect to actions, where the range can be qualitative as well as quantitative, I propose that we view types as extending from the simple *situation types* described by M. A. K. Halliday to modifications of Max Weber's work on the concept of *ideal types*. Halliday's types comprise constructs built up from paradigm cases by which we learn to identify typical social scenarios, like ordering goods or playing games. This process of learning is socializing in two senses: it gives us tools for orienting ourselves, by enabling us to see new situations as variations within the types, and it instructs us in the social or moral forms of behavior expected in such situations.[26] Halliday's interest is in practical contexts where elaborate

26. Halliday, pp. 29–30.

self-reflective analysis or even coherent step-by-step reasoning is unnecessary. Weber, on the other hand, concentrates on types needed for organizing elaborate intellectual inquiries into forms of cultural life where there is no clear, formal, analytic language to provide the necessary general terms. Thus, where Halliday stresses our social learning of types—our being educated into a culture—Weber stresses the need for standing outside one's ordinary contexts and constructing ideal terms which will enable one to analyze the elements of that prereflective order. Just as the scientist needs general laws in order to interpret systematically what he experiences, hermeneutics requires analogous general constructs which dictate relevant lines of further inquiry about particulars:

> In all cases, however, the relationship between such rational, teleological constructions and that reality which is the subject matter of the empirical sciences, is of course not at all that of "law of nature" and "constellation" [of empirical facts], but merely that of an ideal-typical concept which serves to facilitate the empirically valid interpretation by providing a possible interpretation—an interpretive *schema*—with which the given facts are compared.[27]

Types, then, serve three basic functions in Weber's work. Types provide cluster concepts, establishing expectations and possible interrelationships by which to describe and assess a constellation of historical particulars. Conversely, this general comparative context helps clarify the uniqueness of the particulars, by allowing one to distinguish comparatively what basic situational features are not assumable under the types. And, finally, types are central features of established inquiry procedures—for example, type notions of bureaucracy or capitalism—and, thus, they serve to bring into play general contexts of cultural significance and frameworks for showing why it is important to construct particular constellations along certain lines of inquiry. Types mediate between the general concerns of a culture and the details of particular cultural situations.

Weber's ideal types are not features of grammatical understanding. They are specific methodological constructs, which serve for social or historical sciences a function analogous to that served by situation types

27. For Weber on ideal types, see especially "Objectivity," in *The Methodology of the Social Sciences* (Glencoe, Ill.: The Free Press, 1949). I take this quotation from a useful summary of Weber's ideas, Thomas Berger, *Max Weber's Theory of Concept Formation: History, Laws, and Ideal Types* (Durham: Duke University Press, 1976), p. 137. On the role of types in comparative evaluations, see Hampshire, p. 218.

in contexts where ordinary language expectations suffice. However, Weber's types have come to serve something like a grammatical function for those familiar with sociological discourse. Terms like *bureaucracy* retain some of Weber's meaning while also being modified in various ways. Virtually any concept or abstract image of a set of behavioral properties can become a fairly standard type, if it enters the characteristic discourse of a specific community. As I shall develop at length in chapter seven, this is one way works of art serve cognitive functions—they become dense situational examples for modes of action more complex than those covered by standard situation types. In my view, types can be either images or concepts or blends of the two, and they can be transferred from technical contexts or specific artistic structures to serve more general purposes. The more fully one enters a sphere where cultural activity elaborates and preserves concepts or images that become common enough to serve as types, the more fully one develops a vocabulary for characterizing certain kinds of acts—either by direct application of these types or by combining them so they serve as metaphors for making at least rough descriptions of what appears to be an original or unique act.

There are several reasons we need to extend Halliday's situation types into the larger cultural spheres for which Weber's work serves as a metaphor of cultural agents creating what become types. Most obvious is the fact that we understand complex actions which are far too dense for the simple scenarios Halliday explains. Equally important is the way this understanding can require using types on different levels of generalization. Types range from fairly narrow models or classes, with few relevant tokens, to extremely abstract concepts or images, that apply in somewhat different ways to a variety of instances and even of subtypes. Theophrastean characters are a clear example of fairly specific images self-consciously projected as type models. For more elaborate cases, with levels of types embedded in one another, we must turn to encyclopedic systems, where specific types are described and where lines of relationship are established between these types to constitute more inclusive classes. Northrop Frye, for example, describes the second chapter of Yeats' *Vision* as "a perfect circle of literary or mythical types." [28] Each stage in Yeats' *schema*, correlating phases of the moon with the structure of a person's basic imaginative desires, characterizes in highly ab-

28. Frye, "The Rising of the Moon: A Study of 'A Vision,'" in Denis Donoghue and J. R. Mulryne, eds., *An Honored Guest: New Essays on W. B. Yeats* (New York: St. Martin's Press, 1966), p. 24.

stract terms one typical attitude or stance for reconciling the desire to create images and the pressure of objective truth. But one can also group the phases into units marking even more general forces and pressures shaping imaginative behavior. Similarly, Frye's own categories in his *Anatomy,* especially the chapter on *mythoi,* balance within a dialectic of general attitudes a range of particular, yet quite abstract, states. Frye is often attacked for his failure to describe in depth any specific work, but this charge misses the point of his enterprise. His aim is not to describe particular acts, nor is it to provide a rigorous taxonomy. Rather, he proposes a general classificatory scheme which helps locate relevant features of specific acts. To use only Frye's terms for describing an act is to confuse type levels and to lack principles for making discriminations about particulars. But ignoring his model deprives us of ways to bring general tensions that may be reflected in a range of acts to bear on the particular act. Types clarify both general issues and particular cases, by providing terms for identifying acts as particulars and terms for situating those particulars in resonant contexts. This is why type images can be a good deal richer than concepts, even in a moral framework: they establish a range of qualitative oppositions appropriate for seeing what is at stake in the ends that the agent seeks and in the adjectives, like *wise* or *foolish, generous* or *mean-spirited,* we use in our assessments.

Let us take these abstractions back to the simple example of our observing someone who is not eating and declares he is fasting. Interpretation of this act would begin by testing which standard situation type concepts or images afford the most probable correlation with the situational details and the available information about the agent and his intentions. Then a basic identification has taken place, but to know someone is fasting is not necessarily to have a thick or dimensional knowledge of fasting capable of discriminating the qualities of a particular act. Here, at least a cultural grasp of typical accounts of fasting and of the visions it induces would be necessary. Then both the pathos and the glory of the act might become available to one who situates it in relation to analytic discussions of religion and, especially, to structures like Yeats' and Frye's, which provide abstracted images of the structures of desire that come into play in exalted moments of visionary self-reflection. At any point in this sequence, the degree of abstractness and seriousness may prove ludicrous and the agent in fact may be a hypocrite or a rather simple, well-meaning person. But, in a sense, we only know when to stop when we know by contrast how we might go on when our more encompassing or deeper type constructs become relevant.

The full variety of both uses and problems connected with a concept of types, however, requires literary examples. On the one hand, types, and the correlate idea of typology, are often viewed as traps for the spirit: Emma Bovary finds only vulgar types by which to interpret her feelings to herself, and Hawthorne continually tries to work partially free of the confining moral frameworks his culture links to situation types. But, on the other hand, abstract types can represent a higher model of selfhood, free from the contingencies of history. This I assume is a frequent motive for allegory, and it persists in Eliot's and Yeats' very different attempts to discipline their imaginations so thoroughly that they might take on the full identity embodied in saints or figures who live purely in the realm of passionate intensity and become our images for those passions.[29] Writers must free themselves from standard types and yet, as Flaubert's creation of Madame Bovary exemplifies, must do so in a way that enables their own work to become a new type within the tradition they rebel against. Great texts are classics because they create significant classes by articulating the range of problems, passions, and judgments consistently accompanying recurrent human actions. Where lesser works tend to resemble fairly narrow situation types, because they are either confined to restricted perspectives or are indistinguishable from a culture's ordinary level of understanding, the greatest works clarify dimensions of a wide variety of subclasses. It is no accident that one turns to Flaubert and to Eliot for examples of complexities related to typology, and not to Gissing or to Michael Wigglesworth. Similarly, Aeneas provides a perspicuous sample of self-denying responsibility, dense enough to clarify dimensions of almost any conflict between desire and duty, or self-expression and self-abnegation for putative higher purposes.

29. Difficulties in using types involve psychological or epistemological versions of the problem of reconciling identity and differences. In political thought, for example, conservative analyses of situations tend to rely heavily on the authority of types, thus overemphasizing identity and ignoring possible differences as conditions change, while liberal and revolutionary thought tends to see types as at best metaphors, and, thus, it has constant problems in authorizing its interpretive schema. One can locate similar oppositions in theological problems of deciding how much *Old Testament* figures dictate what can be said about Christ, and in the psychological difficulties of reconciling what one takes from or repeats from others and what one genuinely expresses of his "authentic self."

Croce might serve here as the type for theory finely tuned to how the flexibility of types and their capacity to function on many levels dictate the obligations of practical criticism. Simple reliance on received types, Croce argues, confines the critic to dealing only with fragments of a genuinely original imaginative construction, while also encouraging a radical historical reductionism. Characters, for example, become only instances of standard situation types, and a narrow concern for influence replaces a more capacious, timeless sense of how types relate to and with one another. But an opposite stance, that ignores types, also leaves one no power to describe genuine originality. Croce's main concern is to show the limits of historicist reduction of literary images and texts to preestablished type categories. But he also recognizes the limits of Romantic intuitionism, when it ignores the need to use and to transform types. Thus, on the one hand, he shows how foolish it is to reduce Don Quixote to an abstract sum of medieval types, while, on the other, he insists that what gives *Don Quixote* its power is its ability to synthesize these types into a single distinct original image.[30] This image is only intelligible in the context of the types it synthesizes, and that synthesis itself becomes a type within the grammar of other writers (say, eighteenth-century novelists) and subject to their transformations.

Even more instructive, however, at least from my somewhat perversely polemical orientation, are critical arguments that founder because they ignore the ways in which one can use the flexibility of types and type levels to preserve a coherent sense of the actions an author performs and represents in a text. Insofar as my positive case depends on specifically literary matters, a full justification must wait until subsequent chapters, but the stakes can be clarified by examining a subtle, and yet ultimately muddled, textualist essay by J. Hillis Miller. Miller's essay is a reading of Shakespeare's *Troilus and Cressida* based on a skillful and complex deconstruction of Troilus' speech when he sees "Cressida dally-

---

30. See *Aesthetic*, trans. Douglas Ainslie (New York: Noonday Press, 1966), pp. 33–35. Croce's specific argument is against genres here, so I am adapting him to my own purposes. In conversation, Leroy Searle has pointed out to me the importance of distinguishing between ideas of *imaginary* and *imaginative* as adjectival qualifiers of literary texts. The former leads to textualist and Lacanian dualisms, the latter to recovering the import of Croce by fostering a view of literature as model building. For dramatic and thematic readings of how authors encounter problems using types, see the essay by Kermode I discuss in chapter six (from which I take the Hawthorne example above), and Howard Felperin, *Shakespeare Representation* (Princeton: Princeton University Press, 1977).

ing with Diomedes" (act 5, scene 2, 162–85).[31] The speech revolves around the idea that the Cressida he sees "is and is not Cressid," is externally the woman he loves but acts as another, tied to Diomedes. Miller then stresses the way Troilus' double logic, his experience of "two different coherent languages" struggling "for domination within a single mind" (49), calls into question the whole system of western rationality as based on the principle of identity:

When the monological becomes dialogical, the dialogical loses its logoi and becomes alogical. . . . If she makes new vows, she becomes a different person. In the same way, the Troilus who experiences Cressida's faithlessness is himself disintegrated. He becomes not two persons but no person, out of his mind.

If Troilus' speech is taken as a model of narrative discourse, it demonstrates the possibility of a story which is simultaneously two different incompatible stories. These can never be reduced to one by any rule of unity. They can never be simultaneously contained within any one sane mind . . . yet are enclosed within the bounds of one text. . . . This makes possible the "madness of discourse, that cause sets up, with and against itself," that is the madness of a running train of language, a line of argument which is doubled. (51–52)

I cannot avoid the suspicion that Miller's impressive display of intellectual artillery only fires pop-flags. Let us assume that this reading of Troilus' divided mind in the speech is correct, and let us ignore the fact that Miller's analysis depends on the criteria of identity he denies. What, then, is the status of this description, or what level of generality can we attribute to the image of dialogical consciousness Miller con-

31. Miller, "Ariachne's Broken Woof," *Georgia Review* 31 (1977):44–63. Miller concedes in his conclusion (p. 60) that it is possible to understand Troilus' speech as an aberration which is "monologically" interpreted by the play as a whole, but the concession is empty because Miller insists that this possibility is only an alternative in a simultaneous field of dialogical possibilities. That is, one can construct levels of a discourse, but the construction has no authority; it is only another possibility thrown up by a linguistic field. One important reason Miller grants no privileged model for holistically constructing a text is his absolute standard for deciding whether a context is appropriate or not: "How can one stop the widening circle of contextual echoes with a difference," if context "can nowhere be fully identified or fully controlled" (pp. 58–59). As we saw in discussing Derrida, absolutist terms like *fully* only betray an unwillingness to grant any probabilistic criteria. This refusal demands a good deal of theoretical justification it has not yet received.

structs and invokes? The need to ask these questions is one sign that Miller has not concerned himself with distinguishing between possible and plausible descriptions of a specifiable action. That is, there is no attempt to clarify the logic by which one moves from local description to the larger type models required to describe two basic levels of action in the play—that of the character Troilus and that of the implicit author, for whom Troilus is a function in a larger design. In fact, Miller's case for the nonreducible relation of the dialogical to the monological depends precisely on refusing to grant larger types where the oppositions might be resolved. But it is obvious that Troilus' thoughts can be entertained within the same mind. Does not the critic do exactly that? And the dramatically simplest type invoked by Troilus' speech—that of the betrayed, yet submissive, lover—reminds us of how such tensions are the stuff sonnets are made on. Troilus suffers a good deal less from the oscillations of language than from the vacillations of Cressida. Miller's deconstruction supports the general claims I made above, about the ways this critical stance can deepen our understanding of actions—here, by substantially thickening our grasp of the doubleness involved in trying to impose truth on a language of desire. However, without a dramatic focus the critical arguments ultimately cheapen the work. By leaping to abstract problems in language, Miller ignores the complex sources of Cressida's duplicity in her self-protectiveness and in Shakespeare's concern to place in parallel relationship the languages of desire and of heroism, as maddening evasions of Troilus' and our desire to find secure descriptive and commissive utterances. Similarly, he misses the levels of types Shakespeare invokes in order to render and interpret Troilus' divided mind. Troilus submits totally to these vacillations because he is only a boy, a pretender at the roles of lover and warrior. Yet if we take his madness too seriously we miss the ultimate blend of types: Troilus has all the verbal gestures of adult roles, but he in fact neither suffers fully nor acts heroically. All the play's gestures at nobility or even mimetic seriousness are called into question by the ironies around heroism which lead from the dramatic to the authorial act. Since the characters cannot control their destinies or even fulfill their chosen roles, we are lead to look beyond them to the intelligence controlling the irony. Here we project, as a final level of integration, an authorial act like that proposed in Richard Fly's essay on the play: Shakespeare is dramatizing a world divided into dialogical opposites because the characters are unable to fulfill type roles which might sustain some way of mediating the contradictions.[32] If one accepts a proposal like this, one in effect grants the grammatical possibility of understanding—through an authorial act —a purposive, monological interpretation of the dialogical as failed dialectics and of character as built out of tensions among types.

8. Determining the "intention" in an action

My critique of Miller rests on some hermeneutic values that are not self-evident. I have assumed that determining the most probable interpretation of a text depends on treating the text as the product of a complex mental act whose purposes one can recover. I have insisted that this act produces a meaning which is lost if one relies simply on a contemporary theoretical framework not carefully adapted to those purposes. My quarrel is not with contemporary methodologies, but with the failures to use them in a way that situates, rather than displaces, the act's specific qualities. Now I think I can supply the necessary defense in terms of the analysis of defining intentions by means of an intensional language. However, there must be two provisos. I cannot at this point draw adequate links between a general theory of meaning and specifically literary issues. And, in speaking about intentions, I shall have to proceed as if we agreed that meanings can be determinate, so that the only point of contention is how we explain that determinacy. Later, when we are fairly clear on what we mean in speaking about determinate meanings, I shall devote an entire chapter to the ideas of indeterminacy which Miller seems to hold, but which as a general theory is not relevant to the level of analysis in his essay.

If one ignores various forms of indeterminacy theory that base meanings on the interpreter's intentions, we can distinguish two basic ways of establishing the most probable meaning of a text—either it depends on hypothesizing the author's intention from available information, or meaning is an immanent property of the text, by virtue of the conventions it publicly invokes and/or by its properties as an autotelic, self-enclosed structure. The standard arguments for these positions approxi-

32. Fly, *Shakespeare's Mediated World* (Amherst: University of Massachusetts Press, 1976). For a good example of critical work that, without using the concepts, shows how more limited types apparently in opposition to one another can be reconciled with a more general image of behavior, see Stanley Fish's treatment of Herbert in *The Living Temple* (Berkeley: University of California Press, 1977).

mate a classical antimony'in form. On the one hand, philosophers like Strawson and Grice argue that conventions are so general and so multiple that they often will not prove sufficient for our determining the meaning of a speech act. Speech acts, they claim, are determinate only when we can recognize in them both a speaker's specific intentions and his intention to make us see his intention, for speakers use conventions and they, not the conventions, determine the specific relationships that constitute a particular utterance. Max Black makes an equally powerful case for the opposing position.[33] Meaning, he argues, is a public property of an utterance, and, thus, cannot depend on private intentions. The meaning is what the utterance says to someone aware of the relevant conventions; otherwise, we would ignore the obvious fact that people can intend to say all sorts of things that they do not, in fact, say. Moreover, if meanings depend on psychological intentions, we find ourselves in an infinite regress like the one leading early Wittgenstein to embrace an atomistic ontology. In order to know what something means, we must know what a statement of intentions means, which requires a further statement of intentions, and so forth. It seems that we can have secure grounds of publicly determinate meanings only with a pure conventionalism that denies most of what is interesting about human behavior, or we can preserve the depth of person predicates only by challenging the possibility that complex utterances allow a high degree of public agreement.

In the context of action descriptions, however, most of the tensions in this antinomy collapse. Both views treat meaning as defining the principles of selection which justify an interpreter in positing hierarchies of semantic relevance among the details. And both, I think it fair to say, equate the principle of selection with an idea of purpose. So the real issue is not whether a text's meaning requires a sense of intention, but, rather, how we can characterize intention in a way that introduces no problematic ontological properties,[34] remains faithful to the overt textual

33. For references to Grice and Strawson see chapter two. The essay of Black's I cite here is "Meaning and Intention: An examination of Grice's Views," *New Literary History* 4 (1973):257–80. For a concise and fair summary of the dispute, see E. D. Hirsch, *The Aims of Criticism* (Chicago: University of Chicago Press, 1976), pp. 68–71. Hereafter I shall abbreviate Hirsch's book as AC.

34. Of course, what problematic ontological properties are is a matter of dispute: is reductionism a worse danger than mentalism? Again, the crucial point is to bracket these explanatory hypotheses as much as possible in order to describe the phenomena—which probably will continue to allow the same ontological disputes to continue in altered form.

details and structures, explains a motivated selection of details, and avoids endless regress. Conventions seem an appealing answer, because all the data is public and, as Austin shows, conventions involve a sense of purpose without demanding the introduction of psychological information about the agent. Reliance on autotelic structures similarly avoids psychology, by treating the central motive as immanent in the work's use of literary and semantic conventions. But, if I have been correct in the last chapter, there are many cases where conventions are used or manipulated with possible nonconventional implicature. In this chapter, I have tried to secure the claims that for expressive acts or performances one requires a sense of motive that will bear human predicates connected with purpose, and that grammatical competence can be relied upon to test information about intentions in relation to public contexts and types beyond the limited range of conventions. Furthermore, the relevant action in a text need not be purely to say something: any combination of saying something and making a certain kind of object is theoretically compatible with my view of what an intensional language can describe. Both conventions and autotelic structures, then, seem to me limited ways of describing an action, and both can only explain fully how we make specific judgments about motives if they are supplemented by attributing some kind of intention in relation to contexts implicated by the situation. Since conventions account for only some intentions, and since I know no way to make a transition from autotelic structures to a coherent motivated account of the object as a whole without in fact constructing an intentional agent, the equation of meaning with the probable publicly assessable intention seems the most capacious model. In many cases, conventions may provide sufficient evidence for the intention, but, in others, looser grammatical ways of employing contexts must be relied upon in order to flesh out the act performed. In principle, these contexts can remain subject to evidence grammatical competence can adjudicate. The only problem with relying on this flexible sense of intentions is the need to secure the priority of evidence provided explicitly by the text and its publicly assessable contexts. Then we can deny fears that a statement of psychological intentions will be used to reject available evidence about the act that was, in fact, performed. I belabored the case of how actions can be redescribed—in order to assess and often to deny the agent's claims about his intentions—so that we could see the limitations of self-reflexive accounts and thus keep attributions of motivated selection on a level responsible to grammatical evidence.

These abstractions are a prelude to my invocation of Quentin Skinner's distinction between notions of *intention in* and *intention to*, as a clear way of avoiding the problems which give rise to defenses of the alternative views.[35] *Intention in* applies to cases where information from the utterance and contexts it probably implicates is sufficient for attributing purposive agency, while claims about *intention to* assume that a sense of purposes derived largely from nontextual evidence can be applied to a given work, even when the specific utterance does not warrant it. If we take, as an example, cases of nonconventional implicature, like the utterance "I warn you that I shall come," hypotheses about *intention in* the act would consist largely of the integrating of linguistic and pragmatic details I illustrated in the last chapter. One would attribute *intention to* say something, on the other hand, when one takes an agent's statements about his intentions, say, to apologize by means of the above utterance, and insists that the statement of intention determines the real meaning of the act. Skinner, in other words, recognizes the difference between the achievement of a meaning which reveals intentions and the intention to mean which may not be realized. Both are legitimate senses of *mean*, but only the former is sufficient for actually characterizing how the object contains and implicates speakers' meanings in a public sphere.

Intention in, then, is a hypothesis about purpose that derives from constructing internal relations in accordance with a publicly verifiable ratio between the three elements of action description. *Intention in* is a purposiveness that has a public determinacy, like that of conventions (although dependent on probabilistic grounds), which warrants the full force of person predicates. The concept of *intention to*, on the other hand, is significant primarily as a means for identifying problematic cases of intention, and for marking the need to bring one's hypotheses to a discussable argument about *intention in*. A simple hypothesis about intention to do something has no independent hermeneutic value, because neither utterance nor act must mean what someone intends them to. Even if a writer told us he saw in a flash what he had intended to do in his text, we would have no choice but to correlate elements as a

35. The distinction is worked out in his "Motives, Intentions and the Interpretations of Texts," *New Literary History*, 3 (1972):393–408, and applied in a thorough review of essays on the subject in "Hermeneutics and the Role of History," *New Literary History* 7 (1975): 209–32. In "Meaning and Understanding in the History of Ideas," *History and Theory* 9 (1969):28–29, which I discuss in chapter seven, Skinner also makes a succinct statement of the basic terms I employ below in distinguishing meaning from significance.

check that his statement is confirmed by textual evidence. Yet the problem in using this form of intention is less ontological than empirical. We only resort to hypotheses about *intention to* when an·utterance or act is sufficiently ambiguous or lacking in context and detail to warrant a hypothesis about *intention in*. A gap between *intention to* and *intention in* arises either when an agent is actually mistaken about his actual deed or when the interpreter lacks sufficient information or appropriate types to allow correlating intention and deed. In both cases, the interpreter must either show why no strongly probable interpretation is possible, or seek out sufficient information for correlating *intention to* with a situation and type so that a case can be made for *intention in*.

Problematic cases need not invalidate a theory when that theory can explain how the problems arise and how they may be resolved. In my next chapter, I shall demonstrate this by applying my constituents of action theory to a literary text and considering how we determine intention. But this will speak only to practical aspects of problematic cases. Another, more conceptual, challenge to a theory of intention is its need to explain and make use of the circularity in which it finds itself. Both strict intentionalist and strict conventionalist positions are circular to the extent that hypotheses about the determinants of meaning—intention or relevant conventions—depend on selections of details established by the general hypothesis. (Conventions have some independent status —this is the appeal of the theoretical position—but often several conventions might apply, even just on a semantic level, so that convention itself will not allow an independent prediction of relevant details without hermeneutic circling.) If circularity is inescapable, the test of a theory becomes how well it explains conditions of responsibility and synthesis within the circle. Here Skinner's model, as a vehicle for adapting the concerns of action theory, seems to prevail. Because there are three terms one must relate, each one and each pair (for example, situation and type) provides necessary, somewhat independent, features the other elements are responsible for explaining. We do not deal simply with particular events where we need supplementary statements to identify intentions. Rather, we are dealing with a grammar where our statements about particulars involve general expectations and where one can offer cultural evidence for invoking the use of types. The evidence does not preclude further descriptions, but probabilistic grounds, relative to specifiable communities, should be sufficient to dispel charges of vicious circularity. This model of criteria will not satisfy the pure sceptic, but nothing will in these areas, once he denies probabilistic standards.

9. *Meaning and significance with respect to actions*

The concept of *intention in* now enables me to justify my resistance to Miller's too easily imposing a contemporary theoretical construct on a Renaissance text (probably on any text). Once one has a coherent way to attribute purpose on probabilistic grounds in relation to available evidence, it becomes possible also to make at least rough distinctions between internal relations of a speech act and external relations to contexts not directly implicated by the purpose.[36] In other words, we find ourselves faced with the necessary, but problematic, distinction E. D. Hirsch poses between meaning and significance. With the help of Skinner and a philosophical analysis of actions, I think it is possible to restate Hirsch's arguments in a more flexible and defensible form, which escapes his vacillations on the criteria necessary for making the distinctions in particular cases. In order to bring out the significance of Hirsch's distinction, I shall first clarify the kinds of positions it opposes and then I shall show how we can escape the confusions that have led Hirsch to vacillate on possible criteria for applying his model.

There are two basic concepts of interpretive activity that deny one can meaningfully or consistently separate internal relations from the external relations brought to the object by the interpreter's needs, prejudices, and methodological assumptions: a general hermeneutic cultural relativism, and a pragmatic, or methodological, contextualism. The first position now blends with a variety of indeterminacy and intertextuality theories, but its basic formulation is Heidegger's and Gadamer's. Put simply, these thinkers argue that meanings are not objects but constructions by an interpreter from signs. The act of construction cannot avoid being influenced by the *prejudice* or *foreunderstanding* an interpreter has by virtue of his existence in a culture, so there is no possibility of independent meanings not continually revised by man as an inescapably historical creature bound in time. Nor should there be any desire to

36. The best recent discussion of internal and external relations is Kenneth Burke's reflections on the paradox of substance in his *Grammar of Motives*. See also Frye on centripetal and centrifugal structures in the *Anatomy of Criticism*. The fullest grappling with the problem I know is in Hegel's *Phenomenology*, pp. 22–39, where Hegel tries to show that internal relations are possible whenever the subject is expressed by and contained in the predicate. This way lies metaphysical madness, but Hegel's formulation remains a precise definition of organicist ideals for works of art. Moreover, we can make use of it once we distinguish between Hegel's mystified philosophy of nature and his quite useful philosophy of action. I shall return to Hegel in chapter nine.

escape this condition, because it is a testament to the power of great texts that they remain relevant by eliciting and giving form to aspects of the human condition in a particular time and place. If one is less pious, it is easy to shift terms and to stress the violence of interpretive acts, instead of the capacity of great texts to enter into conversation with historically situated human projects.

Methodological contextualism takes, instead, the pragmatic position that all measures of inquiry depend on the observer's relation to his own historical situation. Yet inquiry itself is not bound by prejudice or foreunderstanding: one can specify criteria appropriate to one's questions, and thus develop a model of determinate and yet pluralistic inquiry not trapped in a hopeless pursuit for an essential and fixed object. Because this position marks one direction in which my own concern for procedures can lead, I want to quote Leroy Searle's representative articulation of the position at some length, so that I can show wherein I differ:

> Standards of description can only be expressed as *adequacy* in relation to parameters selected for their significance. Arguments between critics over which of two "interpretations" is correct are thus irresolvable because the basis of disagreement remains unlocated. . . .
> Meaning is a cognitive phenomenon, presupposing a mental act—not a property of a mediating structure. That mental act is sustained in a process of convergence, in which significance is a term that can be used systematically to designate recognizable features which are integrated in the cognitive closure we experience as meaning. . . .
> In examining language *meaning* is determined by focus: for example, articulatory acts are significant features that converge to sustain meaning when one focuses on phonemes. When the focus is upon words, phonemes are significant and so on to sentences and larger structures.[37]

In other words, significance does not depend on a distinct kind of inquiry, but is a function of the relevance of meanings for any coherent inquiry. Significance is the content of a level of operations where mean-

37. Leroy Searle, "Tradition and Intelligibility: A Model for Critical Theory," *New Literary History* 7 (1976):406, 408–10. I cannot do justice to Searle's case by abstracting this claim from his powerful chain of arguments (a condensed functionalist analysis, very close to many of my claims), so I hope this discussion will be seen as reducing him to a representative type. For another version of pragmatist contextualism, see Joseph Margolis, *The Languages of Art and Art Criticism* (Detroit: Wayne State University Press, 1965), pp. 82–144.

ing is integrated within a higher level of generality, as in the example of phonemes.

Hirsch's insistence on the need for an alternative model is based on a very simple, and yet inescapable, argument. If meaning cannot be separated from external relations, there can be no permanent object (except perhaps for a set of physical signs) which one analyzes for its relevant features or deconstructs (AC, 75–85). But if there is no determinate meaning *in* the object, there is neither scandal to deconstruction (since we could never do otherwise) nor any possible authority in the text which warrants testing its relevance. In fact, there is no object to test; there is only relevance or possible interpretations which have no object to which they can do violence. Moreover, given this view, there would be no way to prove claims about cultural situations, since even the proof would have no status independent of the very culture whose limits must be defined. We can only know the limits of a culture's understanding if we can independently understand how other cultures might behave differently. So, in arguing for distinct categories of meaning and significance, Hirsch is not the victim of an anxiety for certainty; rather, he sees that the life of cultural disciplines requires terms for preserving aspects of our past which might have the force of freeing us from the blinders of our ideological assumptions.

There are ways Searle's position can evade Hirsch's charge—for example, by insisting on some core of relevant features common to methods of inquiry—but the model's pragmatism suffers from the serious defect of ignoring differences between natural objects—where there is some warrant for insisting that interpretive procedures determine significance as an aspect of meaning—and human acts. In the latter case, we must assume that the object of inquiry has itself been produced according to an understanding of procedures that are internal to it. Thus, his example of interconnected recursive levels of meaning and significance in the analysis of language makes perfect sense for studying language in general, but ignores what distinguishes acts of giving meanings from the general structure. When a speaker is involved, we expect his act to make certain levels of inquiry more central than others. If we want to know his meaning, for example, it would be very odd to attend to the significance of phonemes with respect to his articulatory act. It would be equally odd to point out, say, how his utterance might relate to some set of frequency tables for the use of semantic and syntactic properties. The point is that as soon as we deal with a purposive act as the object of inquiry, the purpose constitutes the nature of the object and dictates the basic initial interpretive procedures. Once we are clear on the nature or meaning of the object, there are numerous inquiries possible where the relevant criteria are pragmatically established. But unless the object is first constituted, there is no ground for checking the appropriateness of inquiry procedures.

The nature of establishing purposes also enables us to flesh out a second strategy by which Hirsch attacks hermeneutic relativism, because of its assumptions about the nature of an interpreter's bond to his culture. Hirsch states the case in negative terms: there are no relevant metaphysical arguments about the confines of one's culture; there are only various specific situations, whose limits must be empirically established. Action theory reminds us that cultures are sets of practices, neither all dependent on one another nor all subsumable under general claims about epistemé or period consciousness. Strawson's descriptive metaphysics, we recall, shows a relatively permanent core of problems and assumptions that characterize life in any culture, at least any culture we need to consider in discussing Western literary tradition. Moreover, the flexibility and the persistence of types across historical boundaries argue for a notion of period culture as not a fixed object, but as a loose blend of constitutive capacities consisting of many levels of operations and predicates for describing forms of life. It is as silly to assume, with the classical historicism Gadamer rightly rejects, that a writer cannot transcend the ideologies of his time as it is to insist that interpreters are locked into some fixed, determinate culture. When the forms of inquiry in question are the understanding of actions, we find ourselves in a different position from the historian of science or of other specialized languages. Testable scientific paradigms require their users to be explicit about their logic and their presuppositions in a fashion very different from the way ordinary men use type concepts. More important, scientific hypotheses lead to laboratory experiments; hence, there is at any given time a highly codified body of principles which stands and falls as a whole, breeding new test conditions. Ordinary action type predicates, on the other hand, are used in situations which often do not change as society's ideological and economic structures change. People must relate to one another and to ordinary needs in much the same way, whatever the ideological structure, just as they continue to live in a Newtonian world, whatever the prevailing doctrines of physics (at least in Western culture, and perhaps, if we believe the critics of thinkers like Whorf, in most cultures). Moreover, because actions are particular and concerned primarily with practical results, the grammar for dealing with them need not change totally when certain assumptions no longer hold.

One test for this claim is the relative success of translation. To Romantic expressivists, successful translation is a rare feat—but notice how strict are their standards for capturing stylistic nuance, and so forth.[38] It is equally possible, as Newton Garver once said to me, to wonder that some degree of sufficient translation is so often possible. If a lion could speak, we would not understand him, but we usually manage to find sufficiently shared forms of life to understand what other men in different cultures say. We cannot theoretically predict which type predicates persist through cultural change, but we can understand the possibility of their persisting. Take, as a second example, the way certain literary texts survive and others do not. One can say this occurs because they breed reinterpretations, but, as I suggest in discussing *classic*, it is more plausible that they endure because they capture actions and relations between actions that endure (even if the evaluative predicates we apply to them change). What does endure, after all, are texts which themselves seek some purported essential truths, and not those content to mirror or appeal to social fashions. Whatever the cause (and I suspect it has to do with clearly portraying fundamental human attitudes and relations), it is a crucial fact for philosophy and for literary theory that we can appreciate and relate to *Oedipus* and *Don Quixote,* and even to the *Gorgias* and *Symposium,* in ways we cannot to the cosmology of the *Timaeus* or the biology of unnatural natural history. (Yet we can still learn from other features of the *Timaeus*: for example, if we consider its logical account of creation as a possible picture of the psychology of producing versions of the world.)

All this, of course, only shows the possibility of making judgments about meaning which allow a distinction between internal and external relations. Now the difficult task remains of giving criteria for such a distinction. Here Hirsch's scrupulous vacillations indicate the difficulties involved. He cannot decide whether criteria for meaning depend on properties of an utterance or action, or on properties of an attitude the inquirer assumes. In his first definition, Hirsch equated meaning with the signs in a text of an author's probable intention: "Meaning is that which

38. For a recent, noteworthy statement of Romantic expressionism with respect to translation, see George Steiner's *After Babel* (New York: Oxford University Press, 1975). Steiner makes several interesting points, but the differences he points out are often so marginal (and so intelligible to those in this culture) that, as with Quine's intricate case against synonymy, we can be struck by how much of translation is not dependent on specific cultural differences.

is represented by the text; it is what the author meant by his use of a particular sign sequence; it is what the signs represent. Significance, on the other hand, names a relationship between that meaning and a person, or a conception, or a situation, or indeed anything imaginable. . . . Significance always implies a relationship, and one constant, unchanging pole of that relationship is what the text means." [39] Unfortunately, he did not have an adequate concept of intention (as we can see from the above quotation's confused idea of meaning as representing an inner state, and from its vacillations between intention as a function of a person and as a function of what signs represent). He also had no way to handle situations in which intention statements seem not to account for what the text does. Thus, in his later work he simply equates meaning with internal relations and gives no criteria, except a critic's intentions, by which to distinguish internal from external relations: "Meaning is defined *tout court* as that which a text is taken to represent. . . . The important feature of meaning as distinct from significance is that meaning is the determinate representation of a text for an interpreter. An interpreted text is always taken to represent something, but that something can always be related to something else. Significance is meaning-as-related-to-something-else." [40] If, however, there is no test for whether the relation is to something else, questions of significance would only arise when the interpreter admitted he was not concerned with internal relations. This would handle some cases of evaluation, but would not help adjudicate most competing critical claims. Most Freudians or Marxists or historicists would see their interpretive contexts as justified by internal relations.

Hirsch retreats to his later position, I suspect, because he recognizes that it is more important to have this meaning/significance distinction as a test for particular practices than to risk losing its general utility by too narrowly and controversially defining *meaning*. Interpretation may not be primarily an ethical issue, but, as Hirsch shows very well, there are significant ethical aspects in how we approach another's act or utterance, and whether we try to understand what a person might mean or

39. *Validity in Interpretation* (New Haven: Yale University Press, 1967), p. 8.
40. AC, 79–80. In this work, Hirsch vacillates on whether the interpreter has a semantic or simply an ethical imperative for trying to determine intention. The discussion of Grice and Black cited above still conceives intention as semantically necessary, while the explicit discussion of meaning and significance (cf. AC, 87–88) makes it only an ethical imperative. Hirsch's case on the ethical imperative for seeking intentions is a superb one, but it has the unfortunate consequence of weakening the meaning/significance distinction.

simply adapt his statement for our own interpretive projects. In ethics, it can suffice to have distinctions which vaguely mark ideals and are not rigorously grounded, because these ideals function as reminders that in making choices one defines one's character in specific ways. Nonetheless, I think it is possible that our discussion of *intention in* provides a firm intellectual foundation for delineating the respective parameters of meaning and of significance. We cannot have necessary and sufficient conditions, because judgment plays a crucial role here, but we can hope to provide grounds for a clear scenario or imaginative test by an interpretive community to determine which model of interpretive activity is being practiced.

I can best describe the use I propose for Hirsch's distinction by first reviewing my own case. I take the meaning of either a text or a speech act to be a hypothesis about the purposive rationale for selection and organization projected in the specific details and the contexts they implicate, both conventional and nonconventional. Meaning is determined as a set of words which make a semantically coherent statement which one can see in context as embodying or expressing a purpose. We construe the purpose or intention by correlating three aspects of intensional action descriptions—evidence about intention, situational details, and grammatical types—so that the hypothesis about purpose can be shown to account for these attributes in the most comprehensive and economical way. (A coherent description can be offered for an incoherent act, as is all too obvious in ordinary experience as well as in any form of therapeutic practice.) The ultimate criterion for the success of this correlation is a relevant community's agreement that an agent capable of making clear judgments would accept the description of the actual intention in the act because the details, context, and relevant types cohere. This definition will not produce certainty, or even clearly apply in a variety of borderline cases, but it does draw a fairly distinct line between internal and external relations. There appear two clear types of cases where we can say an interpreter is concerned primarily with significance. First, it is obviously not a description of meaning when we ignore or dismiss an author's stated or implicit purposes, without first testing their adequacy to the utterance, because we are concerned only with a given line of inquiry. Similarly, one's concern is with significance, rather than meaning, when she is content to abstract parts of a text to make some general point about an author's character or historical situation. Obviously, one cannot deal with internal relations without taking a text or deed as a distinct entity, itself determining a hierarchy among relevant contexts.

The second type of case is equally obvious in principle, but difficult to adjudicate. It is clearly not an inquiry into meaning when one invokes descriptive predicates which could not be intelligible to the agent.[41] But, as we have seen, it is not correct to define what might be intelligible to the agent in strictly historicist terms, because neither culture nor the human mind is reducible to a given set of ideological beliefs. If we can redescribe an act and agree that an agent might assent to a description of which he was not at the time conscious, we must find a more complex and subtle norm for determining a possible horizon for discussing intention and the internal contexts it makes relevant. I propose that we see this norm as dependent not on psychological terms but hermeneutic ones: criteria for meaning, as opposed to significance, depend on the kind of predicates attributed to the act or text and the kind of evidence one might use to support a description. Hence, we are inquiring into meaning whenever we appeal to the audience's sense that the agent could, in his historical situation, understand the specific descriptive terms used and himself be able to evaluate the type evidence used to support the terms. Inquiries into significance, on the other hand, need not concern themselves with the agent's possible understanding of their methods or criteria.

The difference between these inquiries is clearest when the interpreter relies on a systematic methodology. For here, if the agent is to understand the description, he will have to understand not only the specific terms used but the system which gives them resonance and establishes the criteria for evidence and for connecting the predicates used. When this mode of understanding is required, and when the agent could not historically have been familiar with the system, we are dealing with questions of significance, even if the interpreter tries to explain intentions. We must, for example, invoke concepts and images of family relationships in order to describe both *Hamlet* and *Portnoy's Complaint*.

41. Just as in the distinction between *intention in* and *intention to*, it is important to recognize that an accurate sense of a term like *meaning* depends on understanding the differences implied by the various prepositional phrases we use in connection with it. Meaning *in* or *of* a text is clearly internal (provided we can describe how we determine such meanings); meaning *to* or *for* requires we complete the prepositional phrase, and this will often make clear whether the inquiry is one seeking meaning or significance. I do not develop this in the text because enough is enough, and because *meaning in*, by my argument, is meaning for the agent.

Hence, we can imagine certain modern treatments of the dynamics of the family as applying equally well to the meaning of both texts. But, to the extent that these predicates depend on systematic relationships for their full meaning—say images of the Christian family or Freudian theories—their hermeneutic status would differ with respect to the texts. We can imagine Roth being explicitly aware of the Freudian connotations of terms or systems of relations, and hence we can envision his acceptance of a Freudian reading, at least on some level. But for Shakespeare to accept a particular Freudian concept would entail his knowing the entire system (unless, of course, one manages to state the insight in terms we believe a Renaissance man could understand).[42] Freudian readings of Shakespeare, then, are usually readings of the text's significance, not its meaning. This does not mean that such readings are wrong. It does, however, suggest that they are subsidiary to, and responsible for, a prior description of meaning, and it entails their being subject to different criteria, criteria created by the discipline of psychology rather than constructed to account for authorial purposes. Along similar lines, we normally use taxonomies like Frye's categories in order to demonstrate some features of the significance of a text, since the taxonomy is structured in large part by works and relationships an author does not know or relate as Frye does. Yet we can imagine a description of Frye's symbolic modes stated in analogous Christian terms, which could become one aspect of the meaning of the *Divine Comedy*.

There is one further advantage to my equation of meaning with an intention the author can accept on redescription. It gives us a coherent way of speaking about failed intentions, or features of a text which do not seem to correlate with the implicit intentions—so long as we can imagine the author agreeing. This type of explanation can help us out of cases where we find ourselves relying on concepts of irony in order to make the author responsible for all the features of a work. *Mansfield Park*, for example, is often called an ironic novel because critics cannot imagine Jane Austen simply accepting Fanny Price's eventual subordination to Edmund Bertram. Yet there are so many instances in the text where Fanny accedes to his judgment (and his is the only alternative to the willful blindness of the other characters), that irony seems the wrong concept. I think it makes more sense to say that Jane Austen wanted to try a more conservative solution than she did in the novels where the heroine brings wit and energy to moderate the hero's servi-

42. My argument here is borrowed from Wittgenstein's discussion of Freud in LA, 23–28, where Wittgenstein makes a distinction between causes and motives.

tude to custom. Yet the solution fails, either because Austen cannot so easily restructure our moral resistance to such stiff figures or because she ends up still using the devices which require us to expect a more open world for the heroine to finally enter. In both explanations, we admit Austen's apparent intention, but insist on redescribing it in terms we assume she would assent to. Now the act becomes one we must take as a failed one, but the terms for judgment remain within the text and subject to the agreement of any observer who knows only her other novels and general evaluative associations created by certain character types.

10. *Assessing action descriptions: the jury model*

When one stresses cultural practices, rather than explanatory systems or pure propositions, there is a constant temptation to address the sceptic who haunts merely probabilistic grounds of evidence. My strategy has been to resist attack by attacking first and by attempting to show what the sceptic cannot handle. This strategy is especially needed now, because the criteria of fit and coherence I suggest as appropriate for action descriptions invite the sceptical rejoinder that I turn hermeneutics into a self-conscious rhetoric. There is precious little evidence available outside of the specific formulation a critic gives to an action description. My only possible reply is to accept the charge, and then turn it into a way of further clarifying the image of society which underlies my sense of criteria. There is nothing to fear in acknowledging the critic's need to be rhetorical if we also acknowledge the intelligence of the audience. Most "suspicious" hermeneutics are scandalized by traces of rhetoric, because they theatrically assume that once you don't give an audience only the facts, ma'am, the poor audience will be led into degradation. In the service of "truth," they make it impossible for audiences to judge other forms of discourse and they encourage the temptation to treat social discourse as only the play of wills to power. It then becomes extremely difficult to have any respect for an audience, because the theory affords no common grounds on which disagreement can be resolved in noncoercive terms. But I see no reason why one cannot acknowledge one's rhetoric and trust at least the competent audience I have been assuming to take it into account. This not only treats critic and audience as genuine equals, it also suggests that one can draw analogies between the criteria required for intensional languages and the attributes one can affirm of an audience trained in the reading of these languages. While accuracy remains an important consideration, interpreting actions also requires other dimensions of assessment, like sensitivity, tact, and depth—each subject to distinctions of degree. By exercising powers to make these discriminations, we foster a valuable form of understanding, and, perhaps more important, we learn to trust qualities we can expect of other minds.

The emblem of the scientific model of understanding is clearly the laboratory. I suggest that the equivalent hermeneutic emblem is that of a jury asked to decide on competing descriptions of an action. This suggestion should at least establish a contrast capable of summarizing the themes and implications of this chapter in relation to a practical context.[43] Jury proceedings are concerned with understanding particulars, not with abstracting to laws, and the institution depends on assuming a complex grammatical competence, as the ground on which possible agreement may be reached. Juries, as Aeschylus knew, could not be expected to agree on how and why something is done with the same kind of certitude observers could have when simply describing

43. Ricoeur, in the essay cited above, also uses the jury model (pp. 109–10) and bases it on a very interesting observation. He argues that we can never expect total agreement on rational grounds about an action precisely because it is a particular. Rational arguments depend on correlating particulars to generalizations by making them instances of laws. But if the phenomenon in question cannot be treated as an instance of laws, then it is logically inconsistent to expect any explanation of it to achieve the kind of universal status where complete agreement might be expected (p. 106). Those critics seeking quasi-scientific analogues for literary explanations, like Ralph Rader and Hirsch, might be expected to resist my jury analogy. See, for example, John Ellis, *The Theory of Literary Criticism*, pp. 194–95, who claims that the law court model ignores the fact there is no basic difference between criticism and science, since both have investigative and hypothesis-testing phases. My whole argument, of course, is that actions require different kinds of hypotheses, because of the particular nature of what we try to make coherent.

It is true, as L. Jonathan Cohen powerfully illustrates in *The Probable and the Proveable* (Oxford: Clarendon Press, 1977), that both practical science and juries use an inductive form of probabilistic analysis. But what count as variables, as tests, and as grounds of conviction will nonetheless differ in the two spheres. I will return to these differences in chapter seven. For now, it should suffice that we have no novelistic account of scientific judgments that parallels Dostoyevsky's trial scenes in *Brothers Karamazov*, where both the dramatistic basis of jury assessments and the dangers of decisions based on a model of *fit* are all too evident. In the novel, the lawyer's appeals depend primarily on literary skills. One might, then, easily use Dostoyevsky to argue for the jury analogy as illustrating the will to power behind all interpretive acts. But this would ignore considering what criteria might explain the success of a given will to power. That one is motivated by a will to power does not preclude the need for competing wills to honor grammatical grounds of assessment.

what happened. (His Furies might serve as emblems of justice applied on the basis of extensional language.) But the gain in self-consciousness and sense of community more than outweighs the danger of uncertainty.

If we imagine the literary critic as appealing to a jury, we can clarify several aspects of his activity. First, the jury model gives us a very useful analogy for restating my restatement of Hirsch's distinction between meaning and significance. Speaking very loosely, we might say that in a theory of describing actions Hirsch's *explanations of meaning* become those explanations which are admissible in establishing the truth or falsity of claims about what happened, and, thus, are parallel to what a court takes as relevant in deciding responsibility. Significance, on the other hand, relates to the kinds of considerations that a judge might take into account in deciding on a sentence, or a legislator in deciding on the justice of the applicable laws. *Meaning* relates to demonstrable purposes or formal intentions, and *significance* to explanatory contexts allowing an observer to make hypotheses about the reasons why certain purposes motivated the agent or to use those purposes as instances for a more general argument. Second, this model explains how the coherence we expect from intensional discourse—the coherence of narrative and image rather than inductive or deductive logics—can be institutionally assessed. Juries decide cases on the basis of practical, not rational, inference, and hence must base their findings on type categories which are only provisional and hence easily defeasible. The lawyer appealing to a jury is *bricoleur*, not engineer. Yet juries rarely render verdicts of indeterminacy; they operate in probabilistic terms. Finally, the jury model constructs the role of critic as advocate. His task is to re-present the original act in as complex a qualitative story as he can construct, with heavy reliance on the skills of the rhetorician. In the jury model, the critic-advocate is not an impartial observer; his role is to make a case. Yet if he does not internalize the jury's grammatical expectations and anticipate them, if he has not learned impersonal standards, he will rarely succeed. However provisional the result of jury findings, the institution creates established roles for those who perform within it, gives authority to certain interpretations which, nonetheless, remain open to appeal and to redescription, and provides a metaphor for the joys and the fears attendant upon modes of discourse in which both Greek divinities and the gods of science are banished.

4

A Test Case of Action Description: Interpreting
Williams' "This is Just to Say"

1. *Williams' poem treated as an ordinary utterance* In the abstract discussions so far, I have repeatedly claimed various ways in which my correlation of grammatical understanding and the philosophy of action might prove useful for literary theory. But I have neither tested my case by an extended example nor begun preparing a transition to the distinctively literary issues I shall soon address. This chapter is intended to right the balance. I shall give an example of how an ordinary action description constructs and tests alternatives. But I shall take as my example a literary text, William Carlos Williams' "This is Just to Say," so that I can also indicate those features of action descriptions which depend upon the distinctive literary procedures to be treated conceptually in the following chapters.[1]

I shall treat Williams' poem from two perspectives. First, I shall assume that the poem is simply the note it purports to be and that one can try to understand it in a practical or ordinary context. Then I shall ask about the differences in the status of the evidence and in interpretive

1. This strategy has complex intertextual motives. I am here simplifying and changing an essay on Williams' poem and textualist theory, "Presence and Reference in a Literary Text: The Example of Williams," *Critical Inquiry* 5 (1979):489–510. The changes bring me very close to similar strategies used to reveal the status of literary conventions in Jonathan Culler's *Structuralist Poetics*, chapter eight. However, I differ from him in stressing the properties of action descriptions, and later I shall use the points made here to quarrel with him on the status of conventions.

procedures that occur when one takes the text as a poem addressed to a general audience:

This is Just to Say

I have eaten
the plums
that were in
the icebox

and which
you were probably
saving
for breakfast

Forgive me
they were delicious
so sweet
and so cold [2]

Situating this note involves testing how various scenarios apply. Each scenario involves three kinds of analysis. As Fillmore points out, the information one has about surrounding contexts or what the speaker knows functions in inverse proportion to the density of the scenario that must be imagined. Imagining the scene also requires correlating the details with type hypotheses which bring possible images of the character and purposes of the speaker. These hypotheses in turn must fit with more abstract aspects of the situation, with how we imagine the general problem the agent addresses and how we are to assess the act. Finally, the scenario depends on the interpreter's sense of relevant procedures: one might be content simply to register the fact that an apology has been offered, or one might scrutinize the note more carefully—because of the dramatic situation, because one recognizes aspects of the note which seem worth attending to carefully, or, most obviously, because the note is marked as a literary text.

Let us assume that the observer has reason to scrutinize the note. The obvious focus for the examination is the question: what are the agent's purposes in writing it? Only this question will make it possible to assess the qualities exhibited by the act or enable speculation about the latent desires it betrays. Some aspects of the scenario which an interpreter must construct are obvious. These limit the range of types and inten-

2. In Williams, *The Collected Earlier Poems* (New York: New Directions, 1951), p. 354.

tions we can propose. We recognize that the note's opening marks a casual attitude on the part of the author (whether this is a natural or artificial casualness depends on a more complete scenario), and we understand the bare facts of the situation—that one person, probably living with another, has taken the plums and left a note of apology. Also, if we choose to scrutinize the note, we find ourselves assuming that the relationship it manifests is a fairly close one between equals, probably husband and wife. The warrant for this is strictly grammatical: it would be unlikely for casual relations or relations of different status, like parent and child, intentionally to write notes of apology which another person should read carefully in a qualitative dramatic context.

Now the degrees of probability lessen considerably. There are no ontological constraints against reading the note as a neo-Platonic ladder progressing from eating plums, to reflecting on the language we substitute for them, to some dialectical union of language and plums ("so sweet / and so cold" as words made sensuous) where one reaches a mystically oxymoronic essence of plumness. Yet such a hypothesis would be hard not to take as parody, or as the act of a literary critic desperately displaying his originality in pursuit of tenure. For, without special circumstances, grammatical competence restricts the free play of signifiers. When one ignores the constraints imposed by even the minimal information this note provides, at least without invoking other considerations to justify his departure, we cannot but hope he is offering a parody: all the plausible alternatives place him in a worse light.

Even within general plausibility conditions, however, three interpretations of the note remain possible, depending on the dramatic contexts invoked. First, one is tempted to read the note ironically, if only because we tend to equate scrutiny with suspicion of manifest motives. I imagine a marital or domestic scene ripe with sexual hostility. A coherent explanatory set of types then emerges. The note could present two acts of aggression—first eating the plums and then recounting the act in a tauntingly casual note, a deliberate refusal of face-to-face confrontation which turns empty words asking for forgiveness into an excuse for revelling in the plums as sexual substitutes. On the metaliterary level, the note itself can be seen as the equal of the plums. There, too, one can find sensual pleasure and an aggressive surrogate for sexual relations by enjoying the cold artificiality of this minimal apology. The lover's care becomes the ironist's skill with his pen. How else but ironically can we take an appeal for forgiveness that devotes only one line to expressing concern for the other's feelings? In this self-absorbed context, "Forgive me" becomes a mocking of civilized manners, a bitter reminder of how ineffectual are the shows of concern in light of the intensity of natural desires and the aggressive impulses of wills to power in tension with one another. If we view the note as taking the form of a poem (but still addressed only to one person), the title becomes an ironic undercutting of any ideal meaning in *justice: just saying* is always *only* saying, and thus presents a bitter comment that moral ideals perhaps remain only in the ancient equation between justice and vengeance.

A second reading of the note could emphasize its qualities as an extremely intelligent and tactful form of apology. Here the construction of dramatic and abstract aspects of the situation in terms of serious apology brings with it type concepts, which in turn produce the comparisons and contrasts necessary to define the qualities in the specific act. The speaker seems deliberately to avoid casting the apology in a purely conventional light or projecting his appeal for forgiveness on the basis of a typical moral struggle between temptation and obligation. Instead, the person I shall argue is probably the husband performs or projects his apology in terms that skillfully praise the other person's capacity to understand departures from outmoded moralist postures. The speaker does not begin with his remorse or his sense of obligation. These elements are introduced only by a very casual relative clause in the second stanza and are further distanced by the casuistical "probably." The point is to grant nature its due and to express qualities of honesty and self-knowledge in the speaker which will ultimately justify his appeal for forgiveness. This is no conventional humanistic struggle with temptation; language, and with it self-consciousness, begins only after the fact, after sensual desire has held the field. It seems in the first two stanzas that the role of language is merely to register facts and, even worse, to try to evade their consequences. For I find it hard not to think that the weak introduction to the second stanza and the inclusion of "probably" serve to distance, qualify, and weaken the aspects of moral obligation and cultural constraints they bring into play. The speaker must refuse to consider himself merely a creature of desire, but he seems to want to do so in the way that will least make him subject to cultural guilt. The way to have one's cultural identity and weaken it at the same time is to employ language's capacity for endless qualification, a capacity to turn "certainly" into "probably," and full obligation into weak relative clauses.

These potential ironies about language, however, are only hints in the note because they are neither to win the day nor to produce a cheap dramatic reversal. Their role is to raise possibilities about language which are denied by the subtle shifts that take place in the last stanza: now the past tenses of indicative and subjunctive reporting give way to an explicit illocutionary act in the present tense, and the order of priority between natural and cultural orders is reversed.[3] Now a cultural appeal of a slightly different order, the "Forgive me," precedes the return to natural desire and provides a context for understanding how the two orders relate. The point, then, is to highlight the very different sense of culture and language between the potential casuistry of abstract reflections on moral obligations and the direct present illocutionary act of saying "Forgive me." Notice first that no abstract justification is offered in this appeal. The speaker does not ask for forgiveness because he was especially hungry or because he promises to control his desires better in the future. The justification offered is instead an evocative memory of the plums' sensuous appeal, an appeal that makes it clear similar transgressions will occur in the future, and that threatens to overpower the poem's sense of human relationships. But a profound sense of humanity ultimately prevails because the speaker does not indulge in abstract humanistic platitudes but, instead, merely records his situation. The justness of the speaker's note is its recognition of his weakness and its lovely combination of self-understanding with an implicit faith in the hearer's capacity to grasp and to accept his deed, and, beyond that, to accept his human existence as a balance of weakness, self-knowledge, and concern. The speaker, in other words, recognizes how the performance of meaning can be its achievement. He insists on the expressive qualities of language to sustain and exhibit his performance of qualities of self-awareness as a sufficient sign of his care for the other. In calling attention to his note or act, he completes his apology by implicitly basing it on his appreciation of the other's capacity to understand the subtleties of discourse. This level of understanding, we can imagine him implying, is, after all, what grounds the domestic relation and transcends the lapses each is likely to make.

3. In order to clarify my use of speech acts in discussing Williams' poem, I must anticipate some distinctions which I shall take up later, between acts within a discourse and acts organizing a discourse. I take the poem as a literary illocution that elicits a certain kind of attention to the organizing act on the mimetic level—here, a speech act of making a complex apology. This act is performed in a way that involves expressive implicature. Within the act as a whole, one can also isolate specific illocutions. These are acts of stating as well as the explicit illocution "Forgive me." However, only the whole can produce the desired perlocutionary effects, because it is as a complete act on mimetic and on authorial levels that the utterance carries its expressive implicatures.

A third reading of the note would apply textualist models of interpretation to the dramatic situation. (I assume, of course, that the textualist has been convinced by my last chapter and grants the use of deconstruction as a vehicle for deepening psychological aspects of a situation.) This interpretation would stress the presence of both optimistic and ironic readings, arguing that the words, or perhaps the codes elicited by the concept of forgiveness, force us to vacillate between dreaming that some mutual comprehension is possible and bitterly resenting conditions in which apology seems to be required. This linguistic duplicity, after all, is homologous with a readily available psychological type characteristic —the tendency to resent humbling ourselves that leads to both concealed and overt forms of aggressive behavior.

2. The differences involved in judging interpretations of the work as a poem

Now, which of these interpretations constitutes the best description of the intention in the note? I do not think a strong probable case can be made for any of the three—not because discourse is inevitably indeterminate, but simply because we lack sufficient information. Still, our indecision is theoretically significant. First, it arises from interpretations where we can readily imagine the forms of supplementary information which would establish *intention in*, even though that information would not be given in the text. Instead, the information would change the situation and dictate the probable types to be invoked. If, for example, we knew more about the nature of the domestic relations, especially in connection with how the speaker interpreted those relations, we would be able to make a much stronger case for either the first or the second alternative, in terms of both conscious and nonavowable intentions. Yet even the information we have allows some degree of probability— largely from procedural considerations. The second reading seems to demand more literary scrutiny of the note than most speakers could expect in ordinary circumstances, and it assumes a high degree of conceptual, or at least grammatical, sophistication. Similar reasons also render the third slightly suspect. It does an excellent job of relegating the complexities of a state of mind to a plausible behavioral model, but its complexity seems to ignore the practical demands of the situation, where one of the two alternatives is likely to have priority for the speaker.

The final theoretical implication in this situational indeterminacy is the most interesting. When we begin to take the note as a poem in the full sense—that is, as a text offered to a general audience for reflective purposes rather than as a note to a specific person for essentially practical purposes[4]—the nature of the intention we try to fix changes, the appropriate supplementary information alters, and the second and the third interpretations become more plausible than the first. Now we must deal not with one set of intentions but with two, which must be correlated with one another. We still must understand the dramatic actor's purposes, but they are now situated not simply in a concrete setting but in the purposes of an implicit author who creates the situation for reasons we can only locate if we understand the institutional and cultural practices associated with literary experience. Consequently, the interpreter must invoke different general types. He needs to correlate images of what it is plausible to do in the situation with images that address the question: why should a writer imagine the constructed action as significant for a literary audience?

Simply from the fact that a work is offered as literature we have a significant basis for making hypotheses about probable intentions in the text. To the extent that we have plausible terms for imagining what the author conceived as required by the work's literariness, we have important information on how to situate at least the authorial intention in a basic context. We have a good idea what might count as evidence and often what hierarchies one might invoke for organizing the evidence. Certain facts about the author or the work can extend or deepen these contexts. If a work has been continuously acclaimed as a masterpiece, placed in certain traditions, or especially valued by certain groups, we have a range of assumptions to bring to bear on the text. Certain kinds of acclaim, for example, make it highly likely that the work in question will reward intense reflective appreciation because its linguistic structures carry complex associations and reward forms of analysis that seek rich, metaphorical, emotional and conceptual implications for the dense particulars elaborated on the mimetic level. If we adapt such expectations to this note as a Williams' poem—and I cannot imagine a defensible alternative here—the first reading comes to appear somewhat thin in relation to the others. It does not lead to the forms of complexity or affective and intellectual richness the others do because it cannot make the possible qualities in the experience very resonant. Moreover, the

4. John Ellis, in *Theory of Criticism*, argues (correctly, I think) that this abstracting away from particular, practical, first-person purposes is a necessary conventional attribute of texts taken to be literature.

status of details changes. Not only is there not much cause within the poem for taking "Forgive me" ironically, the reasons for discounting the apology become less convincing. The syntactic features emphasizing and placing that line in a structural whole become crucial complements to any general type assumptions about behavior.

A simple complexity standard would lead to favoring the third alternative. To assert this, however, is to proceed too quickly. We have seen that taking the note as literature changes the status of the action, but we have yet to attempt redescribing the action to fit both levels of intention. Once we adapt this shift in focus, many so far latent features of the poem become significant evidence for my second reading. Take the puns in the title, for example. If we assume a self-conscious, reflective author, we expect the text to make use of these potential complexities. We expect the levels of concrete action to incorporate at least three qualitative implications of "This is *just* to say": *just* is a moral term, a term involving considerations of accuracy, and a term pointing to the causal, momentary, and minimal properties of the statement. These three conceptual contexts should function in correlation with two levels of the deictic "this," which refers to the poem itself, as well as to the speaker's act—that is, to both levels of action I have distinguished.

These levels of action complement one another, because a consistent series of analogies can be drawn between them: speaker and poet each integrate the three aspects of *just saying* in performances which appeal to qualitative understanding, and the speaker's sense of his auditor can be extended to serve as a figure for the cultural grounds enabling an audience to appreciate and to comprehend the implicit features of a linguistic performance. The implicit poet here projects the speaker's act as a sample expressing his artistic ability to render his complex grasp of the nature of apology and forgiveness through the structural patterns he creates. This structure suggests that if the speaker were to say much more, particularly if he were to offer explanations and justifications for his act, he would introduce rhetoric, and, thus, reduce the qualities of honesty, self-knowledge, and faith in the other's understanding which his note exhibits. If he were to say less, he would completely sacrifice his humanity to natural desires. But, by achieving the balance he does, he constructs a powerful example of the relationship between appeals to forgiveness and what I have been calling the grammatical grounds of human culture. For it is probably the case that one ought not be too explicit in asking for forgiveness, because too much argument, too much appeal to the facts (even if it does not then come to seem ironically symptomatic of someone's evading the real issues) makes a person appear to be justifying himself and to be projecting himself as deserving of forgiveness. But the essential feature of forgiveness is a response to another's appeal out of comprehension and compassion. We cannot be argued into forgiveness; indeed, we can only be tempted to withdraw our compassion from someone who thinks his words have power over such situations independently of the qualities of concern they exhibit and appeal to.

Williams' poem, then, can be seen as a direct presentation of the nature of qualities on two levels—it dramatizes the possibility of earning forgiveness by performing the qualities of one's self-knowledge and concern for another, and it evokes in metaliterary terms a general sense of how the justice of poetic discourse is its capacity to capture and make us reflect upon these qualities. This presentation places us, once again, between positivist science and textualism. If positivism were correct, the only adequate way back into the other's favor would be for the speaker to replace the plums or to rest with a formal emotive appeal, "Forgive me." For the textualist, neither gesture would suffice, for both would mask desire and implicate other gestures and meanings.[5]

Defining the nature of this middle ground seems to be the point of the second analogy—between the note's auditor (who, in a literary context is probably best seen as a wife) and a poetic audience. Words can achieve meaning through performance, because implicit meanings are grounded not in objects but in shared features of a life. These shared features, in turn, make it possible to understand how the three dimen-

5. The wittiest and brightest textualist ironic reversal of my case for the expressive quality of speech acts is Roland Barthes' discussion of offering condolences. See his *Critical Essays*, trans. Richard Howard (Evanston, Ill.: Northwestern University Press, 1972), pp. xvii *ff*. Barthes argues that one's real message is simply *condolences*, but a person would not be taken seriously unless he unexpressed the expressible and offered a rhetorical variation on the message. To appear sincere (echoing Sartre's ironies on the theme of sincerity) is to alter the sincere content of one's meaning. Yet, as Kathy Dyson pointed out to me, Barthes' ironies depend on equating the meaning with a possible referent for an emotive term. He ignores the fact that the important feature of the message is the effort one seems to have put into finding an interesting way of expressing his concern. In ignoring the qualitative aspects of performance as a feature of meaning, Barthes makes a typical textualist error that prevents this school from theoretically understanding its own achievements. For irony itself is an intensional term inviting qualitative analysis of a performance. We want to know not only that a statement is ironic, but how deft and precise the irony is. If we read Williams' poem ironically, as I shall speculate below, the ironic aspects of the speaker's treatment of his wife would still achieve meaning as a production of it and would be assessed in similar terms as an adequate response to a situation.

sions of *just saying* may be interrelated in dramatic terms and in terms of the aspects of literary history invoked by the author's metapoetic, self-reflective act. The title places this poem in contrast to Romantic and Modernist poetry's reliance on metaphor, myth, and elaborate (if deprecatingly self-conscious) rhetorical strategies. Williams' poem, after all, is only *just saying*, but because it appears free from rhetoric and forces the poet's creative energies into structurally measuring the experience, it may be the only way poetry can speak justly. Moreover, in denying that any particular subject matter or rhetorical form is necessary to create the effects of poetry, Williams really calls upon deeper expectations elicited by poetry that allow various forms of content to achieve their effects. Just as his speaker eschews conventional ways of explaining and justifying his deed, Williams' poetic act cuts beneath easy interpretations of the poetic to demand that we put into practice what is most characteristic in complete poetic responses—our ability to recognize structural patterns as measures of the quality of an act. Finally, the very bareness of the poem reinforces the figural role of the note's auditor by stressing the analogy between the speaker's and the poet's appeals: poetry, too, is an art of implicit meanings, whose justness cannot be argued for, but must be presented as perspicuous organization of aspects of experience which are intelligible and moving because they rely on a sense of culture as a realm of shared concerns.

The third reading might still be able to give an ironic twist to this authorial situation, perhaps by stressing the ambiguities and mistakes always possible among implicit meanings. However, now, in a literary context, there are two further sets of expectations which provide checks against these claims. First, there is Wittgenstein's reminder (in LA) that a crucial test of an interpretation is how it leads us to perform or stage the text. If we try reading "Forgive me" with a taunting or ambiguous tone, we must also read the final lines in a voice tinged with irony. If we do so, we lose the lovely and slightly pathetic sensuousness created by the contrast between this final memory and the speaker's sense of obligation. There are not many satisfying ways to take the plums as ultimate substitutes for a cultural order, however much we want to distrust language. It is this relation between words and world, in fact, which leads to the most convincing formal reason for rejecting both the alternative readings. Neither allows us to state fully, or to perform, the relationship between mimetic and authorial levels. The ironic view retains a relationship between the levels, but reduces it to an insistence that the *just saying* must call itself into question. There is no further bite in the stylistic opposition to other modern styles and no real point to linguistic economy (since all styles are equally masks for desire). The pure textualist view never allows the mimetic/authorial distinction in the first place, because it gives no place to the implicit purposes of any agent. In the more extreme versions of this position, agents and purposes are only problematic constructs within the linguistic play. Textualism gives us only possibilities for meaning, not deliberate choices, and thus leaves little place for qualities. We measure most qualities because a choice and selection takes place: one is not a hero, or a poet, or perhaps even much of a critic, if he only sees possibilities and does not relate them to the demands to act and to choose in a situation.

We have so far given some weight to a probable case for one intention in the text. Still, the case is not thoroughly convincing and has not yet addressed all the relevant evidence. We know that the poem has a biographical author, so that other forms of evidence about possible intentions to write specific kinds of poems and to work out certain ideas must be tested. These by themselves are not persuasive, but they clinch a case if they correlate with what seems the strongest reading of the details in accordance with literary procedures. In other words, every reading of the text as purposive in terms of internal evidence constructs a type image of the actual biographical agent, which must be correlated with available biographical information. It is always possible, of course, for an agent to depart from his typical practices. But, as is the case with most possibilities, the burden is on the interpreter to construct plausible reasons that can defeat the more probable assumptions. In the case of this poem, the proposed understanding of its understanding of the plain style perfectly fits Williams' general enterprise. His poetic stresses two basic features of that plain style, which are clearly aspects of the authorial act we have identified in the poem. The first is a distrust of abstract interpretation and a corresponding emphasis on the poem's relation to reality as a dramatic *measure* of the correspondence between act and problem situation. Second, *measure* is given a distinctly moral role, based on qualitative features of implicit understandings:

> Without conceptions of art the world might well be and has usually been a shambles of groups lawful enough but bent upon nothing else than mutual destruction. This comes of their partiality. They lack that which must draw them together—without destruction of their particular characteristics; the thing that will draw them together because in their disparateness it discovers an identity. No-

where will this be found save in the sensual, the real, world of the arts.

Every masterwork liberates while it draws the world closer in mutual understanding and tolerance. This is its aroma of the whole. (SE, 199)[6]

3. On moving from the meaning to the significance of the poem

Once the purposes of the acts are plausibly identified, both dramatic and authorial act become available for a wide variety of inquiries into significance. The significance claimed, however, will depend on the description remaining adequate. Williams' poem invites psychoanalytic inquiry into its dependence on oral images. Similarly, it could be a very useful document for feminist analysis of the easy ways in which male authors put on women the burden of understanding and admiring their subtleties. (I am painfully aware here that my own sex may show in my assumption that the author of the note is a male, but the very frame of values a feminist analysis would explore makes it probable that a male author gives that role to a male character, probable at least until evidence to the contrary is adduced.) Moreover, once the purpose is established, deconstruction may do its work—either showing how contrary purposes remain as a subtext or by showing how the note creates complex signifying possibilities which will lead it to be misunderstood and to initiate a chain of aggressive and half-apologetic acts. Finally, the procedures I employed to check the hypothesized intention against Williams' poetic may be reversed and aspects of the poem or its complete structure may be used in exemplary roles to speak of Williams' poetics.

For my general theoretical purposes, there remains one aspect of the poem's significance I cannot resist dwelling upon because it enables me

6. For Williams on measure, see his *Selected Essays* (New York: Random House, 1954), p. 283. For this quotation see the same text, p. 199. And compare also the following passages (pp. 71, 106, 111, 130, 197, 268) to the textualist version of Williams presented by Joseph Riddel, *The Inverted Bell* (Baton Rouge: Louisiana State University Press, 1974). It would be extremely difficult to construct a purposive biographical agent responsible for the descriptions Riddel offers and recognizable as the man who wrote the above passages. Riddel, of course, does not claim to be responsible for original intentions, or even for an objective text meaning, but, while this move saves our respect for his intelligence, it does little to help anyone know how to relate his critical arguments to any actual phenomena.

to summarize the basic implications of the first half of this book for
what follows. Indeed, I have already let perhaps too much of my case
slip into my description of the poem's action. I refer to the possibility of
using Williams' poem as an illustration of the epistemological and ontological status of expressive implicatures in a speech act. I spoke of
both Williams and the speaker as performing certain qualities of their
sensibilities. I consider the term *performance* reasonably innocuous in
my description, but now I want to put pressure on it in ways I have no
reason to believe Williams would accept.

Said, we recall, stated a version of textualist theory of meaning as the
production of meaning which never achieved meaning, because signifiers
displace and extend any secure base on which one could assert meaning
had been achieved. I have returned to his formula ironically, in making
my case for grammatical competence, but now I want to use Williams
to make an explicit defense of my counterclaim and of its implications.
The issue Said raises is one that Derrida and de Man claim lies at the
"center" of Austin's work.[7] If one grants the co-presence of performative
and constative forces, how does he separate the powers of rhetoric from
those of logic? If illocutionary forces and expressive implicatures help
establish the dimension by which an utterance is assessed, how do we
judge the performance without either coming under its will to power or
imposing our own wills?

The cutting edge of this dilemma is most apparent in discussions of
objectivity—both among commentators on Austin's theory of truth and
in the hermeneutic problems we have been considering.[8] A narrower
version of the problem, however, is more appropriate to Williams' poem.
It is a common feature of textualist arguments to pose the issue as: how
do we even locate a common object, when performative discourse displaces that object into a willed and irreducible chain of signifiers? (Again
Wittgenstein's case against simples and Derridean textualism appear
strange allies.) Williams' poem is an apt test case, for it portrays the
process of replacing an absent object, the plums, by a set of signifiers.

7. For de Man, see "Semiology and Rhetoric," *Diacritics* 3 (Fall, 1973):27-33,
and "Action and Identity in Nietzsche," *Yale French Studies*, no. 52 (1975):16–30.
See also Harold Bloom, a more radical Nietzschean, finally, than de Man, "Poetic
Crossing: Rhetoric and Psychology," *Georgia Review* 30 (1976):495–524.

8. For good commentaries on problems with Austin's concept of truth, see the
essays cited above from Fann, ed., and the concluding chapters of Strawson, *Logico-
Linguistic Papers* (London: Methuen, 1971). For a more elaborate treatment of
problems of cultural authority evaded by Said's use of the will to power, see the
version of this chapter in *Critical Inquiry*.

I want to show how our analysis of the poem relies on grounds not subject to this displacement or to a blanket use of the concept of will to power. The stakes here are very high, for, at least in figural terms, civilization itself is a supplement for man's failure to find or rest content with a life based on the presence of objects.

Only a question of significance would put Milton and Williams in the same context, but the pressures of textualist ironies produce just this conjunction and lead us to see how the conjunction addresses the most general aspects of the nature of civilized life. Milton is relevant here, because the theme of *Paradise Lost* is, in general terms, the same relationship as in Williams, between presence/absence and a civilized order. These themes in Milton have not been ignored by textualist scepticism. Here, for example, is Said explaining why we feel in reading Milton that we are witnessing " 'an ontology of nothingness' an infinite regress of truths permanently hidden beyond words" (281):

> ... the Truth is actually absent. Words stand for words which stand for other words, and so on. ... We may take comfort in Raphael's assertion that there had been a Word, a primal unity of Truth, to which such puzzles as "meaning" and "reference" are impertinent. Yet on the other hand we have only his *word* for it, not a thing certainly and not more than an assertion that depends on other words and an accepted sense-giving code for support.
>
> ... To read *Paradise Lost* is to be convinced, in Ruskin's phrase, of the idea of power: by its sheer duration and presence, and by its capacity for making sense despite the absence at its center, Milton's verse seems to have overpowered the void within his epic. Only when one questions the writing literally does the obvious disjunction between words and reality become troublesome. Words are endless analogies for one another, although the analogies are for the most part orderly ones. Outside the monotonous sequence of analogies, we presume, is a primeval Origin, but that, like Paradise, is lost forever. Language is one of the actions that succeeds the lost Origin: language *begins* after the Fall. (280)[9]

But if "language *begins* after the Fall," so does grammatical competence for understanding and appreciating the acts which replace a realm of sufficient objects. Said gives a lovely rendition of the loss of Paradise

---

9. The irony here is that Said is no Derridean. He wants to analyze actual cultural conflicts and changes, but his use of a problematic framework for understanding language undercuts the enterprise.

still yearned for by positivist theories of language—a realm where naming functions and laws will suffice. But Said's model of language has no way of recovering the reasoning that led Milton to take the Fall as a fortunate one. Said can explain the terrors Milton saw in a godless freedom and perpetual exile, but he cannot deal with what men could make of that freedom. What one does with freedom in Milton I take to be a performance of the self before God, in which the qualities of effort supplement the uncertainties of historical existence. By *performance* I mean the self-conscious presentation of self in an act so that its qualities might be assessed in relation to the situation and the laws or procedures appropriate to that situation. The Fall transformed existence from pastoral to drama, but it also gave men the self-consciousness to recognize that the *how* and the *what*, the performance and its object, are irreducible features of his existence. Milton could consider the loss of immediately present origins a fortunate one, because he recognized that once truth becomes difficult to find, men enter an arena where they can discover the joys of making and testing truths as a necessary communal enterprise. Milton also realized that what language loses in direct verifiability it gains in men's need to develop other modes for assessing utterances, modes that would require considerations of the quality of the actions and concerns being expressed by uses of language in specific situations. What men lose in control over nature they gain in their mutual knowledge of their loss and of the moral imperatives for truthfulness this knowledge entails. If a language of origins is impossible, its alternative can be expressive as well as ironic; if men no longer share the names of things, they can learn to share a sense of the quality of the actions they perform as they try to make an order of their middle realm, banished from Eden but potentially superior to the rhetorical world of Hell.

Williams does not have Milton's God, but neither does he have Milton's Eve. There is a considerable loss in rhetorical power, but there is a corresponding gain in recognizing the minimal conditions of human justice. In his poem, forgiveness is only possible if one refuses to name it as his right and refrains from supplementing acts by explanations. *Just sayings* are not just sayings but doings. What matters is what one can *perform himself as*, and that depends in large part on what he trusts his audience to be able to discern. This is ultimately why a radical use of the will to power, as in the work of Harold Bloom, would seem trivial even if it were completely defensible. A will to power that accepts no common terms for assessing the acts that embody it may enable one to live as *ubermensch*, but it gives no framework in which that living can be appreciated and understood. Power without a common interpretive language is mere physical freedom, while a power earned in communal terms is likely to choose to submit itself to flexible forms of those criteria, rather than to submit itself to the endless vacillations of lordship and bondage.

Without God, or even a very coherent culture, Williams must root the terms for mutual recognition of actions in frail domestic contexts. Yet the leap is not a large one to Wittgenstein's shared forms of life. Poems, like interpreters, reach out for significance, and Williams' domestic context ultimately becomes for him a possible metaphor for an "identity" that conquers "partiality" and a condition of "mutual understanding and tolerance" that attends upon imaginative measures of performance. These abstractions of Williams are portentous, almost Miltonic, burdens for so frail a vessel as "This is Just to Say" to carry. Yet it is precisely the minimal qualities of the poem which free Williams' claims from being easily absorbed into sloppy, liberal, humanistic typology. Mutual understanding is not an easy social ideal but a condition gained by careful and concerned performance of the self. A poem can achieve so much by so little explicit content just because its author recognizes how fully performance relies upon and elicits the implicit grounds of grammatical competence which serve as the foundation for achievable and achieved meanings.

TWO

Introduction: Applying a Hermeneutic Based on the Concept of Action to Problems in Literary Theory

Having worked out a general framework for describing meanings and actions, I shall now concentrate on showing how this framework can clarify some of the basic questions in literary theory. To speak of literary theory, one must define literature, or, more precisely, literariness, as a necessary step in locating the procedures relevant to any subsequent inquiry. In chapter five, I shall define a specific literary community fostered by a shared canon, and show how within this community one can identify three standard procedural assumptions that focus attention on the text as qualitative performance of authorial and dramatic actions. The next two chapters will use this notion of performance in substantially different ways. Chapter six will address the questions posed by contemporary indeterminacy theories. These theories at once derive from a failure to describe a defensible model of what might count as publicly assessable interpretations of a common constellation of phenomena, and clarify by contrast the significance of insisting on literary texts as actions. Here I concentrate on the conceptual status of performance as a principle of determinability. In chapter seven I show how it is possible to speak of performance as the principle for coherently naturalizing a text. Coherence is a function of text grammar, and action theory enables us to construct an idealized model of an intensional text grammar which illustrates the determinate ways by which we synthesize the elements of action in the work.

This section of the book involves a good deal of fairly narrow analysis and almost constant argument with a range of other critics. Questions of validity in interpretation require such careful groundlaying. And, more important, I think it is only when we have a clear sense of the issues involved in our disputes that we can develop a practical criticism fully aware of the complexities it should address. We could continue to follow traditions of a literary gentility hostile to theory, but these probably foster the alienation from other disciplines which they complain of, and for the most part they simply fail to account for the richness and depth of the texts they discuss. I insist on this polemical point because it is crucial that we not see concerns for the validity and grounds of interpretation as pedantic or excessively abstract matters. On the one hand such concern for the instruments of perception should lead to richer visions of the objects of criticism, and, on the other hand, the increased self-consciousness of such attention can make it easier to define the powers developed in the subject employing the critical instruments. This last hope informs the shape of my argument as I move from questions of how we can describe texts to those of how we can understand the value of our activities as readers and critics. In other words, I hope to show how careful analytic concerns for intentions and contexts is in the reader's best interest because of the experiences they prepare and powers they offer. Thus, in chapter eight I employ Nelson Goodman on exemplification in order to develop a concept of situated attitudes which can justify traditional claims that literary experience provides distinctive cognitive functions. This view of knowledge, in turn, allows us to indicate one way of understanding how all the interpreting humanities produce and preserve knowledge. In elaborating this point I also prepare for the discussion in my last chapter of how Hegel might be recovered as a model for the ideals of cultural identification and the ends of self-reflection as they are fostered by education into cultural grammars.

5

A Procedural Definition of Literature and the Concept of Performance

In dealing with "This is Just to Say," I simply assumed that I could extend my general semantic position in order to speak of a poem as a performance embodied in dramatic and authorial acts. There are now two ways I can try to support and generalize such an assumption so that it applies to all or most acts of reading literary texts. The first is simply pragmatic. For this the only grounds I need invoke are an audience's sense that such a perspective works or fits, that is, clarifies and connects representative properties one can locate in a wide variety of texts and enables one to relate them to values either proclaimed by the writers or demonstrated in the critical analysis. On this level of argument one hopes to be faithful to the authors who form a loose canon of masterpieces, but there is no need to claim that one is explaining their motives or understandings. The important point is to provide in defensible modern terms an account which preserves both the variety of textual features and the values they seem intended to serve. I can be content with this, but I want to use this chapter in order to push a more ambitious claim—that in fact it is hard to offer a treatment of a variety of literary texts *as* literature consistent with fundamental cultural assumptions unless one attends to texts as performances and treats them not simply as the products of acts but as the embodiment of qualities of acting. This entails providing a definition of literature or literariness. And attempts at definition involve very complex issues, with respect both to how one imagines it possible to check on definitions in the realm of cultural products and to the different ways texts can be construed. Yet the task seems hard to avoid. It is difficult, first of all, to have much confidence even in pragmatic claims unless they are tested against a patient analysis of the particular features theorists have defined as basic to literary experience. Moreover, by attempting a definition I can indicate the kind of work which can be accomplished by my Wittgensteinian perspective and arguments about grammatical competence. Because of my concern with showing the central place we give ideas of performance and the consequences deriving from that placement, I shall be especially interested in developing a theoretical attitude which can combat a variety of positions that leave *literariness* an essentially relative concept. Finally, I see an attempt at definition as provoking competing perspectives to specify the community of readers to which they are applicable and the range of texts or experiences they help to illuminate or make possible.

I shall attempt to argue for and work out what I call a procedural approach to definition. This approach is perhaps clearest in terms of what it is not. Thus I shall spend a good deal of time contrasting my position to two more traditional approaches—assertions of necessary and sufficient or essential properties of a text which characterize a work as literary, and the contrary claim that no perspicuous definition of so flexible a term as *literature* is possible.[1] If they fail the only alternative that

1. Both the essentialist and anti-essentialist positions can be subdivided into roughly humanist and ironic perspectives. The essentialist can claim, with the New Critics, that the specific properties of literary discourse give it a unique cognitive function, or he can follow Paul de Man's vision of the unique property of literature as its self-conscious fictiveness, which gives it only an indeterminate and ironic relationship to existential conditions. In the same way, one can hold an anti-essentialist position either by claiming that literature is central to all humane considerations because it transcends aesthetic categories, or by taking the currently popular position that literary texts are indeterminate because their meaning and value depend on the approaches we choose to take in interpreting them. If there is no essence, there is no privileged approach to meaning. For a thorough statement of this last position see Edward Wasiolek, "Wanted: a New Contextualism," *Critical Inquiry* 1 (1974):627–39, and his response to Lawrence Hyman's essentialist reaction to his essay in *Critical Inquiry* 2 (1975):386–91. In this chapter, I shall concentrate on the humanistic discussions of definition, because the next chapter will be devoted to indeterminacy theories. I should also point out that most critics using Wittgenstein on these questions stress family resemblances among properties and not relations within procedures. Nonetheless, since I worked out this chapter I have read several analyses similar to mine. John Ellis and Jonathan Culler, in particular, helped me sharpen some arguments, in Culler's case in a contrastive fashion, as shall be seen. Now I come across Mary Louise Pratt's very interesting *Toward a Speech Act Theory of Literary Discourse* (Bloomington: Indiana University Press, 1976), which I have not been able to incorporate into my text. There are many respects in which our arguments overlap—her *tellability* and *display* parallel my concern for qualitative performance, and we both stress the significance of speech

remains is a view of definition as capturing not the properties of objects but the expectations or terms of competence that are brought into play when someone uses a term like *literature* or one of its correlates. I assume, in other words, that the humanistic disciplines, and perhaps all cultural practices, share a strange form of circularity, in which we know what counts as a clear instance of the discipline or practice, even when we quarrel about general properties proposed as its defining condition. Within this circle, definition can only proceed by first locating agreements and then testing the effects they have on our treatment of objects. The nature of this circle becomes evident when we ask how a procedural definition may be assessed, since agreement is a vague, flexible concept highly relative to the community chosen. The first condition on such a definition is that it account for a representative set of cases. The limits of a definition are the range of texts or readerly attitudes it cannot handle. But, in making this criticism, one must remain within a circle, because he must be able to show what matters about what is left out. Then, as I suggest above, a judge of a definition might ask about the nature of the community whose agreement is defined. Here the relevant issue is to specify what one can and cannot handle because of the community with which one identifies. The procedures of a group of social realists will rarely allow one to read or value Wallace Stevens, and vice versa.

Understanding criteria for a procedural approach is unfortunately only a first step. Several difficult problems arise in working out a specific account. For example, I shall have to spend a good deal of time distinguishing my way of using Wittgenstein from other procedural approaches, like Jonathan Culler's, which reduce shared expectations to conventions

---

act theory as a way of explaining the power and intelligibility of contexts. Still, as the difference between *display* and *performance* indicates, I think that my attention to properties of action and my interest in a wider theoretical context than she considers allow me to offer a richer account of literary content. I mention all this because we overlap most completely on the subject of defining literariness in terms of competence. Nonetheless, there remain important differences in emphasis. Pratt has a concern I do not share with insisting on the continuity between literature and ordinary language. This leads her to rely largely on analogies with natural narrative and conversational implicature as her foundation for the constituents of literary competence. On the other hand, I am concerned primarily with linking the content, not the language, of literary experience to ordinary experience through the philosophy of action. This enables me to concentrate on features of literary competence arrived at by direct analysis of literary discourse and the act of reading in its complexity and ideality. If, however, one prefers clearly argued analogies from more "scientific" realms of analysis, Pratt's is a superb defense of procedural concerns.

at the mercy of the history of taste. I shall also have to be careful to limit my claims, because the more specific the community in question the more refined and useful will be the expectations one describes. For *community* and *canon* are correlative concepts which establish the field of practices where agreement can be sought. If one were to rely upon the most general sense of *literature* as written matter or as the opposite of nonfiction, there would be very little argument possible among users of the term which would be significant for the concerns of this book. Thus, I shall here treat *literature* as a normative term comprising the canon of works taken seriously by the community I described earlier as the judge I imagine for this work. Then I can specify the relevant community, whose expectation I want to describe, as one consisting primarily of writers and readers self-consciously using, and often revising, the course of a culture's literary history. There may be better ways to distinguish the most sensitive or most morally engaged readers, but the group I envision is one most likely to have a broad sense of the ways literary texts produce meanings and of terms available for assessing the value and basic uses of the kinds of works about which literary theories are usually proposed. Both this community and this canon have ill-defined boundaries, but this is, in fact, an important positive aspect of my model. First, it enables me to concentrate on the central core of texts and readers most likely to influence and appreciate the terms by which we judge more problematic cases. Moreover, it is precisely this flexibility that establishes several important differences between my view and other definitions. Because I identify readers in terms of a shared literary history, I create the possibility (to be developed later) of treating community and competence as categories not tied to specific empirical societies. We can imagine forms of agreement shared by readers who live in very different ideological circumstances. Similarly, by viewing community as something like Quine's network, I can acknowledge the continual tendency within literary history to attempt transcending or transgressing the overt standards of a canonized set of works and readers. Such efforts, like Tolstoy's, are indices of how deeply seated are certain expectations—both because the theorist feels he must take on an entire canon and society in order to authorize a change, and because such efforts usually become appropriated within the very canon they resist. This last condition is a function, I suspect, of the fact that the transgression itself is shaped by and matters primarily to those sharing a sense of responsibility for literary history; hence, it must participate within the discourse and forms of competence it opposes.

Finally, from these literary matters one can draw two philosophical morals to be applied to this chapter. We see how procedural definition cannot be held responsible to necessary and sufficient conditions, because the procedures themselves are often in question when one moves to marginal cases. It is not the procedure, but the relevance of the particulars, which one doubts. The significance of a question like "is *De Rerum Natura* literature" is precisely that we cannot easily answer it. The fact of our perennial questioning marks one of the limits of our clear procedures and indicates that most procedures learned as part of a cultural grammar will involve shadowy areas. The converse of this leads to my second moral. Attempts at the kind of definition I propose are likely to be quite tedious, because the more obvious what I say appears the more likely it is that I am describing precisely what we take for granted as central to the normal working of our literary competence.

Richard Ohmann provides a good starting point in what I consider the best essentialist definition of literature.[2] Instead of locating his necessary and sufficient condition in purely textual features, as did an earlier generation of theorists like Beardsley, Wellek, and Vivas, Ohmann concentrates on the nature of the speech acts represented in a text and largely shaping our sense of relevant properties. (My differences with his treatment of speech acts make his work an especially useful contrast here.) Literature, he argues, may be defined as a species of the genus *discourse* and may be differentiated from other members of that genus by the particular kind of linguistic act it presents:

2. Ohmann's basic essay in definition, which I shall abbreviate as DL in the text, is "Speech Acts and the Definition of Literature," *Philosophy and Rhetoric* 4 (1971):1–19. This essay is the best and most philosophical of a series of essays Ohmann has written on the ways of using the concept of illocutionary acts to discuss literature. I discuss the whole series at much greater length in a paper, "The Poem as Act," *Iowa Review* 6 (Summer, 1975):103–24. There I also develop more fully the concept of *keying*, mentioned later in this chapter. For an interesting discussion of Ohmann, plus a claim for one further defining feature when a work does not fit Ohmann's categories, see Monroe Beardsley's essay in *Literary Theory and Structure*. For the best treatment I know of analytically definable features in literature, see Beardsley, "Aesthetic Theory and Educational Theory," in Ralph Smith, ed., *Aesthetic Concepts in Education* (Urbana: University of Illinois Press, 1970), pp. 1–11. But even so good an attempt will not show that features like unity are a property of texts, rather than a result of the fact we are trained to relate the various elements into a coherent whole (even if the coherence is an image of incoherence) when we read a text labelled literary. I might point out the fact, so curious to one seeking analytic definitions, that there is nothing especially odd in our giving unified interpretations to unfinished poems like "Kubla Kahn" or the second "Hyperion."

A literary work is a discourse whose sentences lack the illocutionary forces that would normally attach to them. Its illocutionary force is mimetic. By "mimetic," I mean purportedly imitative. Specifically a literary work purportedly imitates (or reports) a series of speech acts, which in fact have no other existence. By doing so, it leads the reader to imagine a speaker, a situation, a set of ancillary events, and so on. Thus one might say that the literary work is mimetic in an extended sense also: it "imitates" not only an action (Aristotle's term), but an indefinitely detailed imaginary setting for its quasi-speech-acts. (DL, 14)

This definition, he claims, integrates the valid insights in other definitions of literature: (1) it shows how literature can be called mimetic—not because it copies experience, but because it directs us to recreate imaginatively a world in which the speech acts presented can be significant; (2) it shows how literature is distinct from referential discourse because it structures possible references to an imaginary world; (3) it shows that the emotive properties of literary discourse derive from the reader's need to place the illocutionary act in a full dramatic situation; (4) it shows how literature can be seen as autonomous play, since the speech acts lack their usual force and do not involve author or reader in real obligations and responsibilities; (5) finally, it shows why we tend to define literature as discourse where implicit meanings predominate, since the utterances are freed from normal illocutionary work, and, thus, invite us simply to contemplate the complexities of the experience presented.

The polar opposite of this position is powerfully expressed by E. D. Hirsch, whose recent *The Aims of Criticism* is a more or less silent antagonist for this whole chapter.[3] For Hirsch, the kinds of humane purposes Ohmann hopes to realize are blunted by the attempt to define literature: so long as literature is considered a special mode of discourse, we will be tempted not to take it as the full equal of more discursive and referential modes. Definitions tempt us to narrow our interpretive concerns to methods intrinsic to literary studies and lead finally to replacing moral with aesthetic judgments:

In one respect aesthetic criticism has been distortive. By claiming to be intrinsic to the nature of literature, it implies that the nature

3. Hirsch, *The Aims of Criticism* (Chicago: University of Chicago Press, 1976), abbreviated for future reference in the text as AC. The most relevant section of his book for this section is chapter eight. Hirsch, I should add, follows in his attack

of literature is aesthetic. But, in fact, literature has no independent essence, aesthetic or otherwise. It is an arbitrary classification of linguistic works which do not exhibit common distinctive traits, and which cannot be defined as an Aristotelian species. Aesthetic categories are intrinsic to aesthetic *inquiries*, but not to the nature of literary works. Exactly the same can be said of ethical and psychological categories, or any critical categories whatever. They are intrinsic only to the inquiries for which they are appropriate. (AC, 135)

I am not sure I completely understand this position, since I do not know exactly what *aesthetic* means to Hirsch. But I think I can distinguish a few basic claims on which his case rests. First, while Hirsch grants that the concept of literature is a valid one (AC, 133), he also insists that the term *literature* only came to have its present aesthetic sense in the nineteenth century, and is, thus, not a privileged concept for analyzing the meaning and value of earlier texts. Second, he argues that essential definitions of the term confuse the different kinds of inquiries required to establish meaning and value—neither of which depends necessarily on aesthetic categories. For Hirsch, hermeneutics is only valid as a general rather than a specific or local science; hence there are no privileged procedures for determining different kinds of meanings. Meaning is a property of all intelligible discourse and can be established only in terms of general rules (AC, 44). The single general rule he adopts is the scientific model of verifying hypotheses in probabilistic terms, and he vacillates on what the hypotheses are responsible to. At times he follows *Validity in Interpretation* and argues that the concept of meaning requires inquiry into authorial intentions (chapter six), and at other times he argues that the criteria for meaning depend on the

---

on essential definitions a line of reasoning developed from Wittgenstein, primarily by Morris Weitz in "The Role of Theory in Aesthetics," *JAAC* 15 (1966):27–35, and later writings. And it is because I share Professor Hirsch's values and admire his attacks on literary provincialism and indeterminacy theories that I feel his presence so much in this chapter. Yet, to put these values on firm ground, we need a different philosophical approach and fuller attention to Wittgenstein than we find in Weitz's reliance on the concept of family resemblances. For a good statement of the limits of Weitz's position, which I think supports my procedural approach even though that is by no means the author's intention, see Maurice Mandelbaum, "Family Resemblances and Generalizations Concerning the Arts," in Weitz, ed., *Problems in Aesthetics.* Mandelbaum argues that the defining features of art may be "relational attributes" rather than "specific, directly exhibited" features, and opts for the relevant attribute as the intention to make a work of art, a suggestion I will later develop in my own way.

inquirer's goals—with ethical considerations the only ones capable of defining a hierarchy among goals (chapter five). Value inquiries are even more clearly not intrinsic to putative essences, because values are not determined by the status of objects, but, rather, by the instrumental goals of an interpreter. Criteria for value are established by the questions one asks, and not by an Aristotelian vision of purposes intrinsic in the nature of objects. There are, he admits, aesthetic values intrinsic to aesthetic works, but any claim for the humane values of literature must transcend aesthetic inquiry and pose more general instrumental considerations. So the task of the critic is to maintain a balanced attitude—resisting both the narrow specialization of pure aesthetic inquiry and the easy allure of propaganda and ideology that stems from too readily ignoring the specific aesthetic goals of a work (AC, 138–41).

Finally, Hirsch makes a powerful case for the one feature of an utterance that can privilege claims for intrinsic meaning. Intentions determine intrinsic categories for understanding meaning, because only intentions tell us what kind of object a speech act is. Intentions, we might say, are the only approximation of essence one can establish for objects that are not natural but are created by free agents.[4] From this it follows necessarily that no external or objective category can claim to be privileged, unless its definition can account for all possible authorial intentions within its domain:

> Because an aesthetic approach inheres in the very concept of literature, it appears to be indeed intrinsic. The difficulty is that the concept of literature is not itself a privileged category for the works it embraces. Since literary works were not always conceived under a predominantly aesthetic mode, we cannot assume that stress on aesthetic categories corresponds to the essential nature of individual literary works. Other categories, including instrumental, ethical, and religious ones, may be more correspondent to their individual emphases and intentions.... Whether the inquiry is specially appro-

4. This claim that intentions serve as essences on a human, nonnatural level is never explicit in Hirsch, but it is close to the surface in the writings of Grice, which are very influential on Hirsch. We should also note that Hirsch rightly insists that intentions cannot determine values, as they do meanings, because intentions will not suffice to make something valuable. Here, intentions themselves must be assessed in instrumental terms. Yet I see no way that these assessments can be separated from procedural expectations about the nature of the instrument. My real differences from Hirsch may stem from the tendency in Wittgenstein to treat both meanings and values as instrumental, and, hence, to need procedural criteria for dealing with both kinds of questions.

priate to the nature of a work depends, ad hoc, on the individual case. (AC, 134; cf. 117)

Once we set these views of definition against one another, the question seems to turn on two basic issues: in what way could it possibly make sense to speak of privileged categories for interpreting literary texts, and what possible grounds could establish the force leading us to acknowledge such privileges? We can begin to answer both questions by observing two types of concrete cases which neither theory handles very well. Both reveal forms of privilege, but these are neither *aesthetic* nor dependent on properties of the object or speech act represented. First, if something's being literature were a consequence of intrinsic properties, like an object's being red, we could not explain a phenomenon unique to literature among the humanities—that certain texts which originally had as their primary purpose a nonliterary function came to be taken as essentially literary works in the course of time. A given text may become material for a historian, but it does not become a work of history the way the *Bible, The Decline and Fall of the Roman Empire,* and *The Laws of Ecclesiastical Polity* become works of literature.

The second type of case extends the first by making clear the complexity in ideas of intentions and privileged contexts when we are dealing with such institutional procedures. On the one hand, we tend with literary texts to acknowledge authors' intentions, yet still to give them a different force than the author desired. For example, many contemporary poets, like Allen Ginsberg, seek to break through the idea of persona and present their work as the author's direct personal speech addressing an audience. Yet we read such poems less as personal speech than as performance, to be understood and assessed in terms of the intellectual, moral, and emotional qualities they exhibit in response to what we take as a dramatic situation. We immediately generalize the situation: the poem becomes not simply a man speaking to others, but an image of how one can respond to a situation that is typical of an age, a general human problem, and a particular style of thinking and feeling. In a similar way, surrealist writers desire to break down all conventions, to present the immediacy of experience before language structures it, yet we take surrealist texts primarily as images of a way to organize experience under the influence of certain beliefs and attitudes. We can summarize this second observation by noting that literary attempts to deny the conventions of literature may slightly change the way we read, but we eventually transform these dreams of transforming consciousness into alternative structures of experience, to be treated with the same aesthetic attitude and roughly the same procedures we employ in reading what they attack. T. S. Eliot was right about the principles, if not the contents, of the workings of literary tradition. We might explain this phenomenon by recognizing the need in most literary cases to distinguish two kinds of intentions, which may come into tension with each other. There is the publicly determinate intention to write a work of literature, which involves a specific set of expectations, and the particular intention to offer a certain kind of linguistic experience or message. Contrary to Hirsch, the author may not always be able to control both, either because audience expectations will not allow a consistent union of the two or because, over time, only the larger public intention provides a sufficient context for establishing what counts as the specific speech act. We could not know Vergil's meaning unless we assumed that he intended us to locate patterns of images, character contrasts, and the manipulation of other literary texts.

Ohmann, we must conclude, is right in his sense that taking something as literary can alter our view of the speech acts involved. But he seems to have the grounds wrong. For his commitment to defining literature as a "natural class" of objects with "directly exhibited features of works" entails locating the force in the object. Yet all works are not purported illocutions because of properties they possess; rather, works become purported illocutions once they are taken as literary and adapted to a tradition.[5] In many cases we cannot view the act intended by the agent as a purported illocution. Ginsberg's and Breton's poems are offered as direct addresses, and writers like Tolstoy or Milton have clear perlocutionary purposes. Moreover, the idea of imitating speech acts gets fuzzy in cases like these. Many lyrics offer themselves as direct meditations or even, as with "The Complaint of Chaucer to His Purse," as direct address to a reader, although clearly also as a performance. Ginsberg does not intend to imitate Ginsberg (although the hall of self-reflective mirrors created by literary expectations may make a writer begin to feel that this is exactly what he does). And meditative poems or dream visions are hard to take as speech acts at all, if we concentrate on textual features, because as acts they do not address an audience or bring a social context to bear.

There is a simple way to square Ohmann with these observations, a

---

5. The clearest indication of the limits of Ohmann's position is his insistence that *In Cold Blood* is not literature, because it claims to describe a real world rather than to imitate the act of description. See DL, 15.

way he adumbrates in one instance where he criticizes other essentialist theories for taking as objective properties facts which we recognize as relevant only because they are consequences of our already "knowing the texts to be literary works" (DL, 6, 8). What we posit as significant properties of literary objects depends less on the conditions met by the object than on the methods of projection we bring to the object when we take it as literary. Therefore, if a perspicuous definition is possible,[6] it will depend on specifying the expectations about literariness held by a community of competent readers. We are investigating a term we know how to use, and, indeed, one of which we assume that most creators of literary objects knew the consequences when they decided to offer us works as literary. This case has significant parallels to institutional rules. What objects like pawns or even promises are depends upon cultural expectations, and once the expectations are invoked there is little room for private intentions to alter the properties that will be attributed to the object. Yet we must also be careful to notice the differences from these rules. The more complex the expectations, and the more they are involved in historical disciplines which continually reinterpret themselves, the greater is the likelihood for the set of expectations to become extremely complex, often with several levels that partially conflict with one another. This is one reason we find literary theory so perplexing. Because of this interplay among levels and the variety of concerns they produce, it is difficult to determine whether we can acknowledge the differences fundamental to our literary and social histories, and still locate some guiding expectations on which we can agree.

2. *How we identify texts as literary*

Before we begin discussing questions of privilege we need to see the basis on which one can say that we know texts to be literary, even without necessary and sufficient conditions, and, thus, take up toward them

6. For a good contrary example of posing the questions in a way that admits of no solution, consider Hirsch's statement: the "philosophical difficulty" of claiming a special ontological status for literature "shows itself on a practical level in the contortions that are required when you attempt to accommodate all the important traits and values of literature within purely literary categories" (AC, 137). The "all" here makes demands even the staunchest essentialist would not try to meet. He would be content with typical necessary categories which can be filled in various ways. And the procedural theorist is more abstract: his categories can admit endless variety, because he does not say what the object is but how we look at whatever is there.

attitudes shaped by our learning the relevant grammar for literary methods of projection. My answer is almost embarrassingly obvious, but it has substantial consequences. We recognize literariness from a variety of signs. In contemporary writing these signs consist of features like the presence of verse or allegory or simply a title, or of social attributes that could be statements by the author, or acceptance for discussion by what Arthur Danto has called the "art world." [7] These signs or claims are enough to get a text treated as literary, but they do not insure that it will prove interesting when the conventions of literary analysis are applied. Similar conditions hold for texts of other periods, although here we must add the force of tradition. In problematic cases, like novels which pretend to be histories, we may need to rely on tradition, but often the text itself will invoke literary conventions by dramatizing a self-conscious narrator who provides few facts or scholarly arguments, or by concentrating on events and personages of little historical importance. Finally, there are semantic keys. Imagine a text that begins, "The present King of France is wise." Anyone who knows something about France will immediately take the text as a parody of philosophy or as a work of fiction, because he recognizes (although he may not be able to explain) that any information which will develop this statement must be provided by an imaginary world and set of internal thematic structures.[8]

I take all these signs as illocutionary operators which invoke methods of projection. They are functions, however, not necessarily of the speech act represented in a work, but of what Marcia Eaton calls the translocutionary act of an authorial agent often only implicit in the work. (When we take texts like the *Bible* as literary, or when we take a literary attitude toward Ginsberg's intentions, we take the further step of projecting a translocutionary author different from the intentions in the text, because the external context has the power to dictate operations which enable us to remain consistent with literary expectations.) I speak here of illo-

---

7. George Dickie, *Aesthetics: An Introduction* (Indianapolis: Bobbs-Merrill, 1971), has argued that it is a sufficient procedural definition of *art* to say a work of art is an artifact upon which some representative of the "art world" confers the status of candidate for aesthetic appreciation. But, as Dickie's many critics point out, this definition tells us only what a candidate for aesthetic status is, and does not clarify what procedures it must satisfy if the identification is to be generally accepted and fruitful.

8. Since procedural expectations are only probable, not definitive, the interpreter might, of course, be wrong. Subsequent sentences may show that the opening was a dramatic introduction to a study of seventeenth-century France; but the context would soon make the proper procedure for assessing the work clear.

cutionary operators rather than illocutionary acts because when we push the idea of methods of projection we see complications not ordinarily considered in speech act theory.[9] Some conventional illocutions bear their own signs of the procedures they invoke, for example, the christening of a ship. Others depend for the proper uptake on our recognizing the general discursive practice and institutional features implicit in them and constituting the context. In this type of case, we only know that x counts as y when we understand a context not immediate in the assertion—for example, in the speech of a stage manager within a play, or in the force of terms within most professional groups. I view the illocutionary operators of literariness as signs invoking such a general practice. They serve as semantic forms of a process common on all levels of animal life which Erving Goffman has called *keying*.[10] Keying is the projection of signs which alter our primary frames for organizing experiences and modify the chain of responses normally expected to an act. When animals bite one another, the ordinary frame for this action would call for violent response, but they can give certain signs which redefine the action as play behavior. The response, we might note, is equally typical

9. For attacks on the idea that one can use a concept of conventional illocutions to identify texts as literature, see Margolis, "Literature and Speech Acts," and John Searle, "The Logical Status of Fictional Discourse," *New Literary History* 6 (1975):319–32. Both, however, assume very strict criteria for using the notion of illocutionary force. Searle, for example, claims that the illocutionary act performed is a function of the meaning of the sentence, while utterances in poems do not claim they are poems. Yet he cites games like charades as examples of fictions, and calls literary texts *pretended assertions*, both of which alter illocutionary status without literally referring to the altered status. I take it that something very much like illocutionary force defines the status of procedures in a marked or *keyed* use of language, even if one need not either use the cumbrous and problematic idea of the text as imitation speech act or rely on Pratt's analogies, which Margolis attacks. For literary counterarguments to Searle, see van Dijk, AAD, 285, and notice that Austin seems to support the view of literary signs as creating different expectations from ordinary discourse (HTD, 75). For a good general philosophical case against Searle on explicit performatives, the grounds for his claims about fiction, see Dennis Stampe, "Meaning and Truth in the Theory of Speech Acts," in Cole and Morgan, eds., pp. 3–15. Finally, I borrow the concept of translocutionary acts from Marcia Eaton, "Art, Artifacts, and Intentions," *American Philosophical Quarterly* I (1964): 167–69.

10. Erving Goffman, *Frame Analysis* (New York: Harper Colophon Books, 1974), especially the third chapter. I develop the parallels between Goffman and literary theory, primarily in relation to questions of imitation and of reference, in my essay "The Poem as Act," cited above. There I try to show that keying applies to literature in a way it does not to philosophy because literature normally presents concrete situations and alters response, while philosophy normally presents reflections on concrete situations for which philosophical procedures are the immediately relevant ones.

in the latter case, but involves restraining more "natural" or immediate responses. Goffman uses the concept primarily to define complex levels of keying and recognizing keys in human interactions, but it can also be enormously useful for discussing imitation. Keying explains how actions can retain their concrete qualities and yet, if the relevant conventional signs are evoked, need not lead to typical forms of practical behavior. In effect, Goffman makes the principles of theater, with this blend of apparent concreteness and of internal structures controlling interpretation, a fundamental metaphor for the way we can project acts in contexts.

We need not accept Ohmann's rather narrow model of imitation, as essentially lines of projection between the dramatic speech act whose illocutionary force is suspended and the social act which would take place under ordinary circumstances. Texts do not imitate because of representational properties they possess, but because readers select some properties as ways of understanding how the work can relate to ordinary experience. We can acknowledge that some literary speech acts, like Ginsberg's, are not intended as imitations, while still imposing on them reflective attitudes, in which we treat them as something like imitations to be reflected upon. Similarly, we can transform meditative acts, which need not be represented as speech acts, into structures for reflection which embody the translocutionary acts of an implied author. Both these observations have important evaluative consequences, because they enable us to prepare more flexible and complex forms of situating texts in possible existential contexts than does Ohmann's treatment of imitation as a property of texts. Ohmann's position leads him to argue in other essays that a text's claim to be representative depends upon the readers' identification with the represented actions and judgment of their validity as possible ways of acting. This leads him to defend the position that women students could not recreate a character like Lady Chatterly "without self betrayals" of their own hard-won female identities.[11] A concern for essential properties of texts leaves only pictorial lines of projection between mimetic acts and the world readers bring to the work. But once we see procedure as the governing principle for our treatment of works as imitations, we are free to consider as part of the representative force of a text the relation it projects between authorial desires and the mimetic acts. This, in turn, complicates the range of identifications possible and the blend of identification and judgment,

11. See his "Literature as Act," in Seymour Chatman, ed., *Approaches to Poetics* (New York: Columbia University Press, 1973), p. 106.

which can itself be an object of reflection. Lady Chatterly exists on many levels, best integrated as elements of Lawrence's attempt to project a female figure balancing civility and passion. Her "truth," as we shall see, is not her adequacy as a model for women, but her place in a more comprehensive reading process that reflects upon the model she offers of complex psychosexual tensions, existing at once within a society and as expressions of an authorial effort to define and make sense of social contradictions.

3. *What procedures one can take as privileged: an argument with Hirsch*

I can claim to have demonstrated so far only that it makes sense to view certain recurrent features of how we read literary texts as functions of grammatical procedures, rather than as essential properties of the object. I have yet to show in what ways these procedures are privileged or how they enable us to ground the idea of texts as performances emphasizing qualitative features of actions. In order to do this, I shall have to chart a fairly intricate triangulation. By taking on Hirsch I hope to show the possibility of treating certain features of literary experience as privileged. In my view, Hirsch makes three fundamental mistakes (which parallel his oversimplifying the levels needed to speak about intentions): he ignores the range of terms which might produce a family resemblance sense of literariness; he does not see that a general hermeneutics can include principles specific to given disciplines; and he makes a problematic assumption that if any traits are privileged as literary they must be *aesthetic* and not be capable of serving also as means for focussing a text's moral and philosophical engagements. Yet, if one is to refute Hirsch's claims, one cannot rest easily within the relativistic, convention-bound view of procedures developed by Jonathan Culler. Evading Hirsch's criticisms requires a procedural approach to establish in contrast basic principles within procedures which enable us to treat an aesthetic, contemplative, and pattern-oriented attitude as a means for deepening our full involvement in the text's content. This entails locating levels of procedure that lead us to naturalize texts as performances, regardless of the specific conventions of literariness they invoke.

My first and most general criticism of Hirsch leads immediately to arguing that performance and a concern for qualities are constant concerns within Western literary history. Hirsch does not seem to ask what evidence it would take to support the claim that there are not basic and recurrent attitudes and conventions within Western culture for constituting the way we take a text offered in a form we recognize as literary. Can we really be sure that religious poets, like Milton and Herbert, did not intend their works to be *aesthetic* versions of religious experience? They certainly went to a great deal of trouble if this were not the case. Even if the term *literature* had no aesthetic implications before the nineteenth century, there might well have been other terms or assumptions leading authors to imagine that readers would exercise careful attention to internal principles of organization. To make good on his claim, Hirsch would have to examine all the related terms—*poem, romance, story,* even *essay*—in order to show no common aesthetic assumptions. This is, on the face of it, unlikely, at least for poetry, because, as Thomas McFarland makes clear, the term *poetry* was a widely used one to describe utterances that invoked aesthetic (but not necessarily formal) responses. If we go back to classical defenses of poetry, we find Sidney quite explicit on the conventions that fictional discourse evokes, and we see Milton, the poet who would be least satisfied with a sheerly aesthetic response, nonetheless defining the poetic function with special emphasis on displaying the generalizable qualities of an experience seen as a process: "Whatsoever in religion is holy and sublime, in virtue amiable and grave, whatsoever hath passion or admiration in all the changes of that which is called fortune, or the wily subtleties and reflexes of man's thought, all these things with a solid and treatable smoothness to paint and describe." [12]

While this last consideration probably suffices to refute Hirsch's basic claim, it does not allow us to understand fully either the significance of Hirsch's thinking or the problems that I want to show provide support for my position. For this we need to consider his specific arguments. First, Hirsch is suspicious of appeals to special procedures, because he is committed to a general hermeneutics proposing a simple model of validity for all interpretations. It seems to me, however, that there is no contradiction between having a general model for hermeneutics—say, Popper's idea of falsification—and acknowledging that it can be applied to a variety of modes for organizing semantic properties or emphasizing specific features of a discourse. The crucial issue is simply whether those

12. MacFarland, "The Originality Paradox," *New Literary History* 5 (1974):447–76. For Sidney, "The Defense of Poesie," in Allan H. Gilbert, ed., *Literary Criticism: Plato to Dryden,* pp. 409–17, 439–40, and for Milton, see the selection from *The Reason of Church Government* in Gilbert, ed., p. 590.

using a procedure agree on how falsification might be attempted. In fact, if we recall my discussion of how a psychoanalyst and a lawyer would concentrate on different aspects of speech acts and contexts, it is hard to accept any general hermeneutic that does not acknowledge different methods of projection. We find ourselves repeating Wittgenstein's quarrel with those universally invoking the authority of philosophical logic, now in terms of specifying attitudes writers rely upon in their readers.

Jonathan Culler can now make a timely entrance on the scene, because he offers a powerful example of the differences between the general competence to understand utterances and the grasp of procedures required to appreciate a poem.[13] A simple understanding of ordinary language suffices for grasping the verbal meaning of a work like Blake's "Sunflower." Yet we only comprehend the work of a poem if we have learned to apply what Culler calls conventions but I prefer to treat as procedures for reading. These *conventions* lead us to naturalize the utterance as expressing a representative attitude toward a basic human problem, to relate the images to poetic traditions, to seek ways of making the metaphors cohere as supplementing the attitude, and to project hypotheses which will allow us to see the work as a coherently unified structure of patterns.

The appearance of Culler will not make my imaginary Hirsch retire. Some of the formulations, in fact, would elicit passionate rejoinders. Hirsch could seize upon Culler's repeating the New Critical bias of making poetry paradigmatic for literature (in his book Culler also analyzes the novel, a fact I ignore here for my little drama). More important, Hirsch would feel reinforced in what I assume is his fundamental motive for trying out so radical an alternative—namely, a conviction that claims, like Culler's, to aesthetic ideas of unity impose a quite arbitrary and misleading orientation for readers. Do we really care, or does it really matter, whether *Hamlet* is unified? There are far more interesting and compelling questions to ask about the text. Imagine someone not teaching *Hamlet* because it is not unified. Yet somewhat less dramatic versions of this error are everywhere in the history of criticism—from the neo-Classical unities posited as essential features of great works, to

13. Culler, *Structuralist Poetics*, abbreviated in the text as SP. I depend here on his brief discussion, p. 115. Later in the book he gives a fuller description of these conventions, pp. 164–88. For parallel arguments on the role of conventional procedures in constituting literary objects and the meaning of literature, see Ralph Rader, "Fact, Fiction . . ." and John Ellis, *Theory of Literary Criticism*, chapter two. And for the same arguments in general aesthetics see Sparshott's *Structure of Aesthetics* and the essays by Dickie and Tilghman cited above.

modern failures to find terms for reading or evaluating poems like *The Seasons,* or *Cowper's Task,* or the novels James called "loose, baggy monsters." The saddest irony here is that criticism becomes more embarrassing when it does find organic or thematic unity in such works. In Hirsch's view, if these are the wages of definition, why bother?

Passionate responses to critical temptations, however, ought not lead to passionate oversimplification of the conceptual possibilities within a system. While concern for conventions perennially produces foolishly literal demands, it also perennially produces figures like Samuel Johnson, who see through these mistakes to deeper levels where our literary expectations can, in fact, help us resist such errors and recover the significance of texts. There is no need to take literary procedures as dictating a specific kind of unity. That, I shall argue against Culler, is to have no principles for distinguishing between the history of taste and enduring, underlying expectations about literary experience. Milton says nothing about unity, and very few major writers or critics, even in the post-Romantic era, base their evaluative standards on organic unity per se or, for that matter, on any essentially aesthetic properties. Yet if I have fairly characterized Hirsch's position, there remain two basic ways of showing how it ignores the relation between procedures and the deeper assumptions I am attributing to great writers and critics. Both are, again, questions of levels—one involving how *conventions,* like those positing a concern for unity, work, and the second consisting of his taking aesthetic and other more content-oriented views as necessarily at odds.

If a case for intrinsic properties necessarily constrained one to taking judgments about unity as absolute indices of value and allowed no more comprehensive sense of a text, Hirsch would clearly be correct. But it is hard even to imagine his finding such a programmatic opponent, especially if one makes the further demand of finding significant writers accepting the position. In most theory and criticism we take seriously, the search for unity is heuristic, not prescriptive. We pursue expectations for unity because we want to relate assertions and qualities, and we are ready to allow any simple sense of unity to be frustrated if we can understand why the writer manipulates our expectations. Unity is not an absolute property, not a state a text achieves, but a condition under which we search for meaning. Thus, whether Hamlet is *unified* is not an important question, but that it rewards a search for internal patterns is indeed crucial to our sense of the depth of the play. If, in fact, we turn to critics like Coleridge, who can most easily be criticized for making a fetish of aesthetic unity, we find them attributing such importance less to an aesthetic state than to a neo-Kantian attitude toward unity as signifying active and creative powers of a mind capable of transforming external determinants. Similarly, writers like Wilde interpret aesthetic properties as ends-in-themselves, only to proceed by interpreting ends-in-themselves as signs that one can cultivate a spirit of disinterested nobility, in which style is dignified because it refuses to be bound by utilitarian categories.

If even the most *aesthetic* writers qualify their cases for *intrinsic* aesthetic properties, it is not difficult to imagine there being much less conflict between the intrinsic and the instrumental than Hirsch will admit. It seems obvious, in fact, that it is only if one can make a fairly strong case for connecting intrinsic aesthetic means to larger cognitive ends that one can defend the relevance of literary texts for the larger concerns of which Hirsch wants to remind us. Hirsch harkens back to a time when literary texts could be significant objects of a general criticism devoted to the set of questions around the idea of describing the good or proper like for man. I think that this is still a valid dream but it can no longer be achieved simply within a general criticism because truth criteria have changed, the blend of Platonic ideals and ideals of description at the core of most mimetic theory is now all too apparent, and society no longer grants literature any authority as an arbiter of "truth." Now to give literature currency we must argue for its relevance by making explicit both the properties it possesses and their way of providing forms of wisdom. In order to do this I shall argue that a purely formal sense of the aesthetic is too narrow a reading of what might be privileged as intrinsic within literary procedures. But the primary issue is showing that even if we accept Hirsch's ideals there are no clear reasons why we cannot employ a means-end model and there are strong positive reasons for doing so. The intrinsic after all is not necessarily self-enclosed; it can serve any number of purposes from titillation to edification.

If we concentrate only on the cognitive value of texts, we can still ask what functions could not be served by also acknowledging some structures of internal relations as a privileged principle for constructing literary meanings. If the internal patterns deepened one's sense of the drama of a text or ideas or brought out the qualities of an action, one could continue to read literary texts as serving a range of speculative functions. They could be seen as presenting, provoking, or clarifying ideas, as embodying examples of how ideas can be held, or as projecting possible consequences of ideas and attitudes. (These functions will be the sub-

ject of my penultimate chapter.) The one claim we could not comfortably make about literary texts is that they could enter a truth-functional
calculus or make arguments that were directly testable. The criteria of
such purely referential inquiries demand extensional terms placed within
clearly circumscribed argument functions, and these are not compatible
with the endless qualifications of internal self-referencing and the imaginative sense of possible concrete universality required to appreciate
dramatic contexts as representative. It is, of course, possible to treat
literary texts as particular or conceptual descriptions of states of affairs.
In fact some writers clearly intend their texts to be taken as assertions.
But, as we have seen, literary procedures tend to alter the way we treat
these intentions so that the intention itself becomes part of what we reflect on when we reflect on the text. Once this occurs, we must recognize
the radical differences Russell articulated between the process of clarifying descriptive claims, which entails eliminating all self-referring functions from one's calculus, and the process of recognizing qualities as
properties of the self-consciousness embedded in situations. Hirsch is
perhaps more accurate than he wants to be in combining a suspicion of
internal relations with a desire to see literary texts as quasi-propositional.
We can read this way, but I doubt that such an approach is faithful
either to the most valuable properties of literary experience or to the
challenge they create as contrasts to the narrow exclusiveness inherent in
the kinds of propositions about human behavior which are compatible
with contemporary criteria for defensible truth claims. Even Hirsch's
own claims, both as descriptions of how literature refers and as assertions of what critics should do, require ideas of truth and assessment
different from those countenanced by modern analytic philosophy. But
his way of arguing constitutes a significant attitude which exemplifies a
possible stance toward important existential matters. Hirsch's claims
depend less on what texts are than on a cultural tradition whose values
he attempts to extend to contemporary concerns.

4. The Status of Literary Expectations: A Case for Implicit Purposes within Culler's Semantic Conventions

It should be obvious that one can at least imagine a view of intrinsic
properties emphasized by procedural expectations about literature without reducing that case to formalist arguments about the primacy of
aesthetic features and purely aesthetic response. In order to give sub-

stance to this assertion, however, I must show that an account of expectations based on procedures need not stop with the kind of conventions that encourage formalist theory. Procedural definitions of literature that stop with conventions tend to produce the splits Hirsch complains of and they certainly lack the explanatory power to defend cognitive roles for aesthetic devices. Moreover, if I can show that we can learn from cultural procedures to approach texts with expectations about the purposes they will serve, my discussion has significant ramifications for discussing issues like canon formation where we must distinguish between cultural criteria based on "formal" literariness and those determining discussions of the values we expect the content of the text to serve, whatever its formal structure. This concern for levels is possible within my perspective because I make the object of investigation not texts, whose intrinsic properties can easily be treated formalistically, but actions, a category where intrinsic relations involve purposes and qualities and thus allow us to investigate audience expectations that involve matters of content and value. My case can best be clarified if I contrast it to the idea of procedural definition I take as basic to Culler's work—that expectations about literature are primarily matters of semantic conventions which govern how we read a specific text as literarily structured. Thus, I shall try to show that if the conventions Culler emphasizes like those of seeking unity are heuristic means, it seems plausible to build an argument for distinguishing between conventions tied to historical considerations of genre, style, or ideology and more general grammatical expectations that can be said to govern our critical judgments of period styles. I do not want to claim that these expectations are *necessary*, only that they persist through a good deal of Western literary culture, so that it is now almost impossible to imagine suspending them, because so many other ideas would have to be changed. My arguments will parallel the one I followed in distinguishing between fixed conventions and the more stable, yet flexible, idea of a grammatical competence enabling us to judge and manipulate conventions. In both cases, only by envisioning levels of procedures can we fully preserve differences between human uses of language and those acts performed by computers, whose efficiency is matched by an uncritical docility for which all theory is irrelevant.

Culler's case is essentially textualist and structuralist. Conventions control expectations because they function as structures providing operations for processing semantic information. He distinguishes sharply between the laws for generating meanings, which are systematic and diacritical, and the varying content they organize: "The task of a structuralist poetics ... would be to make explicit the underlying system which makes literary effects possible" (SP, 118). Culler often insists that structuralist theory grows too abstract and unverifiable when it poses no empirical checks for showing that the system actually organizes behavior. But, in the case of reading, he is confident that the systems he proposes can be checked against what competent readers do. However, he must then define competence strictly in terms of decoding operations deriving from structural systems. Therefore he reduces grammar to formal rules, in effect denying the basic distinctions I take from Wittgenstein in my second chapter. The consequences of his so defining competence are enormous, because, once the rules of reading can be distinguished from content, it becomes possible to make decoding operations themselves the object of literary criticism. We can "cease thinking that our goal is to specify the properties of objects in a corpus and concentrate instead on the task of formulating the internalized competence which enables objects to have the properties they do for those who have mastered the system" (SP, 120; cf. SP, 119, 258).

This is not a trivial goal, and Culler accomplishes it superbly. But notice where it leads. The system becomes the end of criticism, even of reading, and not the means for satisfying other nonformalizable purposes and expectations:

> There is a kind of attention which one might call structuralist: a desire to isolate codes, to name the various languages with and among which the text plays, to go beyond manifest content to a series of forms and then to make these forms, or oppositions, or modes of signification, the burden of the text (SP, 259).
>
> By focusing on the ways in which it complies with and resists our expectations, its moments of order and disorder, its interplay of recognition and dislocation, it opens the way for a theory of the novel which would be an account of the pleasures and difficulties of reading. In place of the novel as mimesis we have the novel as a structure which plays with different modes of ordering and enables the reader to understand how he makes sense of the world (SP, 238).

This position seems disappointing, but it is very difficult to state exactly what has gone wrong or to locate an authority for one's criticism. From my perspective the problem is one of confusing means and ends, of treating formal procedures which create literary effects as the primary object of attention rather than as the vehicles for organizing and fore-grounding more existentially directed aspects of the authorial act. Thus, I consider equating a novel with the pleasures and difficulties of reading to be on a par with equating philosophy with the pleasures and difficul-ties of thinking. The position is not wrong but it is emaciated because it does not pay sufficient attention to the problems one thinks about or the desire for thinking and reading to produce an end, even if it be only a momentary stay from confusion or release from the cramps that come when one thinks too long from the same position. In other words, Cul-ler's idea of making sense is far too general. We read particular works to make sense of the way they make sense of specific situations. Our own general ways of making sense are, after all, not very interesting. If we read only for that reason, we would either give up the enterprise once we knew the rules or, perhaps, become Joyce's ideal, insomniac reader of *Finnegan's Wake*. Culler's model simply does not explain why litera-ture has the place it does in western culture, or why we repeatedly turn to and remember specific works. There seems no way to explain why literary texts have been attributed so much significance unless we grant that life, at least outside the academy, does not reduce itself to semantic and epistemological issues. We are concerned with what people do, and with what they know, or think they know, or try to know. This is why the criticism that has endured in our culture deals largely with aspects of content.

If I only make counter-assertions against Culler, I not only mistreat him but I also would glide over an important dimension of my own case. Let us instead ask why Culler is tempted by the position he takes. This question will lead us into the status of the convention of naturaliz-ing texts, the basic point of dispute between us. First of all, there are forms of reading that attend solely to *how* something is written and thus perfectly correlate with Culler's description of attending to how texts manipulate semantic competence. These readings also satisfy a basic methodological commitment of structuralism—they equate the goals of apprehension with the dynamics of the play of the system and thus they require no distinctions between the overt working of the system and hypotheses about the purposes for which people employ the given set of conventions. Finally, Culler makes central in his grasp of literature two basic contemporary values—a sense that all claims to represent the world can be interpreted in terms of the structures informing the repre-senter's behavior, and an awareness of the artificial qualities of literary works which give them forms of internal coherence, or what Roland

Barthes called "textualité," which cannot be turned into purposive predicates. If we concentrate on such textual movements, we can articulate a critical stance from which an emphasis on naturalizing texts seems a reductive denial of the force of conventions and the art qualities of literary constructions.

Although one can read as Culler suggests, I have strong doubts that this is how most competent readers do read or how one can read and still attribute to literature the values which are claimed for it in our humanistic tradition. Culler's problems, I suggest, derive from his method: structuralism allows no talk of purposes informing structures but not clearly accounted for within them, and thus it orients a theorist to resolve all issues on the same semantic plane. That this equalizing is probably not the case appears clearly with respect to the first kind of writing I see as shaping Culler's vision. It is very important that we can identify "writerly" readings which bracket overall intention in order to concentrate on technique. For most writers who practice this form of reading recognize it as a special and distinct process, as something readers can do but not as what they are likely to do if their aim is to fully appreciate the world of the work and the qualities of authorial action within and upon that world. Indeed the appreciation of semantic conventions probably depends on having read the work for the world it offers. One can make similar arguments about reading for textualité or the internal play of artificial patterns and echoes. How much of the practice of writing, the probable motives of writers, or the goals of the readers who have shaped our literary culture will such a perspective enable one to capture or to explain? And how can one move from questions of possible readings to those of preferred readings? What does this tell us about the limits of methodologies?

All these questions lead us to the status of what Culler calls the convention of naturalizing. I claim that insofar as we need to attribute purposes to features of a text—either on the mimetic or the authorial level—we must naturalize. Only the most extreme forms of textualité in which we see the text as passive repository of endlessly echoing overtones are free from such naturalizing. For naturalizing means establishing contexts for attributing motives. There are conventions which govern how authors naturalize, but there is also another level on which we must naturalize in order to attribute purposes to the use of conventions. Thus only when we ignore purposes do we avoid naturalizing. And on some levels naturalizing depends on a grammar deeper than that of specific realistic conventions. This is clearest when we inquire into how naturalizing relates both to the other large practices Culler describes and to specific generic conventions. It is much harder to make purposes dependent on conventions than conventions on purposes. Thus Culler's other three conventions do not, when exclusively stressed, give us much resemblance to the object competent readers construct. To make sense of these other conventions, we must naturalize them by relating them to possible actions and attitudes of characters and authors. Suppose a reader wanted to emphasize the metaphorical structure of a text. We would not understand the relevance of his criticism until it were made the plausible result or expression of an attitude or dramatic process. Similarly, we can imagine literary experience without concern for metaphor, theme, or reference to tradition, but not without proposing attitudes expressed by the text. Even the newest of new novels represents a significant action by the author, at least, if it makes any sense at all. Consequently, if naturalization is a convention, it is one with a central place in dictating the purpose of literary procedures and thus one probably working on a different level from the others.

There is a problem, however, even in thinking of naturalization as simply a literary convention, because conventions can too easily be seen as distinct from general constitutive procedures. Many critics use the concept of conventions with the sense that the materials they structure exist independently of them. It is tempting, then, to see the choice of a particular convention as largely an arbitrary matter. Constitutive rules, on the other hand, are equally dependent on cultural processes, but, because they provide the conditions by which an object exists at all, they tend to project the purposes we have in constructing the object. Here Culler's problem is typical of textualist views of language. Consider the following definition of naturalization: "As a linguistic object the text is strange and ambiguous. We reduce its strangeness by reading it as the utterance of a particular narrator so that models of plausible human attitudes and of coherent personalities can be made operative" (SP, 146). At least two aspects of this statement are somewhat odd. It seems to assume, first, that a text has some real existence before it is naturalized. But until we naturalize a text, it is not strange at all; it is simply a familiar sight of marks on a page. Semantically, the unnaturalized text is not strange but inchoate or *unsinnig*. Strangeness is a product of reading, or more generally of constitutive semantic conventions, not a precondition of them. Texts are not, like desires, forces which we domesticate in reading, but forces we create by reading, and reflecting on problems, etc. These claims become clear as soon as we ask a second question

—what makes a text seem strange? The obvious examples are texts for which we cannot find the appropriate genre, or texts which refuse to admit easy naturalization, like *The Wasteland* or *The Castle*. But with these texts naturalizing is not necessarily opposed to strangeness. In fact, the good critic would be less likely to first notice a text is strange and then naturalize it than he would be to naturalize it by in part showing how and why it is strange. And she would do so by constructing a complex attitude explaining how metaphor, theme, and relation to literary history can be seen as features of the author's purposive act and of her desires as a reader to understand that act.

5. From conventions to more enduring attitudes: treating texts as literary

Attention to performance, I want to argue, is the obvious principle governing naturalization, and thus underlies the level of conventions which are more readily subject to change. Genre conventions, for example, are not in conflict with naturalization, but are means by which we come to construct specific authorial and mimetic attitudes in a variety of texts and times. There are levels of conventions and also levels of competence (for example, some readers only learn to naturalize some modes of literature—I have never felt competent with Shakespearean comedy). Northrop Frye provides another, more important, consideration in his general model of how spiritual authority is located. Frye distinguishes between the social practices of a specific community, where actions rarely coincide with professed ideals and yet are partially shaped by them, and the deeper images of value which the society preserves and honors and which are the continual source of efforts to reform practices and to reinterpret the goals of behavior.[14] The history of taste reveals a similar interplay of forces between specific practices and general visions of the nature and goals of literary activity. These general visions can be seen as constituting the basic procedural assumptions which allow us to understand and evaluate the changes writers propose. In Wordsworth's case, for example, we can only explain the change in taste he wrought by rec-

---

14. Northrop Frye develops this idea of levels of value in several of the essays of *A Stubborn Structure* (Ithaca: Cornell University Press, 1971), especially "The Problem of Spiritual Authority in the Nineteenth Century." Frye's distinctions are necessary, I think, if we are to explain how the past remains a crucial source of values for the present.

ognizing how the change itself is justified in terms of general claims about the permanent expectations men have of poetry, expectations he felt were no longer satisfied by a particular style.[15]

Our construction of texts as performances depends on three deep-level constituents, or what Wittgenstein might call literary ways of going on, which govern the process of naturalization—expectations of contemplative pleasures from attending to both mimetic and stylistic features of a work, a readiness to become affectively engaged in concrete situations without the usual commitments and consequences that accompany emotions in ordinary experience, and an assumption that the text will establish in internal terms (although not exclusively so) relationships that focus one's reflections on the quality and significance of the specific actions presented.[16] None of these procedures is unique to literary discourse. What is distinctive is how recurrently all three are present when we take a discourse to be a literary one.

Claiming three basic procedures is easy, but how can one support such generalizations? One could go on to the tedious task of locating the procedures in critical theories, especially those tradition continues to respect, or one could show how they are projected through common features of literary education, or point out how they are present in critical conversations among trained readers. All these strategies, however, would entail other books. There are simpler tests, which rely only on our imaginative willingness to explore our own competence and to ask if there are really coherent alternatives which we would recognize as reading literature. The first of these tests involves determining how we actually use definitions of literature, for example, when we are confronted with problematic texts. This test is especially important for the general inquiry of this chapter because it measures procedural expectations, and avoids the essentialist techniques of seeking necessary and sufficient properties in an object.

Suppose, then, that someone asks, "Is Spenser really literature?" or, "How can you say Olson's poems or Sollers' novels are literature? They

15. Wordsworth's "Preface" to *Lyrical Ballads* demonstrates the general outlines of his thinking on the need to satisfy a sense of purpose derived from past values and no longer realized in his contemporary literature. This sense of tradition deepens when he realizes in his "Essay Supplementary to the Preface" (1815) that he can only hope to be read fully not by innocent eyes but by those who have been trained on great works from the past.

16. My last suggestion adapts ideals of organic unity to a perspective on reading. So the aim is not some abstract condition of unity, but an intense state of perceiving interrelationships among units of the text.

seem nonsense to me." The one thing we would not say if we wanted to be helpful would be, "Of course they are literature, they have the following properties. . . ." The questioner does not want a taxonomy or an application of abstractions. What he is asking for, I submit, is some help in approaching the text so that it begins to satisfy his expectations about what one finds when he reads literature. *What is literature?* was never really in doubt, or never a relevant question. The real issue is how I can go on to do what I expect to be able to do—how I can find pleasure, engage myself, and reflect upon the author's interpretation of his situation. For a reader begins to resolve his doubts not by understanding general definitions but by shifting the level of problems—by learning how to ask and pursue concrete questions. After reading more of these authors and some good criticism, he may not feel any more adept at telling us what literature is, but the significance of that question recedes once he can see possible answers to questions like, *Why this specific description in this part of the work?* One knows what literature is whenever he can read a text so that it answers the basic questions posed by literary expectations. The general question has real import only for the theorist, and this is perhaps why he has such difficulty answering it.[17]

As posed, this first test shows only the general role of procedures and does not determine the necessity of any specific ones. It is easy, nonetheless, to extend the case imaginatively by trying out different possible procedures one would need to find applicable before feeling satisfied. I will spare my reader working out this exercise, now, however, because there is a better test for specific procedures. In cases where we cannot expect objective definitions but seek to make explicit the grammatical use context for a term, Wittgenstein frequently proposes what he calls intermediate cases. These cases can bring out what we know implicitly, by demonstrating contrasts with other procedures (PI, 122). In the case of defining literature, this tactic has a long history, for it is common, and I think very revealing, to contrast literature to its two closest neighbors in the humanities, history and philosophy. I shall take a slightly different tack on this venerable method, by examining what changes would occur

17. I am using here an argument developed by Stanley Cavell to show analogues between aesthetic experience and Wittgenstein's therapeutic model of philosophical questions being made to disappear. See "Aesthetic Problems of Modern Philosophy," in *Must We Mean What We Say* (Cambridge: Cambridge University Press, 1976):73–96. For the idea that questions like "What is literature?" are used primarily in contexts where a reader is puzzled about how to proceed, see B. R. Tilghman, "Wittgenstein, Games, and Art," *Journal of Aesthetics and Art Criticism*, 31 (1972–73):519–24, p. 77.

if we were to treat conventionally philosophical and historical texts *as* works of literature.

We notice first that a literary approach would involve a different perspective than is usual in these disciplines on what may loosely be called the characters in the work. In the typical ways history is taught as a discipline, characters are seen as people uniquely defined by their specific traits, situations, and choices, and by the effects of their actions, while in philosophy, references to human cases are normally pure examples, shorn of individual traits.[18] A literary approach to the same texts tends, as Ohmann suggests, to see traces of universal attitudes toward experience in historical characters and to find moral principles at play in the relationship between actions and consequences. No reader of modern British philosophy will doubt the difference between its treatment of human characters in examples and literary treatments of character, but we might notice also that as philosophy becomes more psychological and literary, for example, in Sartre, the examples become almost more important and more revealing than the abstract arguments. In pure literary texts, characters raise universal questions and attitudes while retaining our interest in them as individuals.

A second example, drawn from different senses we have of the author of a text and the status of his arguments, makes the contrasts more pronounced. In pure cases, we are not interested in the authorial stance of those who write history or philosophy; we abstract the descriptions or the arguments and measure them against what we can find as the facts or what we take to be the canons of coherent argument. Even when historians or philosophers do attend to the authorial stance and treat the argument

18. I will divide up a series of cases that in practice exist as a continuum, with in fact some literary genres inviting either historical or philosophical inquiry. Nonetheless we inherit abstract ideas of each discipline which continue to shape our basic expectations about the general purpose of each discipline. Philosophers, for example, are adamant in demanding a rigor which eliminates literary and imaginary elements from those more "scientific" modes of discourse. Also, for some sharp points by a literary critic on the differences between literature and history, see Paul Hernadi, "Clio's Cousins: Autobiography as Translation, Fiction, and Criticism," *New Literary History* 7 (1975):247–58. For a good example of differences between literary and philosophical treatments of the same texts, compare the discussions of Hegel in M. H. Abrams, *Natural Supernaturalism* (New York: Norton, 1971), with those by Maurice Mandelbaum in *History, Man, and Reason* (Baltimore: Johns Hopkins University Press, 1971). Also relevant is Kenneth Burke's lovely dramatistic reading of philosophical problems, like the nature of substance, in his *Grammar of Motives* (Berkeley: University of California Press, 1969). Finally, for a literary analysis of historians, see Hayden White, *Metahistory* (Baltimore: Johns Hopkins University Press, 1973).

as at least partially determined by that stance, they root the determining factors either in the author's historical situation or in the logical models or paradigms he employs. A literary approach, on the other hand, attends primarily to the specific ways the author's needs and purposes shape his argument. The critic notices, for example, the fear of a world without values which generates the systems of Kant and Hegel. He is not content with historical or logical explanations; he wants to give the author's struggles to form and overcome his problems the status of a recurrent possibility for the mind's activities. He is not content to describe an action; rather, he tries to indicate how the action itself becomes a possible type or model, not to be abstracted, but to be generalized by developing the dramatic movement of the text as a characteristic means people use to establish imaginative order. When philosophical works are assessed in literary terms, propositional measures of truth and falsity become less important than the qualities of reflection with which the author works out the implications of a specific attitude toward experience, however illegitimate its philosophical foundation. Literary procedures measure dramatic truth, not defensible generalizations, although criteria of plausibility and seriousness remain and can be used to measure the representative qualities of the act. When the status of the act changes, so, too, does the status of its language. Intensional features of the utterance gain prominence, and style becomes a significant aspect of content —not because of some metaphysical unity, but simply because style reveals the qualities and tonalities of the specific attitude presented.

We might generalize these differences in the following way: the reader of history is satisfied when the author is erased and his arguments and descriptions become necessary to gaining a full picture of the situation, while the reader of philosophy desires to have all particulars absorbed into the objective criteria for valid abstract arguments. The reader of literature wants to perform both activities at once—to understand the dramatic situation as a particular experience, and to reflect upon the implicit activity of the author as he imposes his formal and thematic argument on the situation. This is why literature often appears capable of being everywhere and nowhere, of being more philosophical than history and more concrete than philosophy, while at the same time being more empty than history and less rigorous, less useful, than philosophy. Its two basic actions in many cases defer and displace each other, so each becomes problematic.

This inherent instability, I think, must be considered a basic feature of literary experience that stems from the flexibility of literary procedures. Literature produces a good deal of tension between the contemplative and the assertive. Since the expectations I am speaking of are abstract, we have many possible intermediate positions, and often we shift from treating texts as literature to testing their validity as models for governing our behavior or interpretations. The important point, however, is to understand how giving in too quickly to such desires involves adding supplements to literary experience and is not an immediate attribute of it. For if we take literature as primarily providing either historical or philosophical explanations, we find disturbing and scandalous its dramatic presentation of an authorial stance and its strange blend of concreteness and abstraction. We find it necessary, then, to treat literary utterances as failed explanations, and hence as fictions or phantasies masking and supplementing an author's desires. There are simply too many semantic and emotional energies and too many dialectical leaps between the general and the particular operating in a typical literary text to allow us to take it comfortably as referring to independent facts in the world.

We find ourselves realizing in concrete terms the importance of taking literary speech acts as performances. This brings together all the expectations we have been discussing. We can explain why these texts yield more to attitudes of sympathetic scrutiny than to those which test their value as explanatory hypotheses. Performances do not explain phenomena; they articulate, reveal, and create ways men might act upon and react to phenomena. Performances do not explain, but stress the kinds of considerations that might explain phenomena in specific situations.[19] They call our attention to both poles of an interpretive situation —to the needs, desires, and qualities of the actor, and to the complexities in what he encounters—so we can only come to grips with them by assessing the relationship between the poles. We cannot abstract from either pole, because the actor's needs would make his verbal explanations too contextual for philosophy and because the treatment of the situation would be too stylized and focussed on possible typical responses to satisfy the historian. We cannot turn performances into abstract statements, but we can use abstract statements to enhance performances, because they bring contexts to bear which can deepen or complicate our sense of the quality of the particular action. The more we think about *forgiveness* and *just saying*, the more we can appreciate the performance

19. The best discussion of performance I know is one devoted primarily to dance. See David Levin, "The Embodiment of Performance," *Salmagundi*, nos. 31–32 (Fall, 1975–Winter, 1976):120–42.

which is Williams' poem. But the poem has no power to explain either of these ideas philosophically, except perhaps as an example.

How we can relate expectations about pleasure to the procedures I have been discussing is not yet clear. The reason, I think, reveals some of the philosophical complexities in this much-abused or much-ignored concept. When one poses pleasure as a specific expectation, there is a temptation to assume we can locate some distinctive entity. But pleasure is not something we can seek in itself: pleasure is a condition of doing things well or finding our procedures satisfactorily applied. As Mill learned, we cannot successfully make achieving pleasure a distinct end, but must see pleasure as the corollary of purpose, as a response to our recognition that our activity goes well. This is why we cannot specify, in our intermediate cases, a distinct procedure that allows us to achieve literary pleasure. Indeed, this is why talk of aesthetic pleasure, especially Roland Barthes', misses the point and relies on a dense set of metaphoric equations in order to link aesthetic and sexual pleasure. There are distinctive aspects of literary pleasure, but only because there are other procedures to be satisfied. There is, for example, a uniquely aesthetic pleasure that stems from appreciating either engaging descriptions or the skillful manipulation of form—both of which follow from our desire for engagement and our reflection on the authorial act. But aesthetic pleasure is too narrow a concept of literary pleasure, for the same reasons that a purely aesthetic approach to a text ignores our procedural expectations about content.

If, however, pleasure is a corollary of purpose, why do I argue for a distinct third set of procedural expectations involving pleasure? I could claim that there are reasons a distinctive form of pleasure does not manifest itself in our intermediate cases, but then I would not be able to assert also that there are specific concerns for a kind of pleasure. I hope I can avoid this contradiction by arguing that the expectation of pleasure is not a way of constructing content, as are the other two procedures, but an attitude we take toward our relationship to content. The concept of seeking a distinct kind of pleasure, then, serves as an abstract way of including the concerns of the many theorists who discuss *aesthetic attitude* without delaying over their specific disputes. I use the concept of pleasure to include the range of behavioral attributes involved in the particular way literary experience seems freer of practical or argumentative consequences than are other forms of discourse. One of the basic purposes in reading literature, in fact, is to enjoy this freedom—to be disinterested, in the Kantian sense. Thus, while we cannot identify a distinctive psychological object as literary pleasure, there is a distinctive way of enjoying our capacities to engage in and reflect upon actions, because the engagement and reflections need not produce consequences. This disinterest, finally, is why we can be content to allow actions to remain performances, and even to view our own reading as a performance of our sensibilities, without feeling that somehow we ought to do something practical with our activity. We can delight in the nonconsequential, while exercising all the capacities we need to determine consequences in practical situations. We can rest content in reflecting on how literature performs for us our own identities, both those established by our culture and those which partially free us from any specific social structures.

6

Literary Procedures and the Question
of Indeterminacy

1. *Three indeterminacy theories I shall criticize*   If there is any doctrine
that constitutes a shared ideology in recent literary studies, it must be
the belief that substantial aspects of literary meaning are indeterminate.
Where twenty years ago virtually every good graduate student could spin
out intricate arguments demonstrating how verbal and image patterns
articulated paradoxical themes in a literary text, his counterpart now
learns to show how texts respond to perennial problems of language and
authority by declaring their own indeterminacy or at least by rewarding
a wide variety of different reading approaches.

My general discussion of semantic issues has obviously been directed
against this position. Still, the risk of repetition is worth facing in order
to take on the theoretical versions of indeterminacy that have shaped
this climate.[1] I consider it an important test of my perspective that it
can disclose and combat serious flaws in these arguments, and I find
confronting them a useful contrastive strategy for exhibiting the values
in a procedural approach, especially in the description it establishes of
literariness as a specific way of focussing the performance of concrete
actions for empathic and qualitative reflection.

1. E. D. Hirsch is a cautionary example here. His *Aims of Criticism* (pp. 17–49)
offers a convincing case against the most general indeterminacy arguments, by showing that if all discourse is indeterminate, there is no possible truth in saying so, because that statement too would be indeterminate. Hirsch has had little effect, however,
partially because he does not take on the specific formulations of those theories which
have some bite for literary issues and which can take subtle Nietzschean forms,
stressing the critic's will to power.

Our efforts to establish a procedural definition of literariness give us a sense of what an alternative to indeterminacy might look like. Indeterminacy theorists rarely describe in a rigorous way what they oppose. At most, one garners a loose sense that their antagonists are either badly stated versions of organicism or reductions of meaning to thematic patterns. Let this discussion, then, be at least a challenge for them to test their weapons. But let me also clarify the target. In defending a concept of determinacy, I shall not argue that there is a single correct reading for every literary text, even if one takes *literary* in the restricted sense developed above. Determinacy is, as we shall see, a matter of degree and a function of possible communal agreement about assessment procedures. It is a matter of degree because for theory, at least, we must concentrate on probabilistic grounds and on discussions of the general shape of authorial purposes. There will always be indeterminate aspects of texts, like the meaning of Milton's "two-handed engine." But we can consider a text reasonably determinate if we can show that clear public constraints apply to the kinds of evidence that will make a difference for a community, and if there are grounds for agreeing on the level of specific details and on the hierarchy of relationships that establish authorial and dramatic purpose. A general case for determinacy, moreover, must show that in most cases we either have a basic sense of informing purpose or we know the kind of evidence (which may not be easy to get or to prove) which would resolve competing interpretations.

Determinacy is neither certainty nor propositional adequacy to facts. But there remain two theoretical ways of testing for it. Both are matters of judgment. A viable argument for explaining determinacy must describe a basic model of interpretation which postulates a more abstract or general form of synthetic operations than those which foster the conflicts used to justify indeterminacy theories. This shall be the role I ask the concept of performance to play, and this is why I need to contrast this concept to typical discussions of indeterminacy. There is, moreover, strong warrant for relying on a notion like performance because, as we have seen, some semantic operation must be available which frees us from the tautological equation—only textuality, therefore no purpose and no determinacy. The second test involves negative judgments. One can claim a sufficient general model of determinacy with respect to literary texts if one describes a series of fundamental operations which competent readers take as basic to defeating an accepted reading. For, in knowing what counts against a reading, a community reveals implicit criteria it might not be able to articulate fully.

With these matters to contend with, I shall have to ignore arguments for indeterminacy based on considerations of historical change and cultural relativity. The basic theoretical issues involved have already been discussed with respect to meaning and significance and to questions of the limitations of cultural foreunderstanding. Moreover, a grammatical perspective on meaning easily handles specific matters of changes in genre conventions or in the meaning of words, because it insists that awareness of the historical dimensions of a text is a necessary feature of literary education. One is simply not a competent reader who does not know what "vegetable love" meant in the seventeenth century, or who is ignorant of the stylistic conflict between Williams and Eliot.[2]

Those theories I shall consider gain a good deal of their power from confusing and contradictory aspects of the New Criticism. The New Critics greatly expanded our sense of the semantic complexity of a text, but they did not develop adequate ways of showing how this information might be coherently processed.[3] As practical interpreters, they stressed rhetorical and formal features of literary discourse, while as spokesmen for the humanities, they insisted on literature as a special form of intense, complex, concrete experience. The claims to form seemed to give determinate status to a romantic, and ultimately unintelligible, sense of immediate experience, while the claims about experience seemed to circumvent the problems of circularity that attend formal, autotelic criteria for interpretation. We are now witnessing the inevitable breakdown of this unstable synthesis, with each pole claiming its own interpretive methods which necessarily lead to indeterminacy. Each of the models of indeterminacy I shall deal with derives a good deal of its authority from this condition. Psychological versions of indeterminacy, for example, emphasize the difficulty of attributing objective status to the complex experiential impact of literary language. Textualist versions of literary meaning, on the other hand, depend on notions of rhetorical form and the constitutive properties of language, which overdetermine appropriate interpretive contexts and render meanings logically, rather

2. On the determinate quality of historical features of style, see Nelson Goodman, "The Status of Style," *Critical Inquiry* 1 (1975):799–811. On the limits of pluralist versions of indeterminacy with respect to historical issues, see Meyer Abrams, "The Deconstructive Angel: The Limits of Pluralism," *Critical Inquiry* 3 (1977):425–38.

3. Paul de Man makes exactly this argument as justification for indeterminacy claims in the second chapter of *Blindness and Insight* (New York: Oxford University Press, 1971), abbreviated BI. For a very good description of how contemporary criticism still repeats the themes of New Critical theory which it claims to reject, see Gerald Graff, "What Was New Criticism," *Salmagundi*, no. 27 (1974):72–93.

than empirically, unstable. The final model of indeterminacy takes as its focus the way texts themselves respond to dilemmas of correlating formal and experiential aspects of meaning, and, thus, present themselves as "writerly," or subject to a variety of incompatible thematic structures. Each theory in turn tests and clarifies a basic element in my argument— the status of the reading subject, the conditions for contextualizing evidence in order to attribute formal intentions, and the relative priority of action to theme as grounds for establishing meanings.

2. The problem with psychological versions of indeterminacy

There are two distinctive types of psychological indeterminacy theory with a surprising degree of congruence. There are self-consciously empirical developments of I. A. Richards' response theories, which insist that meanings for objects which are imaginatively experienced must be in large part created by the individual reader. The position is clear in the work of Norman Holland and Walter Slatoff and, I think, logically required by Stanley Fish's arguments about affective stylistics, although he denies it.[4] What these critics root in empirical psychology, Paul de Man's earlier writings derive from a phenomenological description of the manner in which an intentional consciousness constitutes meanings from physical signs. Here are Holland and Fish generalizing about literary meaning:

> Meaning—whether we are talking simply of putting black marks together to form words or the much more complex process of putting words together to form themes—does not inhere in the words-on-the-page but, like beauty, in the eye of the beholder. (PIP, 98)

> The stylisticians proceed as if there were observable facts that could first be described and then interpreted. What I am suggest-

4. I have used as my basic text for psychological indeterminacy theories Norman Holland, *Poems in Persons: An Introduction to the Psychoanalysis of Literature* (New York: Norton, 1973), abbreviated PIP, and Paul de Man, BI. Also basic to this position is Walter Slatoff, *With Respect to Readers: Dimensions of Literary Response* (Ithaca: Cornell University Press, 1970). For further readings in Holland and later refinements of his position, see 5 *Readers Reading* (New Haven: Yale University Press, 1975); "Unity Identity Text Self," *PMLA* 90 (1975):813–22; and "The New Paradigm: Subjective or Transactive?" *New Literary History* 7 (1976):335–46. Holland repeatedly denies that his view is a subjectivism and prefers the word *transactive*, but he certainly claims texts are indeterminate and locates the source of the indeterminacy in what he calls a reader's *identity theme*, a position I find hard finally to distinguish from subjectivism.

ing is that an interpreting entity, endowed with purposes and concerns, is, by virtue of its very operation, determining what counts as the facts to be observed; and moreover, that since this determining is not a neutral marking out of a valueless area, but the extension of an already existing field of interests, it *is* an interpretation.[5]

These generalizations depend on three assumptions: (1) that signs are truly objective only as physical data—"A poem taken purely objectively is nothing but specks of carbon on dried wood pulp" (PIP, 2);[6] (2) that the less scientific and referential an utterance is the more its emotive properties can only be reconstituted in individual experience—"a being with a character experiences reality only to the extent he can give it life within that character" (PIP, 161); and (3) that criticism is not objectively assessable but rhetorically expresses individual desires, and consequently is most authentic when seen as self-analysis—"A reader uses the fine, subtle listening 'new' critics have taught these last decades to listen to himself and to others with the same attention to detail and nuance that formerly was reserved for literature as a separate entity" (PIP, 134).

What Holland takes as empirical, de Man derives from Nietzsche, Freud, and Marx: all representations or interpretations are essentially symptomatic epiphenomena of underlying primary structures of desire. Both Holland and de Man, then, place the individual at the center of meaning, but only de Man is sufficiently ironic to recognize that the determining force played by desire threatens our fictions of identity as well as our dreams of objectivity about literary works. De Man's "radical relativist" position on indeterminacy takes its departure from a phe-

5. Stanley Fish, "What is Stylistics and Why Are They Saying Such Terrible Things About it," in Seymour Chatman, ed., *Approaches to Poetics* (New York: Columbia University Press, 1973), pp. 148–49. Fish's other basic statement of indeterminacy principles is "Literature in the Reader: Affective Stylistics," *New Literary History* 2 (1970):123–62. Fish, like Holland, refuses the kind of labels I apply here, but if readers create *what counts as the facts*, we are pretty close to psychological subjectivism, however transactional. I quote here from his response to Ralph Rader's devastating critique of his work, both in "Fact, Theory and Literary Explanation," *Critical Inquiry* 1 (1974):262–72, and in his response to Fish's response, "Explaining Our Literary Understanding," *Critical Inquiry* 1 (1974):960 ff. Rader's work makes it unnecessary to consider Fish here, but I should point out that Rader's basic attack on Fish, for ignoring the conventional procedures by which we construct units of meaning, parallels my general concerns.

6. This view of meaning as constructions from signs and therefore subjective is one of the fundamental themes shared by psychological and phenomenological approaches. See, for example, Fish, "Affective Stylistics," p. 140, and Georges Poulet, "Phenomenology of Reading," *New Literary History* 1 (1969):53–68.

nomenological distinction between natural and human meanings that echoes Slatoff on scientific versus imaginative utterances and both Holland and Fish on the necessary imaginative recreation of mere objective marks on a page. Natural signs always have clear and repeatable meanings, because they hide nothing and follow established laws, while human utterances are always intentional, always both uttered from a point of view not entirely evident in the signs and dependent on the intentions of the interpreter, and therefore always problematic (BI, 10).[7] Intentionality, for him, is not, he says, simply a procedure that transfers content from a mind to a text and then to a reader, as it is for E. D. Hirsch. Rather, intentionality signs a verbal object with the presence of a desire that can never be determinately recovered (BI, 25), for intentionality means that the signs emanate from a point of view, or what Sartre called a surpassing of the object, that can only be recovered from other points of view. Claims about the unity of a text, for example, reside "not in the poetic text as such," for then intention would have the status of a natural sign; rather, they must be proposed "in the act of interpreting this text" (BI, 29). Neither author nor critic has a privileged position on the text, for each has a different spatio-temporal perspective on it and is caught up in one of the two kinds of infinite regress contained in the hermeneutical circle. First, hypotheses about the whole text must continually be modified and displaced by further experience of particulars, and, second, the self who interprets is continually being modified by his changing grasp of both his and the author's intentions (BI, 29–32).

I find these psychological theories of literary meaning extremely useful for elaborating the different ways in which the act of reading is conceived by a procedural approach that emphasizes competence. Questions of procedural competence arise here on the most fundamental epistemological level, and involve us in questions of what *subjectivity* and *objectivity* can mean. For it does not make sense to distinguish sharply between marks on a page as objective content and meanings

7. De Man stresses the subjective construction of meanings in large part because he is led to that position by his early work attacking Romantic dreams of a language that could parallel natural structures. See especially "The Intentionality of the Romantic Image," in Harold Bloom, ed., *Romanticism and Consciousness* (New York: Norton, 1970). De Man's later writings have shifted the forms of indeterminacy from intention to the metaphoric quality of literary texts, that is, from phenomenological psychology to semantics. This is clearest in "Semiology and Rhetoric," *Diacritics* 3 (Fall, 1973):27–33, and "Theory of Metaphor in Rousseau's Second Discourse," in David Thorburn, ed., *Romanticism: Vistas, Instances, Continuities* (Ithaca: Cornell University Press, 1973), hereafter abbreviated TMR.

which are then added by subjects—at least, when the procedure being discussed is the activity of reading. There need be no quarrel that from certain perspectives the fundamental objectivity of a sign resides in its physical properties. These perspectives, however, are usually specialized ones, remote from the kind of objectivity signs have in ordinary experience. Take a picture of a lion in a newspaper. How sensible is it to claim that objectively all we see are certain arrangements of dots and lines which we then subjectively interpret? What if the dots and lines are not substances at all, then do we objectively see only atoms and electrical forces? *Objectivity*, then, may be less an ontological term than one referring to what is fundamental and publicly shared in different modes of inquiry.[8] The kind of objectivity a scientist requires is different from that needed in ordinary behavior, but that does not make ordinary behavior more subjective; it simply makes it less precise, and therefore not an adequate standard for certain purposes. It is not the ordinary purpose of reading to,be clear about the physical properties of words on a page. This is why simple reflection tells us that when we read, we do not ordinarily construe words from letters and empty spaces, nor meanings from words, but take the letters as direct signs of meaningful utterances (assuming, of course, that problematic cases do not arise). It is more difficult not to take letters as objects not transferring meaning than it is simply to read them, and there is obviously quite a gap between our ordinary sense of reading and the kind of behavior we notice when we feel we are subjectively construing such signs (perhaps as reminding us of pictures or hieroglyphs). Our usual meanings of *subjective* and *objective* do not apply to such primary processes as reading ordinary sentences.

The implications of this initial point become crucial when we recognize how a similar notion of objectivity leads Holland and Slatoff to base their analysis on an empiricism that ignores distinctions between natural and institutional facts. They assume that one can establish a theory of meaning by simply observing what readers do in reading. In a rough way, this observation procedure is adequate for a physical science working within established paradigms. However, as soon as the phenomena in question involve education and the corollary possibilities of behavior being judged as inadequate, one must observe not only what people do,

8. The clearest philosophical attack on the idea that words are objective signs which we then interpret is J. L. Austin's *Sense and Sensibilia* (New York: Oxford, 1962), pp. 84–142. For the notion of objectivity as procedurally or situationally determined, see chapter eleven of Austin's HTD.

but the ways in which what they do is judged or defined by the relevant procedures. It follows from our earlier discussion of institutional facts that a scientist from another world could not explain the game of chess by simply observing how people play; he would need to know the traditions and purposes of the game and understand the possible and the good ways of playing it. It seems certain that this scientist could not learn what a promise is by observing a representative sample of promises. He might learn something about promising behavior, but it would be ludicrous to define a promise as a pledge which people seem to keep about seventy percent of the time.

I have made enough abstract claims about competence and procedures. Holland's methods enable us to put the case in concrete terms, for his questions and analyses obviously ignore the relevant issues needed in a description of reading and in understanding the grounds on which we judge the adequacy of such a description. There is, first of all, something very odd in asking one's subjects in an experiment intended to measure the reading of complex texts, "Well, how did you respond?" and "How does the thing make you feel?" (PIP, 70, 91). Not only are these questions heavily theory-laden, they ignore the kinds of considerations that distinguish meanings from simple associative responses. Again, imagine defining chess, or promises, or the enterprise Holland himself is engaged in by correlating answers to questions like these.

The complexities clarified by what Holland does not consider are most obvious in his analysis of one particular respondent, Saul, whose answers derive not from affective states but from his acceptance of aesthetic norms that sound very much like Ezra Pound (PIP, 90–95). Saul's responses, in short, are not immediate, but are mediated by a set of values he has derived from the institutions of literary discourse. Yet while these mediated responses are too complex for Holland's empiricism, they would be judged by most competent readers as naive reliance on a limited moment in the history of taste. We come around again to the complex issue of the nature and the levels of convention. If direct observations of reading activity could tell us the status of literary texts, there would be little point to locating Saul's ideology. But not only can we recognize it, we can see both why he says what he does and what he overlooks. In other words, we confront the facts that there is a history of taste and that there are recursive procedures based on more general conventions which enable us to criticize and to comprehend historical changes. This does not mean that there is a metaphysical essence of reading, for we probably never completely escape our culture. But it does suggest, once again, how flexible that culture is in allowing us to develop a self-conscious critical awareness of our limitations.

De Man is no empiricist. Nonetheless, his Sartrean view of intentionality allies him with Holland on a central thesis of psychological indeterminacy theories—an equation of the intensely personal with the subjective play of desires. De Man recognizes the irony of speaking about *self* at all in this context, since the self is probably a cultural construct, certainly not an empirical entity one can directly experience. Yet the same cultural assumption remains. As Holland puts it, "A being with a character experiences reality only to the extent he can give it life within that character" (PIP, 161).

The force of this claim derives from taking a tautology for a significant truth. Of course, for me to experience *x*, I must have the experience, but it does not follow that I make the meaning. I must personally attribute a meaning, but it is not I who determine what the meaning is. For if each agent determined what meanings to give words and situations, meaning would be entirely private. Holland and de Man confuse having a feeling (which is the act of a subject) with knowing what a feeling is.[9]

There are difficult issues of empirical psychology here, but they do not affect the semantic point made by the private language argument: to be able to speak about a feeling at all involves publicly determinate knowledge of how to relate linguistic conventions to overt situational details we learn to recognize in grammatical terms.[10] After all, we often

9. I take this distinction from Stuart Hampshire, *Thought and Action* (London: Chatto and Windus, 1959), pp. 121–22. Hampshire's book and Anthony Kenny, *Action, Emotion and Will* (New York: Humanities Press, 1963) provide full explanations of how the philosophical attack on the positivist's referential/emotive dichotomy gives us nonsubjective ways of talking about emotional experiences. For another analogue of Hampshire's distinction, consider the intuitive difference between describing a literary work and describing one's response to it.

10. I cannot resist pointing out an obvious case of the dangers inherent in denying the link between the personal and established procedures. It turns out that in "The Significance of Frank O'Hara," *Iowa Review* 4 (1973):102–04, I published a reading of "The Day Lady Died" which almost exactly parallels the one Holland gives the poem to show how his identity theme psychologically conditions his reading (PIP, 110–34). We can, in fact, easily separate in the reading Holland the professional critic from Holland the psychological subject. But the more interesting fact is the difficulty a psychological theory would have explaining both why our readings of the poem are so similar and why, nonetheless, our literary theories are so different. The similarity is easy to handle if one assumes we both know how to read poetry, and that the theorist using a poem as Holland does has no professional obligation to read the specific criticism (that would spoil what he is trying to demonstrate in the reading).

redescribe emotions as we do intentions, a procedure only intelligible if we identify emotions from public contexts. Similar insights led Husserl to insist that intentionality is not a feature of personal relations to situations, but of a consciousness to a noematic object. In other words, Husserl flirted with idealism to preserve a distinction between the determinate relationships an active consciousness has to its objects and the necessarily negative or "unreal" features of subjective intentions later to be stressed by Sartre.

However, it is important to insist that denying the subjective base of our knowledge of emotions does not entail denying that emotions are deeply experienced by persons. The relevant opposition is not between the personally subjective and the objective, but between the personal and the impersonal, both of which admit public determinations. *Personal* is a term that measures involvement, not degrees of hermeneutic objectivity. Again, the relevant structures for the theorist are not ontological subjectivity and objectivity, but the different procedures evoked by different kinds of situations. Moreover, when we are dealing with institutional facts, we must recognize that structures of competence make our experience in large part rule-governed; actors assume internalized roles and do not merely express subjective biases. (The subjective may create particular ways of playing the roles, but these, too, if knowable at all, are publicly determinable.) The roles, nonetheless, can be performed with great personal intensity. One might argue, in fact, that the attack on subjectivity in Eliot's, and especially in Yeats', poetic derives from a sense that personal intensity increases in direct ratio to the subjective baggage one can jettison when he performs the conventions of reading.

3. *Textualist, semantic models of indeterminacy*

De Man's recent work brings us to the second type of indeterminacy theory based on descriptions of the semantically overdetermined quality of linguistic acts. His vision of the failure of the New Critics to control the complexities they revealed leads to complex meditations on the instability of any context an interpreter might pose as an image of controlling form or purpose. For signification, especially in metaphoric discourse, complicates purpose by invoking endless possible paradigmatic sets and affective contexts. These multiplicities are doubled again by the contexts, metaphoric chains, and performative forces inscribed in the interpreter's discourse. To put de Man in the larger textualist frame needed to elaborate the general structure of this model: formalism bred the dream of complex informing structures, which we now must recognize, instead, as aspects of what Derrida calls *structurality*, the capacity to disseminate continual possibilities of structure that never resolve into a determinate context.[11] The simplest, and in some ways the most rigorous, case for reversing New Critical doctrine into visions of textualist structurality is presented by Arthur Moore's critique of *organic form*.[12] Form, he argues, can serve to delimit meaning only if we establish our notion of form independently of a given text. If I mean by form a *sonnet* or a *comedy*, then I have a fixed concept to apply to a text, a concept whose meaning does not depend on what I take the text to mean. But as soon as we try a more organic notion of form, as a concept that establishes what is semantically relevant in a text, we enter a vicious hermeneutical circle that no phenomenological magic can make benign. Organic form is established by our sense of relevant particulars, and we have no facts independent of those we construct in our interpretation with which to control our hypotheses of semantical relevance. We combine advocate and jury, or, as Moore puts it, form becomes "no less and no more than the means by which" a critic "literally recreates the work of art from the potentialities of language."

If I am to represent the logic of textualist indeterminacy adequately, however, I cannot avoid returning once more to Derrida. It is, after all, only appropriate that a position ironically mirroring positivist criteria for secure names (cf. WM, 45, and Diff., 138) should repeat in semantic terms the dichotomy between reference and emotive, or, in this case, associative, discourse that inspired Richards' position.[13] Here I shall presume my earlier discussion of unstable names and concentrate on Derrida's argument that the iterability of writing makes context indeterminate and renders intentions unrecoverable:

11. See Derrida's "Structure, Sign, Play," in Richard Macksey and Eugenio Donato, eds., *The Structuralist Controversy* (Baltimore: Johns Hopkins University Press, 1970), pp. 247–64.

12. *Contestable Concepts in Literary Theory* (Baton Rouge: Louisiana State University Press, 1973), pp. 155–232. It should be noted that Rader, in the essay cited above, makes essentially the same argument against formalism, but in the service of a sophisticated model for verifying interpretive procedures through the use of facts independent of formal analysis. The quote at the end of the paragraph comes from p. 174.

13. The ironic positivism in Derrida has not gone unnoticed. See Warner Berthoff, "The Way We Think Now: Protocols for Deprivation," *New Literary History* 7 (1976):599–618.

A written sign carries with it a force that breaks with its context, that is with the collectivity of presences organizing the moment of its inscription. . . . By virtue of its essential iterability, a written syntagma can always be detached from the chain in which it is inserted or given without causing it to lose all possibility of functioning, if not all possibility of "communicating" precisely. One can perhaps come to recognize other possibilities in it by inscribing it or grafting it onto other chains. No context can entirely enclose it. (SEC, 182)

In order for a context to be *exhaustively* determinable, in the sense required by Austin, conscious intention would at the very least have to be *totally* present and *immediately* transparent to itself and to others, since it is a determining center of context. (SEC, 192; italics mine)

Derrida's claims threaten the center of my arguments, since one can deny his radical opposition between certainty and scepticism only by arguing for probability conditions based on procedures—which in turn require that contexts and intentions be sufficiently determinate to indicate appropriate procedures. Without determinable intentions and contexts, there is no way to affirm a distinction between the ascriptive level of textuality and the purposes that characterize pragmatic uses of language.

Because we are dealing with a specific conceptual issue here, I will assume that one can take Derrida's statements as philosophical claims. Then I will try to show that Derrida poses the issues in ways that have very little relationship to the features of experience where problems of determinate meaning arise. Thus, when we do test his claims against common practices they are neither perspicuous nor accurate. Notice, first, the phrases I have underlined in the quotation above. These reinforcing adverbs insist on absolute criteria, which in effect put questions of meaning in a purely logical universe. Here Derrida (out of context) is his own best commentator: " . . . I become suspicious. This is especially so when an adverb, apparently redundant, is used to reinforce the declaration. Like a warning light, it signals an uneasiness that demands to be followed up" (LI, 175).[14] I am not sure that Derrida is masking uneasiness, but there is certainly cause for suspicion of his adverbial claims. These claims insure the truth of his version of indeterminacy,

14. I note in SEC seven separate sentences relying on these reinforcing adverbs pp. 174, 181, 182, 183, 186, 192, 194.

but they also effectively banish his claims from any practical or testable discourse about meaning. It is tautologically true that all discourse has some degree of indeterminacy—to prevent this, each statement would have to catalogue all the facts, desires, and laws that might impinge upon it. But questions of indeterminate meaning, as they relate to the description of actual language behavior, must concern themselves with degrees of indeterminacy, and, consequently, with purposes and contexts that create specific needs for intelligibility. Statements do not fail because they are not absolutely determinate, but because they are not sufficiently determinate for specific tasks.

Derrida's understanding of intention and context suffers from a similar idealization for the purpose of sceptical reversals. If intentions could ever be "totally present" and "immediately transparent," they would have to have the ontological status of the single objects Derrida and Russell demand as anchors for descriptive names. But who has ever seen a totally present intention? Again, Derrida asks us to suppose that meanings and contexts depend on the most problematic of properties, and, thus, he justifies a tautological scepticism. Yet his view of intention is neither plausible nor intelligible (nor accurate to Austin's).[15] A meaningful attack on intention would have to address the arguments of those, like Anscombe, who show how intention is not a psychological event, but a property we attribute to certain kinds of behavior. From this perspective, Derrida has the relationship between intention and context reversed. As John Searle points out in his powerful critique of what can be abstracted as philosophical claims in Derrida, conventions and contexts enable someone to form intentions to himself and to have them recognized. The intention to write a poem is less a locatable psychic event than a series of choices in a context to which reasons may be attributed.

Derrida cannot recognize the correlation between intention and context, because he has a similarly abstract view of context. For Derrida, contexts are essentially arbitrary frames for a discourse, independent of the speaker's purposes. Thus, he argues as if an utterance can evoke or

15. John Searle's attempt to refute Derrida, "Reiterating the Differences," cited in chapter one, is especially useful on the subject of intention and the problematic notions of writing and absence that support Derrida's claims. There is room, however, also to note the literary mythology informing, or at least leaving traces, in Derrida's speech acts about intention. The absolute demands for presence pose intentions as pure psychic moments of virginal innocence, in which the self might observe itself directly. But then writing comes like Satan to violate the bower with the rude strokes of convention and iterability. See especially SEC, pp. 191–92.

be placed in an infinite variety of contexts, with no qualifying conditions. He claims, correctly, that an ordinarily senseless expression, like "the green is either," is not absolutely determinate as senseless, because it could make sense in some contexts, say as an example of agrammaticality: "The possibility of disengagement and citational graft" exists for every sign (SEC, 185). But possibility is not a normal consideration in interpretation. We do not determine meanings by treating sentences and contexts as independent of one another; nor are contexts necessarily carried along to other contexts simply because a statement is iterable. Contexts are part of the ways sentences come to mean in the first place. We consider "the green is either" to be senseless not in some absolute metaphysical world, but in terms of the ordinary contexts in which we imagine sentences occurring. The fact that the sentence can make sense in some contexts is a sign that we always read its sense through assumptions about appropriate contexts. Indeed, it is a strong argument against Derrida that he can so easily posit the contexts needed for giving sense to the utterance, and that he clearly recognizes how changes in context involve specific changes in what counts as determinate discourse. That different contexts are always possible simply makes no difference to the argument that in given situations we can be reasonably sure of what the relevant contexts are for establishing a sufficient degree of determinacy.

Let me try to link questions of intention, appropriate context, and iterability by developing a simple concrete example. Suppose I write a letter saying, "I will come next week." As a set of linguistic terms this statement is infinitely repeatable and "next week" not a specific temporal reference. Yet a reasonable person would only use this abbreviated statement if he thought the particular context of the letter sufficient for his purposes. He could always specify the date if he felt it necessary. More important, in order to gain an understanding of this letter adequate to act upon its message, there are many contexts and aspects of intention we do not need to know. We do not need to know other cases where the speaker has used the utterance, nor the contexts which made him the kind of person who might make this journey, nor the complex motives he might have in going. There are situations where these might be relevant, but usually not if we wish to understand the basic meaning. The statement is not indeterminate, even though its motives, causes, and possible consequences might be and probably are. Imagine how long one could function in a human community, which is founded on probabilities, not certainties, if each time he received this message he didn't bother to pick the person up, because, after all, he doesn't see it as *ex-*

haustively determinable and is not sure of all the person's motives. Imagine how we could decide that the context is not sufficient—only by assuming that another probable context is the relevant one. It is true that, if we found this letter ten years later, it would be indeterminate as a speech act, though not as a semantic unit. This would be so not because the context is indeterminate, but because there is no relevant context at all. That is, the very conditions of uncertainty clarify the simple probability on which sense depends.

What we adduce about context pertains also to Derridean arguments about the displacing power of metaphor. Derrida claims, for example, that philosophical discourse is inherently unstable, because many of its central terms, like *idea, theory,* and *propre sens,* are inherently metaphorical and multiply contexts. But this assumes that metaphoricity is a property of words, rather than of uses. It ignores the possibility that contexts or conventions can give appropriate fixed senses to these terms, so that their metaphoric qualities are either placed or ignored. The examples I mentioned are by now dead metaphors: philosophers disagree not because the terms are inherently unstable but because they desire to employ them in different kinds of argumentative contexts, like behaviorist or mentalist ones. The terms are defined differently not because of their inherent properties, but because of their generality, which makes their specific meanings depend on an argumentative structure. Moreover, when we consider live metaphors, there need be no indeterminacy. Metaphors cannot easily be elements in referring propositions, but we can understand them as features of a specific expressive speech act. When metaphors displace or complicate reference, they usually do so for an expressive or hermeneutic purpose, and that purpose can normally be inferred from the situation. Metaphors are expressions of an action taking place through the utterance, and if we understand the situation we normally see why the metaphor is used. (In cases where the metaphor cannot be paraphrased, we understand its purpose as creating a certain kind of effect and we assess how effective it is—and here expressive success, not truth, is the relevant dimension of understanding.[16])

Let me demonstrate the determinacy of metaphor by exercising a bit of counterperversity on Paul de Man's brilliant reading of metaphor in

16. For support of my view of metaphor, see Donald Stewart, "Metaphor, Truth, and Definition," *Journal of Aesthetics and Art Criticism* 32 (1973):205–18; Ted Cohen, "Notes on Metaphor," *Journal of Aesthetics and Art Criticism* 34 (1976): 249–59; and L. Jonathan Cohen, "The Role of Inductive Reasoning in the Interpretation of Metaphor," in Donald Davidson and Gilbert Harman, eds., *Semantics of Natural Language* (Boston: David Reidel, 1972), pp. 722–40.

Rousseau (TMR). Rousseau, he argues, claimed that speech originates from one man seeing another and describing him as a giant. Later, the man might recognize his similarity with the other and shift to a generic abstraction like *man*. But, de Man goes on, the expression *man* is actually less accurately referential than the metaphor, because it covers over all sorts of potential differences between the men. The metaphor *giant*, on the other hand, tells us nothing about the realm of objective facts, but, then, it does not pretend to and does not catch us up in bad faith as does the putative description *man*. The metaphor gives an honest expression of a mental state of a given man in a given situation, an expression which does not tempt us to false generalizations, because it is so clear as a particular action.

4. Indeterminacy based on changing ideas of "literariness"

I hope I have made it clear that there are no general reasons why contexts are not sufficiently determinate to allow public agreement on the basic nature of speech acts. One need not so much refute Derrida for this purpose as point out how his claims are largely tautological and self-enclosed. His arguments about meaning are ultimately empty, because they simply do not address the differences between linguistic possibilities and actual linguistic choices. He shows that language as language is indeterminate, because it admits of possible choices, but he does not show that once choices are made there are not probabilistic grounds for deciding what the immediately relevant choices and contexts are. However, while one can dismiss Derrida's relevance for general semantics, the case is not so clear for specifically literary issues. Here we must show that literary texts provide sufficient probabilistic contexts for determining meanings in both the worlds they represent and in the authorial act. Indeterminacy theories specifically devoted to literary matters are likely to prove more perplexing than those based on general psychological and semantic arguments. One must locate principles for synthesizing into a single hierarchy of relationships extremely dense semantic units organized by internal, self-referential contexts. Nonetheless, I have argued that there are procedural considerations that enable us to reconstruct these contexts by naturalizing the text as concrete performance for reflective purpose. The pressure of a third group of indeterminacy theories should allow me to clarify the provenance of this claim and to prepare for the next chapter's discussion of an intensional text grammar.

Because this third group of theories is concerned primarily with practical questions, it does not manifest the clear conceptual organization of the other groups. Thematic claims for indeterminacy may derive from a wide variety of contexts, for example, from a sense of modernity developed out of the conjunction of Nietzsche, Freud, and Marx (as in Edward Said's *Beginnings* and in Roland Barthes' more historical pronouncements), from Paul de Man's insistence that self-conscious writers use indeterminacy to mark the gap between the life of consciousness and the demands of the empirical world, or from Frank Kermode's claims for the inherent plenitude of classic texts that allows them to be reinterpreted according to the demands of different cultures.[17]

I have chosen as a representative example of these theories a recent essay by Frank Kermode on Hawthorne. The essay combines aspects of all the forms of thematic indeterminacy I have just mentioned, and it succinctly exemplifies the way Derridean concerns are domesticated, historicized, and psychologized in some of our best recent practical criticism. Kermode's theme is that Hawthorne is essentially a modern writer, because he recognizes that the very process of representing life in a fiction undermines the possibility of the writer's authoritatively interpreting his materials. Hawthorne employs the conventional typological structures which give an illusion of a writer's authority, but he carefully deconstructs any single thematic coherence within the typology—thus, he suggests that the experience presented can only be given coherence by an individual reader in effect creating his own text. The following comment, on *The House of Seven Gables*, suggests how Hawthorne's metacommentary self-consciously reinforces his awareness of the new hermeneutic world opened up by American scepticism about authority and historical recurrence:

> The text of the novel imitates him in this; its Gothic materials—
> lost maps, inherited courses [*sic*]—its magic, its confusion of the
> "traditionary" and the historical, its allegories cunningly too clear or

17. Said gives a very nice formulation of the five expectations that characterize the classical models of meaning which modern views of intertextuality reject. See *Beginnings*, p. 162. Paul de Man's essay on Derrida in BI provides a good example of a critic trying to subsume Derrida's logical treatment of meaning into a historical and purposive view of the author's thematic awareness of the problems. De Man, in short, makes indeterminacy a possible authorial perspective, and, thus, implies that we can understand it as the action of the implied author. For Kermode, I will concentrate on one essay, "Hawthorne's Modernity," *Partisan Review* 41 (1974), 428–41, where his theory is less qualified than in his recent book *The Classic* (New York: Viking, 1975). I will abbreviate this essay as HM.

too obscure—are all evasions of narrative authority, and imply that each man must make his own reading. The types inscribed on it are shifting, unstable, varying in force, to be fulfilled only by the determinations of the reader; in strong contrast, then, to the old Puritan types. So the text belongs to its moment and implicitly declares that the modern classic is not, like the book of God or the old book of nature, or the old accommodated classic, of which the senses, though perhaps hidden, are fully determined, there in full before the interpreter. In the making of it the reader must take his share. (HM, 436)

It is crucial to this sense of modernity that Hawthorne is not simply a complex writer; rather, he is a consciously indeterminate one, refusing to give his materials any secure interpretations and forcing readers to make "the book according to the order and disorder of our own imagination" (HM, 439). It seems that authors, as well as critics, are trapped between an impossible dream of objective interpretations of experience, on the one hand, and, on the other, a hopelessly solipsistic process of generating fictions which can at best be honest about their own incapacity to understand how other minds make sense of the world.

Kermode's claims are based on a very interesting, and (for my purpose) useful, confusion. He fails to distinguish between an indeterminate text and a quite determinate textual act, which explores tensions that arise from attempting to interpret complex events by simple thematic categories or an insufficient typological grammar. Kermode does not ask whether difficulties of determining the text derive from his model of coherence or from the action presented, and he ignores the fact that it is consistent to offer a coherent, determinate account of a literary text as exploring or postulating an essential indeterminacy in its dramatic situation. What remains determinable is the nature and quality of the acts by which the author develops his claims and suggests their significance—this, at least, is what we buy when we stress competence as the capacity to naturalize a text in terms of a performance we reflect upon for its representative qualities.

In fact, if we look at what Kermode actually does in this essay, we will find strong confirmation for my hypothesis about competence. For, despite his explicit position, he, in effect, demonstrates how to construct a text as a performance. While he takes a share in making the text (an expression that reminds us of Holland's tautology about character), he does not, therefore, arbitrarily impose his own categories. Instead, he offers a very persuasive description of Hawthorne's authorial action that constitutes a comprehensive reading of the textual details. Kermode recognizes the limits of simple moral interpretations of Hawthorne's actions, and shows, instead, how the strands of Hawthorne's fiction make sense as a dramatization of the difficulty of making moral judgments in a social context torn between religious and secular schemes of interpretation. The real power of Kermode's reading is not to release us into subjective readings, but to show how subjective moral allegories only capture us in the hermeneutic trap Hawthorne is depicting. Kermode claims that the reader as interpreter must make his own arrangement of the text's shifting play of signifiers, but, by foregoing moral interpretation for description of Hawthorne's action, he manages to achieve a position where a kind of objectivity is possible, and where the inadequacy of other readings is clearly established. He does this by showing how Hawthorne's problems with typology themselves typify a recurrent human problem.

Kermode, too, typifies a recurrent problem that leads to and informs much of the current interest in indeterminacy. A variety of cultural and academic forces—the enervation of the New Criticism, the desire for relevance, a distrust of formal and aesthetic issues as not sufficiently absorbing for critical work—has led to equating determinate meaning with the possibility of coherent thematic interpretations of a text's details. This emphasis, in turn, fosters discoveries that literary texts are indeterminate. Thematic expectations lead interpreters to concentrate on whether an abstract conceptual model will fit the complexity of event and verbal texture in a work. The results are predictable, especially in a literary culture so aware of the tensions which I have discussed between representation and its other. Moreover, thematic analyses encourage indeterminacy theories, because in their straight form they make it difficult to claim distinctive cognitive properties in literary experience. What depth literary themes provide one can find better stated elsewhere, so it is tempting to root the value of literary experience in other properties—especially in literature's capacity to make themes ironic and to dramatize their inadequacy to concrete situations. (This move ironically repeats New Critical versions of paradox from different epistemological perspectives.) Then there are more subtle pressures at work. Good critics want to stress the complex and intense energies involved in reading a text—both out of respect for the text and out of the desire to perform their own talents. However, if one equates meaning with theme, there is little room now (after decades of interpretation) for the full play of a reader's energies, unless he concentrates on showing how the details contradict any easy generalizations and invite endless reinterpretation. We find this evident in Kermode's reading of the perennial modernism of the *classic* as permanently vital, because always capable of being reinterpreted. This emphasis on reinterpretation preserves the energy of classic texts by denying two of their central features—the necessary *pastness* of the classic, which makes its continuing relevance a testimony to perennial features of human experience, and the relationship between the qualitative depth of classic treatments of actions and their continuing power. It may well be that the term *classic* is significant because the works to which we apply it have the power of generating classes; that is, they become prototypes of basic recurrent modes for imaginatively organizing experience. What matters, then, is less the openness in semantic texture that allows reinterpretation than the depth with which actions are rendered and engage our energies. A text like the *Aeneid* can be read in much the same way Kermode reads Hawthorne—less because it is open to thematic reinterpretation, than because its action typifies perennial problems inherent in interpreting historical change. The implied author must come to terms with the contradictions between the Augustan ideal of the Pax Romana and the danger that the means needed to achieve that ideal threaten to undermine it by repeating the violence endemic to the cultures it wants to supplant; Aeneas himself must continually grapple with reading signs that invoke two contradictory symbolic codes (or texts, in Derrida's formulation), one based on the Trojan values on which he had formed himself, the other requiring faith in a destined new order.

Those very features which lead thematic criticism toward indeterminacy become essentially determinate properties in readings that emphasize dramatistic performative qualities. By contrasting a performance model to Kermode's theses, we can begin to see both what that model can account for and the implications it has for practical criticism. The basic terms for that contrast derive from Kant's attempt to distinguish the status of ideas or themes in art from their status in other modes of discourse: "By an aesthetical idea I understand that representation of the imagination which occasions much thought, without however any definite thought, i.e., any *concept*, being capable of being adequate to it." [18] One cannot be sure exactly how much formalism lies beyond Kant's claim, but it is possible to insist, as Wittgenstein does, that this

18. *Critique of Judgment*, trans. J. H. Bernard (New York: Hafner, 1968), sec. 49, p. 157. For Wittgenstein's position, see LA, 28–40, and Casey, *The Language of Criticism*. The New Critics often tried to define a denotative referent for aesthetic ideas, and, thus, produced claims about truth to nondiscursive experiences.

different status of concepts stems from the fact that, in ordinary experiences, art works are not so much analyzed and interpreted as described and treated as performances. Performances, in turn, cannot be reduced either to verbal constructs or to their informing ideas. These alternatives both serve as means rather than ends, because they make it possible for an interpreter to reconstruct dimensions of an action in a situation. The reader needs interpretive strategies, but these are provisional ways into appreciation of the performance. They are neither substitutes for the concrete enactment nor its goal. Interpretive concepts function more as themes do in music than as explanations do in science or ethics. These concepts become what Whitehead called "lures for feeling"; they are means for bringing large matters to bear in intensifying aspects of a specific irreducible event or situation. One cannot rule out subjective contexts as possible lures for feeling, but for criticism, and ultimately for the reader who internalizes public standards, there remains the procedural test of convincing others that a particular way of conceiving the performance in the text articulates the fullest possibilities inherent in the words, situations, and formal patterns. The criteria for describing a performance, in short, are essentially those by which Kermode persuades us to include Hawthorne's metafictional concerns in our reading of his novels. A text, then, may be conceptually indeterminate because, as Kant says, it admits the interplay of many concepts. But this does not mean we choose among these concepts; rather, we try to establish the action in such a way that we can see how each might affect the nature and quality of what remains a single purposive performance.

Themes, then, contribute to the meaning of a literary text, but do not constitute the meaning. In one sense, this is obvious, because we treat texts as particulars, important as specific organizations of details rather than as primarily instances of generalizations. These texts depend on principles of organization and evaluation which are of a different order of being, and are capable of organizing and using themes. In concrete cases, even with texts whose main purpose is to articulate or defend an idea, this means that as long as we view the text in literary terms—that is, as a significant, self-organizing particular—our largest category of explanation will be *act*, not *theme*. Thus, even with texts based on single organizing ideas, our concern is less with the determinate nature of the organizing ideas than with the purposes the ideas serve. We attend to the qualities of thought by which the ideas are articulated or applied to the abstract and concrete dimensions of the situation. We often find that the nature of the theme—say the idea of justice in *Paradise Lost* or of nature in the *Prelude*—cannot be abstracted from the text. Justice in *Paradise Lost* means the relationships drawn by the text among the various situations in which the concept is used. This, indeed, is why literary texts, as performed correlations among aspects of an idea, so readily transcend the ideological limitations of their historical genesis.

When we insist on the qualitative aspects of even heavily thematic texts, we see that there need not be much difference between classic or readerly texts and self-conscious modernist treatments of indeterminacy. Most literary texts matter because of the properties they hold in tension. These may be dramatic instances, where an author performs a capacity to make fixed ideas resonate in situations—as, say, in Donne's "Holy Sonnets" or in a novel like *Middlemarch*—or they may be situations where ideas themselves conflict and will not be reconciled with one another or with events. In both cases, the texts have determinate and vital existence to the extent that they focus our sympathies and our reflective beings on intense relationships between a human agent and a situation. Thematic criticism can deepen our awareness of that situation, so long as it does not propose too simple a conceptual substitute for it. Then, among other things, it encourages claims about indeterminacy as soon as other features are recognized. These claims are, virtually by definition, reductions of both the dramatic and the conceptual tensions which characterize the power of most texts to move us deeply while rewarding the mind's ability to understand what it is moved by.

5. How a performance model can claim to resolve these problems: the authority of actions

Much of my last argument may have seemed only a rehash of New Critical doctrines. It was that—determinedly and determinately—but with what I take to be the crucial difference that now this doctrine can be put on a concrete basis. Texts have properties of particularity, dramatic tension, and depth because we construe them as specific performances in situations which unfold in time for our sympathy and reflection. Moreover, we now have an imperative for returning to New Critical generalizations about the text as dramatic work, because we can see where the alternative emphasis on thematic content has led. With an essentially Burkean restatement of New Critical views, we can clearly handle what becomes problematic in Kermode's essay. Now we have another way of understanding how a reader's energies might be absorbed.

Reading is only partially thematic interpretation. Equally significant are processes of making qualitative distinctions, assessing acts, and trying to deepen one's grasp of the agents' relationships to their specific and conceptual situations. If theme is central, energies are all connected with decoding operations. But these operations, as we have seen, have nowhere to go but into refined ironies, because the theory provides no other focus for sympathetic and reflective engagement. With action as our center, even the simplest themes can provide place and play for the most intense energies.

A stress on performance can also establish terms for locating and resolving the more general problems that lead to an easy reliance on notions of indeterminacy. Kermode's observations about Hawthorne, for example, can be shown to derive from a basic determinable feature of literary texts which modern writers tend to emphasize. A literary text typically blends two levels of action—a dramatic course of events, and a process of interpretation and judgment carried on by an implicit author, whom Geoffrey Hartmann calls "the voice in the shuttle." Modern writers take advantage of this situation by calling attention to complex aspects of voice which can be set in conflict with the mimetic level. *Madame Bovary* here is the quintessential modern text, for it nicely plays off the authorial voice against Emma's dramatic plight. While she tragically pursues her banal desires, the authorial voice coldly distances itself from that tragic world by using elaborate artifice, grotesque plot manipulations, and obvious control over the dramatic, fictive subjects it creates in order to insist on its freedom from the ironic realm of desire. *Madame Bovary* is not open or pluralistic, but it demands of a reader who is to appreciate it fully that she remain open to the complex interrelationships between the two levels of action. The tensions Flaubert articulates, Kafka brings to one radical extreme, an extreme where indeterminacy is an important concept. For with Kafka, the authorial desire for an adequate stance from which to evaluate, or at least to handle, his dramatic materials becomes the basic action of the novel. There are always more allegorical possibilities arising on the expressive level than can be satisfactorily and coherently applied to the events of the story. But even here the point of Kafka's fables is not to elicit a variety of readings, but to dramatize consequences deriving from the difficulty of determining meanings for events.

Finally—once we can distinguish acts of performing problems involving indeterminacy from indeterminate texts—we can give an adequate description of what is at stake in the fashionable topic of a writer's authority. Kermode is typical of contemporary critics in assuming that authority depends on a writer's ability to make a determinate and accurate interpretation of his materials. It seems more probable, however, that a writer's authority resides less in his generalizations than in the qualities of humane concern his text displays. What gives Hawthorne, Flaubert, and Tolstoy authority—and what denies it to Beaumont and Fletcher or Scribe or Vachel Lindsay—is the fact that the members of the former group make a world serious people can imaginatively inhabit, concern themselves with, and take delight in. Literary authority derives from making problems believable, not from solving them.[19] Indeed, had Hawthorne taken literally the only remarks Kermode seems to think are not indeterminate, had he really believed that "the reader may choose among these theories" (нм, 438), his rendering of the hermeneutic problems which perplex modern man would be far less compelling and his authority that much diminished. On matters like these it is not simply Kermode's authority, but that of literary traditions in general, which is ultimately at stake. So long as we insist that readers can choose freely among alternatives, we simplify and trivialize both hermeneutic activities and the objects that authorize our concern with that activity.

19. There is a simple test for the superiority of a qualitative and question-oriented model of authority, as opposed to a thematic one. In *Beginnings*, Said does brilliant readings of the tension between a writer trying to authorize his text as an interpretation of experience and the pressure or molestation of that authority by the intractable facts of the world or pulls of connotative language. Yet his image of authority cannot handle the basic fact that we can distinguish different degrees of respect for a writer's authority precisely in the honesty and depth with which he presents the ironic forces that molest his desired projection of thematic meaning.

7

Toward an Intensional Text Grammar: The Constituents of Literary Performance

1. *General description of the chapter*   Naturalizing a literary text entails attempting to give it publicly accessible form as the performance of an action. To make good on this claim, however, I must specify the particular features by which naturalization takes place and I must articulate the grounds on which one can assert that an interpretation is sufficiently coherent and perspicuous to warrant claims for determinacy. Rough terms for resolving both of these issues exist in the work of text grammarians like Greimas and Barthes. Yet the work these theorists do is severely limited by their adherence to an extensional, scientific model of analysis. In this chapter, I shall attempt to recast the terms of text grammar so that its description of narrative units and structural functions in a text can be adapted to the intensional properties necessary for interpreting actions. In proposing the shift in emphasis, I will present general structural considerations rather than a formal methodology. What I lose in apparent precision, I hope to gain in a capacity to capture depth as well as coherence and to provide a relatively formal account of what competent readers normally do in largely immediate and flexible ways. The same terms used in suggesting a workable text grammar then lead to a discussion of criteria for judging the validity of literary interpretations. I shall, for the last time, insist that the grammar for dealing with actions requires hermeneutic standards different from the hypothico-deductive model of scientific inquiry. Here, my main purpose will be to clear the way for the next chapter's discussion of the cognitive ends served by this different perspective.

2. Defining actions in literature and
the levels of action in a text

There are two fundamental issues we must clarify before considering questions of text grammars—in what way it makes sense to treat literary texts as acts, not as thoughts or texts or entities that are only products of acts, and what specific kinds of acts or levels of purpose one must consider in giving a full account of naturalization. The first issue is significant, because on it rests the case for treating texts as embodiments, and hence as performances and not simply ideas rhetorically communicated. Much of what needs saying was considered in my discussion of defining literature. Now I think I can bring that discussion to bear here, by considering the place of ordinary distinctions between thoughts about actions and actions themselves. In ordinary behavior, the distinction is usually easy to make. When we discuss thoughts, there is no need to choose among alternatives, to narrow one's options by selecting means, or to worry about responsibility for consequences or assessments by others. We are not responsible for our thoughts until they are seen as constituting purposes and initiating actions. Even then, it is only the specific motive, not the chain of thoughts surrounding it, which is likely to be assessed. With literary texts, however, it is precisely the play of thoughts or processes of reflection which I think we treat as actions. This occurs because of the analogy afforded by expressive implicature and the social fact that this process of thinking is offered to others. Thus, the processes of mind presented imply both selection and responsibility, and these features are best accounted for by treating the work as a self-conscious display of the values in such processes. In order to determine values, in turn, we expect the text to suggest contexts for situating the acts of mind. We find ourselves able, then, to apply to this kind of activity an aesthetic version of A. I. Melden's definition of an action as "a case in which what an individual does can be in principle and in the appropriate circumstances the subject of moral review." [1] I say *aesthetic* version because the relevant category of judgment is the more general idea of qualitative review. As is the case with overt dramatic actions, the thoughts in a literary text take a concrete form, whose particulars imply a way of making choices in definable contexts. The forms of expressing the thought are deeds in every sense of the term, so that even when literary works present an agent as musing or reacting

1. Melden, "Action," in Care and Landesman, eds., p. 27.

unintentionally, we do not dismiss his behavior, but see it as significantly unintentional. He may be blinding himself to something. What is dramatically unintentional we find purposive on the level of authorial action (although it is again possible that the author's intentions do not adequately explain the significance). It is, in fact, an important feature of literary performances that there need be no overt praxis at all, because events are not required to make us pay attention to states of mind. In a meditative religious lyric, for example, we take the mental processes as symbolically representative of mental attitudes significant both in themselves and as indications of how one has composed himself to be ready for any overt action he may need to perform. Similarly with Romantic lyrics or psychological novels, there is no need to concentrate on specific narrative consequences, because we come to understand how a person composes herself for her relationships to nature and to other people. For similar reasons, forms, like comedy, which culminate in a sense of open possibilities focus on changes in attitude and patterns of thinking. What matters more than plot is the qualities of thinking and responding which the agent develops, for this will define what he does in subsequent situations.[2]

In a literary text, what constitutes an action is so flexible that to make even a rough definition it would be wise to adapt terms similar to those Northrop Frye uses in defining a symbol: a *literary action* is any aspect of a text which can become the focus of attention and be seen as significant because of the purposive behavior it reflects, either by a dramatic character or by an implicit author. Once we pose such a definition, it is clear that we will need some supplementary distinctions. This is why we shall have to recast some of the standard philosophical definitions of *purpose*. So loose a definition puts a heavy burden on means for relating these specific units of action into synthetic wholes, whereby we see the specifics as intensionally related to one another and not merely joined as a list of discrete particulars. Moreover, we must be able in these syntheses to distinguish on several levels between *internal relations,* or contexts required by the agent's sense of his own activity, and *external relations,* or contexts brought to bear from features of a text or

2. Elder Olson, speaking of "Sailing to Byzantium," puts nicely the practical implications of taking modes of thinking as acts: "The character is not simply in a passion, nor is he acting upon another character, but has performed an act actualizing and instancing his moral character, that is he has made a moral choice." See "Sailing to Byzantium: Prolegomena to a Poetics of the Lyric," in Crane, ed., *Critics and Criticism,* p. 21.

explanatory systems which clarify for an observer the nature and quality of the action. Here we begin to see one of the complexities with
which this chapter shall grapple, for what are external relations from
the point of view of the characters can well be internal relations when
we construct the implicit author's sense of his own activity. There are
several levels of integration in a text, by which details on one level become symbolically significant constituents on another.

Action philosophers provide one basic concept for producing these
levels of integration. They distinguish between *intentions* and *plans*, or
long-range purposes. Van Dijk, for example, points out that "A purpose
is like an intention but places an action within a broader framework of
other actions, events, and interactions." (AAD, 280). Intentions are normally quite specific and often need not relate to purposes in Van Dijk's
sense. I may decide to go to Toronto only because I am bored. At other
times, it makes sense to ask what long-range purposes inform a specific
decision. The answer to this question in effect interprets the intention
by placing it in a larger context. My going to Toronto may be seen as
part of a research project, and the research project as part of some general plan for achieving success or defining myself as a specific kind of
person. Plans, then, provide the same kind of context for intentions as
intentions do for actions. We determine plans derived to explain a concrete course of action by essentially the same criteria for correlating elements as we use in single action descriptions. In so doing, we make it
possible to employ intensional concepts for a series of actions which
synthesize them all into discrete units, subject to qualitative assessment.
Once we can assess plans in relationship to situations, we have a basis
for bringing in the idea of *character*. Character is a construct for interpreting in human predicates the distinctive projects and styles located
in long-term action descriptions.[3] A person may not be clearly determin-

---

3. Wolfgang Iser, "The Reality of Fiction: A Functionalist Approach to Literature," *New Literary History* 7 (1975):18 ff., provides a useful description of the
way we construct a character's purposes by correlating details in his actions. I do
not see, however, the justification for Iser's insistence that literary texts always work
against prevailing norms and for his sense that the reader's participation produces
indeterminacy. First, I think his sensitive treatment of a text's temporality ignores
the dialectical complement of spatial patterns I discuss above and undervalues the
synthetic role of traditional narrative movements that afford climactic scenes where,
as in the last book of the *Iliad*, we try to synthesize the various strands of knowledge
we have about a character. And second, I think the idea of *an unfamiliar message*
too readily connects freshness of vision with resistance to society. Society provides
several levels of norms, and many texts try to recover, not to disrupt, some social
norms for assessing actions.

able from any given act, but personal identity is inseparable from attributions made to understand extended projects and recurrent attitudes. The corollary of this principle of identity is a diminishing ratio of probable indeterminacy when we describe actions. This helps overcome some of the looseness in my initial definition of a literary action. For however flexible the parameters of a single action, as we try to relate the action to plans we become accountable for a greater number of details. Consequently, there are far fewer possible types and descriptions which can relate the details into a whole. Specific intentions do not often require complex and deep predicate clusters; plans often do, and the greater the complexity, paradoxically, the more limited the possible adequate descriptions of the whole.

We are obviously working toward a definition of *plot*, at least as an intensional account of mimetic actions, but our distance from an adequate definition indicates the limits of standard accounts of actions for literary theory. First, the account of plans and purposes is far too polite. As Paul Grice said in a lecture, philosophers tend to treat the mind's construction of purposes as an orderly stage trial, when the reality requires comparison to a department meeting. In practical life, it is rare when a person clearly decides on an action by deductive practical reasoning from a major purpose and then is totally satisfied with the choice. He normally blends and reconciles conflicting purposes, often unaware of all the considerations that ultimately motivate both the major purposes and the specific act. It is useful, in this respect, to distinguish two basic types of purpose which often conflict—*practical* and *self-regarding* purposes. A practical purpose is a desire to bring about a specific state of affairs in accordance with classical utilitarian measures of one's best interest, while a self-regarding purpose is (loosely) Kantian rather than utilitarian. It is a desire to perform or articulate oneself—both to oneself and to others—as a specific kind of human being who embodies certain standards of sensitivity, intelligence, moral rectitude, and so forth. In literary works, where performance has less narcissistic overtones than it does as an ethical concept, we must further distinguish levels of interaction between mimetic and authorial forms of expressions aimed at satisfying self-regarding desires. Narrative literary forms develop tensions between the levels of practical and of self-regarding purposes, as is most powerfully evident in tragic situations. Oedipus cannot both save his kingdom and maintain his self-image, although he cannot really choose one or the other. Lyric forms, including novels concerned largely with the patterned development of feelings and perceptions, often concentrate on moments where the conditions of one's claim to self-regard can be understood, tested, or changed. Romantic lyrics, for example, test a speaker's desires to achieve through meditation a new condition of power of vision, while traditional love lyrics can be seen as exhibiting both the speaker's and the poet's ability to play an idealized role or to perform his qualities of perception, imagination, and wit to his beloved. Here, whatever its status as a general description of human behavior, Yeats' theory of the mask as a dialectical mode of perfecting oneself provides us with a powerful description of action in lyric poetry.

Even distinguishing types of conscious purposes, however, does not get us to the basic problems, nor will it explain the special role literature can play in making us aware of the relevant complexities. The philosophers rarely consider how the expressive features of actions make us aware of aspects of a person's long-range motivations, which are not explicitly conscious purposes. We need not here enter disputes between determinists and their opponents. For it is a common aspect of literary experience to recognize how the implicit aspects of what one sees and the ways he sees it influence his behavior. Characters are not reasoning machines and purposes are not simply rational ideas. These are truisms, but they are significant because they require a concept of long-range plans on a higher level of generality than the concept of purpose. This concept must be able to account for purposes as themselves constituents of some larger field, in which purposes are correlated with implicit and expressive features of behavior. The best term for this level of analysis, I think, is Sartre's *project*, which denotes the most comprehensive sphere of motivation for behavior and allows us to propose answers to questions about why purposes are chosen and why they often misinterpret or inadequately interpret what the agent actually does. *Project* covers avowable and many nonavowable features of long-range behavior.

A simple literary example will show how these three levels of inquiry can function. From Achilles' early actions we immediately see his basic intentions. He calls the assembly in order to bring order and confidence to the troops, and he quarrels with Agamemnon because he feels insulted. Gradually, we come to see how both intentions participate in two long-range purposes, a practical one to win the war and a self-regarding one to act so that he can consider himself a pure representative of heroic martial virtue. The conflict of purposes is one source of the tragedy. But as we become familiar with Achilles' behavior, we also go back and redescribe his actions in terms of a self he expresses but of which he is not entirely aware. We see, from Odysseus' later behavior in a similar scene, that Achilles could have asked Agamemnon to call the assembly, and, thus, have honored the proprieties and avoided the conflict. And after the visit of his friends in book nine, we suspect that Achilles has a distinctive project for achieving recognition which is morally culpable. He is not content to excel; he wants to be seen as absolutely necessary to his community on his own terms. He is not aware that his image of heroism is incompatible with any form of social existence; hence, the reasons he poses also function in part as symptoms of his blindness.[4]

3. Barthes' text grammar as an example of the limits of an extensional approach

Now I want to show the significance of my concern for distinguishing the role of purposes and the levels of analysis we need for discussing them. From the previous discussion, two principles should be clear. First, it is possible to explain actions in such a way that we relate them to one another in intensional terms on progressive levels of integration which, in turn, require the depth predicates we normally attribute to persons: if a lion had a plan or a project, we could not understand him. Second, as we move toward these larger levels of integration, we enter realms where a story of some kind is necessary for the synthesis. We move to-

---

4. I offer these comments on the *Iliad* as examples for my argument, not as an adequate description of Achilles' character. I am not sure that Homer would understand our concept of character, and, hence, I am, in this respect at least, not a competent reader of this text. I point this out because we have here a case where it is important to qualify one's claims. But even if I am not sure what Homer might have intended, I am not helpless. I can construct an argument for what the shape of the character is and the kind of evidence I use and offer it as a hypothesis to be tested. It seems to me that those classical scholars, like Bruno Snell and Eric Havelock, who invoke cultural arguments to give a very reductive account of the *Iliad* simply do not admit sufficient complexity, which it is hard not to see in the text. Here, in order to construct an adequate account of the text, we must construct an adequate account of Homer and his culture. A further problem we encounter in exaggerated form is the different ways classical and modern texts emphasize purposes. In classical literature the agent is more likely to know his purposes or to be motivated by general, easily abstractable passions. This enables the text to stress the consequences of the action or its social and metaphysical implications. Modern literature, on the other hand, tends to concentrate on the complex attitudes which shape actions and are too subtle and complex to become clear objects of a character's self-reflective acts. Consequences tend to be seen primarily as functions of the way choices are made, rather than of the representative nature of the choice itself.

ward plot and toward analogues between plot and critical accounts of a text. If we were to stop at the level on which we understand a project, we would construct a plot as our account of the agent's behavior. But we would not, at least when discussing a literary text, understand our understanding of the character. For that level of understanding, we must recognize what structures and relationships within the text provide the evidence for our description and give the described project a place in the whole. We need to identify with a level of understanding larger than that of any character; hence, we must shift from dramatic to implicit authorial act. Here plot becomes identified with authorial purpose, and this reminds us that *plot* is a loose term that includes lyric and argumentative structures. (The sceptic will correctly point out that now we will also need a larger level of integration to explain our understanding of authorial understanding. Here, as we shall see, we must resort once more to the concepts of competence and philosophical grammar as our vehicles for explaining how we relate texts to types and to existential concerns which transcend specific texts.)

The best way to show why these principles matter is to relate them to current literary theory. If we are to speak of procedures for naturalizing a text and constructing it as a coherent whole, we obviously want to know how we apply them. I think this, in itself, is sufficient justification for our labors. But we must also face the now-standard model of text grammars, which tries to explain these larger levels of coherence on the model of structural linguistics. The linguistic analogue leads text grammarians to eschew terms like *purpose* and to attempt to describe coherence in purely extensional terms. Consequently, most text grammarians provide terms for recognizing behavior, but not for understanding actions. Without a sense of actions, there is no room for qualitative interpretive questions. The text grammarian ends up concentrating simply on how the author manipulates extensional plot units. We find ourselves trapped again in textualism's stress on writing whose basic purpose is writing. But this perspective is only a consequence of an inadequate methodology, which cannot recover the deeper features of literary discourse. For, as we have seen, categories taken from the ascriptive semantic level of language cannot take us far in describing particular utterances, where we need concepts of a relation between act and context.[5]

5. The basic defense the text grammarians make of their extensional language is Todorov's constant insistence that they are doing poetics, not criticism, and, hence, are not responsible for the qualitative concerns of the critic. Poetics is a science, not

Roland Barthes' influential "Introduction to the Structural Study of Narrative" provides a concise and useful test case.[6] Barthes begins by insisting that literary studies must heed the lesson of linguistics and try to develop a deductive model of the relationships necessary to constitute a narrative structure. There must be, he argues, three levels of integration. The first level parallels morphemes in linguistics. It consists of the basic, independently meaningful, units of a narrative. These can be roughly divided into functions and indices—the former consisting of discrete units that can give a narrative concreteness and atmosphere, and the latter providing signs which will ultimately constitute paradigms revealing character traits, or, in his later terminology, become units within signifying codes. The second level, which focusses and unifies the basic elements into coherent independent units within a specific narrative, he calls the level of actions. Here we have two stages. First, there are *sequences*, logical strings of functional units which form a unity "when one of its terms is lacking an antecedent of the same Kin" and when the last of its terms "no longer entails any consequent function" (ISN, 253). If we integrate these functions, we move to a second stage where we can speak of *actions* proper. These Barthes defines in behavioral terms, as "designating the larger articulations of *praxis* (to desire, to communicate, to struggle)" (ISN, 258). So abstract a formulation allows Barthes to adopt Greimas' strategy of sorting out "characters in narrative not on the basis of what they are but on the basis of what they do" (ISN, 257), and, thus, he can claim to avoid all questions of subjectivity. Characters are functions of large units of praxis and have no independent status (hence, *purpose* is at best a term applying to the most general kinds of desires, with no room for qualitative assessment). Finally, the two prior levels gain their significance from a third, narrative level, which unifies meanings along two axes. One axis is horizontal,

---

a hermeneutic art, and deals with structures, not functions. See, for example, "The Place of Style in Structure," in Chatman, ed., *Literary Style: A Symposium*, pp. 29–31. There is some truth to his claims and some use for this kind of work, but only when translated into functional terms. In essence, Todorov is working not simply from another perspective but within another logic, rather like using ethnology to predict the actions of human beings. For other, more trenchant, logical criticisms of the text grammarians than I give, although essentially for the same lack of concern with contextual functions, see Culler's *Structuralist Poetic*.

6. Barthes, "An Introduction to the Structural Study of Narrative," trans. Lionel Diusit, *New Literary History* 6 (1975):237–72, hereafter abbreviated ISN. One can use Barthes to illustrate the contrast between extensional and intensional approaches to a text simply by comparing the lexia and the commentary in S/Z.

creating the chronological relationships between actions and sequences that constitute a plot, and the other is vertical, a plane of discourse, which gives meaning and form to the horizontal movement.

Barthes' conclusion expresses most clearly the limits of his methodology. Because narratives are so consistent to deductive formal principles, their main source of interest is the way they vary these formal expectations: "What goes on in a narrative is, from the referential (real) point of view strictly *nothing*. What does 'happen' is language per se, the adventure of language, whose advent never ceases to be celebrated" (ISN, 271). The only actor who matters to Barthes is the author considered as craftsman, and he is often conceived merely as a function of language, a move which makes sense only on an abstract tautological and systematic level.[7] This perspective, as we saw in discussing Culler, omits most of what we enjoy in literary experience. So now, instead of quarreling with it, I want simply to point out why it follows from Barthes' method. If there are only extensional linguistic units, there is no room for agents and actors' purposes, and, hence, no place for qualitative existential concerns on either mimetic or authorial levels. If the units of narrative are only formal elements, it follows necessarily that all the author can do is play with manipulating them. There are no dramatic human concerns to understand or take a stand on.

Language per se, however, can only be the source of adventure when a text does not offer signs which can coherently be construed in terms of purposive predicates, but confines its only motivating force to a semantic field. This is, of course, possible, albeit rare. Even the newest of new novels usually implies purposes for its linguistic play, if only in the author's theory of language. Moreover, the concept of integration has little to do unless there are more complex units to relate than Barthes' theory admits. (In practice, Barthes often speaks in terms of dramatic purposes.) Barthes' effort to produce a coherent model of narrative without purposive predicates serves finally to show how narrative itself is a function of plot, and plot is dependent on concepts of situation and purpose which invoke contexts of dramatic or typological plausi-

7. And yet Barthes, unlike most textualists, recognizes the importance of a kind of authorial activity even when a text has no mimetic level: "A novel devoid of any characters, such as *Drame* by Philippe Sollers, turns entirely away from the person, to the benefit of language, but retains nevertheless a fundamental interplay of actants bearing on the speech acts themselves. This type of literature does not do away with the 'subject,' but the 'subject' is, from now on, the linguistic subject" (ISN, 257 n.).

bility and psychological processes.[8] There may then be no very practical extensional text grammar, however much the effort does make clear the elements which authors manipulate for their purposes. But this does not mean that there cannot be a general model of a hierarchy of integrative functions (on the analogue of Russell's theory of types). This model might not explain how texts are constructed, but it can provide a general abstract representation of the considerations that go into defining the coherence of a literary text in terms of purposes.

4. The constituents of an intensional text grammar

We can then sketch in intensional terms these levels of integration, but the variety of particulars (and probably my limits as a theorist) will not admit Barthes' precision. What I lack in precision, however, may be compensated for by the fact that this model applies not only to narratives but to all literary forms of plotting an action. There need be no quarrel with Barthes' description of the first, or morphemic, level of literary constituent units. It is not the units of the paradigms but their final shape which must be revised. On the second level, the units of dramatic action must be considered not as abstract types but as specific forms of purposive behavior. Here the horizontal axis prepares our understanding of character by projecting events and choices in terms of their functions as forming, complementing, complicating, and resisting what we know of the agents' particular desires (AAD, 280).[9] This is the

---

8. Historians seem to have learned this lesson earlier than literary critics, perhaps because Hempel's positivist claims lacked the charm and playfulness of Structuralist deconstructions. See Patrick Gardiner, *The Nature of Historical Explanation* (Oxford: Oxford University Press, 1971).

9. For the fullest treatment I know of how we develop our concept of what a character is, see Charles Taylor, "Responsibility for Self." Taylor's discussion applies on both mimetic and authorial levels. Where Barthes sees character as a function of large units of praxis, Taylor shows that we identify a character by noticing how he defines his praxis. (If a character is what he does, we must remember that what he says and how he says it are important aspects of what he does.) Taylor begins by distinguishing first- and second-order desires. The former is simply a desire for a practical end, while the latter takes the form of a desire to be moved by certain desires rather than others. With second-order desires we refrain from doing something not simply because it is contingently incompatible with another desire (e.g., some people cannot both chew gum and defecate, and so must choose), but because it entails a self-image one wants to avoid. *Refraining* here stems from seeing conflicting desires as involving mutually contrasting images and concepts. One cannot logically, or better *grammatically*, define himself as generous and succumb to selfish desires. Understanding a character, then, depends on observing the con-

process of naturalization on the mimetic level. Simultaneously, a vertical axis of relationships operates in two ways. As we construct the relationship between situations and desires, the dramatic contexts invoke, or are manipulated by an author to invoke, general behavioral type expectations which bring evaluative terms and supplementary psychological predicates to bear. Moreover, the text itself invites the reader, by a variety of formal and structural means, to relate one agent's choices to another, or to relate similar contexts for action within an agent's career. Wordsworth's *Prelude,* for example, gains a good deal of its power from our capacity to recognize and to relate the many ways he responds to sublime situations and to a recurrent set of temptations—either for a dream of apocalypse, or for surrendering himself to the aimlessness of nature and urban society.

The third, and final, level of mimetic integration occurs when the reader can imagine a coherent dramatic and conceptual situation that accounts for the relationship between the projects of the various protagonists in a work and the structural and thematic parallels which focus them. Here, because we are beyond what any agent in the work could possibly see as the nature and meaning of his performance, we must define this level primarily in terms of authorial purposes. Put simply, only a purposive author can stand as both the center and circumference of a text, because only authorial choices are comprehensive enough to establish coherence among all the semantic functions and implicatures. But again we must heed distinctions between *intention in* and *intention to, meaning* and *significance,* levels of purpose, and the possibility of redescribing an act so that the intentions fail or are complicated by what is actually done. The basic strategy for perceiving the necessary sense of authorial activity while still acknowledging the full complexity of both the text and the writing subject can be developed from Kant's distinction between purpose and purposiveness.[10] In essence Kant wants to

---

trastive patterns constituting a person's idea of the good. His projection of himself as a person is a self-conscious articulation of purposes in accord with this contrastive vocabulary (and, as Taylor does not sufficiently stress, his acting according to his definitions). Self-definition (and, I add, coming to define another as a person) is a continual process of seeking greater articulation of a person's preferences and making them commensurate with one another. In literary texts, what Taylor sees as explicit self-definition depends on implicit expressive aspects of behavior. But the crucial point remains: we construct a character (or an author) by becoming articulate about his articulations in words and in behavior, of preferences and of the contrastive structures his stories about his purposes reveal.

10. *Critique of Judgment,* sections three, four, and especially ten.

separate a form of authorial activity that can be treated by abstractions about overall communicative design from the sense of immanent authorial activity continually making choices in terms of a feel for relationships which cannot be subsumed under single abstract concepts. Purposiveness, in other words, is the sense of intentionality that correlates with viewing the object as comprising an aesthetic idea, while purpose is a sense of intentionality we attribute to rational actions. If we accept Kant's rejecting purpose for purposiveness as the appropriate sense of intentionality in art, we find ourselves constrained to the aestheticism Hirsch rightly rejects. Writers clearly have Kantian "purposes," especially if we acknowledge levels of purpose. Art works can be the result of purposes to communicate an idea in a certain way or purposes to make a certain kind of object. In the latter case the purpose in the making could be to perform self-consciously the desires and qualities informing the specific mode of communication or it could be to manipulate narrative situations or emotional responses. There are, in other words, a broad enough range of levels and kinds of purposes that the concept remains applicable to aesthetic objects. Yet the sphere of judgment this concept invites requires a different kind of attention than does purposiveness. So the two can complement one another. Kant's purposiveness makes the most sense if we view it not as a condition of intentionality appropriate to the work as a whole but as a condition expressed in a variety of ways as the work reveals the imaginary engagements of the author within it. Where the idea of purpose suggests an author who stands apart as desiring agent from a cosmos he has ordered by immanent laws, the idea of purposiveness suggests a Greek god actively taking sides within the dramatic events and not necessarily capable of restraining particular attachments because he knows the overall design. Purposiveness, then, is a concept for handling the traces of many states of desire within or working through the authorial subject and released by a designed imaginary world. Purposiveness, like all states of imaginary attachment, is not likely to have the coherence of rational, communicative or aesthetic purposes. But neither should we allow the play of purposiveness, with its contradictions and tensions, to blind us to the traces of overall design which organize the text and set the dramatic stage for recognizing the complexities of authorial desire.

These distinctions about purpose are crucial because the fuller our idea of authorial agency the richer can be our discourse about intentions. The idea of intention consists in treating the evidence for authorial action in a text exactly as we treat evidence for predicating character on the text's dramatic level. Hirsch, for example, must qualify his strong case for the biographical author by admitting that the same principles hold for anonymous texts. They too must be construed by positing "a particular subjective stance in reference to which the construed context is rendered probable." [11] Interpreting literary texts, in other words, means positing for them modes of coherence that can bear expressive implicatures and can be situated in terms of types for purposively responding to situations. Thus, while I agree with Hirsch, I think we must give a fuller account of what it means to construe a probable context, in a way that enables us to have a locus for attributing qualities to the act that establishes coherence. I view authorial purpose, then, as the hypothetical projection of a human agent responsible for the expressive dimensions of a work. Because the agent is a constructed character, he or she will bear qualitative predicates relevant to aspects of style and sensibility, and will provide a locus for models of coherence as varied and as complex as we can attribute to any existential act, plan, or project. In particular, we construct this authorial agent as a principle of motivations for at least three levels of the text—local, foregrounded aesthetic choices; general stylistic patterns; and an overall interpretive presence, which gives coherence to the text and allows us to situate the text as a representative act in historical or typological frameworks.

The first realm of choices is the most obvious, and least theoretically taxing, because it consists simply of those aspects of the text where we become conscious of the author's presence as a craftsman. This presence is foregrounded both by the author's manipulation of formal properties and by her standing forth as the creator or manipulator, rather than simply the reporter, of the dramatic situation. One could, in fact, develop a form of close reading that emphasized accounting for each major choice an author makes by considering what options her previous choices leave her. This stress on choice, and a consequent playful relationship to the reader in which the writer keeps trying to outwit his expectations,

11. Hirsch, "Objective Interpretation," in Perry, ed., p. 106. Hirsch also (p. 105) sees that there are several levels of integration in reading a text, the most inclusive being the authorial act. The best discussion I know of the different contexts involved in describing mimetic and authorial acts is Barbara Herrnstein Smith, "Poetry as Fiction," pp. 274–81. She does not, however, see a need to integrate mimetic and authorial levels. We can also see Northrop Frye's categories in the first two analytic essays of the *Anatomy* as a possible taxonomy of authorial acts. As a context for the various ways I invoke Frye, see my "Northrop Frye and the Problem of Spiritual Authority," *PMLA* 87 (1972):964–75, and "Some Uses of Frye's Literary Theory," *The CEA Critic* 42, no. 2 (1980):10–20.

is a major component of the novelistic tradition which runs from Fielding to Dickens to Joyce to Barth and Pynchon.

If we try to establish patterns of significance among a writer's aesthetic choices, we shift to a second integrative level, which can loosely be equated with the implicit author's stylistic activity. Style is a very complex topic, of course, but it is worth taking up briefly here, because I think my general model can clarify two important questions—how we determine which linguistic aspects of a text are stylistically significant for its meaning, and how we understand the roles stylistic choices play in constituting literary meaning. In order to be brief, I shall begin with a definition of stylistics with which I agree, and then I shall try to show how this definition can be expanded by means of this discussion of integrating levels of action. The definition is by Ruqaiya Hasan, in the best theoretical essay on style I know: *stylistics* is the "study of literary language for the purpose of showing how it is related to the internal organization of literary texts, how the text is made to cohere in one unity and how the elements of this unity are brought to one's notice." [12]

The full significance of this definition depends on its polemical context. First, Hasan excludes several possible questions about style. She ignores affective or non-avowable aspects of style that cannot clearly be shown to function as elements of a text's intended meaning. Then she interprets style as the property of a single work, neglecting larger questions about the nature of an author's style or general features of period or genre style.[13] She so limits the inquiry because she desires a clear

12. Hasan, "Rime and Reason in Literature," in Chatman, ed., *Literary Style: A Symposium*, p. 323, hereafter abbreviated RR. Hasan follows in general the functionalist approach of Halliday (who is also represented in this volume), which is the mode of stylistic theory most compatible with my approach. Halliday argues (implicitly against Todorov and Jakobson) that stylistics is essentially concerned with function rather than structure. With this functional approach we do not need to ground discovery procedures for establishing semantically relevant stylistic features in terms of abstract patterns or norms and deviations. Relevance is a function of what the critic can show to be consistent with an overall structure of authorial purposes. In other words, what controls linguistic effects is not simply other linguistic patterns as patterns but the purposive contexts they elicit. There is clearly a circularity in this procedure, but it is a circularity common to any attempt to correlate purposes, types, and situational details.

13. Seymour Chatman, "On Defining Form," *New Literary History* 2 (1971): 219 ff., argues that style proper is a manner of expression characteristic of a particular writer. He suggests using a term like *local texture* for linguistic effects operating in specific texts. It does not matter what terms we use, so long as we are clear that there are aspects of style relevant to meaning (and, hence, a function of specific texts) and those clearly matters of significance (that is, defining an

focus on the central issues perplexing contemporary stylistic theory—
how we establish what features of a text are stylistically significant for
its meaning, and what criteria we use to determine relevance. The
standard procedure, rightly attacked by Hirsch and by Stanley Fish, is
what might be called an inductive expressionism.[14] This strategy tries to
interpret which features of a discourse are stylistically relevant on the
basis of purely linguistic information. If style is a pattern of choices, one
can distinguish a significant choice either by searching out deviations
from an inductively established norm (as Michael Rifaterre does), or
by invoking transformational grammar. This grammar, after all, is designed to identify variations from a norm in the deep structure, and to
trace the paths by which the variation comes to make sense. Even if we
locate a norm, two problems remain. We cannot find significance in
ordinary and recurrent syntactic structures (at least in Rifaterre's
model), and, more important, linguistic information brings no supplementary contexts to serve as criteria for our hypotheses about the meaning or *motivation* of stylistically significant features. As a consequence,
we get a tendency to treat these features as immediately significant and
expressive in themselves, with very little sense of their particular place
in larger informing contexts, whether textual or cultural.

Fish is a superb critic of these tendencies, but his own solution indicates the depth of the problem. For he, in effect, denies that there are
any significant contexts not provided by the affective response of an
individual reader. Hasan tries to avoid this radical step by insisting that
stylistic choices must be interpreted in relation to larger regulative purposes we establish by seeking out the authorial intention *in* the text. The
critic's task is to recover the central regulative purpose informing a particular fictional hypothesis, and then to describe the fit between this purpose and supplementary linguistic features and patterns (RR, 309–11).
This model may sound mechanical in its rejection of expressionist views
of linguistic effects because there is no clear basis for their relation to
meaning, but we should remember that she speaks of critical acts and

---

author's style, a project I assume would have to take into account the changes
created by various specific authorial situations). The primary question for the theory
of literary meaning is obviously the question of the place of linguistic effects in a
single text.

14. For Hirsch, see AC, chapter four; and for Fish, see especially, "What is
Stylistics" in Chatman, ed., *Approaches to Poetics* (New York: Columbia University Press, 1973). For other references to Fish's essays on style, see my footnote
to chapter 6.

does not claim that texts are created this way. (We should also observe how subtly she uses her theory.) Still, I do not buy the model. It is necessary to take a broader view of the authorial presence as an expressive or purposive project, and not simply as conscious purpose. But any corrective will probably need to use two crucial insights she offers— first, the stress on an internal norm conceived as authorial activity, and, second, the specific justification she gives for positing this norm, namely, that if there is to be such a discipline as stylistics at all it must be different from general linguistics (RR, 300).[15] We ask questions about style only when we desire a form of knowledge which a linguistic description alone cannot provide. The difference, I think, rests in the status of rules in the two disciplines. Linguistic rules are general and repeatable in a variety of contexts. This is why we cannot successfully determine stylistic meaning from purely linguistic information: there is not enough specific context. Stylistics is, of course, dependent on linguistics, but it is also, in effect, the casuistry of linguistics. Its emphasis is not on following rules for making sense, but on constructing particular objects which use those rules for purposes that express more than simply linguistic information. *Linguistics* explains how sentences make sense; *stylistics* discerns how writers or speakers use the capacity to make sense in order to express a specific perspective on the process of making sense. Linguistics can be descriptive and extensional; stylistics is interpretive and intensional, and, hence, assumes a level of purposive behavior not accessible to purely linguistic analysis. If there is to be stylistics at all, there must be, as the focus of the discipline, an emphasis on how an agent's behavioral, as well as semantic, purposes are expressed and realized in his linguistic choices.

Given this logic for deciding the basic way to determine norms for stylistic inquiry, the value of my action model should be clear. First, it enables us to conceive the purposes and projects determining stylistic

15. Hasan locates the difference between stylistics and linguistics as the demarcation between literary and ordinary language. It seems wiser, however, in deference to Fish's superb essay, "How Ordinary is Ordinary Language," to draw the line between interpretive purposes that deal with expressive aspects of language and those content with the message. There are clearly expressions in ordinary behavior which invite or reward stylistic as well as linguistic analysis. Hasan cannot admit this, because of her narrow sense of purpose. In her scheme, the author must invite stylistic analysis as the means for appreciating his intended meaning. If we accept the purposive act as a project, and see the imperative to recover stylistic effects as dependent on conventions of interpretation, which are intrinsic to literature but applicable elsewhere, we avoid her problems.

effects in terms of a full authorial presence, of a person and not simply of a maker of hypotheses. Here, the mimetic level functions as an apt analogue for the relationship between style and project. Stylistic effects are one means we have for constructing an image of a character. They indicate how a person processes information and how he projects himself in relationship to other people, for example, how Hamlet responds differently in monologues, in conversations with Rosencrantz, and in dialogue with Horatio. We recognize these traits of character by correlating linguistic information, typological expectations about style, and knowledge of context and of a person's projects.

When we move from characters to more general stylistic effects—say, in a lyric voice, or in a narrator, or in structural patterns—we apply the same procedures to the implicit author. The one difference is that we are more apt to take the effects as deliberate, as intended to be recognized and related to other information about his general purposes (although many stylistic effects remain features we take as disclosed, rather than directly intended). Style becomes one of the means the implicit author has for interpreting his mimetic situation. Hence, the analysis of it, as Hasan argues, requires a general sense of his intentions. More important, the analogue with the mimetic level explains how style becomes a feature of a text's overall meaning. Style may contribute to our sense of the thematic import of a text, but its more basic function is to characterize the authorial stance by focussing our attention on the full expressive human project as it engages with the dramatic situation. Style does not so much communicate additional meaning as dramatize the specific desires of the author to construct a pattern of meanings and evaluations in a distinctive way and to perform his qualities of mind and sensibility. Finally, because style is a dramatic feature of authorial action, we can understand the significance of the last clause in Hasan's definition: her insistence that stylistics must show how the elements of a text's unity are brought to a reader's notice. I take this to be an attack on transformational stylistics, and for good reason. For style to express authorial attitudes as a dramatic element in the text, the stylistic features must be phenomena observable in the process of reading. Only in this way can they consistently characterize the authorial stance or be correlated with other features of the text that define the author's purposes. We can understand the implications of the abrupt and imaginative imperatives in Othello's opening speeches because their overt form expresses his character. Transformational grammar may explain how this form is linguistically possible, but there is no warrant for giving any expressive weight to the purely linguistic operations which generate the imperative. The transformations may help clarify unconscious aspects of the authorial project, but they introduce a plethora of possible relationships which play a small part in the reading experience and are so abstract as to be extremely difficult to relate coherently to any purposive norms.[16] Transformational linguistics does not easily become transformational stylistics, because it depends on a level of analysis where the distinctive features of stylistic questions and the criteria for judging stylistic hypotheses are lacking.

Discussion of stylistics leads easily into the third level of authorial activity, which manifests itself in what Hirsch calls the total subjective stance. Here we locate the most general dramatistic structure making the text a distinct entity: we posit a coherent human project which accounts for the interpretive patterns the author employs in drawing parallels among mimetic acts and in imposing narrative and thematic structures on his imaginary world. One obvious example of this type of construct is the brief description I gave in the last chapter, of how Flaubert interprets his own authorial freedom in dialectical relationship to both his disdain and his sympathy for Emma Bovary's attempts to satisfy her desires in the empirical world. A fully integrated description of *Madame Bovary* first constructs a coherent set of mimetic relationships, and then explains how the implicit author presents and interprets his own complex behavioral project in relation to that world. This project includes the nature of Flaubert's aesthetic choices, his style, his purposive investments, his implicit valuation of the meaning of his realistic commitments, and his intellectual and emotional interpretation of his materials.

In proposing a sequence of increasingly general interpretive acts that culminate in authorial purposes, I am not asserting that the author follows such a sequence. Nor do I insist that the mimetic acts are inde-

16. In Richard Ohmann's "Literature as Sentences," *College English* 27 (1966): 261–67, for example, the brief reading of the last sentence of "Araby" makes a useful point, but ignores the obvious way the sentence functions thematically (and alliteratively) to stress the past participles. Joyce's probable purpose is to capture the paralysis of self-consciousness as the boy comes to see himself as object of psychological and cultural forces, rather than as successful purposive agent. Style here expresses what Sartre would later describe as the essence of experiencing shame. A similar oversight occurs in the sentence Ohmann analyzes from Conrad's "Secret Sharer." In stressing the many levels of transformation, Ohmann spatializes the sentence and ignores its dramatic movement, which carefully registers a progression from contemplating the mysterious departure of the Sharer to recognizing in a more direct mode of expression his moral achievement.

pendent of authorial intentions. I am offering only a logical reconstruction of how an interpreter might characterize the elements of the text in order to establish its coherence. I rely, then, on the widely acknowledged principle that criticism should distinguish between represented speakers and an authorial presence, and I add that we usually view that presence as projecting, for qualitative assessment, ways of engaging in the imaginary world that is constructed.[17] From a logical perspective, it is clear that both the situation and the signs of authorial presence are constructs of an authorial act. The mimetic situation is created for and ultimately inseparable from the interpretive purpose, because the author creates a situation warranting his interpretive stance. Only in conventional omniscient novels can one clearly distinguish a logic of events from the explicit authorial perspective, but even here the authorial stance is justified by how the author creates his mimetic world. Thus, a more accurate formulation of the relation between mimetic and authorial levels would characterize the text as a whole as a purposive authorial act, which for purposes of interpretation we separate into a level of represented courses of action and a level of representing and interpretive acts. Notice that even with texts which purport to be pure representations or presentations, like the naturalist novel or the imagist poem, we attribute significance to the impersonality. Because we expect to locate an attitude, impersonality is a marked relation to mimetic materials and it invites qualitative assessment. Given these qualifications and my limited purposes, I think I am justified in taking the two levels for granted without specifying the actual terms in which they interrelate in specific texts. These terms will vary enormously, say between allegories, naturalistic novels, and objectivist lyrics, but we only know what we are looking for—or why it matters—if we have a workable general picture of how to characterize coherent authorial presence.

Once we have principles for distinguishing and integrating levels of agency, we can also further develop the concept of situating. Situating leads in two different directions, often dialectically related to each other. One direction involves placing the actions in imaginative worlds that

17. For a good summary of what he takes as now "the normal" maneuver of distinguishing fictional and authorial or real world speakers, see Michael Hancher's review of Pratt, "Beyond a Speech-Act Theory of Discourse," *MLR* 92 (1977):1092–96. I give a more extended practical analysis of the use of authorial and mimetic levels in *Madame Bovary* in "Image and Act in Modern Poetry." For the best practical analysis I know which uses these levels of analysis, see Ralph Rader's essay on Joyce cited below.

allow us to fully appreciate their qualities, while the other consists in imagining how the imagined worlds might involve significant consequences if one were to treat the stance projected as a way of responding to typical existential concerns. One form of situating is primarily a question of meaning, the other of significance. We must, however, be careful to preserve the possibility of reversing these emphases. We can argue for the existential significance of imaginary sites or, more often, we can use the possible significance of a text as a dialectical means to elicit the nature and value of the qualities it possesses as a meaningful work offered for imaginative contemplation. The existential dimensions of situating lead to questions of knowledge and exemplification which I take up in my next chapter. So here I will concentrate on situating as a feature of meaning, a feature I must repeat, which involves matters of significance in the guise of possibilities the author may or may not take into account.[18]

The best way to explore the activity of situating is to attempt to put on a theoretical basis the levels of description I used in reading "This is Just to Say." Each level of integration requires a corresponding process of situating the act so that one understands its probable context and can assess it. This justifies a somewhat melodramatic and figurative insistence that every work of literature is to be taken absolutely literally, with the critic's problem being to locate the world or situation where such literalness is possible. Once we locate this world we can show clearly why artists do not want their work paraphrased: this would change the force and degree of abstraction of particular representations and substitute interpretations for images. Modernism, in fact, can be seen as a demand on all the arts to explore new strategies for situating the action presented. We must try out Cubist ideas of a fourth dimension or a poet's experiments with literally stationing the mind within myths. There are also cases, like the *Waste Land*, where we now feel we understand the poem despite its virtually unintelligible dramatic structure (is Teiresias really the speaker of the poem?), because we know what Eliot's problems are and how his imaginative stance enables him to occupy a space where the allusive texture becomes symbolically resonant and leads to his subsequent poems. Even a poet as traditional as Yeats makes similar demands. When, in "For Dorothy Wellesley," he speaks of seeing "the Proud

18. For a fuller treatment of situating complex expressionistic lyrics see my "The Poem as Act." For a good general discussion of the problem of poetics as discovering the site of poetry, see the first chapter of Riddel's book on Williams, *The Inverted Bell*. Barthes' description of finding the subject of Sollers' *Drame* (above, note 7) addresses the same problem of situating the new novel.

Furies each with her torch on high," he is not simply offering a metaphor for an intense state of vision. The whole project of the poem is to construct a possible state of emotional and intellectual intensity, by which a noble woman comes to share a vision once available literally to the heroic Greek consciousness. Similarly, when Rilke sees his angel, or Stevens speaks of lighting the first light of evening as in a room, or Ashbery spins his meditations on a portrait, the crucial critical act is to understand from what perspective such equations can be intelligible and valuable.

When we turn to novels or dramas, (as well as to some virtual or representational features of poems), this construction of purely imaginary sites usually becomes less significant. There are important exceptions— we must recognize how the imaginative space of an *Othello* involves ritualistic dimensions not applicable to realistic novels or theatre, and we need to see how Lawrence's expressive novels or Joyce's complex play of voices demand interpretive attitudes different from those we adapt towards "realistic" fiction. Nonetheless, situating extended texts that implicate the contexts and logic of ordinary or historical experience requires a more familiar idea of literalness which warrants the provisional use of significance terms borrowed from existential contexts. We situate such works as possible stances towards the range of concerns we grammatically associate with the language and events represented in the virtual space we learn to bring to narrative and theatre. Here the crucial critical step consists in identifying both methods of projection allowed by convention and forces of projection that indicate the nature of the authorial stance towards what we can construct as potentially significant on the mimetic level.

5. A criticism of Ralph Rader's holistic model for interpretations

We cannot simply discuss such complexities without making clear the demands they make on our notions of hermeneutic criteria. Contemporary discussions of this subject indulge in an odd replay of the 1940s. Then, there were two basic views of interpretation in sharp opposition —that of the New Critics, who in practice, although not in their best theory, stressed the irreducible density of segments of literary texts, and that of the Chicago Aristotelians, obsessed with questions of how texts form affective wholes. The radical induction of Fish and Holland, along with deconstructionist suspicion of any concept of integration, have been breeding a reaction similar to that of the Aristotelians. I will not here repeat myself on the problems with radical induction, but I think it is necessary to point out the dangers in the competing holistic perspective of critics like Hirsch and Ralph Rader, whom I very much admire. They insist that interpretation should define wholes in terms of principles of coherence consistent with the concept of falsification developed by Karl Popper. In my view, this creates the danger that they may purchase coherence at the cost of ignoring the complex situating required to account fully for the multiple levels of meaning and the loose edges of authorial involvement in the mimetic world we find in the richest literary texts. Too rational a model for holistic explanation tends to produce too rational an image of authorial purposes and too narrow a sense of aesthetic purposiveness. In order to right the balance, I want to oppose these deductive models by arguing that, in conceiving the text as performance, we are responsible instead to looser forms of criteria embodied in our grammatical understanding of how types might be invoked and adapted in intensional ratios with hypotheses about the authorial situation. In general my arguments lead to a claim that in complex action descriptions it is often impossible to make explicit the principle of coherence which allows one to deduce the constituent elements, even only as a feature of an explanation with no claim about actual methods of inquiry. In these cases we recognize coherence not because of some larger principle held in common but because a certain chain of thinking and situating enables us to see the relations among parts as significant. We determine adequacy of explanation not because of models which can be made explicit but because we feel that certain concepts or descriptions of some features bring to bear concerns and ideas which enable us to go on to a deeper grasp of others. To adapt what Wittgenstein says somewhere with regard to ethics, coherence can be a function of fit without the fit depending on our recognizing some underlying foundation or model. Assessments then, of an interpretation, depend less on whether one can falsify particular building blocks than on demonstrating relative adequacy to produce a sense of fit and mutual resonance among the details we accept as central elements of the act.

In order to pose the issues clearly, I shall take some time to elaborate, and then respond to, some recent essays by Ralph Rader. I consider Rader's work one of the most significant (and unfortunately one of the most ignored) positions in contemporary theory. His general strategy is to establish criteria for holistic explanations by making flexible and subtle use of the Chicago Aristotelians, but with much more awareness of the cognitive aspects of literary experience than we find in Olson's and Crane's affective sense of plot.[19] Rader's model of meaning is similar to Grice's: understanding a nonnatural meaning entails constructing from an utterance immanent purposive signs, which enable us to take it as a whole (CG, 91). He defines his method as deductive, moving from hypotheses about wholes to testing the hypotheses' power to explain particular details, and opposes himself absolutely to Stanley Fish's radical inductivism. Fish, he sees, is forced to indeterminacy because he grants no form of shared competence for posing and testing integrative concepts. Rader then argues that we characterize a text as a purposive whole by registering its similarities with and differences from other texts in the same basic genre and by proposing a hypothesis about the most general authorial purpose which might explain the differences: "The overall explanatory commitment ... is that each work be generally differentiated from the others within their common likeness as literature, with the most general unique literary feature serving, in turn, to define the particular form of the work in a way that (in principle) permits the clear deductive explanation of all its specific features and the resolution of any special problems independently associated with its interpretation" (FT, 253).

Rader then offers three ways of determining superiority among competing explanations. The first criterion is deductive coherence and generality: "The specific conception of the individual work must imply all its particular features and permit the strict deductive elucidation of them" (R, 905). This deductive model is not one of necessity, as in physical science, but of consistency, where "the more general classes do not imply the less general, but the less general must imply and be constrained by the specifications of the more general" (R, 905). In other

19. I shall refer to the following essays by Rader and employ the abbreviations given: "The Dramatic Monologue and Related Lyric Forms," *Critical Inquiry* 3 (1976):138–52—DM; "Fact, Theory and Literary Explanation," *Critical Inquiry* 1 (1974):262–72—FT; "Critical Responses," *Critical Inquiry* 1 (1974):901–10—CR; "The Concept of Genre and Eighteenth Century Studies," in Philip Harth, ed., *New Approaches to Eighteenth Century Studies* (New York: Columbia University Press, 1974), pp. 79–115—CG. I should also point out that Rader's specific literary analyses save me the work of showing how we can synthesize a text in terms of immanent authorial purposes. See, in addition to DM and CG, "The Comparative Anatomy of Three Baggy Monsters: *Bleak House*, *Vanity Fair*, and *Middlemarch*," lecture at Berkeley, Spring, 1975, and "Defoe, Richardson, Joyce, and the Concept of Form in the Novel," in *Autobiography, Biography, and the Novel* (Los Angeles: Papers Read at Clark Library Seminar, 1973), pp. 29–72. For his critique of other Aristotelian theorists, see "Comparative Anatomy," p. 2.

words, the fact that a work deals with love implies nothing specific, but
a critical description of particular features of an expression of love must
explain them in terms constrained by a more general hypothesis. The
second criterion is the ability of a reading to avoid the circularity of
formalism by testing itself against independent facts, which are aspects
of our literary experience (like the different ways we relate to the speakers in "My Last Duchess" and "Elegy in a Country Churchyard"), or
of general circumstances we know about a work's production or con-
sumption (FT, 246–47). Finally, there is a literary version of Popper's
falsifying procedures: one reading proves itself superior to another if it
can account within its deductive scheme for the observations most basic
to its opponent's case. Thus, ironic readings of the role of the Houyhnhnms or of Milton's God can be falsified if one sees how the data
supporting such readings can be absorbed into another schema in better accord with independent facts, like Milton's reputation as a religious poet or Swift's claim that he intended *Gulliver's Travels* to vex
and not divert the reader. In both cases, the data for ironic readings can
be explained as unintended consequences of the author's fundamental
choice. For Rader, placing God as an agent in a poem at all is to run
the risk of making him seem cold and impersonal, and to write a universal satire entails the creation of a norm which is in many respects
inhumanly rational (for a human norm would exempt some humanity
from the attack).

I have two basic problems with Rader's theoretical work, both of
which derive from his concern with deductive explanations of the text's
coherence. First, the deductive ideal leads him to assume that the only
intentional activity implicit in the text consists of an overall plan to
construct a particular object in relation to a particular genre. This reduces the full behavioral presence of an authorial project to abstract
signs of purpose, and comes dangerously close to transforming purposiveness into merely thematic unity for a text. He leaves no room for the
kinds of descriptions I offered of Flaubert's engagement in the dramatic
process of his work, or for instances where the text seems to contradict
implicit authorial intentions and requires a redescription of the relationship between actual achievement and desires.[20] Moreover, the more

---

20. This stricture is against his theory; in practice he often treats the implicit
author as a presence for whom we can construct complete behavioral attitudes,
especially in his reading of Joyce. Here, though, is a representative passage theoretically describing authorial presence: "Just as in our real life examples language is

one abstracts the author from the processes of the text, the easier it is to equate authority only with unified, thematically resolved, structures.

If Rader ignores the import of action theory in his description of authorial purposes, he contradicts it when he proposes his deductive norms for holistic explanation. It is crucial in action theory that there are imagistic and narrative ways of articulating an act or text, so that coherence and consistency are not necessarily reducible to logical relationships. To deny this is to lose some of the possible depth provided by implicit features of an action. More important, this denial deprives us of a crucial means for resisting historicism. As we have seen, it is because action types are not formal paradigms that they endure when ideologies require a shift in paradigms. Rader is correct to argue that one's vision of the whole must "imply all its particular features," but he does not seem aware of how tricky a concept implication has become in recent philosophy. Wittgenstein, for example, shows that we must distinguish between *explanatory* and *descriptive* implication. The former depends on an accepted discursive system, which provides criteria in terms of a formal method of projection, while the latter depends on intuitive and grammatical criteria, on shared forms of life rather than shared systems of inquiry. In this latter case, as we have seen, there is no more formal criterion possible than a notion of fit, a notion that the description enables an observer to proceed and feel satisfied that the details form a single chain of related acts.

Two specific problems in Rader's work will give some substance to these generalizations. The first is largely a quibble, but it reveals important differences between deductive and dramatic models of coherence. Rader argues that the best reading of "My Last Duchess" treats the poem as the Duke's self-conscious "warning his new wife through the envoy without seeming to warn her, because to warn her would be to stoop when he chooses never to stoop" (DM, 4). The Duke, in short, performs his arrogance rather than expressing it as an unconscious symptom. Rader offers three reasons for his reading: "the Duke's motives become" more completely cogent and more deeply hidden; if there is a possibility of reading the poem this way, the less self-conscious alterna-

---

intelligible only by reference to a significant intention inferred within a communicative situation, so in literary works the language is intelligible only in relation to the author's presumed intention to realize an inherently significant representational structure" (CG, 89).

tive leaves too much "unexplained in terms of motive"; and the blend of iambic pentameter couplets and run-on lines concealing the rhyme suggests a sense of "submerged pattern running, like the Duke's hidden purpose, through the whole" (DM, 10)[21] It seems to me that, despite his claims, Rader here prefers breadth to depth. His third, and only concrete, point relies on a critical assumption that bringing various features under a single pattern is at least as important as concentrating on models of coherence produced by dramatized motives. Yet on a simple dramatic level, the obviously relevant type is of a Renaissance man, whose blind egoism precludes him from reflecting on motive at all. As I see it, the point of the poem is that the Duke is as blind to the reactions of the envoy as he was to the suffering and eventual disaffection of his wife. Instead of deliberately controlling responses to his act, he completely disregards other terms for judging his behavior. Rader buys a clever dramatic performance at the cost of consistency between the Duke's implicit past behavior and his speech. In opting for self-conscious motive as the deeper alternative, he ignores the possibility that symptomatic motives might well be, for Browning, more historically representative and more morally significant.

My arguments against Rader take a kind of deductive form, but on the basis of considerations about character and motive which themselves derive only from grammatical assumptions. We each claim a plausible image of behavior, but Rader's claim quickly leaps to rhetorical terms and logical connections, while mine insists on dramatic coherence between features of the various elements of the Duke's behavior of which we become aware. We also each claim a plausible image of the implicit

---

21. The two basic facts in the poem Rader uses to support his reading are much easier to read differently than is the general image we have of the Duke. He makes a good deal of the speaker's blend of imperiousness and politeness as a sign of a tension between casual surface and hidden control. But Browning's sense of the Duke as a Renaissance figure adequately explains those combined traits. And Rader calls attention to the statement, "I said / Fra Pandolph by design, for never read / Strangers like you that pictured countenance . . . But to myself they turned . . . And seemed as if they would ask me, if they durst, / How such a glance came there" as evidence of design behind apparently casual statements. But to me, the purposes behind this statement are to develop the Duke as one who thinks he understands others' reactions and to capture his inability to distinguish life and art. Formal conventions make us especially conscious of this last tendency because of the lovely irony of the last "cast in bronze for me," a passage Rader reads as deliberate, not unconscious, irony.

author. This level of analysis is crucial, because the ultimate choice is between an author desiring to portray a single moment of clever behavior representing Renaissance *sprezzatura* or an author making of a single moment a summary expression of moral attitudes which reflects an entire life and perhaps a culture based on imperious will. Even if the dramatic evidence supported Rader, this choice of authorial attitude is difficult to make deductively without first choosing appropriate types as major premises and recognizing the lines of inference they create. Rader tries to escape this, by reading the enjambed couplets and the possibility of purposive irony as strong evidence of intentions one can rationally reconstruct. But we can much more readily adapt Rader's unintended consequences to both his claims than we can dismiss our impression of consistency in the Duke's character or of moral analysis on Browning's part. It is, in principle, always possible to take the irony in a dramatic monologue as a deliberate rhetorical strategy of the speaker, because this requires only that we shift levels of consciousness we normally attribute to an ironic author onto the character. Obviously, there are many nondramatic reasons for using enjambed couplets; surely, enjambed couplets do not usually supplement dramatization of a character's hidden control. Rader's arguments are possible, but they have none of the plausibility that derives from relating specific textual elements to the behavioral expectations produced by type images and signs of repeated situations. In fact, these expectations ultimately constitute somewhat independent criteria for organizing internal evidence.

Similar problems of overvaluing deduction enter into Rader's specific examples for using arguments from unintended consequences and independent facts. His principles are valid and valuable, but he has no adequate way of saying why they are valuable, or what kind of defeasibility conditions apply to their use. There are, I grant, relevant independent facts, and Rader is at times brilliant in developing metaphors for getting us to admit that we all do have the same basic experience of the text. In one case, for example, he asks us to imagine how differently we would film the speech acts in "My Last Duchess" and "Elegy in a Country Churchyard," in order to demonstrate how differently we see the relationships between implicit author and speaker in the two poems (CC, 94–95). But there are, I suspect, no logical principles for deducing what constitutes genuinely independent facts, distinguishable from vagaries in the history of taste or unrealized psychological intentions. Again, we have a kind of circularity: what counts as a genuine independent fact—

and not a history of misreading—depends on one's reading of the text.[22] We avoid total circularity only by resorting to the connection between coherent actions and typical, nonformal expectations about relevant contexts which I developed earlier, and these connections are matters of fit, not of deduction.

Rader is correct in thinking that most coherent explanations of an action can be posed in ad hoc deductive terms, but, when deductions so freely adapt first principles, there is little point in using the term. Moreover, its use tends to conceal the actual grounds of the coherence one seeks to describe and to neglect certain explanatory constraints imposed by those grounds. Consider, for example, Rader's use of the concept of unintended consequences. Is it true that the only constraints on this kind of argument are deductive and empirical? I doubt it. I think we have strong biases toward taking hypotheses about unintended consequences as provisional and immediately defeasible by any treatment equally adequate to the facts which treats the major elements of a text as deliberately expressive. We expect a masterpiece to turn its difficulties to expressive purposes, and we find it hard to resist procedural conventions which lead us to take such large elements of a text as the nature of the Houyhnhnms or the coldness of God as essential to the whole. Finally, the more one stresses the author's intentions as immanent and formal, the more he is constrained to accept such features as internally significant. There are procedural and grammatical not empirical, reasons why an interpretation of *Paradise Lost* which explains God's coldness in purposive dramatic or authorial terms is immediately preferable to Rader's alternative. We expect to describe texts as complete renderings of an intention located within the details, and we can understand why even so good a Christian would grapple with the remoteness of God as a problem. Thus, we are not likely to be content unless we can locate possible conscious, or even unconscious but avowable, intentions informing the choice of rendering God as cold. This particular example is actually not difficult to handle, because it is perfectly coherent with Milton's general purposes to see God's coldness as an emblem of the fact that men must not expect ultimate truths to coincide with their desire to project God as an extension of human social values. It is Satan, we remember, who cannot accept a universe not in accord with his im-

22. This is the real point of Stanley Fish's "Response" to Rader in *Critical Inquiry* 1 (1974):883–91, which is marred by excessive self-defensive rhetoric.

mediate personal desires. If men are to be perfected, they must learn the place of cold reason.

6. A *return to circularity: types, covering laws, and the logic of situations*

In the next chapter, I shall show how action theory, especially the notion of types, warrants claims for the cognitive role of literary experience. The previous discussion of Rader enables me to set the stage for those arguments by providing a contrastive context, in which we can clearly see the central role a grammar of types plays in humanistic inquiry. For only a notion of types can release us from the difficulties inherent in employing either inductive or deductive models for holistic explanations when the goal of an inquiry is intensional description of a complex particular act. Inductive models, as we saw in discussing Holland, cannot explain the properties of public intensional facts, especially with the established institutional frames basic to literary interpretation. Deductive models, on the other hand, provide terms for holistic explanation, but only by endangering the complex internal relationships which characterize the actual hierarchy among particulars constituted by an authorial presence.

The only alternative to these models is a form of the idealist concept of concrete universal, in which types at once provide a representational abstraction connecting particulars to grammatical understanding and serve as flexible principles one can adjust to specify the originality of the particular action. Types, in other words, perform a task analogous to general laws warranting deductive explanations, because their properties are not dependent purely on particular situations. How we correlate details depends on a grammatical understanding of possible connections which is independent of a particular grasp of the situation. Yet what remain independent are not isolated facts (whose independence we have seen is problematic) but flexible terms we can adjust to actual details.

These claims do not so much offer a way out of hermeneutical circles as suggest the role of judgment in rendering the circle benign. Yet I can see no other alternative. The problem we saw in Rader's work derives from a logical difficulty, which is clearest in Karl Popper's exemplary description of deductive explanations in disciplines concerned with analyzing particular actions. For Popper, a deductive model is a necessary form for any testable assertion, because it clearly delineates the link between independent general warrants and specific predictions.[23] In pure or generalizing sciences, one seeks to discover a general law of nature which can be correlated with details or *initial conditions* to show how a specific result is predictable. If the result occurs, and is not falsifiable in terms of irregularities or unrecognized complexities in the conditions, we can take the explanation as provisionally valid. Thus, a general law that *thread breaks under certain tensions* can be shown as valid if the initial conditions of a thread and a tension exceeding the predicted breaking point produce the expected result. If, on the other hand, one accepts the law and wants simply to make a particular judgment about a piece of thread, the law serves as a means rather than as an end— often without requiring a conscious deductive analysis. The analysis, nonetheless, can be produced.

Popper, then, applies the model of particular judgments to action descriptions. Recognizing there are very few perspicuous general laws for explaining human actions, he saves the deductive model by positing a *logic of the situation*, which substitutes for a general law: our actions "are to a very large extent explicable in terms of the situation in which they occur," because situations dictate what we can predict as rational behavior. Rationality is not an abstract hypothesis. Rather, we develop standards about what might be rational for a human being to do in a situation. As I read Popper, this means that insofar as we could explain an action, it would have to fit what our general expectations would predict—for example, of how consumers use purchasing power to satisfy certain obvious expectations.

The basic problem in using the general law model at all for situations is determining a predictable relation between the nature of the law and the density of a situation. The more thoroughly one tries to account for a specific situation, say a specific decision to buy something, the more qualified becomes the general law of the logic of the situation. Ultimately, the law involves essentially the same qualifications on character and specific desires as one must use to describe the situation, so that the logic of the situation becomes an ex post facto description of the per-

23. For Popper on deduction, see especially *Objective Knowledge* (Oxford: Clarendon Press, 1972). For a discussion of the concepts of *situational logic* and *historical explanation*, see Popper's *The Open Society and its Enemies*, 4th ed. (London: Routledge and Kegan Paul, 1962), vol. 2, chapters fourteen and twenty-five. I take the example below from p. 262 and I quote from p. 97. My perspective here parallels that of Patrick Gardiner, *The Nature of Historical Explanation* (New York: Oxford University Press, 1961). Gardiner opposes theories of historical explanation, like Carl Hempel's, which insist on deduction from general laws.

son's context and choice. The law has descriptive, not explanatory, power. Popper's model only works at a level of predictive generality like that of behavioral sociology, where broad expectations about the preferences of a class of people might be specified. Types raise the same problem, but the concept brings no illusion of laws and less of a tendency to focus only on what a general logic of the situation might predict of the act. By maintaining the illusion of quasi-scientific prediction, Popper encourages the tendency we noted in Rader to rely on aspects of situations which do not involve concrete images of behavior, or complex interconnections among details whose plausibility depends on narrative rather than rational considerations.

I find the most striking example of the differences between a type model of holistic explanation and a deductive one in Rader's use of metaphors. Were he true to any notion of deduction as a rational procedure, he would avoid metaphors, because they complicate the choice of deductive principles. Metaphors invoke more than one principle for organizing details. They work because they make connections which relate details to norms we understand in nonrational terms. Critical metaphors bridge a gap between concrete internal relationships in a text and typological frames based on other grammatical terms needed to make the relationships intelligible. We can understand why imagining different ways of filming "My Last Duchess" and "Elegy in a Country Churchyard" (CG, 92–95) offer different generic approaches to the dramatic monologue, because our conceptions of the respective speakers depend on different general typological expectations for dialogue situations and meditative situations. Density is both a problem for and a result of the circular processes fundamental to the workings of grammar.

8

Literary Reference and Literary Experience
as a Means of Knowledge

1. *My general case and some qualifications on my claims*   In my last two chapters, I want to turn from specific questions about the nature of meaning to the implications my arguments have for larger issues. I do not think that the pleasures of close analysis can forestall facing E. D. Hirsch's challenge to contemporary theory—that it specify the contributions it can make to education and to social issues.[1] Under this pressure, the logical first step is to describe the possible cognitive functions literature might provide. There are other alternatives—one could speak about modifying sensibilities, or sharpening perceptual powers, or even of freeing us from Hirsch's nostalgic moralism. But these claims quickly grow vapid, unless they are tied to the fundamental question of literature as a form of knowledge. Moreover, I consider it an important feature of my emphasis on action, performance, and philosophical grammar that these concepts lead easily into an argument for the kind of knowledge literature affords, and, hence, for the educational role it might play in a culture. My argument, however, shall be somewhat limited in scope. I understand *knowledge* in the spirit of Nelson Goodman's remark that often on leaving an art exhibition, "We see what we did not see before, and see in a new way. We have learned." This learning can take many

---

1. I slightly modify here Hirsch, AC, 139–40. Hirsch's answer to his challenge is largely a call for concerned teaching of writing. I see this as a sign that even moralist critics now despair of describing cognitive roles for literary studies. In my view, both student interest.in writing and their development as writers depend largely on the ways we teach humanistic knowledge.

forms, all of which are comprised in a broad sense of *cognitive*.[2] Nonetheless, I shall be concerned only with a limited version of knowledge that follows from the way I have been describing the text as performance. I do not insist that such knowledge is a necessary condition of literary experience, or even a necessary justification for literature's place in education. My account, I hope, helps make one of many possible justifications for literary studies. Finally, claims about knowledge must be distinguished from arguments that literature directly serves moral functions, in the sense of cultivating values more specific than a desire to know or to experience rich and complex phenomena. I understand knowledge as simply a form of power which may clarify moral issues, but like any other power, may be used for moral, immoral, or amoral purposes.

One of the many ways Plato and Aristotle remain vital contemporary figures is their articulating a conflict at the core of literary theory: literature seems too important to culture not to be seen as conveying some kind of knowledge, yet if we put too much analytic pressure on the forms of representation literature offers we may well lose its special qualities and treat it only as inferior social science, psychology, or philosophy. The history of literary criticism is largely an elaborate intellectual dance between these two claims—that literature gives knowledge and that literature is different from philosophy and science in its way of presenting its existential materials, and thus in how its contents can be assessed. This dance has its pleasures, but it has become a somewhat tedious marathon. Yet our efforts to escape it tend only to sustain it or to create visions of an impoverished world we want to flee, even back to old partners and movements. This history suggests that one be cautious about his claims, but its very threat to absorb our arguments motivates my desire to show how a performative approach can integrate both claims and thus at least enable us to shift the dance to a new level. My project entails working through two specific analytic problems which confront any attempt to describe the nature of the knowledge literary texts can provide—what

2. This statement is from Goodman's reply to a set of discerning essays on his work. All are contained in *Erkenntnis* 12, nos. 1 and 2 (1978). I shall use the abbreviation E in my text to cite Goodman's replies; here the quotation is from p. 173. Worth special mention in this collection is Monroe Beardsley's essay " 'The Languages of Art' and Art Criticism," pp. 95–117, a useful critique of Goodman's aesthetics which I shall abbreviate in the text as LAAC. Goodman's two major works mostly on aesthetics, with the abbreviations I shall employ, are *Languages of Art* (New York: Bobbs-Merrill, 1968)—LOA; and *Ways of Worldmaking* (Indianapolis: Hackett Publishing Company, 1978)—WWM.

properties of literary texts make knowledge claims possible and what form this knowledge might take. Thus we must engage the question of reference, or more loosely and more manageably, what lines of projection or matchings can one draw between the full aesthetic, self-referential aspects of a text and objects or attributes of the realm of ordinary experiences we take as real or existential. Leroy Searle puts this theoretical issue succinctly as the need to discover "an explicit means for connecting the intentional strategies of texts with basic relationships literature can establish between people and their own experience." [3] The attention we have paid to these internal, intentional features seems to me to have taken us a long way towards fulfilling this ideal. The task now is to concentrate on ways that the set of concepts around treating texts as performances afford us fresh ways of addressing questions of reference. These questions in turn are largely attempts to give philosophical weight to ancient claims that literature instructs as well as delights, a claim whose looser formulation I find actually more appropriate than modern concerns for "reference." Here, though, I shall address both reference and instruction primarily by developing for my own purposes Nelson Goodman's concept of exemplification. There are important similarities between Goodman's general philosophical position and Wittgensteinian themes, like the attack on simples and the importance of a concept of fit, so I shall concentrate on these while largely ignoring differences that arise from Goodman's relativistic nominalism. Goodman's demonstration that there are at least two modes of reference, descriptive denotation and exemplification, is what matters here. Exemplification, as a general semantic concept, makes it possible for me to show how literary texts implicate and extend a grammar of attitude types. Thus, the cognitive impact of literature consists largely of enabling us to make more complex and more varied discriminations about actions than may occur in ordinary experience. Because I am concerned only with actions, I shall neglect other modes of exemplification that interest Goodman and I shall make claims that his nominalism and insistence on an extensional language will not tolerate. But my object of analysis is literature, not Goodman. The test is not whether he approves, but whether one can go on to make further applications. Here, that will involve elaborating distinctions between different cognitive uses which we give the exemplified actions in a text. The cognitive nature of the immediate act of reading

3. Searle, "Tradition and Intelligibility: A Model for Critical Theory," *New Literary History* 7 (1976):406.

involves largely the exercise of grammatical powers, while the long-term effects of a sustained literary education produce a range of models, and of interrelationships among models, that deepens our capacity to situate and to reflect upon particular actions. Finally, an adequate notion of these long-term effects provides a perspective from which one can counter a historicism like Quentin Skinner's and can argue for the perennial force of rich literary actions because they constitute representative type attitudes. In this respect at least, it makes sense to speak of a philosophical dimension to literary experience.

2. Problems basic to discussing the cognitive functions literary texts serve

There are several ways of talking about cognitive uses of literature. Literary texts, or parts of texts at least, do sometimes make referential claims about historical phenomena,[4] and these texts are themselves historical phenomena that one can treat as monuments expressing various cultural values or depicting historical conditions and thus affording a kind of knowledge. But the crucial issue basic to claiming full knowledge of a work as a monument is describing the cognitive impact of the text understood as a dense semantic and pragmatic interplay of aesthetic, descriptive, and projected interpretive acts.

Even on this last point, there are almost as many accounts of how the

---

4. For a good technical discussion of how parts of texts can denote while the text as a whole must be treated as self-referential, see Joseph Margolis, *The Language of Art and Art Criticism*, pp. 155 ff., especially p. 155. Margolis ends up, however, essentially denying that the self-referential text has cognitive value. The New Critics, on the other hand, managed to claim cognitive value for self-referential texts by insisting that their nondiscursive structure of internal relationships enables them to present directly the complexity of experience. The boldest claim of this nature, by Cleanth Brooks, is *The Well-Wrought Urn* (New York: Harcourt, Brace, 1947), pp. 211–12. A similar desire leads Ransom to reduce Kant's position to a kind of aesthetic realism. The best New Critic at claiming nondiscursive texts provide a direct knowledge of *reality* is Allen Tate. See *Essays of Four Decades* (New York: William Morrow, 1970), pp. 191–94. But even Tate ignores the fact that texts are constructs, however much they seek objectivity, and not direct presentations of anything one can take as true, actual states of affairs. Texts cannot *be:* as forms of languages they must denote in order to relate to states of affairs. But they need not denote as descriptions or representations; seeing this is Goodman's great contribution. Not seeing this is why the New Critics had such trouble in at once denying the adequacy of empiricist models of reference and still posing cognitive claims for literary experience.

text as a whole implicates non-textual realities as there are available theoretical frameworks for rationalizing critical practice. Yet despite our ambition and inventiveness, we continue to run into basic problems we have not adequately handled. On the most general level, the basic types of contemporary theory all fail to make full correlations that capture the possible cognitive import of both the authorial acts and those represented on the dramatic level of the text. Aristotelian theories of catharsis, for example, provide a powerful account of how the dramatic shape of an action imitates plausible patterns of action and consequence in order to purify moral understanding. But they limit cognitive functions to moral (or, in Crane, affective) knowledge, and they overlook both complex features of authorial presence and immediate dramatic qualities of those texts which offer themselves as simple presentations of acts of mind in meditative settings.[5] On the other hand, the many forms of expression theory developed in order to account for works in the Romantic tradition—for example, Heideggerean, Projectivist, or thematic psychoanalytic approaches—abstract a version of expressive force or authorial presence from the full interplay of structural and mimetic elements embodying that act in a specific imaginative situation. The former makes rhetoric too self-consciously purposive, and the latter ignores the necessarily rhetorical perspective literary procedures elicit even when works promise to present direct confrontations with experience. Finally, even though textualist theory explicitly mocks any conventional idea of knowledge, because of the displacing power of writing and of metaphoric language, textualists frequently bring knowledge claims back in connection with the possibility of becoming self-conscious about the properties of writing as free play. We find both arguments, like de Man's, for a distinctive form of self-consciousness fostered by writing which makes us aware of the gaps between conceptual and empirical selves and several versions of Culler's claim that literature reflects for us the possibility of recognizing the duplicities and traps inherent in our signifying conventions. Yet when these theories consider authorial purposes at all—for often they attribute our knowledge simply to properties

5. My reading of Aristotle here derives from Francis Ferguson, "Introduction" to *Aristotle's Poetics*, trans. S. H. Butcher (New York: Hill and Wang, 1961), and from Leon Golden and O. B. Hardison, *Aristotle's Poetics: A Translation and a Commentary For Students of Literature* (Englewood Cliffs, N.J.: Prentice-Hall, 1968). Barbara Herrnstein Smith's "Poetry as Fiction" is a good non-Aristotelian discussion of *mimesis*. I might also point out that I give a much fuller account of the nature and weaknesses of mimetic and expressionist concepts of literary meaning in my essay "The Poem as Act."

of textuality—they collapse the variety of possible authorial projects into a single thematic framework, which simply does not account for or warrant the scrutiny we afford a wide range of texts and aesthetic forms. Pure textualism cannot even fully account for the problems inherent in using signs, because the terms of the problems involve concerns for purpose and situation.

These general outlines, however, do not reveal what I consider the most important problem in describing the cognitive role of literature—that of stating the lines of projection between text and world in a way that can finesse the models of knowledge which in our society create our basic criteria for using terms like "truth." Most professional critics, and most readers, see reading as extending their powers to understand experience or even, as Gerald Graff puts it, to develop "a conceptual apprehension" of the "propositions" offered by the work. However, they usually state that vision in terms which seem either nostalgic for an older, pre-scientific order or ludicrously ambitious paeans to the imagination. I hope to put the case for literary knowledge in a different, more secure foundation, but we probably will only appreciate the qualifications required if we first work through the specific dangers one faces in the enterprise. Let us begin with the strongest possible case, a work like Tolstoy's "Death of Ivan Illych." Here we need not infer some unconscious representation of some ideology or social conditions. It is plausible to assume that the author intends to communicate knowledge by offering a picture of an experiential sequence which his audience might find true. Also we have a case where the mimesis is not a case of simple denotations but involves our grasp of the work as a whole. These ambitions, however, make us ask just what in the text can be true to what and how do we justify calling the concepts or images we derive "knowledge." Graff, for example, speaks about "representation" but he never specifies whether the textual elements represent forms of behavior, ideas about behavior, or ideals for behavior. I suspect that he does this because there is no single account possible—either of how texts reflect states of affairs in the world or how we can call the representation "true." Tolstoy's story clearly does not accurately represent some empirical condition since all men do not act as Ivan does or learn what he does. We could say that the text represents an idea, but this only puts the same problem on another level because we must ask how do we know to whom the idea applies or how to judge it. This leaves us an option of asserting only that the idea or image is true of some people. This, however, trivializes Tolstoy and ignores the fact of how many different modes or levels of experience there are in which we can identify the image as true of us. More important, this search for referents makes clear what a straightforward mimetic account misses—that Tolstoy is less concerned with the actual empirical conditions of human lives than with possible, normative ways of coming to terms with those conditions. In order to capture this moral force, we need to speak of the qualities of accuracy Tolstoy performs because these are elements we use in assessing the nature of concern and reflection which have gone into the moral judgment. But Tolstoy's moral claim as such is neither a representation (say of some objective moral truth) nor a proposition; rather it is an appeal to resist all the typical representative attributes of Ivan's life and a demonstration of the ideal forms of thinking and acting this involves. Ivan is made to seem typical not primarily because accuracy is an end but because the accuracy makes us see the importance of and desire to imitate an action which is not at all typical. "Truth" here is at best a rhetorical stage for intensifying features of the text that ultimately invite very different kinds of assessment.

If we present a sociologist or psychologist with a description of a man like Ivan, he has clear ways of testing both the accuracy of the description and the possible uses of it as a representative version of social conditions. But the literary image leaves us in very different straits. First of all we notice that if we attend more closely to specific objective details we do not get closer to relevant testable propositions or quantifiable features whose probability can be measured. Nor do we necessarily gain a clearer picture of any social truths Tolstoy intends to communicate. In Tolstoy much of the description is not intended to specify reference but to deepen our involvement in synecdochic features which emotionally reinforce the general moral vision. Similarly, if we try to imitate the social scientist's ways of assessing truth claims we would put ourselves in an odd anomaly (for which only Marxist social theory has an analogue). For here the relevant literary assessment demands suspending the particulars so that their lack of accuracy does not contaminate the general import. The crudest example of this is our need to abstract the "representative" qualities of older (or wilder) texts like the *Iliad* or *Jerusalem* from details that are no longer relevant to its "literary" truth. Moreover, most literary critics will differ from the other disciplines in often encountering situations where they value equally two texts which give competing interpretations of quite similar states of affairs, while not expecting the contradictions to be resolvable. Finally, we find our literary analysis tempted to take into account dimensions of individuality and intentionality which would make any scientific assertions about representativeness very difficult to apply. I have assumed that we can take at face value Tolstoy's desire to make a picture of a state of affairs. But literary procedures tend to have us treat the desire to communicate a moral truth as itself a condition of the performance we are asked to reflect upon. I might add that this orientation is not simply a matter of convention. It enables us to value variety and thus treasure the multiplicity literary history offers, and it allows us to be responsive to the ways writers like Tolstoy make their own artistic activity in structuring and controlling the story an element we are to appreciate as part of the work's coherence. If, however, the performative quality is part of the expressive meaning, how do we state what is represented in the text so that we can judge what it is true of? Does the text demonstrate how it feels, or what it entails, to see, say, think, or write the plight of Ivan as a potentially representative moral example? Even specifying what would be represented in this case leads us into the quandary of having to select an act to be taken as the representative one among the range of verbs that enter into the description of writing in terms of its purposes and purposiveness. The only other option is to take as representative the full complexity of the act, but this greatly reduces the possible existential parallels.

I do not intend to discount the power of Tolstoy's work to engage us in existential matters. Quite the contrary. I hope to have shown that the more we worry about questions of mimesis as truthful representation of particulars or concepts, the more we take up a critical stance which at best captures rhetorical elements and misses the sources and possible values of the existential implications projected by the text. Insistence on representational terms of mimesis tends only to repeat polarities which make purely aesthetical positions or emotivist claims seem unpretentious and defensible, if not quite satisfying. More important, the very effort to insist on "truth" in literature without necessary qualifications only reinforces suspicions that literature is only fantasy or only offers in sloppy form concerns which require for accurate statement and assessment more analytic disciplines.

In this critical climate I think that the arguments I shall develop can play two roles. First the emphasis on qualities and performances identifies areas of existential implication which do not so readily invite equating reference or relevance with "truth" claims and the empiricist apparatus we associate with them. This allows a broader model for treating implication based on the exemplification of properties and ways of correlating features of action so that we can understand not truths about experience but possible uses of images and concepts as instruments for clarifying experiences. My alternative will not depend on truth claims but show how literary texts help foster ways of thinking and grammars for describing actions which can also be used as terms in referring propositions. Literature enhances a capacity to employ complex predicates but it need not, in itself, be the means for determining precise statements which can be judged for truth values. We need no single model for making truth claims because literary texts are least confusingly employed simply in showing us questions and predicates which deepen our propositions and may reveal the limitations inherent in our need to rely on testable propositions in order to feel our beliefs are justified.

In this critical climate the argument I have been making, about naturalizing literary texts as performances, plays an important corrective role. First, it focusses attention on the necessity of correlating mimetic and authorial acts into a single, self-referential structure which still, as an action, implicates ordinary experiences. Also, it reminds us that both expressive and descriptive features of discourse are publicly determinate and can be placed in contexts derived from the "objective" world, once we recognize the appropriate grammatical frame. Finally, by stressing the role of grammar in establishing the nature and intelligibility of acts, my argument characterizes literary content in a way that does not demand that we conceive of reference solely in empiricist, descriptive versions of denotation.[6] It is largely this narrow model of reference that

6. Gerald Graff, *Literature Against Itself* (Chicago: University of Chicago Press, 1979), p. 71, and pp. 151–65. Graff's basic argument is that it is the denial of mimesis in modern literature and theory that contributes to literature's loss of authority in our world. He then tries out several formulations of the mimetic, without really articulating any, because the moral idea of literature's relevance seems more important to him than any strictly analytic case. His most sustained argument (pp. 151–65) is for imagining literary texts as stating or implying general propositions, which he opposes to the idea of presenting dramatic images. His concept of propositions, however, consists largely in emphasizing very general beliefs one can construct from the text. This ignores all the technical questions about propositions and gives no sense of why stress such an enterprise as especially useful for literature. It is illuminating that Graff's evidence consists almost exclusively of the fact that critics use general statements in their work. Of course one can derive belief statements from texts, but this does not show that their meaning or fullest use leads to such statements. The possibility of articulating qualities or filling out conditions of actions gets lost. Graff makes explicit probably the most common reductive feature of academic criticism and he shows how we are tempted to it by our sense of high purpose. He is excellent on the social and intellectual problems characterizing the current plight of literature and literary criticism, but the power of his analysis makes it very

produces radical splits between viewing art as descriptive and prosaic, or as autonomous and purely self-referential. Given the limited sense of valid connections to experience such models of reference entail, claims about knowledge from literary texts encounter a host of standard problems—why bother with literature when other modes of discourse descriptively denote more clearly, in explicitly testable ways, and how does one explain valuing texts whose explicit truth claims contradict one another, and, thus, do not directly provide standards or rational motives for action? A broader model of reference, on the other hand, makes it possible to distinguish between descriptions of external states of affairs and a knowledge of what I shall call properties displayed in performance. Then it makes sense to speak of self-referential features of a text not as ends but as means for deepening our grasp of these properties as we make dense correlations among situations, types, and evidence about intentions. It becomes the correlations, not the denotations, that link literary and practical experience.

3. *Applying Nelson Goodman on exemplification to literature*

Again I have proffered large claims. Here, though, Nelson Goodman's two books devoted primarily to aesthetics, *Languages of Art* and *Ways of Worldmaking*, provide a way of making good on them. Goodman's relevance begins with his analysis of two ways pictures can be seen as making references. When we are clear about the projections involved, we might view a picture as depicting (or describing) something it symbolically represents, and we might ask of the picture what "sort of representation (or description) it is. The first question asks what objects, if any, it applies to as a label, and the second asks about which among certain labels apply to it" (LOA, 31). A picture of Wellington may be seen as representing him, and also as characterizing him in relation to certain labels, predicates, or properties one finds in other pictures, or, more loosely, in our ways of talking about pictures. The latter case is a paradigm for reference by exemplification, in which the particular object functions as a sample of the labels which it possesses and which denote

---

important that we not be tempted to solutions which might further impoverish what we do by tying ourselves to views of literary knowledge that are both indefensible and reductive.

it. Goodman provides the following formulation of the distinction in
directions of reference: "While a picture describes what it represents,
and a predicate denotes what it describes, what properties the picture or
the predicate possesses depends rather on what predicates denote it"
(LOA, 51). Correspondingly, each mode of reference involves a different
mode of assessment. Descriptions and representations are true or false
in relation to a given state of affairs, but samples and examples are
judged in relation to measures of appropriateness, fairness, perspicacity,
and so forth (WWM, 132–38).

A concrete example should make Goodman's distinctions clear. One
may take a swatch of red-and-white cloth and see whether it represents
or describes the pattern and color of the suit June is wearing. The swatch
denotes what it refers to, and is (depending on one's canons of accuracy) either truly or falsely applied to the suit. But one may also take
the swatch of cloth to look for similar shades and patterns in a pile of
assorted fabrics. Here the swatch functions as a sample. It is not used
to describe, but refers to the labels one might employ in describing it.
The swatch instantiates a label for some of the properties it possesses;
it does not represent a particular object. When we use the swatch as a
sample, we usually do not treat it as exemplifying all the properties it
possesses. The weight or size or material of the sample were irrelevant
in my example, although in other contexts one might use the same object as a sample of these label categories. Possession of properties is a
necessary, but not sufficient, condition for exemplification. Two other
features are necessary: a principle for attributing a role to the sample,
and a principle for what Goodman calls *projectibility*. We must know
why the sample is being used, and we must know some standard conditions or established practices, if we are to recognize the properties exemplified and to use them in a relevant or perspicuous way. Finally, one
can complete a picture of the features that characteristically accompany
exemplification by describing typical forms of assessment. Goodman's
ultimate criterion for assessment is a general notion of fit that can take
a variety of forms. If, for example, one assesses a sample of the mixture
of grass seed in a barrel, the relevant measure is one of fairness. Here
the basic criteria would involve showing that the sample has been drawn
so that pains were taken to make it an unbiased illustration of the contents (WWM, 135). More complex samples may involve several dimensions of fit with the labels or predicates that denote it, but all involve
the adequacy of projection relative to purpose. In art, where the purpose
is usually to create an object for contemplation, the measure of fit be-

comes the capacity of the example to produce fresh and discriminating renderings of a way of viewing the world (cf. LOA, 255–62).

We are finally coming around to the basic issue of how Goodman fits our discussion about literature. What makes Goodman so exciting an aesthetician is his demonstration that the arts provide a form of knowledge through the kinds of examples they establish. Insofar as an art work exemplifies certain properties or qualities, it "makes manifest, selects, focuses upon, exhibits, heightens in our consciousness" the properties it shows forth (WWM, 65). These exemplifications need not be assessed by the denotative standards of truth claims, because works "function as symbols for features they possess literally and metaphorically" (WWM, 105). Thus, they help establish powers to employ discriminating labels or to adapt fresh ways of sorting, identifying, weighing, ordering, and supplementing what experience may present (cf. WWM, 4–17). By exemplifying, works of art become instruments of worldmaking: "after we spend an hour or so at one or another exhibition of abstract painting, everything tends to square off into geometric patches or swirl in circles . . . or vibrate with new color consonances and dissonances" (WWM, 105). Similarly, while a written portrayal of Don Quixote does not denote the person it describes, it creates a sample that can serve the function of metaphoric denotation, because the direction of reference is "by what possesses to the property possessed" (WWM, 32). Thus, what Don Quixote exemplifies "effects a reorganization of our familiar world by picking out and underlining as a relevant kind category" a model "that cuts across well-worn ruts." Fiction applies metaphorically "to actual worlds": "Whether a person is a Don Quixote (i.e., a quixotic) or a Don Juan is as genuine a question as whether a person is paranoid or schizophrenic." Indeed, Goodman says the former question "is easier to decide," presumably because the fictive label creates a more penetrating and discerning kind.[7] Goodman recovers in defensible terms, with no talk of intuition or spirit, the point of Croce's expressionist rejection of mimetic theory, and yet he maintains rich lines of relation between literary texts and actual worlds. Once we see how an expressive act exemplifies, we also see how it fulfills the spirit, at least, of mimetic theory. Indeed, Monroe Beardsley seems bothered by Goodman's affinities to mimetic theories, because they lead Goodman to ignore aesthetic criteria for evaluating works (LAAC, 96–114). But Goodman, in my view, has the last word, because he can argue that aesthetic properties may be

7. My paragraph here is essentially a recasting of WWM, 103–04.

the means for articulating inventive, subtle, and perspicuous exemplification (E, 173). In a formulation Goodman would never countenance, although Aristotle might, art serves the actual world because of the qualities it projects in ideal terms.

I still have a reasonably long way to go before I can fully adapt Goodman for my argument about texts as performances which extend our grammatical capacity to situate and assess acts in ordinary experience. The lines of this correlation should already be clear, but several details and problems need further elaboration. There are, first, practical problems in actually applying Goodman to specific literary texts. As Beardsley points out, Goodman is not really concerned with questions of practical application, and he leaves us few guidelines for "determining which labels, if any, are exemplified by a work that comes his way." For one thing, we know the label involved in the swatch of cloth, but it is hard to know what labels apply to art works, because we lack the practical context and the presence of the concrete cloth for which the swatch serves as a label (LAAC, 103–04). Second, there are problems in connecting my intensional language and concern for acts to Goodman's criteria for exemplification. I shall briefly work through these matters, but I would like to suggest that specific problems, in using Goodman or in reconciling my arguments with his, probably do not invalidate his general model of how art works may implicate actual worlds. Goodman is not very concerned with matters of practical criticism, because the ultimate use of his work is less to develop a way of examining art works than to articulate a model for evaluating them which is consistent with his general philosophical position. In this respect, Goodman's aesthetics are somewhat like Kant's: they both gain coherence and suffer a myopia from looking in two directions—at the needs of a system and (sporadically, for Kant) at art works. In each case, we may have to be content with a vision powerful enough to motivate lines of research it cannot itself define within its systematic confines.

Two specific difficulties in Goodman's arguments about exemplification help justify the modifications I need for correlating his model of exemplification with my concerns for actions and grammatical competence. The first involves problems Beardsley raises about how we define the fit between a work and labels it exemplifies, and the second consists of asking how we know which properties are exemplified and in what relation they stand to one another within a work. The swatch of cloth, Beardsley pointed out, clearly refers to labels in a public domain. Similarly, we know how to test a sample of grass seed for fairness. But if we directly apply this version of samples to aesthetic theory, we will have a mimetic perspective about as rigid as social realism. Goodman avoids this trap by allowing for figurative exemplification, where the label need not be clearly a copy of some original. Works of art are often like samples of water from the sea, rather than seed from a barrel. We need not measure fairness in relation to a previously determined whole. Rather, the measure of the example's adequacy is one of the *coordination of samples*. Works "literally or metaphorically exemplify forms, feelings, affinities, contrasts, to be sought in or built into a world." Thus, the test is not fairness to a determined set of properties, but a process of projection "in discovering and applying what is exemplified": "what counts as success in achieving accord depends upon what our habits, progressively modified in the face of new encounters and new proposals, adopt as projectible kinds" (wwм, 132).

If I understand Goodman's general semantic theory correctly, these qualifications to admit originality create difficulties in relying only on a model of labels. Given the capacity of art works to construct new ways of seeing, I think one must say that they refer not to specific labels (as loa, 54–59, argues), but to the relevant range of labels or vital categories we characteristically use for the appropriate mode of symbolization. An original shade of red, or a fresh image of character traits, cannot refer to labels. These signs constitute or become labels, so they refer to, or, perhaps better, implicate, relations among labels, because they invite us to rearrange and extend our grammatical capacity in relation to the situation and contexts elicited by the sample. We must distinguish between the grounds by which the original label gets identified, and the form of denotation possible when we know what the label is or can be used for. The grounds for the initial identification must be adjustable, must be more like a system of relations than a distinct label. Only after we can describe the work and, to some extent, define what it exemplifies does it become a distinct label which, ultimately, refers to the very properties we see that it exemplifies. Then we can use Don Quixote for figurative denotations, because taken as a sample he refers to the features he has in the text, just as the sample of grass seed refers. We can also employ levels of the type: this kind of behavior is one of the things Don Quixote does.

We can now see and handle the impact of Beardsley's insistence that there are instances of property-exemplification which are not cases of label-exemplification. If the work as a constitutive example challenges our capacity to use only the labels we possessed before we encountered it, the qualities of the work, as Beardsley puts it, tend to outrun available predicates (LAAC, 101–02). Again, we need a distinction between reference to labels one has available for scrutinizing a work—where properties of the work are likely to evade the labels—and the result of manipulating those labels so that we recognize what the work exemplifies and can use the work itself as the referent for labels we employ in describing other phenomena. This distinction needs more careful work, but it should indicate the need for considering examples in relation to the general workings of a grammar as a flexible process for correlating samples and testing new ways of applying them.

We now enter an even more perplexing problem, where it seems we need to extend our sense of the grammar required by Goodman's case to include judgments about intention. Goodman is superb on how we might use art works as examples and labels, but he is not, to my mind, completely satisfying on how we determine what is exemplified. He sees that exemplification cannot be simply the mention of a label or property. The work, like the swatch of color, must possess the properties it exemplifies. Possession can be either literal (a color or a shape) or figurative (the possession of sadness by virtue of the way we read some literal configuration of properties as an expression) (LOA, 50–51). Conversely, a work does not exemplify all the properties it possesses. Some properties of a painting, like its weight or price, usually do not exemplify in aesthetic contexts, while properties of color and line do. Exemplified properties must be determined by the work's ability to function as a symbol, not just by its physical existence. Exemplification depends on the nature of the world the object inhabits. Goodman sees no large theoretical problems raised by these strictures.[8] There may be problems

8. Goodman's caution on the issue of defining what properties of a work are exemplified seems to me to betray a worry that his extensional language will not suffice. But he will brook no leaps to intention. See LOA, 78, and WWM, 37. He is careful to insist that his is a special sense of expression, reserved for cases "when the property belongs to the symbol itself—regardless of cause or effect or intent or subject matter" (LOA, 85; also LOA, 91). However, caution is no substitute for presenting an account of what belongs to the symbol itself. This is why I assume below that Goodman accepts an autotelic view of how art symbols function as wholes. The real issue, though, is the subject of intention, which I shall discuss in a moment. Here is Goodman's most candid remark on the subject: "Since I am often accused of overlooking the fact that only as a result of a user's acts and intentions does a symbol refer at all and refer to what it refers to, I should say once more that my apparent neglect is itself intentional. Of course a mark or a painting becomes a symbol, as a piece of wood becomes a railroad tie, through actual or intended use ..., but the characteristics and functions of symbols as of railroad ties can be studied quite apart from the acts or beliefs or motives of any

in determining what is exemplified in particular cases, but, in general, one can say that by virtue of "practice or precept" the applicability of expressive properties to an art work "is not arbitrary" (LOA, 88; as related to style properties, cf. WWM, 37). *Precept* and *practice* resolve for Goodman primarily into knowing how to manipulate the general symbol system controlling a work's functioning. (Symbol systems seem to include principles for treating works as something like autotelic structures; cf. LOA, 85–91.) Goodman will not grant that attribution of intention or purpose are in any way necessary for determining this symbolic functioning or for deciding on the nature of the properties possessed. This, for him, would deny the objectivity of the properties and would involve an intensional language. Thus, Goodman insists that the identity of a work can be established in purely extensional terms—a literary work, for example, can be identified with its script, its spelling as a particular text (LOA, 208–10, and chapter three). Style is defined basically as consisting "of those features of the symbolic functioning of a work that are characteristic of author, period, place, or school" (WWM, 35). There is no place in his analysis of style for specific choices that may be described as motivated by patterns in a given work, or that may be seen as deepening other thematic or qualitative dimensions of that work.

In the spirit of Goodman's relativism, I must point out that his is a perfectly consistent account, but it may have some unfortunate consequences and may allow only a rather limited range of projections. By not allowing a language that can fully handle purposive features of a particular work's symbolic functioning, Goodman seems to ignore, or actually to deny, possible solutions for three basic needs of at least a

---

agent that may have brought about the referential or mechanical-relationships involved" (E, 162). The problem here is that railroad ties are not usually complex expressive particulars. Their function is purely determined by practices, in a way not comparable to symbols, whose specific functioning as a unique object is the object of inquiry. With art works, the same general symbolic function, say of properties in landscape, can play different particular roles once we describe how the work as a whole qualifies the landscape properties. For a discussion of this matter, see Guy Sircello, *Mind and Art: An Essay on the Varieties of Expression* (Princeton: Princeton University Press, 1972), pp. 16–46. Sircello also helps explain some of the weaknesses in Goodman's theory of expression, because Goodman in many ways shares the description of expressive properties Sircello criticizes as the now canonical view. The canonical view conceives expression in terms simply of properties of the object. Sircello, in contrast, makes a powerful case for considering expressive properties as implicating an agent for the work, and, thus, he provides welcome support for my arguments about positing human motives as principles of intentional agency.

literary theory: he gives no adequate general methodological perspective for distinguishing between treating works as bundles of exemplified properties and as coherent interrelationships among the properties; consequently, there is, from his perspective, no way to address the basic critical problem of establishing and describing a hierarchy among the exemplified properties, so that they all contribute to and are modified by a coherent whole; he also allows no theoretical room for treating whatever it is that may constitute the whole, like an authorial act, as itself exemplified, and, hence, as serving the function of establishing perspicuous labels or models for sorting experiences.

These shortcomings are most apparent in Goodman's infrequent discussions of literary texts, probably because an extensional language will not take one far in establishing the nature of a work in language or in defining the properties exemplified. (Paintings, Goodman's preferred illustrations, have a broader range of properties available as extensional features—there is a sense, for example, in which the whole is clearly displayed—but similar problems of interpretation will eventually arise.) Goodman's theory of labels neatly gets around the problem that texts literally exemplify only names, because for him all exemplification exemplifies the names of properties (LOA, 238). This is not much help in deciding how symbolic functioning establishes the relevant exemplifications. Goodman's illustrations project a fairly wide variety of cases, but not much depth. Texts exemplify formal properties, like being a sonnet, so that they can be used in making discriminations with respect to other uses of the form (WWM, 33). Literary texts also apparently exemplify expressive attitudes: Goodman suggests that a text may be drab or slow or "electric" (LOA, 91–92) and that Macbeth exemplifies horror and revulsion (LOA, 250). But I recall only his example of Don Quixote as approximating an analysis of exemplified properties that are typically of interest to literary critics. Yet even here, Goodman treats what the character exemplifies as largely independent of the text's internal structure. Don Quixote is, in his discussion, not qualified by his relation to Sancho Panza or seen as exemplifying Cervantes' complex sense of the value and pathos of fiction. So Don Quixote becomes a label that can help identify certain traits, but the label lacks the depth that helps complexly situate and interpret what it identifies.

Thus, Goodman casts a fairly broad net, preserved from the damaging tears a more speculative language might create. But such a net may not be strong enough to catch anything more powerful than a minnow. Goodman's net sorts properties into conjunctive sets, but it only distributes properties, without delineating procedures for or qualities of integrating them. In order to capture the potential for density in a figure like Don Quixote, I think it is necessary to speak about authorial purposes. Then one can show how texts fully use the instruments for world-making that Goodman describes. Purpose establishes a coherent test both for properties the text possesses when it is read and for its particular ways of using symbol systems (cf. WWM, 35). Furthermore, as I have shown previously, purposes are inherently integrative concepts. When we construct a text as an authorial act, we are not content with making a conjunctive list of properties. Instead, we try to correlate the properties, and the types they elicit, into a single structure of relationships organized as a series of emphases and mutual modifications. We not only identify the work as possessing properties that function symbolically, we also ask what part the properties play in the symbol as a whole. By understanding what Cervantes was trying to do, we know what relational roles to attribute to various aspects of Quixote's character and the modifications context puts upon these traits. There is no reason why one cannot separate properties to concentrate on the labels they exemplify, but in so doing one is simply not addressing the fullest capacity of an art work to be appreciated or to constitute significant samples. .

One final issue remains. Have I not destroyed the spirit as well as the letter of Goodman's work, by introducing ideas of intention and integration? How can a text possibly be said to possess what in an extensional account would be at best quasi-properties? And how can a text show forth properties of authorial intention as examples (cf. LOA, 85–86)? Here I think it is sufficient to recall two features of my previous arguments. First, I have been careful to claim as an intention only what can be shown to serve as what Skinner calls *intention in.* Therefore, if a text can figuratively possess expressive properties, which depend on constructing a represented scene, I see no reason why it cannot figuratively possess the intention by which we characterize and situate it as an act. In both cases, what allows figurative possession is a relevant method of projection. So, if the conventional framework for reading literature elicits our constructing intentions, these intentions are figuratively perceived as features of the text. *Women in Love* exemplifies a Laurentian stance.

The method of projection also accounts for the next step in my argument. Intentions are not merely attributed to a text. Rather, because they serve as the most comprehensive integrative level of the text, they are displayed as central for a reader's reflections on the authorial performance. The work as a whole becomes an expressive act, because it displays qualities of a performance. What a symbol system, or, as I prefer, method of projection, emphasizes as displayed in ordinary aesthetic contexts must also be viewed as being exemplified. Just as it would be odd not to take features of color as typically part of the expressive exemplification of a representational painting, simply because we expect that particular correlation in paintings, it is odd not to treat what we take a text as displaying as central to its status as an example. It is likely, in fact, that a central trait of most symbol systems distinctive to human culture is our need, in learning them, to develop the capacity to recognize how certain properties implicate possible purposes and lead us to posit agency for the act the system articulates.

My use and modification of Goodman pertains to only one of the many forms of exemplification that he argues all serve cognitive functions. I am interested here only in the grammar for recognizing and assessing actions, as it can be developed from the characteristic practices of literary critics and trained readers. I think it is now fair to claim support from Goodman for arguing a distinctive cognitive role for literary experience, because he makes it possible to show how what I call types are exemplified in literary texts. This model, moreover, allows us to retain a sense of the flexible, multilevelled discriminations types afford, since different texts provide examples which sort and situate actions with various degrees of generality. Finally, we can see that most of the traditional claims of mimetic theory can be recovered and extended, so long as we grant that *reference* is not the descriptive positing of truth claims, but consists in working out features of examples that refer to what denotes them. This shift in the direction of reference both explains the basic qualities of mimetic analysis and provides a framework for describing the broader parameters of denotation contained in expressive authorial acts. Thus, in discussing the mimetic level of "This is Just to Say," we treated the poem along the lines of an Aristotelian reading. We correlated situational details with plausible grammatical type qualities that enabled us to describe the act as a specific qualitative version of an apology. We performed an absolutely standard act of practical criticism, but we emphasized a different direction of fit—not from poem to specific existential conditions, but from the poem's rendering of an imaginary situation to our capacity for developing ways of characterizing existential conditions. The poem is *in the world* by revealing ways to talk *about the world*. With the authorial act, on the other hand, we must rely more fully on a framework like Goodman's if we are to rationalize critical practice and defend knowledge claims. For there the direction of reference is not to standard images of behavior, but to a variety of abstract predicates connected with attitudes toward literary history, the nature of poetry, and the relations between the theory of language and typical properties of poems. While these are not the standard terms of mimetic analysis, they depend upon lines of reference similar to those involved in describing the apology, and thus make it possible to situate the expressive act in relation to grammatical understanding.

In effect, we can recover the cognitive impact of mimetic theories without tying mimesis to claims about resemblance, or positing for the ideal quality of representations some corresponding ideal ontological realm (as Romantic theorists of imagination as well as Aristotle are prone to propose). Reference involves only the operational realm of grammatical predicates, whose functions in experience are phenomenologically determinable. By these moves we do lose the idea that art has some special truth it discloses by intuition or transcendental abstraction. But what is hard to substantiate is not painful to lose, especially when, through Goodman, we recognize that, in many ways, the condition for appreciating specific truth claims is the possession of a grammatical sense for recognizing the fit or appropriateness of a particular claim. If we lose the ability to assert that art reveals specific or special truths, we gain the power of recognizing how art works reveal the nature and the possible uses of the ways agents frame the worlds within which truth judgments are proffered. If we cannot speak easily about the truth of a poet's vision, we do know how to talk about its possible uses—a more limited and yet more capacious perspective.

4. Attitude as the basic form of literary exemplification

Because I am concerned only with one form of exemplification, I want to replace Goodman's vocabulary with a more literary one. For my purpose, the basic cognitive content of literary samples is their capacity to function as a particular kind of type I shall call *representative attitudes*. First of all this concept of attitude seems uniquely appropriate to the issue of what we can know from literary texts even though we cannot take them as offering propositions. It establishes an object for knowledge which preserves both the properties and diversity of expressive acts as basic features of meaning. An attitude, considered as an aesthetic concept, is a concrete stance which is frozen for contemplation. Thus it contains concrete properties it can exemplify, and it fixes in a form something we can examine abstractly for possible representativeness. We have, in short, a way for describing actions when they have been interpreted: attitudes are actions held in the mind as contemplative objects. Thus attitudes have the same range as actions. A simple purposive gesture or an elaborate project worked through a series of events can both become concrete objects of reflection. Similarly, one can treat any aspect of the mimetic action of a work as an attitude, but the work as a whole can be preserved only by constructing an authorial attitude. I insist on this primarily as an analytic point: insofar as the coherence of an utterance is a distinctive feature of its meaning, or something more than a simple semantic fact about sentences, then we must locate the coherence in an expressive actor. For many works of art, however, the authorial attitude is not the most pronounced dramatic fact, and from a cognitive point of view there is no need to emphasize only authorial attitudes. The example of mimetic attitudes, in fact, enables me to emphasize another crucial point about the concept. Because attitudes are concrete, texts do not only project attitudes, they also can be seen as testing them, as working through imaginary situations that explore the relevance and possible use of qualities the actor exhibits. Attitudes become representative, in large part, by inviting and rewarding such projective tests. Thus attitudes are perhaps best seen not as abstractions from the text (although some abstraction is necessary) but as ways of preserving for the abstract space of thinking the energies and conflicts of both the mimetic and the authorial actions. This reflective abstraction, in turn, allows one to explain how attitudes at once employ types and themselves become types which can be employed to clarify subsequent experiences. It is in this context that I want to absorb the psychological uses of the term "attitude" while I hope resisting the behaviorist frameworks within which it is ordinarily employed. If attitudes can exemplify and serve as types then we have a principle for what I call text-psyche correlations. That is, we can show how what we construct in reading becomes an object with a place in our general mental activity. Finally, because the concept of attitude plays a significant role in modern philosophy, we can situate our discussion of literary knowledge in relation to other basic models of inquiry.

I. A. Richards is the first modern theorist to make significant use of the term *attitude* as a vehicle for discussing problems of literary reference. He defines attitudes as "imaginal or incipient activities or tendencies to action." [9] Attitudes are not actions or expressive stances, but mental states which mediate between emotions or the body's awareness of its impulses and the overt behavior which can set these impulses to rest. In Richards' behaviorism, these attitudes are not objects of cognition but dispositions of a subject created by stimuli, not properties of the text but of a responding subject. They are important because they can be enjoyed in themselves: civilization is a process of learning to enjoy, on the level of attitude, what might be harmful or disturbing if allowed to be expressed in physical actions. In fact, all needs to adapt attitudes to specific actions limit consciousness. In ordinary behavior, satisfying one set of impulses entails denying another, and actions must be limited by the constraints of social morality. Only in the imagination are the discontents of civilization mollified and made creative. Here, moral constraints are not so powerful (since there is no fear of consequences), and, more important, in aesthetic contemplation we can be content to experience more complex attitudes, because we need not simplify them to fit the constraints of acting in the world. If one acts, she must choose between contradictions; if she rests content in the disposition to act, she can enjoy the presence of contradictory aspects of the attitude, and, hence, experience her full psychic powers. Where the actor need say "yes" or "no," feel pity or fear, the aesthetic response can say "yes *and* no," feel pity *and* fear in relation to a specific situation.

From the perspective of the New Critics, Richards was the founder of a genuinely modern criticism, open to the complexities of attitudes, and was also its first heretic. For Richards could develop his sophisticated sense of a text's complexity only by defining it in opposition to the clear and distinct propositions needed if one wants to make claims about knowledge. Propositions refer by denoting, and, hence, constrain the mind's energies to simple tests of truth and falsity. But *because* literary texts do not claim referential truth, they are free to create complex affective attitudes. Richards was often regarded as denying the high seriousness of literature, because he refused to take it as providing knowledge. However, it is more accurate to see him as denying the high seriousness of truth claims by showing how only a form of discourse free of

9. I quote from Richards, *Principles of Literary Criticism* (New York: Harvest Books, n. d.), p. 112. The discussion below also makes use of his *Science and Poetry*, 2nd ed. (London: K. Paul, Trench, Trubner, 1935). See also Wallace Stevens, *The Necessary Angel* (New York: Vintage Books, 1965), p. 128: "Every image is a restatement of the subject of the image in terms of an attitude."

the narrow criteria of empirical truth can give adequate expression and resolution to the complex and various energies at work in the psyche.

We need Richards' insistence on the limits of empirical reality-testing, but we need not, therefore, banish attitudes to the realm of affective discourse, whose basic function is restoring psychic wholeness. As Goodman shows, our knowledge is not reducible to tests of denotative reference, so psychic wholeness need not be simply an affective state. It may be possible to have reflective knowledge of the various attitudes which compose that wholeness, and which a culture develops over time in order to become aware of its affective states. Richards' equation of *attitude* with *response* ultimately simplifies the very complexity he desires. For, as his many critics have pointed out, unless one tries to distance himself from the text and interpret it as public performance, he can attain neither the subdued and reflective emotion that allows one to register complexity, nor the internal dialectic which forces one to check and revise simple or stereotyped responses.[10] Immediate affective response is too crude and amorphous a state of mind to serve Richards' purposes.

By virtue of their paradoxical efforts to define attitudes so that they might be separated from propositions, Richards and his early positivist allies actually help illustrate the cognitive status an expression of attitude might have. In order to know what the attitudes are that they are banishing, the positivists must use illustrative samples and rely on grammatical understanding. Here, for example, is Carnap dismissing any truth claims for utterances that confuse attitudes with propositions:

> What gives theoretical meaning to a statement is not the attendant images and thoughts, but the possibility of deducing from it perceptual statements, in other words, the possibility of verification. . . . Metaphysical statements—like lyrical verses—have only an expressive function, but no representative function. Metaphysical statements are neither true nor false, because they assert nothing. They contain neither knowledge nor error. . . . They express not so much temporary feelings as permanent emotional or volitional disposi-

10. Wittgenstein's argument, which I suspect is directly aimed at Richards, is simple and powerful. If one were really concerned only with an art work's creating emotional responses, he would make statements like, "Since I want to feel sad any one of this group of works will do." The fact that this is not the case, that we read specific works for specific experiences, suggests a very different common attitude toward art. It suggests that we desire to contemplate concrete actions and movements and that the specific emotions raised depend on complex understanding of the attitude constructed. See LA, 34; p. 35 goes on to speculate about attitudes both in the work and in the responder.

tions. Thus, for instance, a metaphysical system of monism may be an expression of an even and harmonious mode of life, a dualistic system may be an expression of the emotional state of someone who takes life as an eternal struggle.[11]

The blend of precise intelligence and vulgar simplification in this quotation is all too typical of those who equate meaning with propositions and verification. Carnap's lack of concern for the complexity and uses of attitudes continues even in speech act philosophers, like Searle, who try to domesticate Austin within the confines of analytic philosophy. The fashion now is to recognize that attitudes play a role in most discourse, but then to define them as propositional attitudes, which can safely be prised off the proposition, leaving it intact and verifiable. These attitudes are equated with large adverbial classes characterizing modes of expression like belief, doubt, fear, and so forth. Thus, "I fear John has come" and "I hope John has come" are statements that present the same proposition under different propositional attitudes. The reductive attitude to attitudes is probably motivated by the laudable desire to preserve a realm of distinct, referring propositions, verifiable in standard empirical and logical ways. But, again, we see methodological principles merging into ontological ones and denying the significant complexity of other, equally public, dimensions of discourse that require different modes of assessment. There are many expressive acts where attitude is a crucial aspect of content, and thus cannot be so easily separated from the assertions. Even Carnap clearly assumes that he understands the permanent attitudes of metaphysicians, although as coherent attitudes they cannot be reduced to perceptual statements. (One perceives behavior, but interprets attitudes.) Yet, perhaps in order to approximate a perceptual statement, Carnap oversimplifies the attitudes expressed by philosophers. Even if Plato and Spinoza were equable fellows, and Descartes a contentious one, not every person with a harmonious attitude writes or even thinks like Plato or Spinoza, and not every lover of conflict earns Descartes' specific place in Carnap's inferno. Carnap, then, can neither specify the distinctive qualities manifest in the specific movements of mind and feeling of these philosophers, nor explain their cultural importance. This importance, moreover, is not simply historical, even if we cannot accept their conclusions as true. The philosophers exemplify significant questions and significant styles of

11. Rudolf Carnap, "The Rejection of Metaphysics," in Weitz, ed., *Twentieth-Century Philosophy*, pp. 209, 215.

questioning. They form part of a tradition which keeps alive an image of what philosophers can do and how they might do it. In so doing, they reveal not only permanent dispositions but permanent possibilities for thinking through certain problems. Stuart Hampshire, for example, has recently shown Spinoza's relevance to modern discussions of the concept of freedom, and Strawson has made it clear that, while no one might now be strictly a Kantian, it is hard not to be in some sense neo-Kantian.[12] The alternatives for attitudinal statements are not only true or empty. If we were to take Carnap literally, we would be forced to say that Socrates merely exemplifies the contentious style of berating others we might expect of a man with a shrewish wife. Yet it seems closer to the truth to see him as an exemplar of the dramatistic foundations of philosophy—both as a mode of inquiry and as an ethical project worthy of respect in a society.

These dramatistic foundations have significant ethical implications which, in turn, clarify the distinctive properties of attitudes. Ethical discussions face the inevitable problem of determining whether rational analysis can actually determine moral ends, or whether ends derive from custom or from individual preferences. The framework of this study will not help us resolve this dilemma, but it can make clear the role attitudes play in the second alternative. For, if reason does not determine ends, exemplary attitudes, like the image of Socrates we have been discussing, must play a crucial cultural role. First, attitudes actually constitute ends. Wittgenstein, for example, argued in the *Tractatus* that, in any area of experience where values are in question, it is not what arguments say but what agents show in behavior that can affect one's sense of moral ends. Science describes facts; images project and authenticate values which have no status as facts. In his case, the example was Tolstoy, a figure whom Wittgenstein tried to imitate because he represented the noblest attitudes toward wealth and toward *das mystiche*. Second, exemplary attitudes can clarify the properties of moral choice, and of moral agents. Ethical discourse is itself largely a matter of self-performance (albeit under strong sincerity conditions), because it involves projecting oneself as a moral being in terms of the qualities of concern one exhibits and the humane significance of the goals one pursues. There will probably always be moral disputes, as Hannah Pitkin

12. Hampshire, "Spinoza and the Idea of Freedom," in P. F. Strawson, ed., *Studies in the Philosophy of Thought and Action* (New York: Oxford University Press, 1968), pp. 48–70, and Strawson, *The Bounds of Sense: An Essay on Kant's Critique of Pure Reason* (London: Methuen, 1966).

argues, because there is no guarantee that every problem allows only one course of action which can be rationally discovered. Yet this does not make moral discourse impossible, but, rather, makes it absolutely necessary, although on grounds requiring a complex grammar of attitudes. The point of moral discourse, she says, is "successful clarification of two peoples' positions vis à vis each other." [13] The actors must, if they wish to be taken seriously as human beings, be able to satisfy three conditions: they must display adult moral attitudes, they must be able to give reasons for their principles, and they must give careful scrutiny both to their reasoning and to the situation. Actors can give various reasons for their acts, but not any reason will command respect. The terms for our ability to request and grant respect depend on our knowledge of other exemplary attitudes and on our ability to judge whether that knowledge is, in fact, applicable to a given situation. Without an adequate and complex grammar of attitudes, we can neither represent ourselves to ourselves with any refinement nor recognize the possible justifications (or lack of them) for another's behavior.

It will not be a large jump from this point to the argument that, in complicating our grammar of types, literature prepares for moral understanding without necessarily affecting moral behavior. Now, however, I want only to emphasize what the moral case shows us about the properties of attitude types. *Contra* Carnap, attitude types constitute an absolutely necessary aspect of public human language, because they enable certain kinds of mutual performances and recognitions in areas where propositional agreement is impossible. They also cannot be separated from the propositions that characteristically embody them; they function grammatically as a complex blend of the abstract universality of concepts and the flexible degrees of complexity locatable in concrete images. They are at once constituents of judgments and objects of them. Again, Wittgenstein is the most perspicuous commentator on their ontological properties as features of experience. He speaks of scents and emotions, complex properties which likewise admit no separation between being and quality: "The atmosphere that is inseparable from its object—is not an atmosphere" (PI, 183). This could be a precise reply to Carnap and an index of what we preserve from experiencing writers like Socrates. It is not simply with emotions, or with sensations like pain, that expression, attitude, and complex public forms of recognition prepare grammatical understanding. Attitudes are the analogues of a conceptual vocabulary

13. Pitkin, *Wittgenstein and Justice,* pp. 140–68. For the performative aspect of self-descriptions, see Charles Taylor, RS.

in expressive spheres of human behavior where atmosphere is essential.[14]

In "This is Just to Say," for example, there are considerable differences between taking either mimetic or authorial acts as presenting concepts of forgiveness and as projecting exemplary images of an attitude toward a situation where apology is required. In the former case, the poem would be simply an instance exemplifying the thesis that forgiveness is not something we can command. As an exemplary attitude, on the other hand, a stance toward forgiveness implicates other aspects of experience, like relations between nature and culture and a sense of the evasive properties of language. More important, the poem is less concerned with defending a truth than with projecting a concrete, representative sample of qualities that may enter into very different conditions once one is aware of them. The type becomes a potential constituent of other type constellations and, by implicating the grammatical features needed to make sense of a particular act, it has the potential of focussing these as means of referring to acts which have not yet taken place.

5. *Two basic forms of literary knowledge:*
   powers and frameworks

If the cognitive status of literary texts is the refinement and extension of a grammatical capacity for constructing performances into samples of representative attitude types, we can distinguish two basic forms of

14. Wittgenstein, PI, 531, nicely uses the concept of expressive attitudes to posit two distinct forms of knowledge and verification. For representative passages on expression, attitudes, and ways they support the need for a grammatical model of culture to supplement a view of understanding emphasizing propositions see PI, 527, 329, and Z, 191, 164. I want also to point out here that this atmosphere Wittgenstein speaks of introduces a possibility for speaking about emotive aspects of attitudes, which I ignore in my argument. Because attitudes are concrete dramatic instances, they often project emotional and evaluative dimensions of the stance presented. Figures like Don Quixote or Emma Bovary, or authorial stances like Joyce's or Dickens', are not simply modes of classifying actions in an abstract taxonomy. The attitude organizes kinds of situations and contexts which contain and elicit emotional involvements in what is presented. Thus, an important cognitive function of many literary attitudes is making us aware of how, and sometimes why, we can respond to experiences with particular, complex feelings. I ignore this in my exposition, because the basic case is easier to make in terms simply of identifying stances and because working out the correlation between emotions and images can get very complicated. I should add, however, that Wittgenstein's concept of grammar and a weak version of his attack on private languages provides a very useful context for discussing how we can learn modes of feeling. For Wittgenstein, we learn modes of feeling when we learn the possible uses of terms. Thus, when

knowledge developed by a literary education.[15] Each form is based on an aspect of the activity that takes place in reflecting on performances of specific actions. The first concerns the immediate activity of constructing coherent descriptions, and the second develops from a long-term process of reflecting upon, using, and comparing the attitudes one has constructed.

The form of knowledge we acquire from the actual process of reading is best considered a kind of power or disposition. We develop capacities for relating various explicit and implicit features of a performance to one another and for constructing coherent wholes. Here we can give conceptual grounds for attributing to literary activity the cultivation of powers like sensibility, taste, and tact. In the context of constructing qualitative features of a performance, *sensibility* can be seen as the capacity to register as significant subtle and implicit features of an action, *taste* as the ability to see how different aesthetic structures might render and qualify these actions in different ways and with different degrees of success, and *tact* as the internalization of criteria for interpretive activity so that a person can synthesize features of an expression in economical, coherent, and plausible terms. These powers are sharpened by reading, because conventional procedures dictate that one try to understand the action as fully as possible. It does not suffice to grasp it only to the degree that one can make a desired practical response, as is the case in ordinary experience. Moreover, this project of literary understanding differs from ordinary behavior in leading us to pay special attention to the specific duration or unfolding of the action. Actions are

---

we see how attitudes are appropriate to certain complex situations, we, in effect, come to recognize how those situations might warrant or elicit characteristic feelings. For a good discussion of the relevances of Wittgenstein for emotional aspects of literary experience, see John Casey, *The Language of Criticism*, chapters one, two, and *passim*.

15. The best recent essay I know on the nature of literary knowledge is Hilary Putnam, "Literature, Science, and Reflection," *New Literary History* 7 (1976):483–92. He argues that the closest parallel to the kind of knowledge given in aesthetic experience is moral knowledge. Both forms of knowledge are practical, rather than theoretical, because their contents are not clearly derivative from empirical or deductive propositions. Both are conceptual, rather than empirical, because they involve knowledge of possibilities, of how things can or might be, rather than of what is a general and provable fact about the world. And, finally, he sees that one cannot make propositional claims based on literary knowledge, because the text's concern is not with the world per se but with the world as constructed from a given point of view. Putnam, in short, makes exactly the claims I do—not surprising since we work out of the same tradition—but he does not fully articulate the grounds for and implications of these claims.

seen not as simple events but as processes whose movement qualifies and complicates content.

When we attempt to isolate powers, we find ourselves at once echoing and extending Richards' claims about the attitudes developed in readers. We are speaking less of knowledge created by interpretations than of ways of acting as an interpreter, where reading carefully becomes itself a kind of attitude which we can carry over into practical experience. Then, the more contemplative, less immediately affective the stance toward the text, the more plausible it is to expect reading to develop powers that have long-term effects. Stuart Hampshire, for example, reminds us that a "policy of seeing round and of testing an intention by alternate descriptions in any given case, is itself a maxim of conduct, a part of a particular moral outlook." [16] Similar ideals occur within literary texts, as the author's implicit image of a desired result for his work. It is likely, in fact, that poetry in the Romantic tradition requires a critical vocabulary of situation and attitude, because its own basic goal is less to achieve either convincing argument or formal closure than to display stances and mental strategies exemplifying for a reader modes of attention toward real numinous powers, within and outside the imagination. The aim is to train the reader's sensibility through aesthetic experience, so that it becomes capable of visionary experience in its own right. In many novels, analogous ideals take ethical form. Attentive reading becomes the text's own metaphor for the proper way of engaging in interpersonal relationships. Even when reading becomes an ironic theme, as it does in Pynchon's equating it with a half-justified paranoia about plots and significance, the text usually propounds the general values of an ironic consciousness as a form of power. The power may be also a trap and a liability, but it remains the text's only source of authentic sensibility and of an approximation of sanity. Thus, while modern writers may make more cautious and ambivalent claims, it is hard not to conceive the proper way of reading one's text as a privileged way of stationing oneself in the world.

If we view the exercise of this power as taking place over an extended period of time, we can see how processes of careful reading also produce distinct objects of knowledge. For, by constructing and reflecting upon attitude types, critical attention can lead to the development of a complex grammatical sense of the possible range and depth of these types. Our cultural possession of a range of texts makes available a com-

16. Hampshire, *Thought and Action*, p. 215.

plex body of knowledge. It is Richards, again, who sees the importance of such long-term effects, although his vocabulary does not allow a full development: "A more reliable but less accessible set of signs can be found in the readiness for this or that kind of behaviour in which we find ourselves after the experience. Too great insistence upon the quality of the momentary *consciousness* which the arts occasion has in recent times been a prevailing critical blunder.... The after-effects, the permanent modifications in the structure of the mind, which works of art can produce, have been overlooked." [17] From the point of view of my discussion of samples, the crucial point is not the structure of the mind but the availability of specific structures to the mind. When we consider literary texts as cultural possessions, as themselves samples the mind can employ, we must recognize that *in memory*, the distinctive, subtle features we encounter in the process of reading will be lost. What will remain is a sense of the general shape of the attitude as a form of grammatical knowledge, in which representative images serve as concepts. Here we have a general sense of possible character types, of relations between emotion, tone, and situation, and of strategies for interpretation reflecting distinct possible modes of mental activity. Here expressions are understood simultaneously as stances of mind and as ways of becoming conscious of and describing particular phenomena. Literature as cultural possession is a basic constituent in our dramatistic grammar, and, hence, it expands our horizons for both situating and understanding existential attitudes. Most important, by constantly placing complex attitudes in relation to one another, it makes possible the senses of depth involved in knowledge as a dimension term. The relationship among attitudes prepares a transition from a simple grasp of attitudes as propositional states to a comprehension of attitudes as profound existential conditions. We find it possible to restore a dialectical dimension to cognitive experience. In Derrida's framework, an initial attitudinal term like *love* becomes lost and displaced when it is submitted to the variations of literary expression, as in the sonnet tradition. But it is more plausible to see that these variations function in a roughly Hegelian fashion, to negate one's initial sense of the attitude as incomplete, to preserve a sense of the varieties inherent in human experiences of the attitude, and to prepare for rich new syntheses when we are confronted with complex performances like Shakespeare's sonnets. The clearest evidence for this process is the way puzzles in these complex performances are gradually

17. Richards, *Principles of Literary Criticism*, p. 132.

resolved into coherent images, which, in turn, qualify one's openness to subsequent experiences. These subsequent experiences, I should add, can be reflective as well as practical: we take up attitudes toward practical situations and we assume reflective attitudes for interpreting our practical behavior or for speculating on its possible significance.

6. Attitudes versus Quentin Skinner's historicist view of speech acts

I have so far set the case for knowledge of attitudes only in contrast to Carnap's positivism. By shifting contexts, I can clarify the stakes involved in this discussion. For within analytic philosophy, as well as within textualism, an increasing attention to properties of rhetoricity and of speech acts has developed. Yet this work remains locked in opposition to a sense of what propositions do, with the consequence that theorists of rhetoricity have no adequate language for discussing the significance or use of the speech acts they describe. I shall here ignore textualist versions of rhetoricity, since I would only repeat myself, and I shall take my contrasts from the analytic work of Quentin Skinner. In one respect Skinner is a hero of this book. He exemplifies a dramatistic attitude which insists, against easy claims about timeless concerns, on the specificity and thickness of historical acts, and he provides sharp concepts for articulating the nature of this work. But in my view his opposition to a facile universalism blinds him to other ways of stating claims for something like universals on a grammatical level. I shall therefore argue against him that dramatistic concern for speech acts need not confine one to matters of archaeological record but can produce another kind of knowledge which continues to be vital as a means for interpreting present experiences.

Skinner's many essays on interpretation have their common origin in the principle that "no agent can eventually be said to have meant or done something which he could never be brought to accept as a correct description of what he had meant or done." [18] This principle, which I employed in distinguishing meaning from significance, is crucial to

---

18. I refer to several of Skinner's essays in chapter three. Here I shall rely on "Meaning and Understanding in the History of Ideas," abbreviated MU in the text. I quote from p. 28. The claim made here is qualified in his later distinction between autonomous and heteronomous texts. See "Hermeneutics and the Role of History," pp. 209–15 and *passim*.

Skinner, because it combats what he sees as the two basic conceptual mistakes plaguing the history of ideas. Most historians of ideas subordinate intentions to social contexts, or reduce the role of intentions by basing their inquiries on a concept of perennial questions which tempts the interpreter to search out the author's position on questions he never posed for himself. In reaction, Skinner denies that meanings are timeless (MU, 32), and insists that a recovery of intentions entails capturing the specific illocutionary forces the author wanted his audience to recognize (MU, 37, 46):

> To understand a text must be to understand both the intention to be understood, and the intention that this intention be understood, which the text itself as an intended act of communication must at least have embodied. The essential question . . . is what its author, in writing at the time he did write for the audience he intended to address could in practice have been intending to communicate . . . [The] appropriate methodology of the history of ideas must be concerned, first of all, to delineate the whole range of communications which could have been conventionally performed on the given occasion by the . . . given utterances. . . . (MU, 48–49)

The consequence of this emphasis, on specific meaning and communication, is a sophisticated form of radical historicism. Concern for dramatic representativeness, Skinner argues, returns us to perennial problems and ignores the only defensible use of historical analysis—the development of a sharp sense of the differences between past and present: "The classic texts . . . help to reveal . . . not the essential sameness, but rather the essential variety of viable moral assumptions and political commitments. . . . To discover from the history of thought that there are no such timeless concepts, but only the various different concepts which have gone with various different societies, is to discover a general truth not merely about the past but about ourselves as well" (MU, 52–53).

It does not follow, however, that if there are no perennial problems, or at least if it is dangerous to proceed initially by searching out a perennial problem, there are not perennial strategies and attitudes, as I argued in my discussion of Carnap. Skinner assumes that variety and differences are primarily a function of historical change, and not of changing situations and possibilities in the realm of experience considered horizontally or spatially. This leaves him vulnerable in two ways. Empirically, his insistence on historical situation oversimplifies the nature of many authorial intentions. Many writers do not take their sense of identity and role, or even the strategy for their arguments, from their immediate culture, but imagine themselves as repeating or altering an attitude whose nature and authority derive from the past. Machiavelli is trivialized if we ignore his self-projection into the tradition of classical Republicanism, and Blake's power depends largely on our ability to see how he not only imitates but actually becomes in his own eyes an incarnation of Milton (albeit Blake's Milton). The spatial realm of exemplary attitudes often functions as a basic element in the specific ways an author both interprets his contemporary situation and constructs his response to it. More important, it is common for authors to assume that their rhetorical project and their audience are not limited to given historical situations. Philosophers, for example, are likely to think that their project depends on a series of eternally valid arguments, not on specific historical contexts (which are obviously necessary for interpretation, but do not entail concluding that the author has only a contemporary audience in mind). It is plausible that Hobbes is less interested in defending a specific political order than in articulating a set of arguments which define the nature of law and of civil society.[19] (The result of these arguments may be a support for one political order in preference to another, but this can be a largely contingent effect. Hobbes could have changed political allegiances without altering his general case.)

Where philosophers intend an ideal status for their arguments as constitutive of a true theory, independent of history, authors of literary texts often intend to achieve this status by means of the dramatic attitudes they construct. Writers need not simply address the concerns of their age. They can construct a performance of a representative stance toward perennial human problems, or they can articulate their historical condition so as to provide an interpretation of it for subsequent ages. This is why the concept of communication is so difficult to apply to literary texts. The intended audience need not be an empirical, historical one. Many writers appeal to ideal audiences, or imagine their task as the construction of artifacts which might, over time, change the tastes of the audience. One important aesthetic norm, in fact, is the ability of a writer to understand and interpret his own historicity, to determine a

19. For this observation on arguments as constitutive of truth in philosophy and the example of Hobbes, I am indebted to Richard Friedman. It is a further consequence of this argument that the *Rezeptiongeschichte* of theorists like Jauss is inadequate. No empirical analysis of an audience will provide a sense of how the author constructs his image of possible auditors. Determining a specific image of an audience requires formal analysis of a text and its implicit contexts.

shape by his act for forces that in normal experience are determinations of thought and behavior.[20]

Finally, Skinner's version of hermeneutics does not give sufficient importance to the past or to historical inquiry.[21] If the main value in studying the past is developing a sense of its difference from the present, there is no imperative for continuous, careful, and wide-ranging inquiry. As we saw in discussing Culler's textualist claims about literary cognition as knowledge of conventions for making sense, once one recognizes the general principle of difference and the basic shapes it takes, there is little reason for further inquiry. In Skinner, as in Culler, particulars have little value in themselves and have no relevance as distinct acts for an interpreter's contemporary situation.

Despite his concern for attitudes, Skinner arrives at his limited position in large part because he assumes that only the actual propositional content of a work has a claim to transhistorical status. Thus, if speech acts reduce propositions to very specific questions, there is nothing that transcends those specific conditions. He gives no attention to exemplary aspects of attitudes and strategies. With philosophers, this clearly ignores a significant role their work plays as a cultural possession. Socrates, for example, represents one permanent mode for the struggle to espouse values independent of social practice, and Kant a permanent attitude, with its attendant conceptual strategies, expressing the need for and the possibility of locating grounds of moral obligation in conceptual a priori terms. (John Rawls' recent work illustrates the exemplary value of Kantian strategies, and Rawls' use of these strategies in turn provides a model for reinterpreting the logical grounds earlier contract theorists, like Hobbes, have relied upon.)

The more important issue here, however, is the cognitive status of literary texts. I want to argue, by analogy with the philosophical attitudes just mentioned, that literary performances may provide perennially rele-

20. In "The Limits of Historical Explanations," *Philosophy* 41 (1966):213, Skinner seems to concede this point: "The qualities of intelligence and presentation which make a writer the best illustration in a philosophical picture will make him in an historical picture the worst." He goes on to say historians can define contexts in great detail, but not necessarily the uses made of those contexts.

21. It is interesting to note that on this point Gadamer is Skinner's radical opposite. But Gadamer offers a case for perennial knowledge that reduces the past to propositions, collapses meaning into significance, and relies on a vague notion of tradition. Gadamer, in effect, posits an inverse historicism, in which the past becomes a timeless repository of truths and all change is located in a narrow sense of the cultural limits impinging on the interpreter. For what I hope is a better use of the Hegelian tradition Gadamer relies on, see my next chapter.

vant literary samples which have distinctive philosophical import. Here, the previous discussion of Wittgenstein, on *showing* as opposed to *telling,* provides the necessary context, because it illustrates that there are areas of philosophical concern where propositions will not suffice. In these areas, representative literary attitudes serve two functions. The obvious function is to present concrete samples that test, extend, and give depth to philosophical claims.[22] But the more interesting cases are those in which writers try to perform directly philosophical roles, by stressing the quality of questions or the nature of stances and attitudes which the mind employs to situate itself in relation to traditional philosophical issues.[23] This is clearly the motive in the emphasis which Romantic poetry and poetics place on the presentation of meditative acts of mind, operating in terms of what Coleridge called poetic logic. But an equally powerful, and more concise, example can be offered by comparing the philosophical aspects of two writers reflecting on essentially the same problem—John Stuart Mill and George Eliot.

It is clear that there is not much point to reading Eliot's *Middlemarch* as an articulation of the arguments about liberalism and free will which Mill also makes. Why not just read Mill, where the evidence and logical structure are directly given? Eliot's novel, as a concrete, yet representative, structure of attitudes, provides a sense of liberal ideas *in practice* which Mill cannot match. In her dramatic development of states of consciousness shaping her characters' actions, and, above all, in her capacious, tolerant, and understanding narrative voice, Eliot expresses the

22. For a good example of using literature as examples in philosophical arguments, see Jesse Kalin, "Philosophy Needs Literature: John Barth and Moral Nihilism," *Philosophy and Literature* 1 (1977):170–83. Kalin's essay is especially interesting, because it shifts from reducing Barth's texts to arguments to final comments on a different, distinctive contribution the texture of the novels makes to philosophy (pp. 180–83). These last pages make a good case for the philosophical significance of concrete aspects in the articulation of an attitude.

23. In his very interesting *Wittgenstein's Language* (The Hague: Martinus Nijhoff, 1973), Timothy Binkley argues that Wittgenstein's *Investigations* are best read in a literary tradition. The form of argument and basic metaphors require our learning to renounce propositions and to situate the mind in such a way that one sees how to approach a philosophical problem in order to make it dissolve. In my terms, Wittgenstein challenges boundaries between literature and philosophy to the extent that he is tempted by the possibility that the source of problems in philosophy is not bad arguments, but the kind of stance one takes up when he is philosophically puzzled. His *Investigations* then dramatizes a set of representative procedures for recognizing and dissolving these puzzles. In this context, the goal is not truth, but a *way* of acting, free from error and aware of the structures giving significance to particular situations. One must remember, however, that Wittgenstein gains authority for his dramatic stance by some pretty sharp argument.

kind of mind needed to create and maintain a liberal society. Moreover, in the interplay between narrative voice and characters, she exhibits a sense of limit and of ironies making necessary a distinctive tone, aware of tragedy, but also of the compensations that come from such an awareness. This attitude may be a necessary feature of any possible faith in liberal ideals. Yet there is no way to argue analytically for such a tone, or, if one could argue, to make the tone appealing and available to others. What gives Eliot's novel a particular philosophical value is the fact that liberal concepts of society are not so much its theme as its situation for authorial activity. This situation makes the narrative activity representative, while allowing it to eschew arguments in favor of displaying strategies for achieving self-knowledge, accepting limits, tolerating differences, and admitting social obligations. It allows Eliot finally to supplement all the age's philosophers by understanding the despondently melioristic tone which, unlike Mills' optimism, might actually enable one to escape despair over such fragile yet necessary ideals.

I find this comparison especially useful, because it admits one more twist. If we turn from Eliot to Mill, we see that Mill was not without literary ambitions, nor without a philosophical use for them. From the time of his essay on Bentham, Mill found himself in a difficult situation. As son of James Mill, he could grant philosophical authority only to arguments that could be stated in propositional form, and yet, as critic of Utilitarianism, he found himself committed to values involving predicates—like nobility or psychological fullness—not easy to place in his inherited philosophical language. One consequence of this tension is simply a tendency to contradiction, to sometimes pose moral issues as reducible to propositional analysis and at other times to insist that the grounds of moral choice were beyond argument. But the nature of the tension is far more important. For Mill labored under the early stages of the dichotomy between propositional statements, which could be verified but could say nothing about value, and exemplary attitudes, which were both the focus of ethical discussion and the means for making philosophy applicable to human behavior. Mill's vacillations were later formalized in Wittgenstein's early work (see especially NB, 72–91) and were fundamental to Russell's inability to reconcile his analytic and his ethical commitments.[24] Given these tensions, the importance Mill

---

24. For a good general statement of this dilemma with respect to Russell and analytic philosophy, although without the context of dramatistic inquiry, see Stuart Hampshire, "Russell, Radicalism and Reason," *The New York Review of Books*

attributed to his *Autobiography* (which later ages have acknowledged by treating it as his basic work) reveals his own need to attempt what Eliot could do in her novels. The aim of the *Autobiography* was to provide the dramatic context and exemplary attitudes which were necessary to illustrate the significance of his analytic work.

Mill's *Autobiography*, in fact, serves as a powerful literary sample for pointing out and clarifying a characteristic modern philosophical stance. Mill dramatizes a now-pervasive tension between the desire to preserve the authority of logical analysis and the fear that claims to truth depend largely on exemplary self-presentations and rhetorical skills. He inherits a tradition in which the truth and authority of philosophy depend on the powers of the mind to be logical, and on logic somehow representing either the order of things or the necessary order of inquiry. Yet he also finds himself recognizing the claims of historicism, in which views of logic are epiphenomena of social conditions and truths are relative. Thus, he is forced to grapple with the moral relativism which is a logical complement of historicism. Mill, then, both needs and distrusts philosophy, needs a framework in which descriptions can be objectively justified and verified, and suspects that the real power of descriptions lies in their rhetorical effectiveness as dramatic gestures. This is evident both in his quandaries about the foundation of morality and in his desire to reconcile descriptive truths with what he finds morally acceptable.[25] The exemplary dramatic power of Mill's work derives from his ability to stand between pressures which would soon create an absolute dichotomy in Western philosophy: the analytic tradition would soon embrace a radically extensional language, irrelevant to most questions about human behavior, and the Continental tradition, from Bergson to Heidegger, Sartre, and Derrida, would so stress the nature of expressive features of behavior that visions of shareable truths and articulate responsible inquiry appear nostalgic evasions of primary forces which cannot even take determinate dramatistic forms.

Exemplification of problems is perhaps not the highest philosophical function, yet it has important precedents in the work of Socrates and

---

15 (Oct. 8, 1970):3–8. These comments on Mill derive from two observations by Richard Friedman. He pointed out to me that Mill's probable intention in his *Autobiography* was to fix the way his philosophical works would be read, and he suggested that the crisis chapter in this work is probably in large part fiction, aimed to show that Mill was not simply a "reasoning machine," but had experienced a less mystical equivalent of Carlyle's "Everlasting NO."

25. For examples of this problem in Mill's *Autobiography*, see his discussion of his rejection of religion on moral grounds and his discussion of determinism.

Wittgenstein, and it at least serves the role of deepening our grasp of what explicitly philosophical arguments must solve. In fact, given the temper of modern analytic philosophy, it may be that all we can expect of philosophical import with respect to problems perennial in the literary tradition are these dramatistic performances. If this is the case, if traditional philosophical issues do not admit clear propositional solutions, the examples of Mill and of other writers remind us that there remain dramatic encounters in which permanently available questioning stances become virtual exclamations celebrating the powers of philosophically informed acts of mind for their own sake.

9

Self-Reflection and Reading as
a Source of Social Values

1. The need to capture self-reflective aspects of literary experience   A
model of literary knowledge affords an instrumental response to Hirsch's
challenge, and it concludes my direct arguments based on a dramatistic
semantics. Yet there is a good deal more to say, or to gesture at. One's
sense of value is rarely exhausted by descriptive and instrumental accounts, especially when the object of attention is aesthetic and contemplative. I have described the text's capacity to perform attitudes, but
there remains a horizon to our grasp of these attitudes, an "attitude toward attitudes," perhaps, where the stance we take reveals some important dimensions of literary experience. In this chapter, I want not to
examine texts or competence, not to attend to objects or direct acts of
interpretation, but to speculate on the values we become conscious of
if we reflect upon the powers we exercise in reading and the cultural
identifications implicit in the possession of those powers.[1] Instead of
describing competence in reading, I want to construct two ideals that
can be seen as possible conditions of self-knowledge and attitudes toward culture, made available by reflecting on what is involved in taking
texts as performances which constitute a qualitative cultural grammar.

---

1. J. R. Findlay describes this shift from description to reflecting on self-reflection
in his "The Methodology of Normative Ethics," in his *Language, Mind, and Values*
(London: George Allen and Unwin, 1963), pp. 248–56. I shall later use Findlay's
attempts to secularize Hegel for modern philosophy in *The Philosophy of Hegel*
(New York: Collier Books, 1962) and *Values and Intention* (London: George
Allen and Unwin, 1961).

I insist on terms like *speculate* to describe my stance in this chapter, because I do not want to make any normative or descriptive claims. I am only projecting a possible way to appreciate and draw consequences from what readers do. Yet, if my speculations are plausible, they can serve three important functions—clarify social attitudes and perspectives on community, inherent as potentials of a literary education;[2] give a final way of understanding and valuing the circular processes that I have been arguing are basic to the humanities; and indicate how my model in this book builds upon and interprets traditional humanist ideals of *culture* (or high culture) as forming mental powers needed for what Frye calls the work of civilization.

The first of the two values, or ideal self-reflective attitudes, I shall concentrate on can be stated in simple terms: because it develops powers to describe actions, literary education can be seen as also fostering a capacity to bestow on human agents (and by analogy on the self) attributes traditionally associated with ideas of dignity and nobility. We can appreciate what such pieties involve and we can reflect on our commitment to them by briefly considering a casual statement made by Carl Dennis during a poetry reading. The literary imagination, he said, tries to do justice to human lives, often when the agent represented would, in reality, lack the terms and faculties for doing so in his or her own right. The idea of justice makes me leery, since it admits radical ironic reversals. But Dennis identified what is to me an extremely significant aspect of literary experience—an attitude committed to taking seriously the purposes, qualities, and achievements of the agents represented. Because we reflect upon their acts, we cannot easily take up the casual stances we often do in daily life, and, because we attend to qualities, we are not content with impersonal explanations that can treat lives as symptomatic reflexes of external conditions. Even when persons are represented as defeated by these conditions, most of our best literary texts make us understand that defeat from within a character's attitude so that we can fully sympathize with it or at least understand it as a significant state of mind. So an attitude of seriousness toward actions leads to a sense of how agents outside literature can be valued.

My second self-reflective stance extends this concern for individuals to a more abstract and general concern for the nature of cultural life and the way that life can be seen as satisfying the mind's needs. The focus here will be on understanding the forms of identification made possible

2. I address the issue of positing ends for criticism much more fully in a still unpublished essay, "Taking Ends Seriously," written after this book was completed.

by considering how we can connect texts to one another and define our own powers in relation to those texts. This framework of interrelations, on which we depend for identifications, will be my vehicle for describing the significance of circularity in the humanities, primarily because discovering it will require invoking the exemplary figure of Hegel in the *Phenomenology of Spirit*. His concepts of *Geist*, self-understanding, and dialectic are to me necessary for articulating the full humanistic implications of a dramatistic perspective. Moreover, the framework I have been developing from action theory affords ways of separating the parts of Hegel that are valuable and defensible in a loose empirical way from the more problematic teleological assumptions in idealist thought. I shall take Hegel as strictly a philosopher of the development of a dramatistic grammar and of the forms of self-reflection made possible by this grammar. He shows what is involved in the mind's knowing itself with respect to a cultural sense of community, and he, thus, establishes a transition from discussing the ends of practical criticism to the more general and abstract possibilities of literary education.

These are not easy matters to discuss with precision, but the price for not attempting the discussion is high. First, that would entail equating the humanities with methodological and instrumental issues which do not exhaust the speculative energies created by the experience of beauty or of complex performances. These energies lead us at once back to the consequences of a performance model and out to the general sphere of how culture cultivates and provides not only examples, but exemplary ways of using examples. Putting this same point differently will show another reason why Hegel matters so much to my work: because literary procedures invoke complex acts of identifying with and assessing performances, an account of them is incomplete unless it considers dimensions of self-consciousness, as well as ways of dealing directly with objects of interpretation. Literary attitudes allow, even encourage, transitions between the terms for self-regard posited by the performances of those whom Taylor calls *strong evaluators* and the processes by which readers identify their own purposes and commitments.

There are probably many different ways these states of self-consciousness of self-regarding evaluations take place—so many, in fact, that theorists have despaired of bringing order to the subject. However, it seems clear that if one does not now take up the question of how literary culture cultivates values, one grants domination to deconstructionist positions, the only stances that have fully articulate and definable relationships between the act of reading and the values criticism serves. The

Derridean line, for example, is best exemplified in *Glas*, where deconstruction as interpretive strategy becomes a vehicle for preserving the freedom of imagination to adapt itself to cultural monuments which have become, if taken literally, mere mausoleums to dead images of man and of human values. The only defense of culture, as an academic General Westmoreland might say, is to destroy it and to build a new performative arena for free play out of its fragments. More political versions of Nietzsche, like Said's and Foucault's, on the other hand, offer consistent connections between a hermeneutics of suspicion and a general model of culture as the manipulation of sign systems to satisfy wills to power. In both models, the emphasis on specific forms of interpretation projects a clear image of the kinds of power an educated mind has with respect to its cultural heritage.

The case with traditional defenses of humanistic values is quite different. Many of the best literary theorists have withdrawn from large speculations about culture and cultivation, in order to propose defensible versions of smaller questions, like the nature of meaning. Here the temptation, as we have seen, is to rely on philosophies of scientific explanation which have no contributions to make to a general account of humanistic knowledge or even to the humane goals of practical criticism. Full-scale defenses of the humanities provided by the previous generation of theorists have come to appear depressingly lame—partially because of internal contradictions or inadequate philosophical frameworks, and partially because they cannot handle textualist challenges.[3] The blend of Arnoldian humanism and Romantic epistemology which characterizes New Criticism, for example, had by the 1960s collapsed into an academic formalism or reductive stress on original thematic readings, with no articulate sense of the significance of such enterprises. Even the best statements of this position, as de Man points out, have not developed an adequate philosophy of mind to account for the nature or the importance of the complex aesthetic dimensions their methods of reading disclose. One effect of this failure is that inadequately defended concepts of culture and of the mental powers employed in close reading make

---

3. Murray Krieger's response to Derrida in his last chapter of *Theory of Criticism* (Baltimore: Johns Hopkins University Press, 1976), is an interesting and complex case here. In order to resist textualist challenges to aesthetic autonomy, Krieger ignores his own general Kantian stance and grants a Derridean case for ordinary language. To return to the military metaphor I used above, this move wins a battle by losing the war. Once one loses faith in a general model of interpretive mind, he has no way of describing the use of what he preserves in aesthetic terms; we get a literary coherence divorced from humanistic praxis.

claims about culture and taste seem to be mere masked defenses of established social and intellectual authority. Bad philosophy always invites sceptical explanation of the position as motivated primarily by symptomatic needs. The other major twentieth-century defense of humanistic values—the neo-Kantianism of Cassirer and Langer—suffers from an opposite problem. It bases its defenses of man as a symbol-making animal on an all-too-explicit philosophy of mind, which in my view is inadequate for contemporary concerns. By overstressing the active, creative mind, it gives us no coherent way to show how creativity depends on grammatical frameworks, or language on complex internal systems. Its emphasis on symbol and symbolic form tends to pose in epistemological terms solutions which are so vague they only repeat the conditions of the problem they are to solve. We need to know why certain objects are read as symbolic forms, and how this makes a difference in what we know or can say about the experiences presented.

2. Taking actions seriously: the means for understanding dignity

I have so far dealt with action essentially as a semantic category. Yet it is obvious that actions are also the primary focus of our emotional involvement in texts and our subsequent reflections upon them. I want now to consider this larger framework and to treat my first ideal in terms of a specific sense of values we can locate in our self-conscious reflection on these engagements. I take the hermeneutic task to consist of getting a text to fully display its performance, by mediating between the concrete qualities of the acts of mind presented and the interpretive capacity of an audience. As we fill out and situate the actions, we can reflect upon the attitude this leads us to take toward purposive agents. Put simply, we take human agents seriously, at least to the extent that we find dramatic or authorial persons producing and taking responsibility for the course of action they carry out. This idea of seriousness is not innocuous; it brings us to the spirit, if not the letter, of Arnoldian humanism, and for good reason. If we abstract seriousness from particular cases, we can see that it leads in two significant directions—out toward more general questions of human dignity, and in toward a renewed sense of the obligations of criticism, if it is fully to articulate the terms on which dignity is to be grasped.

The question of dignity or nobility has always been a fundamental humanistic concern, although its specific grounds and contrastive base often shift. For our purposes, the crucial shift creating the pressure which makes literary experience relevant for these questions took place primarily in the eighteenth century. For Christian humanism, dignity and nobility could be predicated of lives that resisted temptations to sin or to negate social responsibilities. In the eighteenth century, the external threat to self-possession became philosophical rather than dramatic. One lost dignity not only or even mainly as a result of any act, but because of a philosophical sense that human behavior was shaped by external determining forces, and hence no meaningful action was possible. So the very possibility of purposive action became philosophically significant. From Kant to Wallace Stevens to Chomsky, dignity depends on demonstrating a capacity to exert a counterpressure to the pressure of reality. Now, when we situate literary actions as serious, purposive responses to problems, we in effect construct expressive models of self-definition. Because the performances we attend to are fictional, we cannot base our sense of dignity on arguments which we can prove. But we do cultivate an attitude for viewing actions which keeps alive the experience of registering and following up on purposes, so we establish at least a perspective which can be the object of philosophical arguments (such as those posed by teleological theorists). Perhaps more important, we develop ways of viewing dignity that depend neither on Kantian ethics nor Arnoldian pieties. We locate dignity and seriousness in the energies of self-conscious expression. It is precisely the depth and qualities of purpose carried through in an action that we identify as an agent's claim to our attention and respect.

It is important to mark the differences between Kant's and Arnold's equations of seriousness and dignity, on the one hand, and, on the other, the expressionist view consistent with an emphasis on literary performances. In the latter case, there are few constraints on content, no universal laws, and no Arnoldian tendencies to privilege certain genres or dismiss the significance of ironic or comic stances. Seriousness and dignity depend solely on the power to project purposes a person can embody in his acts and on the qualities of judgment and sensibility those acts reflect. Seriousness as a criterion for criticism, in turn, would depend on the depth and significance one can illustrate are relevant to the action one is describing. These expressive concerns will lead in a few moments to my attempt to adapt Hegel, but for now a literary example should make clear both the difference from Kant I am after and the effects critical acts can have on our capacity to posit dignity and nobility.

Flaubert's work is, in general, deeply resistant to any traditional moral account of actions or even any self-regarding role supported by traditional humanism. Yet the critic can construct an attitude describing the purposes and details in Flaubert's work in a way that enables us first to see Flaubert's purposes as serious, qualitatively significant human ones, and then to recognize the kinds of situations where a person might represent her own actions as worthy of concern because they share both the concepts and the forms of interpreting experience typified by Flaubert.[4] This would be done by understanding the contrastive nature of Flaubert's performance, where the lucidity of writing is set against the banalities and self-deceptions of the characters' moral self-images. Dignity, in short, resides not in the simple following of moral precepts, but in the qualities of consciousness one can see deliberately expressed in a performance. Within the parameters of an expressionist set of values, situating becomes the precondition for moral as well as aesthetic experiences.

3. *Some consequences of a seriousness criterion for literary hermeneutics*

We have seen Leroy Searle's argument that a literary theory should link properties of aesthetic experience to an audience's existential concerns. A corollary claim might be that, once we see possible existential results of a way of reading, we can make a case for imposing some criteria for the forms of attention cultivated by close readings. The criteria will hold only to the degree that we value what seriousness provides, and we must recognize the possibility of other values producing other models. But even with this proviso, we can develop a powerful catalogue of practical and speculative consequences that follow from basing work on the values associated with seriousness. First, this procedure obviously defends a dramatistic concern for situating the purposes embodied in texts. We can draw relevant contrasts to textualism, where an obsession with metalinguistic concerns confines criticism to one level of situating and allows little basis for significant dramatic extension of the textual duplicities revealed. Deductive theories offer almost the opposite contrast.

---

4. I want to make it clear that the representative aspects of attitudes are not most effectively brought out by tedious statements about a text's use for us. *Representativeness* is largely an implicit feature of work by a mind informed by representative concerns and using a language sufficiently general to suggest the ramifications of a description without belaboring them. This is obviously the source of most of the pleasure we in fact derive from good practical criticism.

They establish seriousness by insisting on the overall coherence of the author's artistic purpose, but in so doing they reduce the range and depth of situations we can attribute to both author and dramatic characters. The characters tend to be confined to thematic structures, and the artist is projected as confronting primarily aesthetic choices not fully connected to existential desires and confusions the text may be attempting to work out. Finally, response theory reveals an interesting problem in assessing the power of a theory to situate the seriousness of a text. I refer here only to Stanley Fish's *Surprised By Sin*,[5] because Holland's form of indeterminacy theory grants no self-conscious control of purposes. Fish's early work concentrates on the author's manipulation of audience response, so it clearly establishes significant purposes for the author. But, by stopping on the level of response, it greatly limits the nature of the authorial act the audience can reflect upon, and, correspondingly, it diminishes what one can predicate as significant or serious about the author's purposes. For, while Fish is brilliant in describing how the audience is controlled, he gives the audience no power to recognize and reflect upon Milton's manipulations as part of the act Milton offers us. This is especially problematic in Milton's case, because insofar as his strategies are presumed to function without the reader's awareness of being manipulated, they put the implicit authorial attitude in a strangely unChristian light. The author must fool us in order to save us. Yet we lose none of Fish's astute observations if we conceive of Milton as desiring us to see his strategies as consciously and overtly designed to represent a serious Christian attitude toward making moral discriminations. Then the authorial act represents the epistemological drama in which any Christian must learn to participate, and we have a strong contrastive base for relating the stance Milton creates to other, less discriminating, models for representing oneself to oneself as a Christian. This point, put in more general terms, suggests that, all other things being equal, a critical position is to be preferred to the extent that it makes available the fullest possible dimensions of authorial consciousness as samples an audience can situate and reflect upon in existential terms.

The means for such situating will frequently involve a good deal of interdisciplinary work. Thus, the second consequence of my proposed seriousness criterion is that it affords a coherent conceptual place for interdisciplinary work and, more important, for interdisciplinary educa-

5. Stanley Fish, *Surprised by Sin* (New York: St. Martins Press, 1967). My point below actually derives from arguments with my colleague Allen Fisher.

tion. In fact, insofar as describing actions is the focus of critical activity, it is necessary to speak of the humanities as inherently requiring knowledge of the various subject matters and procedures now absurdly divided into narrow specializations. We require disciplines because there are distinct modes of discourse with appropriate procedures and basic traditions, which usually inform authorial purposes and constitute basic aspects of meaning. Yet, in order to develop the representative seriousness of actions in intensional terms, one must be able to situate the act and the problems confronted in several interlocking contexts. (As a contrastive counterexample, consider the poverty of Harold Bloom's reductively literary psychodynamics.) At least history, psychology, and philosophy are usually necessary to reconstitute the depth of a problem or to clarify the nature of questions asked, as well as to illuminate the distinctive qualities of awareness displayed in a literary performance. Obviously, too ready a reliance only on these supplementary contexts ignores the purposes defining an act as a specific one and collapses the act into the interpreter's structures for establishing significance. Literary texts become only evidence or documents for historians, psychologists, and philosophers. But action theory enables us to distinguish between inquiries into significance and attempts to situate the representative seriousness of distinct purposive acts. This enables us to treat subsidiary disciplines simply as interpretive contrasts or lures for feeling, so that (without indeterminacy) we maintain and sustain a rich pluralism among possible forms of seriousness.

We have already considered the instrumental role of this grammatical pluralism. Now, however, we view it from a different, self-reflective perspective. So the crucial point to consider becomes the values served by this pluralism, with respect to the ways it enables us to recognize the range of actions we can take seriously and the effect these realizations have on our own sense of cultural identity. Dorothy Walsh states concisely two poles of this vision, which will require Hegel for full articulation. The testimony of literary art both reminds us of how complicated the range of psychic states we can recognize is and makes possible our realization that in such states we find "man's distinctive presentation of himself to himself" establishing his "visibility" or potential identity "as a total person." [6]

If Walsh is correct, our reflections on grammar lead to a position on expression and supplements very different from Derrida's. Derrida makes

6. Dorothy Walsh, *Literature and Knowledge* (Middletown, Conn.: Wesleyan University Press, 1969), pp. 107, 140.

an important contribution, in insisting that expressive acts derive from and supplement previous acts. But if one has terms for situating these acts as purposive reinterpretations which can display their own rationale, *supplement* is less displacement than self-conscious adjustment, and the history of attitudes is not a mausoleum, but a dynamic contrastive context for description and judgment.[7] The line from Milton to Wordsworth to Arnold to Eliot, for example, may be viewed as a series of displacements of a paradise myth, or as a continual ground of conflict on which individual poets prove their strength by swerving from the parent in creative misreadings. However, misreading is a trivial form of competition—one can only prove strength by trying to master his opponent's actual performance—and displacement is a passive model of behavior which does not allow us to take the agents very seriously. Derrida can still reply that we only delude and flatter ourselves when we desire to take human agents seriously. Yet it is tempting to say that it is difficult for a Derridean not to flatter himself with the seriousness and lucidity of his refusal of seriousness, so why not accept a more pluralistic range of acts one grants as displays of the agent's serious stature as a human agent? Even without such a move, it remains plausible to view this line of poetic acts differently, and to use a contrast with Derrida as a means for clarifying what claims to seriousness involve. We can view each poet as turning to his predecessor's terms for dramatizing significant qualities of the psyche, and then as imposing on them a performance displaying the seriousness of another perspective—on the implicit grounds that the latter perspective at once accounts for the other's power and adapts it to a richer or different sense of situation. The claim to a richer content, in turn, sustains the attitude's appeal to embody a sense of dignity that we attribute to fully facing up to the difficulties of one's surroundings. Stevens offers the best summary: nobility is a function of how an agent confronts the pressures of reality and constructs an attitude which preserves the freedom and vitality of full imaginative encounter.[8]

Because seriousness ultimately depends on the constitutive force of

7. The best general statement I know of this use for literary analysis is by Stuart Hampshire, *Thought and Action*, pp. 59–66: "Moods, states of mind, feelings and sensations have to be described, the particular quality of them communicated; and to find more and more effective ways of describing them is the most serious of all the necessary refinements of language. It is serious because moods, states of mind and feelings must be distinguished and identified in a society before they can be facts that enter into men's practical intentions and manners" (p. 65).

8. Stevens, *The Necessary Angel*, especially pp. 20–27, 33–36.

an entire history of predicates for representing the human features of humanity, we see the deepest reason why discourse in and about the humanities must be circular. What can be expressed about the human is not something we read off the natural world or off machines. We know what we are looking for only because *knowledge* is a dimension term, given depth by complex possibilities of situating and relating attitudes in terms passed on by tradition. The less we know this tradition, the less fully we have gone through the complexities of the circular predicates we need to describe certain actions, the easier and more tempting it becomes to succumb to the pressure of reality and to view ourselves as simple creatures of biological necessity, without history or the corollary potential to make, as well as to suffer, history. By adapting seriousness as its criterion, criticism participates in that tradition's primary process of keeping a distinctive sense of man alive and flexible. As Hegel put it, in his own confrontation with reductive analytic models, "The more paltry the conception of Spirit ... mental properties become fewer ... [and] more detached, rigid, and ossified, and therefore more akin to characteristics of the bone, and more comparable with them." [9]

4. *Hegel as a model for describing the identifications made possible by literary education*

My arrival at Hegel is not fortuitous. As one shifts from descriptive to speculative arguments, one crosses a threshold where one must change guides—in my case, from the tutelary presence of Wittgenstein to that of Hegel. Hegel's thinking in his *Phenomenology* contains for me the fullest and deepest exposition of the nature and implications of dealing with questions of the values afforded by a dramatistic perspective. Hegel both exemplifies how criteria of seriousness and representativeness apply to the analysis of attitudes, and treats the corollary theme of circularity as the basis for his discussion of dialectics. In working out these ideas, Hegel also articulates a vision of the mind I consider necessary for any discussion of educational functions and powers derived from critical reflection on attitudes. Hegel's *Phenomenology* can be seen as an extended meditation on the question I posed for this conclusion— what is it we know when we try to reflect on the nature of the powers we accumulate and organize by virtue of a series of specific dramatistic

9. G. W. F. Hegel, *Phenomenology of Spirit*, trans. A. V. Miller (Oxford: Clarendon Press, 1977), p. 202. This text shall hereafter be abbreviated PS.

analyses? For Hegel, there are discrete acts of knowledge and there is a nonthetic (or self-reflective) horizon to these acts of knowledge, which we can bring to awareness by reflecting on the overall structure and interrelationships among our critical acts. This mode of reflection, moreover, permits a transition from practical to teleological questions, because it establishes an image of what particular acts of knowledge can produce in relation to a general sense of the mind's powers. We do not think only about attitudes, we think about our thinking, and about how we are changed or modified by what we know. Hegel gives a powerful model of how we can view our relation to history and to other minds, in relation to the dramatistic knowledge we acquire and the powers we exercise in these interpretations.

I am as uncomfortable as most readers with Hegel's vocabulary and some of his metaphysical claims. But I think we can modify, as well as use, Hegel when we are discussing the consequences of action theory, because that theory enables us to reduce the relevant features of Hegel's thought to a defensible core. We can read Hegel as speaking only about features of self-consciousness with respect to the understanding of actions. We need no unsupportable claims about dialectical properties in nature and in history. My version of action theory, in other words, seeks to put Hegel back on his feet by eliminating the major elements which attracted Marx. I shall read Hegel's significance in terms that are purely idealist—that is, not as claims about a dynamic nature, but, rather, as simply an account of how the mind takes on powers and a form of self-knowledge through dramatistic analyses. The crucial feature of Hegel's *Phenomenology* is its account of expression and of what knowledge of expression consists. Thus, if we restrict Hegel to the realm of analyzing actions and attitudes, where there are phenomenological and intuitive tests for claims he also applies to nature and to history, we find ourselves going over, from a broader perspective, the concept of attitude types discussed above in relation to Yeats and Frye. Hegel shares their concern with reflecting on spirit in terms of the ways its expressive productions manifest a range of attitudes that constitute dense perennial types for classifying and making discriminations about human actions. But only Hegel combines a philosophical account of what these attitudes reflect with a comprehensive image of the properties of mind necessary to make sense of how we reflect upon our cultural possessions. Hegel treats expressive activity as the articulation of the mind's powers, and makes dialectic the process of recognizing how we can identify with and find identity in what attitudes reveal about those powers. The

Phenomenology, then, can be read as a model of the values in and self-reflective uses for dramatistic analysis. Hegel gets into trouble in his attempts to characterize an immanent ground for nature and history as they determine the expressive powers of mind. But his error is easy to specify: he treats all propositions as if they ultimately belonged to a dialectical logic, which is in fact appropriate only to intensional aspects of experience. Hegel treats nature in a fashion only applicable to human actors. Yet, perhaps because of his blindness, he provides a rich account of how expressions become a form of objective knowledge—subject neither to Carnap's dismissal of attitudes, nor to Derrida's version of dialectic as only supplement and displacement—and he typifies an ideal attitude for reflecting upon the total grammatical structure developed by a full humanistic education. For Hegel, desire takes form in performance, and knowledge of the range of human performance is ultimately awareness of the self's full identity as concrete agent and participant in universal capacities and structures.

Restating Hegel's significance in defensible modern terms requires two major modifications of his thought. The first is obvious. Claims about an absolute mind, constituted as a scientific grasp of the internal relationships among the moments of *Geist*'s development, are impossible to state in falsifiable terms or to defend.[10] At best, as Findlay argues, the absolute is a useful supreme fiction, an image of a never-to-be-realized goal of self-reflective inquiry. Then, once one rejects a principle of absolute reason, he must restate Hegel's version of the elements that produce this principle. Here my arguments about grammar and attitudes come into play. Instead of taking Hegel's stages of the development of *Geist* in historical terms (even as a logically reconstructed history, which is what I believe Hegel intended), I take his specific analyses as dense descriptions and situatings of very general attitude types. There is, then, not a simple dialectical progression, but a timeless grammar, capable of infinitely varied interrelationships, to be used for identifying specific acts and projecting contrastive accounts of their representativeness and depth. As Sartre and de Man exemplify, the unhappy consciousness is

10. Yet see James Ogilvy, "Reflections on the Absolute," *Review of Metaphysics* 27 (1975): 520–46, for a very good review of discussions of the absolute and a nontheological defense of it. Even if one does not buy Ogilvy's view, Hegel's version of an immanent absolute makes an interesting mythical dramatistic analogue to Wittgenstein's *das mystiche*. The mystical to Wittgenstein (in TLP) is a sense of the world as enclosed by all and only the possible true predications that can be made of it. To Hegel, the absolute encompasses the world as enclosed by all the self-reflective acts that can be performed as expressions of it.

not an attitude limited to early Christianity. Similarly, a good deal of post-modern poetry (and contemporary culture) is in large part a reen-actment of Hegel's description of the limits of seeking pure empirical freedom and self-expression. And Hegel's types may have their order reversed, and be used simply to stress relational features in performances or philosophical positions. By developing interrelations between unhappy consciousness and scepticism, one can show how and why Derrida works himself out of Sartrean dualistic *angst* and yet still retains traces of metaphysical nostalgia in his Nietzschean free play. Or one can, as Lionel Trilling has done, make Hegel's discussion of the tensions in *Rameau's Nephew* the exemplary type for fundamental contradictions in modernism.[11] For strategies like these, Burke is Hegel's obvious heir (perhaps with Derrida playing Edmund to Burke's Edgar).

The second modification involves more narrow and difficult philo-sophical issues, difficult to separate from Hegel's vocabulary. For what follows, I beg the reader's indulgence and remind him that the first modification already contains the essential points. Hegel's idealistic path from nature to absolute mind is based on a concept of substance and subject—or objective being and active, negating mind—as immanently identical, but needing the course of history to make that identity deter-minate and significant:

> For they [the ancients] rightly saw the moving principle as the neg-ative, though they did not as yet grasp that the negative is the self. Now, although this negative appears at first as a disparity between the "I" and its object, it is just as much the disparity of the sub-stance with itself. Thus what seems to happen outside of it, to be an activity directed against it, is really its own doing, and substance shows itself to be essentially subject. When it has shown this com-pletely, Spirit has made its existence identical with its essence; it has itself for its object just as it is, and the abstract element of imme-diacy, and of the separation of knowing and truth, is overcome. (PS, 21)

It is, as a totality, a syllogism or the movement of the universal through determination to individuality, as also the reverse move-ment from individuality through superseded individuality, or through determination, to the universal. It is therefore, in accordance with

11. Trilling, *Sincerity and Authenticity* (Cambridge, Mass.: Harvard University Press, 1972).

these three determinations that consciousness must know the object as itself. (PS, 480)

What we can know of substance depends on the state of spirit: in this sense, ideas are constitutive of reality. But at any given moment before absolute knowledge is achieved, the mind experiences itself largely as a negative force, a power not fully determined by the objects and completed attitudes it confronts. Yet negation gives the mind fresh perspectives on substance, so that progressive degrees of identification take place between knower and known, until complete truth, which is by definition identity of mind and object, has been achieved. Then the mind's universals are recognized as fully immanent in natural and historical order. This means that the ultimate stage of knowledge is pure self-knowledge, a grasp of one's deepest potentials to structure experience, made possible because these structures have been objectified. Hegel offers, then, a radically expressionist metaphysic:[12] the grounding force is the desire to know oneself in terms of the qualities of one's active being which can be objectively displayed: "Substance is charged, as Subject, with the *at first* ONLY *inward* necessity of setting forth within itself what it is *in itself*, of exhibiting itself as *Spirit*. . . . The I is not merely the Self, but the *identity of the Self with itself*; but this identity is complete and immediate oneness with Self, or this *Subject* is just as much Substance" (PS, 488–89).

If one takes nature and history as unfolding themselves expressively, then one must posit some form of general, immanent, purposive force which motivates the transition from substance to subject. This is the function of *Geist*. There are, however, more limited views of expression, based simply on the concept of action, which fit Hegel's general perspectives, while requiring only a desire to understand the various properties of human behavior that get articulated in performances. If we adapt such a position, we can replace Hegel's metaphysics with two basic human motives for expressive activity—the desire of persons' to create themselves by acting and taking responsibility for acts, and their desire to understand what actions reveal. Even a modified Hegel provides a powerful image of these two processes, through his concepts of action, actuality (or *wirklichkeit*), self-consciousness, and dialectic.

Action, for Hegel, is the process of articulating individual being so

---

12. For a trenchant account of Hegel's concept of expression and its relation to concepts of the self, see Charles Taylor, *Hegel* (Cambridge: Cambridge University Press, 1975), pp. 11–29.

that there emerges a "unity of objectivity and Being for Self" (PS, 138). In action, one gives public being to his purposes and qualities, and, in taking responsibility for them, identifies them as self-consciously willed objective signs of his spiritual being (PS, 416). Action is, in behavioral terms, a rich analogue to artistic practice because it is the means by which spirit presses itself out into substance and substance is given meanings for consciousness: "It [action] is the pure form of transition from a state of not being seen, and the content which is brought out into the daylight and displayed, is nothing else but what this action already is in itself. It is implicit: this is its form as a unity in thought; and it is actual—this is its form as an existent unity" (PS, 237). As expressive of spirit, an action is *wirkung* which constructs a world one sees as *wirklichkeit*. Cultural forms become objective expressions of the way in which spirit gives itself shape as actuality within history. Action is the production of a sign "through which the individual only makes known what he really is, when he sets his original nature to work" (PS, 186).

We return again to an account of origins that counters Derrida,[13] for expression theory depends on the fact that the production of meanings becomes achievement of meaning by transforming origins into cultural forms. The telos of this transformation is self-consciousness. Self-consciousness is a process of creating differences or negations which unfold aspects of the self, and then recover them as not different but as expanding aspects of a single dialectical process: a spiritual being "repels itself from itself, posits itself as an inner being containing different moments, but for which equally these moments are immediately *not* different—*self-consciousness*" (PS, 103). "Spirit is the knowledge of oneself in the externalization of oneself; the being that is the movement of retaining its self-identity in its otherness" (PS, 459). One comes to know what the negation revealed, and, hence, identifies it as part of the determinate and determining shape of spirit expressed in its self-objectification. Because the self-knowledge correlates immediate existence with the universal predicates characterizing mental life, consciousness of self is also a potential for grasping identity in larger cultural terms. One grasps

13. A good deal of Derrida's argument, however, restates Hegel in terms of a structuralist Saussurean model of representational structures. Derrida's discussion of *différance* and doubling probably derives from early sections of the *Phenomenology* describing the relationship between consciousness, appearance, the supersensible, and self-consciousness. His concepts of supplement and trace are ironic versions of Hegel's *aufhebung*: every expression breeds as its completion an antithetical one, but, instead of a dialectical synthesis, Derrida sees only endless proliferation of differences.

himself as simultaneously concrete and universal, because the differences defining one's particular circumstances become intelligible only by virtue of general interpretive structures (for which language is a central, but incomplete, metaphor): "Spirit has in it the two sides which are presented above as two converse propositions: one is this, that substance alienates itself from itself and becomes self-consciousness; the other is the converse, that self-consciousness alienates itself from itself and gives itself the nature of a thing, or makes itself a universal Self" (PS, 457).

These more encompassing forms of self-knowledge and communal identification constitute the telos of consciousness as it reflects upon the *wirklichkeit* its negations and expressive reintegrations have produced. The form taken by this reflection, which fulfills the need of self-consciousness to understand the two sides of spirit, is the process of dialectical thought. Hegel calls it "the education of consciousness to itself" (PS, 50), and bases the education into the self's nature on a three-stage drama. First, as consciousness reflects on its performance, it negates the adequacy of that activity by recognizing what it mistook or could not include. The performance objectified only some of what one desired to be a total identity. Then, the mind comes to understand the terms of what the action lacked, and, thus, to preserve the state as one specific determinant of the development of consciousness. Finally, when one has terms for preserving the state as a determinate meaning, one can also *transcend* that partial state by recognizing its place in relation to other attitudes. Only in this place does the performance become fully meaningful, because one can locate the role it plays as a feature of the full identity which spirit works to achieve. A dialectical model of education, then, emphasizes transitions from a limited sense of one's identity as a specific actor to a realization of the place one's actions have in the universal grammar, which makes them ultimately intelligible in a structure of determinate relations. When one grasps his actions as concrete participations within a larger structure, he comes to realize his identity in and identification with a larger transhistorical community. For Hegel, this final stage of knowledge is a scientific grasp of necessary relations, and, hence, establishes identity of the self with absolute rationality. However, we probably gain more than we lose by limiting these claims to grammatical knowledge and a view of full education as dialectically clarifying one's dependence on and participation in an ongoing shared cultural enterprise. The following account of the spirit's "insight into what knowing is" certainly preserves a good deal of its imaginative force even in these modified terms:

This past existence is the already acquired property of universal spirit which constitutes the substance of the individual, and hence appears externally to him as his inorganic nature. In this respect formative education, regarded from the side of the individual, consists in his acquiring what thus lies at hand, devouring his inorganic nature, and taking possession of it for himself. But, regarded from the side of universal spirit as substance, this is nothing but its own acquisition of self-consciousness, the bringing about of its own becoming and reflection into itself.... The length of this path has to be endured, because, for one thing, each moment is necessary; and further each moment has to be lingered over, because each is itself a complete individual shape, and one is only viewed in absolute perspective when its determinateness is regarded as a concrete whole, or the whole is regarded as uniquely qualified by that determination. Since the Substance of the individual, the World-Spirit itself, has had the patience to pass through these shapes over the long passage of time, and to take upon itself the enormous labor of world-history, in which it embodied in each as much of its entire content as that shape was capable of holding, and since it could not have attained consciousness of itself by any lesser effort, the individual certainty cannot by the nature of the case comprehend his own substance more easily. (PS, 16–17)

5. How an idealist approach to criticism can project social values

In this discussion I have simply presumed Hegel's power at concretely analyzing attitudes and interrelationships among stances and situations. I have concentrated instead on a grammatical and dramatistic restatement of his central ideas, in order to provide the largest context I know for illustrating the self-reflective implications of my arguments about critical seriousness. Hegel shows us what we can claim to do and to know when we seek long-term literary education, and probably humanistic education in general. In so doing, he enables us to shift our focus from the practical power attained by developing a complex grammar to the self-reflective power of knowing and being able to state what we possess in such an education. I have no delusions that my restatement has independent philosophical validity. Instead, I am content to take Hegel as a useful myth or set of terms which gives a plausible account of how literary theory might represent its own goals to itself. In other words, Hegel's seriousness is a model attitude we can employ in performing or showing the values we affirm and are willing to accept as describing our responsibilities. There are, then, three specific implications of this model with which I shall conclude. Each clarifies a basic feature of the status of literary criticism, considered as a way of pursuing distinctive forms of knowledge, and, thus, as affording a means of reflecting on what we learn and desire to promulgate in our work with literary traditions.

Hegel's expressionist account of the dialectic between substance and spirit provides a clear, deep foundation for explaining the cognitive status of action descriptions. These descriptions are not propositions and do not necessarily conform to rational deductions, because one accounts not only for events, but for a relationship between purposes, types, and situations applied to specific contexts. From a modified Hegelian perspective, one can assert that *propositions* and *attitudes* each have distinctive grounds for explanation, because the latter refer not to independent facts, but to what men make of facts. As Goodman helps articulate in a more empirical way, the grounds of dramatism are the grammatical principles which render those acts of making intelligible and come to constitute a flexible set of terms eliciting further performative constructions.

Here it becomes possible to make a conceptual move analogous to Frye's shift from mythic to anagogic forms of symbolism.[14] In normal practice, one simply uses a grammar of attitudes to describe, and, at times, to assess, specific acts. But it is also possible to attend to the working of the set of attitudes as a whole, so that expressions are situated in relation to other possible attitudes. Attitudes become possible forms for constructing experience, and their meaning comes to depend on their relationships to one another. Here culture itself becomes the ultimate object of literary reflection—as Frye's anagogic texts exemplify. There may be no absolute, but there are, within the acts of reflecting on our cultural possessions, strong imperatives to imagine a supreme fiction, by which we would see the necessity and power of all our possible attitudes in internal relationship to one another. The possessor of this *Geist* is Stevens' Major Man.

14. See *Anatomy of Criticism*, pp. 115–30. There are also many ways in which Frye's notion of *concern* informs my discussion of seriousness. For Frye's general understanding of the *educated imagination* is ultimately a Hegelian one. See in this respect my essay, "Northrop Frye and the Problem of Spiritual Authority," *PMLA* 87 (1972):964–75.

If the status of attitudes as objects of knowledge is clear, one need not turn to Stevensian speculations in order to recognize the centrality for the present of reconstituting serious representative performances from the past. The basic Hegelian principle applicable here is his definition of the teleology of self-consciousness as the pursuit of identity between the knower and what he knows. Again, this principle is defensible only in speculative reflection on the nature of actions. But in this sphere it gives a powerful dramatic model of the dialectical procedures one can apply to appreciating what he possesses from literary experience. Hegel's dialectic derives from the issues raised by Skinner, on the one hand, and by deductive theorists, like Rader, on the other. Historicism, for Hegel, reduces all history to tragedy, by conceiving the monuments of past cultures as empty tombs, irretrievably different from present needs and concerns. Rationalism, on the other hand, reduces history to farce, by abstracting from concrete performances only those features which fit fixed logical categories and principles of derivation. To escape these alternatives, Hegel felt one needed a speculative view of history dependent on two basic notions. Actions had to be seen as the progressive dialectical unfolding of something, *Geist*, of which they were ultimately expressions—so that the knower and the known might share a common ground of identity. And the relevant features of *Geist* had to be imagined in such a way that they would require dense particular descriptions before their place in the whole would be clear and significant. Now, with respect to actions, it still makes sense to claim that consciousness is "explicitly the *Notion* of itself" (PS, 51), and that this notion depends on the constitutive terms consciousness employs in representing what the mind makes of the world. These terms are the history of ideas and attitudes worked out by a culture's continuing efforts to describe, situate, and assess human actions. Because the grammar for these terms emerges historically from acts of interpreting the past, it is plausible to imagine the deepest grasp of these attitudes as a dialectical appreciation of their interrelationships. Because this dialectic applies to the terms history affords for our own self-representations, dramatistic knowledge is a vehicle by which the self finds a portion of its identity in its grasp of the history of purposive performances created, preserved, and supplemented by other selves. Expressive acts at once bring a world into being and become constituents of self-understanding, which, in turn, involves recognizing what one shares with other consciousnesses. How we read determines what we can say about the mind and the grounds of community.

Hegel's expressionism serves finally to put dramatic flesh on Kant's notion of the way an ethical city of ends is symbolically present as a horizon of aesthetic judgment:

> Now I say the beautiful is a symbol of the morally good, and that it is so only in this respect ... that it gives pleasure with a claim for the agreement of everyone else. By this the mind is made conscious of a certain ennoblement and elevation above the mere sensitivity to pleasure received through sense, and the worth of others is estimated in accordance with a like maxim of their judgment. That is the *intelligible* to which, as pointed out in the preceding paragraph, taste looks, with which our higher cognitive faculties are in accord, and without which a downright contradiction would arise between their nature and the claims made by taste. In this faculty the judgment does not see itself, as in empirical judging, subjected to a heteronomy of empirical laws; it gives the law to itself in respect of the objects of so pure a satisfaction, just as the reason does in respect of the faculty of desire.... Taste represents the imagination in its freedom as capable of purposive determination for the understanding. ...
>
> The propaedeutic to all beautiful art, regarded in the highest degree of its perfection, seems to lie, not in precepts, but in the culture of mental powers by means of those elements of knowledge called *humaniora*, probably because *humanity* on the one side indicates the universal feeling of sympathy, and on the other the faculty of being able to communicate universally our inmost [feelings]. For these properties, taken together, constitute the characteristic social spirit of humanity....[15]

This is as humane as the Kantian model of community gets, because his vehicle is the concept of a universal will at the core of any ethical decision. For Hegel, on the other hand, aesthetic experience brings self-consciousness to recognize the full dramatic content, by which these feelings are expressed, and serve as the constituent features upon which individual judgments depend. For Hegel, one desires to take the expressions of others as seriously as possible, because in and through them he recognizes others in himself and himself in others. Even without a Spirit in history, there remains a communal identity present for those respon-

---

15. *Critique of Judgment*, sections 59–60, pp. 198–201 in Bernard's translation.

sive to purposive agents as they attempt to perform the stances by which history and nature become an intelligible legacy to the present.[16]

What Hegel proposes philosophically, Dante disposes poetically. In the *Commedia*, Spirit takes the form of God's love as it is perceptible to a dialectical consciousness becoming aware of the grounds for its ultimate identity. This dialectical project demands that Dante as protagonist come fully to know "come si covenne / l'imago al cercio e come vi s'indova" (how our image coexists in [God's] circle and how it there situates itself).[17] God contains the totality of permanent human types, held in an eternal moral hierarchy by reason, and in knowing him one sees finally how the containing forms of behavior are themselves contained in a set of structural relationships. The structure, moreover, is not simply abstract and logical, but manifested in fully concrete images, each in its place. Dante's growth is coming to understand the dialectical form of this structure, by recognizing how each partial attitude is preserved and transcended by subsequent ones and by the internal relationships they manifest.

Without God, we cannot share Dante's faith in a single hierarchical structure. But we can recognize and share both the desire for relationship and a sense of the ideal form, constituted now by simply our capacity to reflect upon the multiple interrelationships of our grammar as potential aspects of our individual identities. Cosmic order must yield to a mere image of a possible aesthetic order, true only in partial connections and only for the contemplative mind. But even aesthetic orders glimpsed in aesthetic contemplation of the grounds of interpretive activity can have ethical consequences. Even a speculative sense of an ideal human form, contained in culture considered as a possession, provides a fresh perspective on the nature of the self, an image of one significant

16. The sense of community created in reflection on acts of knowledge, however, is not a directly empirical or ethical one. Both Kant and Hegel construct ideal communities in large part as responses to the collapse of any actual social community warranting one's allegiance. (Hegel unfortunately retreats from this position in *The Philosophy of Right*.) This contrast between empirical and ideal communities is one reason I hesitate to equate knowledge with moral action. It may be that repeated experience of the best that has been thought and said with respect to human behavior will inculcate ideals needed for a more humane society. But it is just as likely that contemplation of these ideals and of intense, refined moments of qualitative expression has antisocial effects, by making people aware of the gulf between imaginative life and the dullness and consistent compromise in empirical situations. Literary knowledge expands one's sense of the grammar of his culture and often gives one an enlarged sense of identity, but the society it puts us in contact with is abstract and speculative.

17. Dante, *Paradiso*, Canto 33, ll. 137–38.

goal in literary education, and a possible vision of the goals of social practice. On the basis of this kind of speculation, we can imagine the self not as a psychological cogito, but as constituted by the capacity to assume as wide a variety of attitudes and roles as a person can master imaginatively. These attitudes repose in a public domain, and, hence, are at once potentially shareable with others and, as Kant points out in his discussion of the value of social life, dependent on our observations of and sympathy for other actors. Given this vision, we can use the image of shared identity as one powerful model for the values of literary education. We may not thus transcend the world to see God, nor will we find any ontological imperative for our labors, but this image establishes one possible secular mode for transcending our limited identities. One cannot argue the values of such an enterprise, but he can try to display them by reflecting on the nature of our interpretive grammar. In inquiring about the shape of human purposive activity, we are perforce asking what it means to be human and to be capable of acting deliberately, and we are reflecting on the grounds of our ability to comprehend those actions.[18] The ethical correlate of this mode of inquiry,

18. When dealing with such pieties, it is difficult to avoid the temptation of humanistic rhetoric. I have borrowed two statements in order to satisfy this desire. The first is from a modern phenomenologist, F. Olafson, "Merleau-Ponty's Philosophy," in Edward Lee and Maurice Mandelbaum, eds., *Phenomenology and Existentialism* (Baltimore: Johns Hopkins University Press, 1967), p. 89; the second from a discussion of attitudes in C. S. Lewis, *An Experiment in Criticism,* (Cambridge: Cambridge University Press, 1961). "I would say that the movement from the natural to the transcendental attitude is one through which I gradually come to appreciate the fact that I am, so to speak, the owner and operator of a total conceptual system. This requires, as the late John Austin said, 'a prising of language off the world,' i.e. a break with the naive conceptual realism that submerges conceptual and meaning conferring activity in the flux of experience; and it leads through an appreciation of the unity of the systems of meaning which we have, as it were, been unconsciously applying to an understanding of the thorough going parallelism between the various forms of objectivity and the intentional acts by which they are constituted.... In the final apotheosis of transcendental subjectivity, I even overcome the condition of finite selfhood by constituting a milieu of transcendental intersubjectivity in which the perspectives of individual human beings are harmoniously related to one another to form a single public world that is the true correlate of the systems of meanings we employ.

"Literary experience heals the wound, without undermining the privilege, of individuality. There are mass emotions which heal the wound; but they destroy the privilege. In them our separate selves are pooled and we sink back into sub-individuality. But in reading great literature I become a thousand men and yet remain myself. Like the night sky in the Greek poem, I see with a myriad eyes, but it is still I who see. Here, as in worship, in love, in moral action, and in knowing, I transcend myself; and am never more myself than when I do."

finally, is a possible feeling that man's task, like the task of Hegel's *Geist*, is to realize these abstract possibilities in the concrete world by creating social conditions amenable to a variety of expressions and to the speculative freedom to appreciate what these expressions display. This final reflection is far too abstract to help much in resolving particular ethical problems. But, as a possible attitude, it has a different function: it articulates one way of constructing the terms in which we can create qualitative standards for evaluating ourselves as ethical performers, and, hence, it can shape the actual purposes we bring to concrete ethical situations.[19]

19. As I have indicated above, I think that the basic role of ethical discourse is creating terms within which one can construct images of self-regard to which she can be held responsible, both as a measure of her subsequent acts and as a measure of how fully she understands her human situation. For a good use of this kind of thinking to replace ontological models of contract, see John Rawls, *A Theory of Justice* (Cambridge, Mass.: Harvard University Press, 1971), pp. 17–52.

Bibliography

Abrams, M. H. "The Deconstructive Angel: The Limits of Pluralism." *Critical Inquiry* 3 (1977): 425–38.
———. *Natural Supernaturalism*. New York: Norton, 1971.
Alston, William. "Meaning and Use." Reprinted in *Readings in the Philosophy of Language*, ed. Jay Rosenberg and Charles Travis. Englewood Cliffs, N.J.: Prentice-Hall, 1971.
Altieri, Charles. "From Experience to Discourse: American Poetry and Poetics in the Seventies." *Contemporary Literature* 2 (1980): 191–224.
———. "Going on and Going Nowhere: Some Uses of Wittgenstein for Literary Theory." In a forthcoming book, ed. William Cain.
———. "Northrop Frye and the Problem of Spiritual Authority." *PMLA* 87 (1972): 964–75.
———. "The Poem as Act: A Way to Reconcile Mimetic and Presentational Theories." *Iowa Review* 6 (1975): 103–24.
———. "Presence and Reference in a Literary Text: The Example of Williams." *Critical Inquiry* 5 (1979): 489–510.
———. "Some Uses of Frye's Literary Theory." *The CEA Critic* 42, no. 2 (1080): 10–20.
———. "Wittgenstein on Consciousness and Language: A Challenge to Derridean Theory." *MLN* 91 (1976): 1397–1423.
Anscombe, G.E.M. *Intention*. Ithaca: Cornell University Press, 1969.
Aune, Bruce. *Reason and Action*. Boston: David Reidel, 1977.
Austin, J. L. *How To Do Things With Words*. New York: Oxford University Press, 1962.
———. *Philosophical Papers*. New York: Oxford University Press, 1970.
———. *Sense and Sensibilia*. New York: Oxford University Press, 1962.
Barthes, Roland. *Critical Essays*. Trans. Richard Howard. Evanston: Northwestern University Press, 1972.
———. "An Introduction to the Structural Study of Narrative." *New Literary History* 6 (1975): 237–72.

————. *S/Z*. Trans. Richard Miller. New York: Hill and Wang, 1974.

————. "Style and Its Image." In *Literary Style: A Symposium*, ed. Seymour Chatman, pp. 3–14. New York: Oxford University Press, 1971.

Beardsley, Monroe. "Aesthetic Theory and Educational Theory." In *Aesthetic Concepts in Education*, ed. Ralph Smith, pp. 1–11. Urbana: University of Illinois Press, 1970.

————. "The Languages of Art and Art Criticism." *Erkenntnis* 12, nos. 1 and 2 (1978): 95–117.

Berger, Thomas. *Max Weber's Theory of Concept Formation: History, Laws, and Ideal Types*. Durham: Duke University Press, 1976.

Berlin, Isaiah, ed. *Essays on J. L. Austin*. Oxford: Clarendon Press, 1973.

Bernstein, Richard. *Praxis and Action*. Philadelphia: University of Pennsylvania Press, 1971.

Berthoff, Werner. "The Way We Think Now: Protocols for Deprivation." *New Literary History* 7 (1976): 599–618.

Binkley, Timothy. *Wittgenstein's Language*. The Hague: Martinus Nijhoff, 1973.

Black, Max. "Meaning and Intention: An Examination of Grice's Views." *New Literary History* 4(1973): 257–80.

Bloom, Harold. "Poetic Crossing: Rhetoric and Psychology." *Georgia Review* 30 (1976): 495–524.

Booth, Wayne. *Modern Dogma and the Rhetoric of Assent*. Chicago: University of Chicago Press, 1976.

Brooks, Cleanth. *The Well-Wrought Urn*. New York: Harcourt Brace, 1947.

Burke, Kenneth. *Grammar of Motives*. Berkeley: University of California Press, 1969.

Carnap, Rudolf. "The Rejection of Metaphysics." In *Twentieth Century Philosophy*, ed. Morris Weltz. New York: Macmillan, 1972.

Casey, John. *The Language of Criticism*. London: Methuen, 1966.

Cavell, Stanley. "Aesthetic Problems of Modern Philosophy." Reprinted in *Must We Mean What We Say?*, pp. 73–96. Cambridge: Cambridge University Press, 1976.

Caws, Peter. "Critique of Structuralist Semantics." *Diacritics* 3 (1973): 15–21.

Chatman, Seymour, ed. *Approaches to Poetics*. New York: Columbia University Press, 1973.

————. *Literary Style: A Symposium*. New York: Oxford University Press, 1971.

————. "On Defining Form." *New Literary History* 2 (1971): 217–28.

Cohen, L. Jonathan. "Do Illocutionary Forces Exist?" In *Readings in the Philosophy of Language*, ed. Travis and Rosenberg, pp. 580–98. Englewood Cliffs, N.J.: Prentice-Hall, 1971.

————. *The Probable and the Proveable*. Oxford: Clarendon Press, 1977.

————. "The Role of Inductive Reasoning in the Interpretation of Metaphor." In *Semantics of Natural Language*, ed. Donald Davidson and Gilbert Harman, pp. 722–40. Boston: David Reidel, 1972.

Cohen, Ted. "Notes on Metaphor." *JAAC* 34 (1976): 249–59.

Cole, Peter, ed. *Syntax and Semantics: Pragmatics*. New York: Academic Press, 1978.

Croce, Benedetto. *Aesthetic*. Trans. Douglas Ainslie. New York: Noonday Press, 1966.

Culler, Jonathan. "Literary History, Allegory and Semiology." *New Literary History* 7 (1976): 259–70.

————. *Structuralist Poetics*. Ithaca: Cornell University Press, 1975.

Davidson, Donald. "Actions, Reasons and Causes." In *Readings in the Philosophy of Action*, ed. Norman Care and Charles Landesman, pp. 179–98. Bloomington: Indiana University Press, 1968.

——. "The Logical Form of Action Sentences." In *The Logic of Decision and Action*, ed. Nicholas Rescher, pp. 81–95. Pittsburgh: Pittsburgh University Press, 1967.

Davis, Steven. *Philosophy and Language*. Indianapolis: Bobbs-Merrill, 1976.

Davis, Walter. *The Act of Interpretation; A Critique of Literary Reason*. Chicago: University of Chicago Press, 1978.

de Man, Paul. "Action and Identity in Nietzsche." *Yale French Studies*, no. 52 (1975): 16–30.

——. *Blindness and Insight*. New York: Oxford University Press, 1971.

——. "Intentionality of the Romantic Image." In *Romanticism and Consciousness*, ed. Harold Bloom, pp. 65–76. New York: Norton, 1970.

——. "The Purloined Ribbon." In *Glyph One*, pp. 28–49. Baltimore: Johns Hopkins University Press, 1977.

——. "Semiology and Rhetoric." *Diacritics* 3 (Fall, 1973): 27–33.

——. "Theory of Metaphor in Rousseau's Second Discourse." In *Romanticism Vistas, Instances, Continuities*, ed. David Thorburn, pp. 83–114. Ithaca: Cornell University Press, 1973.

Derrida, Jacques. "Freud and the Scene of Writing." *Yale French Studies*, no. 48 (1972): 74–115.

——. "Limited Inc." Trans. Sam Weber. In *Glyph Two*, pp. 162–254. Baltimore: Johns Hopkins University Press, 1977.

——. *Of Grammatology*. Trans. Gayatri Spivak. Baltimore: Johns Hopkins University Press, 1976.

——. "The Purveyor of Truth." *Yale French Studies*, no. 52 (1975): 31–114.

——. "Signature, Event, and Context." In *Glyph One*, pp. 172–97. Baltimore: Johns Hopkins University Press, 1977.

——. *Speech and Phenomena: Introduction to the Problem of Signs in Husserl's Phenomenology*. Trans. David B. Allison. Evanston: Northwestern University Press, 1973.

——. "Structure, Sign, Play." In *The Structuralist Controversy*, ed. Richard Macksey and Eugenio Donato, pp. 247–64. Baltimore: Johns Hopkins University Press, 1970.

——. "White Mythology: Metaphor in the Text of Philosophy." *New Literary History* 6 (1974): 5–74.

Dickie, George. *Aesthetics: An Introduction*. Indianapolis: Bobbs-Merrill, 1971.

Donato, Eugenio. "The Idioms of the Text: Notes on the Language of Philosophy and the Fictions of Literature." In *Glyph Two*, pp. 1–13. Baltimore: Johns Hopkins University Press, 1977.

Eaton, Marcia. "Art, Artifacts, and Intentions." *American Philosophical Quarterly* (1964): 167–69.

Ellis, John. *Theory of Literary Criticism*. Berkeley: University of California Press, 1974.

Fann, T. K., ed. *Symposium on J. L. Austin*. London: Routledge and Kegan Paul, 1969.

Felperin, Howard. *Shakespeare Representation: Mimesis & Modernity in Elizabethan Tragedy*. Princeton: Princeton University Press, 1977.

Fillmore, Charles. "Entailment Rules in Semantic Theory." In *Readings in the Philosophy of Language*, ed. Rosenberg and Travis, pp. 533–47. Englewood Cliffs, N.J.: Prentice Hall, 1971.

———. "Topics in Lexical Semantics." In *Current Issues in Linguistic Theory*, ed. Roger W. Cole, pp. 76–138. Bloomington: Indiana University Press, 1977.

Findlay, J. R. *Language, Mind, and Values*. London: George Allen and Unwin, 1963.

———. *The Philosophy of Hegel*. New York: Collier Books, 1962.

———. *Values and Intention*. London: George Allen and Unwin, 1961.

Fish, Stanley. "Literature in the Reader: Affective Stylistics." *New Literary History* 2 (1970): 123–62.

———. *The Living Temple*. Berkeley: University of California Press, 1977.

———. "Response to Ralph Rader," *Critical Inquiry* 1 (1974): 883–91.

———. *Surprised by Sin: The Reader in Paradise Lost*. New York: St. Martin's Press, 1967.

———. "What Is Stylistics and Why Are They Saying Such Terrible Things About It." In *Approaches to Poetics*, ed. Seymour Chatman, pp. 109–52.

Fly, Richard. *Shakespeare's Mediated World*. Amherst: University of Massachusetts Press, 1976.

Foucault, Michel. *Discipline and Punish*. Trans. Alan Sheridan. New York: Pantheon, 1977.

———. "Nietzsche, Freud, Marx." In *Nietzsche*, pp. 183–92. Paris: Editions de Minuit, 1967.

———. *The Order of Things*. New York: Random House, 1970.

Frye, Northrop. *Anatomy of Criticism*. Princeton: Princeton University Press, 1956.

———. "The Rising of the Moon: A Study of 'A Vision.' " In *An Honored Guest: New Essays on W. B. Yeats*, ed. Denis Donoghue and J. R. Mulryne, pp. 8–33. New York: St. Martin's Press, 1966.

———. *The Stubborn Structure*. Ithaca: Cornell University Press, 1971.

Gardiner, Patrick. *The Nature of Historical Explanation*. New York: Oxford University Press, 1961.

Garver, Newton. "Derrida on Rousseau on Writing." *The Journal of Philosophy* 74 (1977): 663–74.

———. Introduction to *Speech and Phenomena*, by Jacques Derrida.

Geertz, Clifford. *The Interpretation of Cultures*. New York: Basic Books, 1973.

Goffman, Irving. *Frame Analysis*. New York: Harper Colophon Books, 1974.

Golden, Leon and Hardison, O. B. *Aristotle's Poetics: A Translation and a Commentary for Students of Literature*. Englewood Cliffs, N.J.: Prentice-Hall, 1968.

Goldman, Alvin. *A Theory of Human Action*. Princeton University Press, 1970.

Goodman, Nelson. *Languages of Art*. New York: Bobbs-Merrill, 1968.

———. "Response." *Erkenntnis* 12, nos. 1 and 2 (1978): 171–76.

———. "The Status of Style." *Critical Inquiry* 1 (1975): 799–811.

———. *Ways of Worldmaking*. Indianapolis: Hockett Publishing Co., 1978.

Graff, Gerald. *Literature Against Itself*. Chicago: University of Chicago Press, 1979.

———. "What Was New Criticism?" *Salmagundi* no. 27 (1974): 72–93.

Greene, Marjorie. "Life, Death, and Language: Some Thoughts on Wittgenstein and Derrida." *Partisan Review* 43 (1976): 265–79.

Grice, Paul. "Further Notes on Conversation and Logic." In *Syntax and Semantics: Pragmatics*, ed. Peter Cole, pp. 377–88. New York: Academic Press, 1978.

———. "Logic and Conversation." In *Syntax and Semantics: Speech Acts*, ed. Peter Cole and Jerry Morgan, pp. 41–58. New York: Academic Press, 1975.

———. "Meaning." *Philosophical Review* 86 (1977): 377–88.

———. "Utterer's Meaning and Intentions." *Philosophical Review* 78 (1969): 147–77.

Halliday, M. A. K. *Language as Social Semiotic: The Social Interpretation of Language and Meaning.* Baltimore: University Park Press, 1978.

———. *Learning How to Mean: Explorations in the Development of Language.* New York: Elseveir, 1977.

Hampshire, Stuart. "Russell, Radicalism and Reason." *The New York Review of Books* 15 (Oct. 8, 1970): 3–8.

———. "Spinoza and the Idea of Freedom." In *Studies in the Philosophy of Thought and Action,* ed. P. F. Strawson, pp. 48–70. New York: Oxford University Press, 1968.

———. *Thought and Action.* London: Chatto and Windus, 1959.

Hancher, Michael. "Beyond a Speech Act Theory of Discourse." *MLN* 92 (1977): 1089–98.

Hasan, Ruquaiya. "Rime and Reason in Literature." In *Literary Style: A Symposium,* ed. Seymour Chatman, pp. 299–326. New York: Oxford University Press, 1971.

Hegel, G. W. F. *Phenomenology of Spirit.* Trans. A. V. Miller. Oxford: Clarendon Press, 1977.

Hempel, Carl. "Rational Action." In *Readings in the Philosophy of Action,* ed. Norman Care and Charles Landesman, pp. 281–305. Bloomington: Indiana University Press, 1968.

Hernadi, Paul. "Clio's Cousins: Autobiography as Translation, Fiction, and Criticism." *New Literary History* 7 (1975): 247–58.

✓ Hirsch, E. D. *The Aims of Criticism.* Chicago: University of Chicago Press, 1976.

———. *Validity in Interpretation.* New Haven: Yale University Press, 1967.

Holland, Norman. *5 Readers Reading.* New Haven: Yale University Press, 1975.

———. "The New Paradigm: Subjective or Transactive." *New Literary History* 7 (1976): 335–46.

———. *Poems in Persons.* New York: Norton, 1973.

———. "Unity Identity Text Self." *PMLA* 90 (1975): 813–22.

Hollis, Martin. *Models of Man.* Cambridge: Cambridge University Press, 1977.

Hymes, Dell. "Models of the Interaction of Language and the Social Life." In *Directions in Sociolinguistics,* ed. John J. Gumperz and Hymes, pp. 35–71. New York: Holt, Rinehart and Winston, 1972.

Iser, Wolfgang. "The Reality of Fiction: A Functionalist Approach to Literature." *New Literary History* 7 (1975): 7–38.

Jameson, Frederic. "Marxism and Literary History." *NLH* 11 (1979): 41–74.

✓ Kalin, Jesse. "Philosophy Needs Literature: John Barth and Moral Nihilism." *Philosophy and Literature* 1 (1977): 170–83.

Kant, Immanuel. *Critique of Judgment.* Trans. J. H. Bernard. New York: Hafner, 1968.

Kenny, Anthony. *Action, Emotion and Will.* N.Y.: Humanities Press, 1963.

———. *Wittgenstein.* Cambridge: Harvard University Press, 1973.

Kermode, Frank. "Hawthorne's Modernity." *Partisan Review* 41 (1974): 428–41.

Lemaire, Anika. *Jacques Lacan.* Trans. David Macey. London: Routledge and Kegan Paul, 1977.

Levin, David. "The Embodiment of Performance." *Salmagundi* nos. 31–32 (Fall, 1975–Winter, 1976): 120–42.

Lewis, C. S. *An Experiment in Criticism*. Cambridge: Cambridge University Press, 1961.

Louch, A. R. *Explanation and Human Action*. Berkeley: University of California Press, 1969.

MacFarland, Thomas. "The Originality Paradox." *New Literary History* 5 (1974): 447.

Mandelbaum, Maurice. *History, Man and Reason*. Baltimore: Johns Hopkins University Press, 1971.

Margolis, Joseph. *The Languages of Art and Art Criticism*. Detroit: Wayne State University Press, 1965.

———. "Literature and Speech Acts." *Philosophy and Literature* 3 (1979): 39–52.

Mehlmann, Jeffrey. "How to Read Freud on Jokes: The Critic as Schadchen." *New Literary History* 6 (1975): 439–61.

Melden, I. A. "Action." In *Readings in the Philosophy of Action*, eds. Norman Care and Charles Landesman, pp. 27–47. Bloomington: Indiana University Press, 1968.

Miller, J. Hillis. "Ariachne's Broken Woof." *Georgia Review* 31 (1977): 44–63.

Moore, Arthur. *Contestable Concepts in Literary Theory*. Baton Rouge: Louisiana State University Press, 1973.

Moore, G. E. "Wittgenstein's Lectures in 1930–33." In Moore, *Philosophical Papers*, pp. 247–318. New York: Collier, 1962.

Moravcsik, J. M. "Appreciation, Care and Understanding." Unpublished; to appear in different form in two essays in *Dialectica*, 1980, 1981.

Oglivy, James. "Reflections on the Absolute." *Review of Metaphysics* 27 (1975): 520–46.

Ohmann, Richard. "Literature as Sentences." *College English* 27 (1966): 261–67.

———. "Speech Acts and the Definition of Literature." *Philosophy and Rhetoric* 4 (1971): 1–19.

Olafson, F. "Merleau-Ponty's Philosophy." In *Phenomenology and Existentialism*, ed. Edward Lee and Maurice Mandelbaum, pp. 179–206. Baltimore: Johns Hopkins University Press.

Olson, Elder. "Sailing to Byzantium: Prolegomena to a Poetics of the Lyric." In *Critics and Criticism*, ed. R. S. Crane. Chicago: Chicago University Press, 1963.

Pitkin, Hannah. *Wittgenstein and Justice*. Berkeley: University of California Press, 1972.

Popper, Karl. *Objective Knowledge*. Oxford: Clarendon Press, 1972.

———. *The Open Society and Its Enemies*, 4th ed., London: Routledge and Kegan Paul, 1962.

Poulet, Georges. "Phenomenology of Reading." *New Literary History* 1 (1969): 53–68.

Pratt, Mary Louise. *Toward a Speech Act Theory of Literary Discourse*. Bloomington: Indiana University Press, 1976.

Putnam, Hilary. "Literature, Science, and Reflection." *New Literary History* 7 (1976): 483–92.

Rader, Ralph. "The Comparative Anatomy of Three Baggy Monsters: *Bleak House*, *Vanity Fair*, and *Middlemarch*." Lecture delivered at Berkeley, spring, 1975.

———. "The Concept of Genre and Eighteenth Century Studies." In *New Approaches to Eighteenth Century Studies*, ed. Philip Harth, pp. 79–115. New York: Columbia University Press, 1974.

———. "Defoe, Richardson, Joyce and the Concept of Form in the Novel." In *Autobiography, Biography and the Novel*, pp. 29–72. Los Angeles: Clark Library, 1973.

———. "The Dramatic Monologue and Related Lyric Forms." *Critical Inquiry* 3 (1976): 138–52.

———. "Explaining Our Literary Understanding." *Critical Inquiry* 1 (1974): 106–09.

———. "Fact, Theory and Literary Explanation." *Critical Inquiry* 1 (1974): 262–72.

Rawls, John. A *Theory of Justice*. Cambridge, Mass., Harvard University Press, 1971.

Rescher, Nicholas. *The Coherence Theory of Truth*. Oxford: Clarendon Press, 1973.

Richards, I. A. *Principles of Literary Criticism*. New York: Harvest Books, n.d.

———. *Science and Poetry*, 2nd ed. London: Kegan Paul, Trench, Trubner and Co., 1935.

Ricoeur, Paul. *Conflict of Interpretations*. Ed. Don Ihde. Evanston: Northwestern University Press, 1974.

———. "Husserl and Wittgenstein." In *Phenomenology and Existentialism*, ed. A. Lee and M. Mandelbaum. Baltimore: Johns Hopkins University Press, 1968.

———. "The Model of the Text: Meaningful Action Considered as a Text." *New Literary History* 5 (1974): 91–117.

Riddel, Joseph. "From Heidegger to Derrida to Chance: Doubling and Poetic Language." *Boundary 2* 4 (1976): 571–92.

———. *The Inverted Bell: The Counter-Poetics of William Carlos Williams*. Baton Rouge: Louisiana State University Press, 1974.

Rorty, Richard. *Philosophy and the Mirror of Nature*. Princeton: Princeton University Press, 1979.

Royce, Josiah. *Lectures on Modern Idealism*. New Haven: Yale University Press, 1919.

Said, Edward. *Beginnings: Intention and Method*. New York: Basic Books, 1975.

———. "Reflections on Recent Left American Criticism." *Boundary 2* 8 (1979): 11–30.

Schaefer, William. "Editor's Column." *PMLA* 93 (1978): 354–55.

Schiffer, Stephen. *Meaning*. Oxford: Clarendon Press, 1972.

Searle, John. "Indirect Speech Acts." In *Syntax and Semantics: Speech Acts*, ed. Peter Cole and Jerry Morgan, pp. 59–82. New York: Academic Press, 1975.

———. "The Logical Status of Fictional Discourse," *New Literary History* 6 (1975): 319–32.

———. "Reiterating the Differences." In *Glyph One*, pp. 198–211. Baltimore: Johns Hopkins University Press, 1977.

———. *Speech Acts*. Cambridge: Cambridge University Press, 1969.

Searle, Leroy. "Tradition and Intelligibility: A Model For Critical Theory." *New Literary History* 7 (1976): 393–415.

Sircello, Guy. *Mind and Art: An Essay on the Varieties of Expression*. Princeton: Princeton University Press, 1972.

Skinner, Quentin. "Hermeneutics and the Role of History." *New Literary History* 7 (1975): 209–32.

———. "The Limits of Historical Explanations." *Philosophy* 41 (1966): 199–215.

———. "Meaning and Understanding in the History of Ideas." *History and Theory* 9 (1969): 3–55.

————. "Motives, Intentions, and the Interpretation of Texts." *New Literary History* 3 (1972): 393–408.

Slatoff, Walter. *With Respect to Readers: Dimensions of Literary Response*. Ithaca: Cornell University Press, 1970.

Smith, Barbara Herrnstein. "Poetry as Fiction." *New Literary History* 2 (1971): 259–82.

Sparshott, F. E. *The Structure of Aesthetics*. Toronto: University of Toronto Press, 1963.

Sperber, Dan and Wilson, Diedre. "Les ironies comme mentions." *Poetique* no. 36: 399–412.

Stampe, Dennis. "Meaning and Truth in the Theory of Speech Acts." In *Syntax and Semantics: Speech Acts*, ed. Peter Cole and Jerry Morgan, pp. 1–39. New York: Academic Press, 1975.

Steiner, George. *After Babel*. New York: Oxford University Press, 1975.

Stevens, Wallace. *The Necessary Angel*. New York: Vintage Books, 1965.

Stewart, Donald. "Metaphor, Truth, and Definition." *JAAC* 32 (1973): 205–18.

Strawson, P. F. "Austin and Locutionary Meaning." In *Essays on J. L. Austin*, ed. Isaiah Berlin, pp. 46–68. Oxford: Clarendon Press, 1973.

————. *The Bounds of Sense: An Essay on Kant's Critique of Pure Reason*. London: Methuen, 1966.

————. *Individuals*. Garden City: Doubleday/Anchor, 1963.

————. "Intention and Convention in Speech Acts." In *Readings in the Philosophy of Language*, ed. Rosenberg and Travis. Englewood Cliffs, N.J.: Prentice-Hall, 1971.

————. *Logico-Linguistic Papers*. London: Methuen, 1971.

Tate, Allen. *Essays of Four Decades*. New York: William Morrow, 1970.

Taylor, Charles. *The Explanation of Behavior*. New York: Humanities Press, 1964.

————. *Hegel*. Cambridge: Cambridge University Press, 1975.

————. "Interpretation and the Sciences of Man." *Review of Metaphysics* 25 (1971): 3–51.

————. "Responsibility for Self." In *The Identities of Persons*, ed. Amélie Rorty, pp. 281–300. Berkeley: University of California Press, 1976.

Tilghman, B. R. "Wittgenstein, Games, and Art." *JAAC* 31 (1972–73): 519–24.

Todorov, Tzvetan. "Structuralism and Literature." In *Literary Style: A Symposium*, ed. Seymour Chatman, pp. 153–68. New York: Oxford University Press, 1971.

Tormey, Alan. *The Concept of Expression*. Princeton: Princeton University Press, 1970.

Trilling, Lionel. *Sincerity and Authenticity*. Cambridge, Mass.: Harvard University Press, 1972.

van Dijk, Teun. "Action, Action Descriptions and Narrative." *New Literary History* 6 (1975): 273–94.

Walsh, Dorothy. *Literature and Knowledge*. Middletown, Conn.: Wesleyan University Press, 1969.

Warnock, G. J. *English Philosophy Since 1900*. 2nd ed. New York: Oxford University Press, 1969.

Wasiolek, Edward. "Wanted: a New Contextualism." *Critical Inquiry* 1 (1974): 627–39.

Weber, Max. *The Methodology of the Social Sciences*. Glencoe, Illinois: The Free Press, 1949.

Weitz, Morris. "The Role of Theory in Aesthetics." *JAAC* 15 (1966): 27–35.

White, Hayden. *Metahistory*. Baltimore: Johns Hopkins University Press, 1973.

Williams, William Carlos. *The Collected Earlier Poems*. New York: New Directions, 1951.

Winch, Peter. "Introduction: The Unity of Wittgenstein's Philosophy." In *Studies in the Philosophy of Wittgenstein*, ed. Peter Winch, pp. 1–19. New York: Humanities Press, 1969.

Wittgenstein, Ludwig. *The Blue and the Brown Books*. New York: Harper Torchbooks, 1965.

————. *Lectures and Conversations on Aesthetics, Psychology and Religious Belief*. Ed. Cyril Barrett. Berkeley: University of California Press, 1972.

————. "Lecture on Ethics." *Philosophical Review* 74 (Jan. 1965): 3–12.

————. *Notebooks 1914–1916*. Trans. G.E.M. Anscombe. New York: Harper Torchbooks, 1969.

————. *On Certainty*. Ed. G.E.M. Anscombe and G. H. von Wright. New York: Harper Torchbooks, 1972.

————. *Philosophical Investigations*. Trans. G.E.M. Anscombe. New York: Macmillan, 1958.

————. *Tractatus Logicus-Philosophicus*. Trans. D. F. Pears and B. F. McGuiness. London: Routledge and Kegan Paul, 1961.

————. *Zettel*. Ed. G.E.M. Anscombe and G. H. von Wright. Berkeley: University of California Press, 1970.

Woolf, Virginia. *A Room of One's Own*. New York: Harcourt Brace, 1929.

Index

Earlier versions of portions of this book have appeared as essays in the following publications: "Wittgenstein on Consciousness and Language: A Challenge to Derridean Theory," *MLN* 91 (1976); "A Procedural Definition of Literature," in Paul Hernadi, ed. *What Is Literature?*, Bloomington: Indiana University Press, 1978; "Against Indeterminacy: A dissent from the New Orthodoxy," *New Literary History* 10 (1978); "Presence and Reference in a Literary Text: The Example of Williams," *Critical Inquiry* 5 (1979) (reprinted by permission of The University of Chicago Press); "The Concept of Expressive Implicature: A Modification of Grice," *Centrum*, in press. A selection from "As We Know" by John Ashberry, copyright © 1979 by John Ashberry, is reprinted by permission of Viking Penguin Inc.